Pass the CDL Exam

Everything You Need to Know

Pass the CDL Exam

Everything You Need to Know

Van O'Neal

Alice Adams

DELMAR
™
THOMSON LEARNING   Australia Canada Mexico Singapore Spain United Kingdom United States

Pass the CDL Exam: Everything You Need to Know
by Van O'Neal and Alice Adams

DELMAR STAFF:

Business Unit Director:
Susan L. Simpfenderfer

Executive Editor:
Marlene McHugh Pratt

Acquisitions Editor:
Paul Drougas

Developmental Editor:
Patricia Gillivan

Executive Production Manager:
Wendy A. Troeger

Cover Design:
Pomona Artworks

Cover Photo:
Erik Berthelsen

Executive Marketing Manager:
Donna J. Lewis

Channel Manager:
Wendy E. Mapstone

COPYRIGHT © 2002 by Delmar, a division of Thomson Learning, Inc. Thomson Learning™ is a trademark used herein under license

Printed in the United States
3 4 5 6 7 8 9 10 XXX 06 05 04 03 02

For more information contact Delmar
5 Maxwell Road, P.O. Box 8007,
Clifton Park, NY 12065

Or find us on the World Wide Web at http://www.Milady.com

For permission to use material from this text or product,
contact us by
Tel   (800) 730-2214
Fax   (800) 730-2215
www.thomsonrights.com

Library of Congress Cataloging-in-Publication Data
O'Neal, Van.
   Pass the CDL: everything you need to know/ Van O'Neal, Alice Adams
      p. cm.
   Includes index
   ISBN 0-7668-5015-3
   1. Truck driving—United States. 2. Truck Drivers—Liscenses—United
States. I. Adams, Alice. II. Title

TL230.3 .O54 2001
629.28'44'076—dc21

NOTICE TO THE READER

Publisher does not warrant or guarantee any of the products described herein or perform any independent analysis in connection with any of the product information contained herein. Publisher does not assume, and expressly disclaims, any obligation to obtain and include information other than that provided to it by the manufacturer.

The reader is expressly warned to consider and adopt all safety precautions that might be indicated by the activities herein and to avoid all potential hazards. By following the instructions contained herein, the reader willingly assumes all risks in connection with such instructions.

The Publisher makes no representation or warranties of any kind, including but not limited to, the warranties of fitness for particular purpose or merchantability, nor are any such representations implied with respect to the material set forth herein, and the publisher takes no responsibility with respect to such material. The publisher shall not be liable for any special, consequential, or exemplary damages resulting, in whole or part, from the readers' use of, or reliance upon, this material.

Contents

GRE

LSAT

Preface

When you pass the Commercial Driver's License (CDL) examination, you become a member of one of this country's most important professions. Professional drivers supply each and every citizen of this country—no matter how rich or how poor, how young or how old—with many of their basic needs.

The saying, "If you've got it, a trucker brought it!" applies to everyone, from the darkest corners of the inner city to the wealthiest suburbs in the land. Each consumer item the American public needs and uses every day is available because it was loaded onto a truck and delivered to docks, warehouses, and stores around the country.

This book was written to help you pass the CDL. More important, it was written so that you will be "the expert" when it comes to trucks, driving skills, and the responsibilities of a professional driver.

But this book is more than a study guide. It is a window into the transportation industry, providing up-to-date information on the "real world" of the professional driver. After each chapter and in the Appendices, you'll find valuable information—information that may be helpful today or five years from now.

Take time to find out about the multiple opportunities in this industry and more about the benefits. What are companies offering today that they didn't offer five years ago? Get to know the business. Get to know the major players.

As you review this book, keep in mind the legions of men and women who have paved the way for today's professional drivers. Also remember that as a professional driver, you have entire communities counting on you to do your best job, to make deliveries on time, and to maintain security and safety for every load on every road you travel.

America's quality of life depends on you, your knowledge of the laws, and your driving skills. Delivering items—from emergency medical supplies to Halloween candy—is the everyday responsibility of professional drivers. They take this responsibility seriously—and so should you.

We, the authors, welcome you to this highly skilled and respected profession and wish you Godspeed down life's highway.

PART

I

The Basics

1 Everything You Need to Know About the CDL—Before You Start Studying

At one time or another, you have had to study for a test.

Whether you have been out of school for two years or 20, studying for your CDL test will require two things: (1) a plan to study regularly, and (2) sticking to that plan.

We suggest dividing the 18 chapters of this study guide into comfortable chunks of information. You may want to cover a chapter a week. You may decide to spend two weeks on each chapter. So, depending on how much time you have to study, make a study plan and stick to it! If you get behind, find time to catch up and then try to stay on target.

How to Get the Most Out of Your Study Time

Most learners get more out of studying for short periods of time. Don't try to "cram" for the CDL over a few days.

Decide now how much time you can study—three times a week, five times a week, or more. Study for 30 minutes, take a break, and then study for another 30 minutes. Study at your own pace and you'll be surprised at how fast the time flies.

Most people learn best by reading information and then writing it down. The authors recommend that you read each chapter and highlight the most important information. Then go back and write down what you have highlighted. This way, you automatically review the information twice.

After reading, highlighting, and taking notes on each chapter, you'll find 10 review questions at the end of the chapter. These are to help you make sure you've absorbed the important information in the chapter. Read each question and mark the right answer. Then check your answers. If you need more study in one area, go back and reread that section of information.

One week before taking the exam, go back over the highlighted chapters, go over your notes, take the sample final exams—and you should be ready to go.

See how easy it is?

A. Read the book and highlight the most important information.
B. Go back over each chapter and write down highlighted information.
C. Take the test at the end of the chapter and check answers. Review material that is not clear to you.
D. Before taking the CDL exam, go back over each chapter, read your notes, and take the sample exams at the end of the book.

Now, let's get busy!

What Is the CDL and Why Is it Important?

The Class A Commercial Driver's License grants the holder permission to legally operate certain vehicles, including:

- Vehicles with Gross Vehicle Weight Rating (GVWR) of 26,001 pounds or more.
- Trailers with GVWR of 10,001 pounds or more.
- Vehicles carrying placarded hazardous materials.
- Vehicles (buses) with a capacity of 15 or more people (including driver).

What CDL Classification Should You Choose?

This really is a simple choice. The CDL classifications are divided into three categories:

Class A—Combination

All tractor-trailer drivers must have a Class A CDL if the trailer Gross Vehicle Weight Rating (GVWR) (amount of weight for which the vehicle was designed) is more than 10,000 pounds. So, when you add the weight of the tractor the Gross Combination Vehicle Weight Rating is more than 26,000 pounds.

If you plan to pull double or triple trailers, you must have a Class A CDL.

In certain states, if a tow-truck operator tows vehicles that exceed a GVWR of 10,000 pounds or if the combination of the tow truck and the towed vehicle exceeds 26,000 GCVWR, a Class A CDL may be required. Check with your state Driver License Division (DLD) for specific requirements. Figure 1-1 shows Class A vehicles.

Figure 1-1   Class A vehicles.

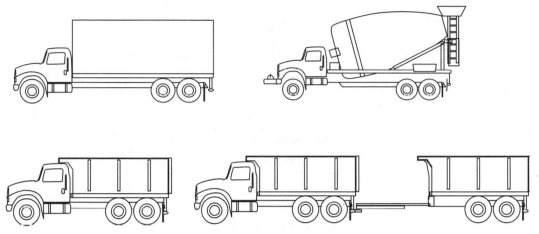

Figure 1-2   Straight line trucks (class B).

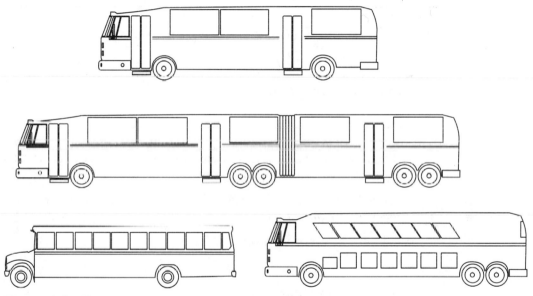

Figure 1-3   Buses.

Class B—Heavy Straight Truck or Bus

If you plan to operate a large straight truck or bus with a GVWR of 26,000 pounds or more, you need a Class B CDL. You may pull a trailer as long as the GVWR is not more than 10,000 pounds. Articulated buses also are in this category. Figure 1-2 shows Class B vehicles. Figure 1-3 shows types of buses.

Class C—Small Vehicles

A person who drives a small van, minibus, or car, requires a class C CDL, depending on the type of cargo, not the weight.

Figure 1-4   Class C vehicles.

- If you are transporting hazardous materials requiring hazardous materials (HazMat) placards, you need a Class C CDL, no matter how small or how heavy the vehicle is.
- If you operate a small vehicle, or one designed to carry more than 15 people, including yourself (the driver), you will need a Class C CDL. Figure 1-4 shows some types of Class C vehicles.

What the CDL Test Looks Like

The CDL test is divided into two parts—the Knowledge Tests and the Skills Test.

The Knowledge Tests

The Knowledge Tests are written tests. Contact the Driver License Division in your state of legal residence to find out when and where the Knowledge Tests are given, how much time they take to complete, and the costs. You must answer 80 percent of the questions correctly to pass the Knowledge Tests.

Note: The DMV (Department of Motor Vehicles) is where you get your vehicle licensed, not always where you take the tests.

There are seven Knowledge Tests:

The General Knowledge Test

All CDL applicants must take this test. It reviews general safety rules for driving a commercial vehicle carrying various types of cargo.

The General Knowledge Test is made up of 50 true-false or multiple-choice questions with four possible answers. You must have 40 correct answers to pass. After passing the General Knowledge Test, you are eligible to take the Skills Test, unless the vehicle you will be driving while taking the Skills Test requires one of the following endorsements:

Combination Vehicle Test—for articulated vehicles or if you plan to pull a trailer. The Combination Endorsement Test is made up of approximately 20 questions. You must correctly answer 16 to pass.

Air Brakes Test—for operators of any vehicle equipped with air brakes (road test required). This test must be taken if you plan to drive any commercial vehicle equipped with air brakes. If you take the Skills Test in a vehicle without air brakes or if you fail the air brakes test, your CDL will indicate you are not qualified to drive a vehicle with air brakes. There are approximately 25 true-false or multiple-choice questions on this test. You must correctly answer 20 to pass.

Note: To receive the Class A CDL you must pass the General Knowledge Test, Air Brakes Test, and the Combination Vehicle Test.

Endorsement Tests (Four)

Endorsement Tests are dependent on the type of vehicle you will be driving. Each Endorsement Test covers knowledge of a specific type of commercial vehicle, including:

- **Passenger Vehicles (Bus)**—needed by operators of all motor vehicles designed to transport 15 or more passengers, including the driver.
- **Tanker**—for operators of vehicles transporting liquids or gas in bulk.
- **Double or Triple Trailers**—for operators of vehicles pulling two or three trailers. This endorsement requires a Class A CDL.
- **Hazardous Materials (HazMat)**—for operators of vehicles transporting hazardous materials. Must be trained and retested every two years. You must also be 21 years or older for a HazMat Endorsement.

What Do the Endorsement Tests Look Like?

When you pass an Endorsement Test, your CDL will carry a special marking (or endorsement), indicating you are qualified to drive a particular commercial vehicle.

- **The Passenger Vehicle Endorsement Test** has approximately 20 questions, 16 of which must be correctly answered for a passing grade.
- **The Tanker Endorsement Test** is made up of approximately 20 questions, and 16 correct answers are required to pass.
- **The Doubles and Triples Endorsement Test** has approximately 20 multiple-choice questions, and you must correctly answer 16 to pass.
- **The Hazardous Materials Endorsement Test** is made up of approximately 30 multiple-choice questions. You must correctly answer 24 to pass.

Most drivers take only three of the four Endorsement Tests, but it is best to take all the Endorsement Tests while the material is fresh in your mind. In addition, prospective employers look for applicants with all Endorsements. And you never know when you will need an additional Endorsement.

The Skills Tests

There are three types of Skills Tests that must be taken in the state of your legal residence and in the vehicle you wish to be licensed to drive. These tests are usually given by appointment only, so an examiner can be scheduled. Contact the Driver License Division in your home state for more information.

The Pre-Trip Inspection Test is given to see if you know whether the vehicle is safe to drive. On this test, you may be asked to do a pre-trip inspection of your vehicle and/or explain to the examiner what you would inspect and why. Some states require only a written pre-trip test. However, the main reason for a complete pre-trip inspection before each trip is to ensure that you, the driver, are operating a safe piece of equipment.

The Basic Control Skills Test evaluates your basic skills in controlling the vehicle. The test involves exercises including moving the vehicle forward, backing, and turning maneuvers. You will be scored on how well you stay within boundaries (marked with lines or cones) and how many pullups (stopping and remaneuvering to the correct position) you make as you park your vehicle.

The Road Test evaluates your ability to drive safely in a variety of on-the-road situations. The test course includes left and right turns, intersections, railroad crossings, curves, up and down grades, rural or semi-rural roads, city multi-lane streets, and expressway driving. You will be scored on specific tasks, including turns, merging into traffic, lane changes, and speed control as well as signaling, spotting hazards, and lane positioning. You will also be scored on how well you "start and stop" the vehicle, shifting, braking, and clutching.

The Commercial Vehicle Safety Act of 1986

The United States Congress passed the Commercial Vehicle Safety Act of 1986 (CMVSA/86) to increase highway safety. Among other things, the Act requires all 50 states to meet the same minimum standards in testing and licensing of all commercial drivers. These standards require that all commercial motor vehicle drivers must pass the required tests and obtain the CDL.

The reason for this requirement is to ensure that anyone operating a commercial motor vehicle has the skills and knowledge required to operate it safely on the highway.

Therefore, all professional drivers must take the CDL Knowledge Tests as well as appropriate Skills Tests (by driving the vehicles they are being licensed for with an examiner).

What You Need to Know About the CMVSA/86

1. As of April 1, 1992, it is illegal to drive a commercial vehicle without a CDL. If you do so, you may be fined up to $5,000 or jailed for breaking this law.
2. Commercial drivers may have only one license. The fine for having more than one license can be up to $5,000 or possible jail time. Your CDL must be issued by the state of your legal residence.
3. If you are an experienced commercial driver and have a safe driving record, you may not need to take the Skills Test to transfer your CDL to another state. Check with the local licensing authority or the Department of Motor Vehicles to verify your state's requirements.
4. Testing and licensing of all commercial drivers is required.
5. All commercial drivers are required to report all moving violations to their employers and to their state of legal residence within 30 days of conviction.

   Drivers must also report license suspension, revocations, cancellation, or disqualification before the end of the business day on which the driver receives notification. This notification is required, whether you are driving a commercial vehicle or an automobile when the violation occurred. This does not include parking violations.

6. When applying for any commercial driving job, commercial drivers must give information about all driving jobs held over the past 10 years to the new employer.

7. All states will share information about CDL drivers via a universal computerized database.

8. Your employer cannot allow you to drive any commercial vehicle if you have more than one license or if your CDL has been suspended or revoked. The penalty for doing so is a $5,000 fine or jail time for your employer.

9. You will lose your CDL for at least one year if
   - you drive a commercial vehicle while using alcohol or other controlled substances.
   - you leave the scene of an accident involving the vehicle you are driving.
   - if you use a commercial vehicle to commit a felony.

10. You will lose your CDL
   - for at least two months if you have had two serious traffic violations involving a commercial vehicle within a three-year period.
   - for at least four months for three serious violations within a three-year period.
   - for one year for first offense of driving under the influence of alcohol (Blood Alcohol Concentration [the BAC limit] is 0.04 percent or more). If your BAC is less than 0.04 percent and there is any detectable alcohol in the bloodstream, you will be taken out of service for 24 hours.

      Note: A 180-lb. person consuming two drinks will have a BAC of .04 percent, so drinking two beers may cause you to lose your CDL—a high price to pay!

   - for one year for leaving the scene of an accident while driving a commercial vehicle.
   - for life if you have a second offense of driving after using alcohol or other controlled substances.

11. "Serious violations" include excessive speed, reckless driving, and traffic offenses committed in connection with fatal traffic accidents.

12. Individual states may add to this list and their penalties may be more severe.

13. Your state may have additional rules, which you must know and obey.

Let's Review

Read each question and all of the answers provided. Place the letter of the correct answer in the space provided or write your answers on a separate piece of paper so you can use these questions again as you review for the CDL. Once you have answered all the questions, check your answers against the answer key that follows.

_____ 1. The penalty for being convicted twice for driving under the influence of alcohol or controlled substances is losing your CDL for
(A) 120 days;
(B) lifetime;
(C) until the company allows you to return to the road;
(D) three years.

_____ 2. The Commercial Motor Vehicle Safety Act of 1986 (CMVSA/86) required that all states
(A) license all commercial vehicle drivers;
(B) allow doubles and triples to operate on state highways;
(C) charge tolls for all commercial vehicles;
(D) none of the above.

_____ 3. If a commercial vehicle driver is stopped and his or her blood alcohol concentration is found to be .04 percent or higher, the driver will be
(A) ticketed;
(B) given a warning;
(C) arrested for driving under the influence;
(D) reported to their employer.

_____ 4. If you are planning to drive a vehicle equipped with air brakes, you must
(A) take the Skills Test in a vehicle equipped with air brakes;
(B) pass the Air Brakes Knowledge Test;
(C) earn the Air Brake Endorsement;
(D) all of the above.

_____ 5. The "P" Endorsement is required on your CDL if you plan to drive
(A) a van with a seating capacity in excess of 15;
(B) a school bus;
(C) a commercial bus;
(D) all of the above.

_____ 6. If you do not obtain a CDL and are stopped by authorities while driving a commercial vehicle, you will be fined
(A) $5,000;   (C) $15,000;
(B) $10,000;   (D) none of the above.

_____ 7. If you are convicted of a moving violation, the CMVSA/86 requires you to notify your employer within
(A) 24 hours;   (C) 2 weeks;
(B) 30 days;   (D) 21 days.

_____ 8. The Class A CDL grants the holder
(A) the right to legally operate vehicles with a GVWR of 26,001 pounds or more;
(B) the right to operate trailers with a GVWR of 10,001 pounds or more;
(C) the ability to operate a vehicle equipped with air brakes;
(D) all of the above.

___ 9. A BAC of .04 percent can be achieved in a 180-lb. person by
(A) drinking 6 beers;   (C) drinking 1 beer;
(B) drinking 2 beers;   (D) drinking 1 wine cooler.

___10. True or False: When applying for any commercial driving job, the driver must give information about all driving jobs held over the past 10 years to the new employer.

Answers to Let's Review

1. B; 2. A; 3. C; 4. D; 5. D; 6. A; 7. B; 8. D; 9. B; 10. True

Terms You Need to Know

The following terms have been taken from the contents of Chapter 1. Review them. If you see any you're not sure of, check the definition in the Glossary at the back of the book. If it helps you, keep a written list of the words and their definitions (or write in the definitions here) and review them several days prior to taking the CDL tests.

Air brakes

BAC

CMVSA/86

Doubles

Endorsement

Hazardous materials

Knowledge test

Placard

Pre-trip inspection

Pullups

Skills test

Tanker

Triples

THE DISPATCH BOARD

Every trucking company has a "dispatch board." Some are chalkboards. Some are white boards. Some are computerized. The "dispatch board" was developed to provide information to drivers during the course of their shift. Some of the messages came from customers. Some were reminders from dispatchers. Some of the messages reminded the drivers to pick up a gallon of milk before returning home.

At the end of each chapter, "The Dispatch Board" will provide some additional information for the professional driving applicant. It might be useful, although you will not be tested on it when you take the CDL tests. So, you may choose to read this information or you may skip it and go on to the next chapter. It's your call.

When a Driver is More Than a Driver   Twenty years ago, I drove a cab for a living. It was a cowboy's life, a life for someone who wanted no boss. What I didn't realize was that it was also a ministry. Because I drove the night shift, my cab became a moving confessional.

Passengers climbed in, sat behind me in total anonymity, and told me about their lives. I encountered people whose lives amazed me, ennobled me, and made me laugh and weep. But none touched me more than a woman I picked up late one August night.

I was responding to a call from a small brick fourplex in a quiet part of town. I assumed I was being sent to pick up some parties or someone who had just had a fight with a lover, or a worker heading to an early shift at some factory for the industrial part of town. When I arrived at 2:30 AM, the building was dark except for a single light in a ground floor window. Under these circumstances, many drivers would just honk once or twice, wait a minute, and then drive away.

But I had seen too many impoverished people who depended on taxis as their only means of transportation. Unless a situation smelled of danger, I always went to the door. This passenger might be someone who needs my assistance, I reasoned to myself. So I walked to the door and knocked.

"Just a minute," answered a frail, elderly voice. I could hear something being dragged across the floor. After a long pause, the door opened. A small woman in her eighties stood before me. She wore a pillbox hat with a veil pinned on it, like somebody out of a 1940s movie. By her side was a small nylon suitcase.

The apartment looked as if no one had lived in it for years. All the furniture was covered with sheets. There were no clocks on the walls, no knickknacks or utensils on the counters. In the corner was a cardboard box filled with photos and glassware.

"Would you carry my bag out to the car?" she said. I took the suitcase to the cab, and then returned to assist the woman. She took my arm and we walked slowly toward the curb. She kept thanking me for my kindness. "It's nothing," I told her. "I just try to treat my passengers the way I would want my mother treated."

"Oh, you're such a good boy," she said.

When we got in the cab, she gave me the address, and then asked, "Could you drive through downtown?"

"It's not the shortest way," I answered quickly.

"Oh, I don't mind," she said. "I'm in no hurry. I'm on my way to a hospice."

I looked in the rearview mirror. Her eyes were glistening. "I don't have any family left," she continued. "The doctor says I don't have very long."

I quietly reached over and shut off the meter. "What route would you like me to take?" I asked.

continues

THE DISPATCH BOARD *continued*

For the next two hours, we drove through the city. She showed me the building where she had once worked as an elevator operator. We drove through the neighborhood where she and her husband had lived when they were newlyweds. She had me pull up in front of a furniture warehouse that had once been a ballroom where she had gone dancing as a girl. Sometimes she'd ask me to slow in front of a particular building or corner and would sit staring into the darkness, saying nothing. As the first hint of sun was creasing the horizon, she suddenly said, "I'm tired. Let's go now."

We drove in silence to the address she had given me. It was a low building, like a small convalescent home, with a driveway that passed under a portico. Two orderlies came out to the cab as soon as we pulled up. They were solicitous and intent, watching her every move. They must have been expecting her. I opened the trunk and took the small suitcase to the door. The woman was already seated in a wheelchair.

"How much do I owe you?" she asked, reaching into her purse.

"Nothing," I said.

"You have to make a living," she answered.

"There are other passengers," I responded.

Almost without thinking, I bent and gave her a hug. She held onto me tightly. "You gave an old woman a little moment of joy," she said. "Thank you." I squeezed her hand, then walked into the dim morning light.

Behind me, a door shut. It was the sound of the closing of a life.

I didn't pick up any more passengers that shift. I drove aimlessly, lost in thought. For the rest of that day, I could hardly talk. What if that woman had gotten an angry driver, or one who was impatient to end his shift? What if I had refused to take the run, or had honked once, then driven away? On a quick review, I don't think that I have done anything more important in my life.

We are sometimes taught to think that our lives revolve around great moments, that our memories go back to only the great moments of our lives—graduation, a significant relationship, or our first jobs.

As a professional driver, you will touch many lives. Often it will be in passing, as you make a delivery or a pick-up. Most of these relationships will be strictly business. But, as in all our lives, there will also be some great moments—those times when we don't realize how our lives and our actions impact another, those times that often catch us unaware—beautifully wrapped in what others may see as an unexpected gift.

People may not remember exactly what you did, or what you said, but they will always remember how you made them feel.

2 Welcome to the New Millennium of Professional Driving

After passing the CDL, you will enter a profession much different than professional drivers found two decades ago. The changes made in the transportation industry during the last quarter-century have created an environment of increased professionalism and continuing opportunity.

Here's what one retired driver had to say about his tenure in trucking from 1948 to 1980:

> I was lucky. I worked for a carrier who tried to stay at the forefront of the industry, so when something new was available, we were usually the first to get it, but we still had trucks we held together with baling wire. And, until the last years I worked, there wasn't the emphasis on safety that there is now.
>
> In the old days, getting a load delivered was everything—and that still holds true today, except the driver's health and well-being also plays a role now. Back then—when I first started driving—I drank a lot of coffee and drove a lot of hours I probably shouldn't have, just to be on-time.
>
> And back then, I usually felt like the Lone Ranger out on the road. Dispatchers today have some empathy. But when I first started, their word was law—no if's, and's or but's. I remember wanting to come home so I could be with my wife while she had our first kid. But delivering that load came first, so I got home a few days after the baby was born.
>
> When we got CB radios, now that was a positive change. We only called home once a week because long-distance could eat up your paycheck in a hurry. With the CB, we could communicate with other drivers instead of going hundreds of miles and the only conversation would be with the waitress at a restaurant at what eventually became a truck stop—but back then, there were a couple of gas pumps and a "greasy spoon" type of café, which is probably why I have trouble with my stomach—even today.

Truck drivers today will find a totally different environment when they go to work for most carriers, and today's carriers are continuing to find ways to improve the driver's quality of life.

To give you a wider view of professional driving today, here are some frequently asked questions about the transportation industry:

Q. Are there driving jobs where I can be home every night?

A. Absolutely, and many of these jobs provide a tremendous foundation for your professional driving career. "Local" or "regional" carriers usually cover about a 200-mile radius from their home base, which makes it fairly easy for a driver to take a load, deliver it, and return home in the same day.

The drawbacks these jobs offer: some don't pay as well as over-the-road jobs, but drivers *are* home every night or, at the most, every second night.

Q. **If I take an over-the-road job, how long will I be away from home at one time?**

A. Depending on the company, some work to have drivers home every two weeks, whereas some assignments put you on the road for as long as three weeks out of every four.

Q. **Do any companies allow my spouse or partner to come with me over the road?**

A. Many companies allow wives to travel with their husbands. And many companies have liberal policies so that a driver's children (age 12 and over) can travel with them over summer vacations or Christmas break. A few companies even have policies where a pet can travel with the driver.

Q. **Are there opportunities for women as professional drivers?**

A. Absolutely! Professional driving schools report that a larger percentage of each class—12 to 15 percent—is female and more women are going over the road. Some companies, as you'll read later on, are buying trucks with automatic transmissions so that more women will drive. And some companies train a driver's spouse, partner, or significant other to drive so that couples can drive in teams.

Q. **What if my wife or husband has to stay home with the kids?**

A. Many of the major carriers offer special hotlines so that your wife or husband can contact you immediately if they need to talk or if there's a problem. Some companies give phone cards so you can call home more often. In the "old days," drivers might have been allowed one long-distance call home at company expense. Today, thanks to QualComm, the Internet, and cell phones, drivers can talk to families and friends every night of the week, and "phone home" programs are more popular than ever before.

Q. **What if there's a special event that requires my attendance at home?**

A. Some companies—but not all—do everything possible to get drivers home when they need to be there for weddings, funerals, graduations, the birth of a child, and other special occasions. Drivers also help each other out by offering to take loads so that others can be home for family events. But there are also some companies that guarantee drivers will be home for special occasions, even if it means flying them back at company expense.

Q. **What about banking, getting paid, and paying my bills while I'm on the road?**

A. Some companies make it possible to see each paycheck, via the Internet, even if the driver has direct deposit. This tells the driver how much is going into his or her bank account. Drivers with partners sometimes allow the partners to take care of their bills for them. However, with the advent of laptop computers, Internet banking, and automatic bill-pay services offered by some banks, paying monthly bills has become easier for over-the-road drivers.

Q. **What about a laptop computer? Do I need one if I go over-the-road?**

A. Actually, there are a couple of options here. Some companies provide on-board computers with the ability to receive and send e-mails. However, drivers who use their personal laptops prefer their privacy. The ability to keep in contact with friends and family through e-mail is a must, according to drivers who pack their own laptops or hand-held computers. Some drivers also report success using the capacity of sending and receiving e-mail over their cell phones.

What Some of America's Top Carriers/Trainers Say

Here's what some leaders in the transportation industry say about professional drivers and driving in the new millennium:

Bob Hirsch, President, Truckload Carriers Association (TCA)

"We are the national association for the long-haul, over-the-road, for-hire motor carriers. Our members pick up and deliver truckload freight, which means when they pick up freight from a single shipper, the load either weighs out or is cubed out to occupy the entire vehicle.

"Last year, TCA initiated partnerships with the national office of La Raza and the National Urban League. In working with these groups, we are recognizing many cultural issues within the ethnic populations that this industry will have to overcome. We hope that our work with these groups will bring more drivers from various communities into the industry.

"According to the information we have, the driver shortage as of Fall 2002 will be about 80,000. That means every year for the next several years, 80,000 new drivers will be needed to keep America's trucks rolling.

"As companies grow and as older drivers retire, there will be ample numbers of seats that have to be filled. And projections are that traffic is going to increase. With that increase, we will need more drivers and we're competing heavily with other industries to get the best talents into the transportation industry.

"In terms of opportunities, you will find that opportunities in trucking run the gamut, depending on the type of carrier you want to work for and the operations particular to each carrier.

"You've got dry vans, household goods, tankers, reefers—and they all have needs unique to that segment. There are also opportunities with long-haul and regional carriers and with many carriers operating within a particular commercial zone. There's not a stereotype operation—not a one-size-fits-all operation.

"Traditional long-haul carriers have continued modifying operations to better accommodate their particular workplace needs, and this adds new dimensions to what over-the-road carriers offer in the way of opportunities.

"What can you do with driving experience after a couple of years? You can go into other branches of transportation, and that includes administration, operations, recruiting, training—the opportunities run the gamut like any other business and many times, opportunity depends on the size of the business. In a smaller company, sometimes you wear a number of hats and have a variety of responsibilities, from driver, maintenance, human resources, chief executive, dispatch, safety, recruiting, maintenance, sales, routing—all areas related and all requiring different levels of expertise.

"At the Truckload Carriers Association, we think professional driving is only the first step in a long and rewarding career. We wish each new driver a long and exciting experience in an industry that offers challenges, rewards, and a lifetime of opportunities."

Bruce Buscada, President, Diesel Driving Academy and President, Commercial Vehicle Training Association

"Professional driving can be a great career, but it depends on the individual and what they're looking for. Being away from home and learning how to live on the road is one of the challenges of driving today. We teach a lot of this in our schools—how to handle things on the road, like time management. Some drivers lose a lot of time by sitting in a truck stop, talking for two or three hours at a time and then having to really hit it to make up that time. We also talk about managing the diet, resting, and how to accomplish tasks as simple as cleaning your own clothes.

"We're hearing recruiters from various trucking companies say their carriers are doing more and more to make life on the road easier. Some of the better companies work every day to make professional driving a positive experience for families across the nation.

"Drivers today have knowledge the previous generation of drivers didn't have because communications has become so important. You have to learn how to get in touch with people quickly, how to get your messages faster, and how to get messages to your family in faster ways, too.

"Typical students at the Diesel Driving Academy average 31 years of age—they can be married or separated but most have kids. Fifteen to 20 percent of the classes are women."

Buscada said more and more wives are coming to train with their husbands. Their kids may be finished with college or out on their own, so many couples cope with the "empty nest" syndrome by getting out on the road together. However, there are more and more young couples training together so they can drive as a team until they're ready to start a family.

Paul Strohm, Operations Manager, McCurdy & Co., a Refrigerated Carrier Based in Houston, Texas

McCurdy finds a lot of their new drivers are in professional driving programs, like Houston Community College's Professional Driving Program, and the company also runs ads in *The Houston Chronicle*. Most of the new-hires have never seen a refrigerated (reefer) unit before, and for two months after hire, they ride with an experienced driver.

The most challenging part for McCurdy is getting drivers to understand what the company is trying to do—taking a perishable product and getting it to market while it is still fresh. Most receivers expect delivery when it is scheduled, and if a driver has mechanical problems or problems picking up the load, they should call the McCurdy dispatcher for help. Some do. Many don't. "If something goes wrong on the road, the dispatcher will help the driver find a solution," said Strohm.

As the largest reefer carrier based in Houston, McCurdy offers competitive pay, newer equipment, good maintenance, and a goal of getting drivers home once a week.

Strohm said that in the early part of the new century, getting and keeping drivers has been easier. "The ones we're hiring are staying and we're having more candidates apply when we have openings," Strohm said.

Don Lacey, Director of Safety and Recruiting, P.R.I.M.E., Inc., Springfield, Missouri

"When we're recruiting, one of the first things we ask is, 'Are you prepared to be gone four weeks out of the month?' Just being prepared for it and doing it are two different things. P.R.I.M.E. runs the entire U.S. and Canada, but we also have a liberal passenger policy and some people even 'home school' their kids on the truck. That works out well while the kids are still young."

P.R.I.M.E. recently constructed Millennium Center in Springfield, which serves as corporate headquarters for the carrier. Those working there or coming for training can leave their children each day in a child care facility staffed by professional child development specialists. The Center also offers concierge services, a CPA firm to help drivers with money matters, a banking service, a mail center, shopping center, movie theater, private rooms for meetings, basketball court, fitness center, shuttle service around town, and a place to nap, which, Lacey points out, you can't do at the airport.

"If you're used to visiting your old auntie on Sundays, you won't like it here," Lacey said, "but we have a liberal passenger policy, we provide phone cards at a low rate, and we have e-mail set up for every driver.

"In our driver services building at Millennium Center, P.R.I.M.E. drivers have free access to the Internet, soundproof phone booths, and the company operates two motels to house drivers who come in for repairs or for training."

The carrier hosts two major events each year, a sit-down dinner and a family picnic. P.R.I.M.E. also has a message center where operators relay QualComm messages to the truck for the driver to call home if a problem arises. And about 1000 people are on the carriers CabCard, an e-mail system through QualComm.

Lacey says it takes a special person to be a top professional driver, although some drivers report that being home only a week out of the month makes every trip home seem like a honeymoon.

Kelvin McKelvy, Vice-president of Recruiting, Contract Freighters, Inc., Joplin, Missouri

Are you suited to become a professional driver?

CFI's Kelvin McKelvy says many may be capable, but professional driving jobs are for people who are willing and able to spend long hours and many days traveling and away from home. Salaries range from $40,000 to $50,000 per year, but McKelvy says, "It's a tough job—physically, emotionally, and mentally—although it looks easier than it is."

Why is it tough? When it starts to hit you that you're missing your kid's Little League play-off game or your dad's 72nd birthday, the emotional aspect takes a toll.

McKelvy says drivers either make the adjustment because they fit the professional category or because they adapt to it through a somewhat painful process.

When hiring new drivers, CFI looks for people who keep and maintain a clean vehicle, people who can get good fuel mileage and low, out-of-route percentage. They want drivers who have a good safety record, can deliver loads on time, who have strong customer service skills, and show courtesy on the highway to four-wheelers. "Professional drivers know that it's not just about shifting gears and knowing how to back up to a dock," McKelvy said. "And like CFI, there are companies out there who will support you. If you're going to work for the best, you have to be among the best."

"We have periodic programs and are sensitive to the needs of our drivers," he said, "and we want to be inclusive of the driver's family, so we have a rider's program and we encourage couples to drive in teams whenever they can. That program gives the family a double income and keeps the family together. From our standpoint, that's a winner and that's why we started our automatic transmission training program."

CFI has also developed a "take your spouse to work" program, allowing partners to accompany professional drivers on the road. The new program gives the partner a perspective on what life is like on the road. "They may have the perception that their partner sits around in bars, drinking beer, and stuffing dollar bills into G-strings when, in reality, they're out there driving 10 hours a day, living in a sleeper, unloading trucks, and fighting traffic. And the driver's perception may be that their partner is hanging out with a best friend and drinking beer at the local bowling alley when they're really diapering kids, driving carpools, and doing laundry at all hours. We think when the two worlds come together, both partners increase their perspective and increase their understanding."

This motor carrier has always encouraged drivers to keep in close contact with home, and its call home program offers liberal long-distance time. "If they [drivers] can keep in touch frequently, those inevitable disasters aren't as big. And if a partner can reach the driver when they need to, they are less anxious," McKelvy said.

All CFI trucks are outfitted with cellular service and if there is an urgent triumph or tragedy call, drivers can call home as soon as the message is transmitted—and just knowing that service is available makes being away from home less challenging.

At CFI's headquarters, family members can call an 800 number and ask to talk to a spouse, son, daughter, or parent. The CFI operator will contact the driver immediately—no questions asked—and ask them to call home. Knowing that capability is there lessens the anxiety.

" 'You can call me and I can call you' doesn't sound like a big deal, but it's a security blanket for everyone involved," McKelvy said. "It's not that the at-home partner couldn't handle it, but they may want input from the driver. And it may be something like 'The car won't start. Should I call a wrecker or your brother?' So, this asks for the driver's insight. It shares information, it lets the driver know his or her input is important, and it allows partners to handle situations as partners."

McKelvy said CFI has a couple of thousand drivers and when they pull together to help a fellow driver, this is one of the best parts of the business. CFI works hard to create a sense of family among drivers, significant others, and their families. "Once a year we host a family night and open our main offices for everyone," McKelvy explained. "Drivers and everyone bring families to see where they work, to see the red racer, to climb over the trucks, and to meet dispatchers, maintenance personnel, safety personnel, and other drivers. We raise money for local charities for children and senior citizens, and we think when families see how and where a driver works, more empathy and understanding develops."

Ron Dowdy, President Ronnie Dowdy, Inc., Batesville, Arkansas, and Chair, Driver Recruitment and Retention Panel, Truckload Carriers Association

In the year 2000, the Truck Carriers Association found the average professional driver's salary was at $40,800. For individuals completing their CDL, training and finishing, they can, within a five-year period, be making $50,000. In addition, there is also the opportunity to build seniority and eventually move up to management.

This industry has much to offer. For people who have driven professionally, their training and experience can be used to get into middle management and other opportunities as they grow and mature with the industry.

"This nation's goods are going to move by truck," Dowdy said. "I don't know who the companies will be who will do the hauling, but I do know that our goods are going to move by truck and that means there will be jobs and opportunities.

"I know that industry publications prior to this year (2001) projected a shortage of 80,000 drivers every year. With the economy down turning, some of those seats will be filled, but there will always be jobs for good, professional drivers."

Terry Brown, President, Allied Drivers, a Driver Leasing Company Based in Houston, Texas

Terry Brown's father owned trucks and because he had no sons, he taught his daughter Terry to drive and took her on the road when she was old enough. "When I went with my dad, I got to eat pancakes and drink orange soda for breakfast and shippers gave me toys," she remembers. "That was it for me. I was hooked."

Brown drove for 22 years and still holds a fully endorsed Class A CDL, because, as she says, "You never know."

After she hung up her CB and driving gloves, she opened Allied Drivers and now works with companies when drivers are on vacation, during busy periods, or when companies want to hire an experienced driver. She says clients come to Allied Drivers to try out drivers before hiring them full time. This also gives the drivers an opportunity to see if they like working for an outfit before they sign up full time. "You may have seen a truck or know of an outfit and you may want to try it. If it doesn't work for you, you haven't lost anything."

Brown said some people have a misconception about lease drivers. "The people I hire are full-time, professional drivers," she said. "That's what they do for a living—and we have really high standards. We're not hiring warm bodies with CDLs, five accidents, and three drug violations around here. We want people who can get out there, do a good job, deliver their loads, and bring the trucks back in one piece. And my files are open so customers can come in and check out a driver's credentials any time they want to.

"We go by the book around here and then some. So, the hardest part of my job is finding qualified drivers—but if that were easy, everybody would be doing it," she said.

By "qualified," Brown means good, verifiable work experience, no more than two violations in the last three years, and no drug use. "We don't promise them the moon, just to get them through the door," she said. "But we don't promise anything we can't deliver either."

Anyone can tell by talking to Terry Brown that she loves what she does, and she says someday—when her kids are grown (her husband is also a professional driver)—she just might swing up into the cab and take off down the road one more time.

Randy Scheel, Director of Driver Development, CRST Van-expedited Division, Cedar Rapids, Iowa

"We're considered a truckload hauler, running coast-to-coast, and all our freight is van truckload general commodities. We have over 400 trucks that are solos—people who work within a specific region of the country, and out of our 1,400 trucks, 300 are owner-operators.

"What we do specifically is try to create career paths for people to meet individual needs and goals, and we do offer training, partnering with community colleges, like Houston Community College professional truck driving school. We sponsor training for students and pay tuition and, in turn, we ask for a one-year commitment after completion.

"In our system, for the first year minimum, a new driver must run team. Once someone is driving with us two or three years, they have several options. They can switch to solo division. And we do have a lease-purchase program that will help them get into a truck with good financing terms. If they want to buy a truck on their own and lease back to us, they can also do this.

"If a driver wants to be over-the-road, they can go into our lead driver program, which provides training to new drivers or they can go into operations. Right now, three departments are headed by former drivers, our safety department, driver development, and our operations department.

"Trucking today has a dynamic focus and is such a wide-open field. So, I think there will always be a demand for trucks, regardless of the economy. People will still have freight to move across the highways.

"To meet the demand for drivers, CRST employs a number of husband-wife or family-member driving teams. We also have a guaranteed home policy—[drivers] tell us when [they] need to be home and we'll guarantee to make that happen, even if we have to fly or bus them to get them there.

"We are also talking about a spouse support network. We try to involve the spouse with newsletters and feedback on how their significant other is doing and we are going to be doing more to communicate with a driver's home base, such as recognizing important anniversaries and sending birthday cards to the family.

"We realize that driving a truck is a non-typical job, not a standard 8-hour a day, 40-hour-a-week job. We also recognize that some working conditions are often beyond the company's control and beyond the driver's control: weather, construction, traffic, customers who may not be driver-friendly, equipment issues such as breakdowns, etc.

"On the other hand, when you're moving down the highway during the evenings, there's a sense of isolation that goes with that. This is the part that appeals to people who are tired of factory work, tired of having their boss standing over their shoulder. Basically, when you're a professional driver, you're unsupervised and you have a lot of freedom.

"That's why it appeals to such a broad variety of people. We have applicants from junior high educations to master's and PhD degrees. In a few years, they'll make $40,000 to $50,000 a year. Professional driving gives people a chance at a better earning potential than any career they could choose.

"In 1992-1993, one woman who was a family practitioner—an MD—went through truck driving school and drove for us. She was eventually featured on NBC Nightly News. And after driving for us for a couple of years, she became our company doctor. We also hire empty nesters who have always thought about driving a truck, raised a family and now husband and wife can see the country together, drive a truck, and earn money while doing it. These teams call themselves 'paid tourists.'

"So, as you can see, driving offers something for everyone. It's a win-win for the right people."

Mike Ritchie, Executive Vice-president, Stevens Transportation, Dallas, Texas

Stevens began training drivers in 1991 or 1992, and about six to eight years ago it began trying to shrink time on the road from four weeks. Now the company targets two weeks in getting drivers home, thanks to the help of software packages that help relay trucks and identify trucks crossing enroute so they can repower and get people home on a timely basis.

When dispatchers get ready to staff, the Stevens' software lets them know how many days each driver has been home, so they don't dispatch a driver who just got home.

On the road, drivers can e-mail home and each other and there are also voice mailboxes that the drivers can check throughout the day.

When a driver goes to Stevens' professional driving school, they are assigned to another driver and to a fleet manager who can work with them on payroll issues and personal problems.

"And we've taken that a step further," said Ritchie, "because we also have driver counselors. These are personal go-to people—where drivers can talk about problems and find resolution. They are also there for drivers and contact them two or three times a week, just to see how they're doing. Then we meet every Friday with the counselors to find out where we can help."

This program has paid off, and drivers have stayed with the company just because they wanted to be in "the family." And, if the driver has problems with fleet managers, payroll or operations, or a fellow employee, the counselors bring them together to work these things out.

Ten or 12 years ago, professional drivers were treated like second-rate citizens, but Ritchie sees an entirely new picture. "These people are our lifeblood—they pay my salary. They are our company when they make a delivery, when they pick up a load. Drivers are the heartbeat of this industry."

"We furnish shirts and ballcaps and have a semi-dress code: long pants, no flipflops—and we work with our new employees on how they dress, how they present themselves, and how they manage themselves on the road," he said.

"We're concerned with fuel costs, but also we're concerned with the comfort of drivers at fuel stops and we align ourselves with better chains—with clean showers, hot meals—versus pump your fuel yourself, get a hotdog, and take off.

"If you think about it, we've got a big investment in every driver, aside from their training. Every time they go on the road, they take $100,000 worth of equipment and $1 million worth of cargo. We've got a big investment out there, but it goes beyond that. If we've got an unhappy driver out there, they're a safety risk. So, we encourage dispatchers to listen to the driver's tone, and if the driver sounds distracted, we ask them to talk to them before they get off the phone.

"We encourage our drivers to bring their wives around and our counselors talk to the partners by telephone," Ritchie said. "Once a month, the counselors send the drivers' partners a postcard, just asking how things are going."

Counselors are typically people who started out as Stevens drivers, so they know what it is like on the road, but they are also qualified to help people.

Greg Adkinson, Safety Director, Builders Gypsum Supply, Houston, Texas

"When we hire drivers, we basically sit down and talk with them to find out their attitudes and values toward life. We also want to see if they are physically qualified, review their motor vehicle record for accidents, and see what type of vehicle experience they've had. Then, we verify their work history—for past driving experience and what kind of equipment they've operated—and then we go to the companies to talk about their performance.

"Our company offers the opportunity for growth as the company grows. And we're in an aggressive building period right now. We like to promote from within, so drivers can come into our warehouse operation, into our dispatch, and we have different locations around the state, which is an attractive option for anyone who likes to move around.

"We also have remedial training and any driver can further their education, depending on their job classification. A lot of our work is labor intensive. They are classified as driving motor vehicles but once they get to the work site, they then drive boom trucks or move drywall wherever the customer wants it.

"We pay tuition for those who want to further their education because we do take the more inexperienced individuals. We occasionally hire under-21 drivers for our class B work.

"We have a bonus program at the end of the year. We deduct for any accidents that could be prevented—but if a driver has no write-ups, they get the full bonus, and most of our drivers are home nightly, which is bonus in itself.

"Our work environment is also a plus because the owners of the company take pride in their employees, so there's a personal interest and off-the-wall type benefits—barbecues and meetings. Our drivers all have a feeling of being an important part of the team, of belonging somewhere. When you work with us, you're not just a number.

"Our most senior drivers have been with us about 15 years, and a good portion of our team has been with us 7 to 15 years. We have a very low driver turnover ratio—

they have to be physically fit, but we have 60-year-olds working with us who are in better shape than most 25-year-olds I know.

"Our starting salary, for Class A level, is between $20,000 and $24,000 . . . in this region of the country. In other areas of the country, that could be $30,000 to $35,000."

Next Stop: Great Opportunity!

Trucking is one of this country's most important industries. Without trucks, people's quality of life declines. Without trucks, costs skyrocket. Trucks move food, furniture, books, clothing, automobiles, refrigerators, and medicine.

Currently, there are more than 9.6 million people driving and supporting the transportation industry in the United States. Together these workers generate more than $372 billion a year hauling 6.7 billion tons of freight.

The trucking industry uses more than 4.5 million trailers and more than 1.7 million tractors as they travel over 118 billion miles every year.

Trucks include step van delivery vehicles, straight trucks, tractor trailers, doubles, and triples. Trucks also pay more than $28 billion in federal and state highway user taxes and more than 38 percent of all federal highway taxes that go to pay for those roads.

In the United States, there are now approximately 458,000 trucking companies. Some have only one truck, whereas others use thousands of vehicles to do business. About 88 percent of these companies can be classified as small businesses, while others are large, publicly-traded firms or closely held businesses, including partnerships and sole proprietorships owning only one or two tractors and trailers.

A serious driver shortage has plagued the industry for years and to solve this problem, trucking companies are offering better pay, better equipment, more benefits, and bonus programs to attract and keep good drivers. Compensation runs $22,000 to $26,000 per year for starting drivers and an average of $36,000 for more experienced drivers.

To qualify for a driving job, you must be 18 years of age or older and you must have a valid CDL. Drivers must be able to pass a complete Department of Transportation physical every two years and may not have suffered the loss of a hand, arm, foot, or leg and should not have any other physical defect that interferes with safe driving.

Anyone who has been diagnosed with diabetes requiring insulin for control cannot drive a truck but certainly can work in any other capacity within the industry.

Drivers must be able to speak and write English well enough to communicate with law enforcement authorities and the general public. Some companies have additional educational requirements.

The industry has strict regulations against the use of alcohol or drugs prior to or while operating any commercial vehicle. Negative results (clean) on alcohol and drug screenings are often a condition of employment.

Drivers may not have a felony conviction involving the use of a motor vehicle or have been charged with a crime involving drugs, driving under the influence of drugs or alcohol, or a hit-and-run accident resulting in an injury or death.

Men and women who have passed the CDL and who meet the requirements to become professional drivers have seen doors open for additional responsibilities, increasingly higher pay, and respected positions within the companies for which they work. It is not unusual to find vice-presidents and CEOs of transportation companies who began as drivers in this challenging and rewarding industry.

Now it's your turn!

THE DISPATCH BOARD
Road Rage: A Deadly Game

by Ron Adams, Ph.D.

Bob slows and eases his rig into line for the Border Patrol inspection. He glances at his watch. "If this doesn't take too long, I should be in San Antonio by midnight," he says to himself.

After the inspection, the miles glide by and as traffic increases, Bob knows he is nearing San Antonio. He slows for the Loop 1604 exit. "Not much traffic this time of the night."

Bob knows this route well. He's driven it for the past 10 years.

East on Loop 1604 and then north, crossing over I-10, Bob can see the lights of the I-35 exit only a few miles ahead. "I wonder why my stomach is churning?"

"Well here it is, I-35."

Since NAFTA began, this 250 miles to Dallas—right through the heart of Texas—is one of the most traveled highways in the country and, it seems to Bob, most of it is under construction.

Bob eases up on I-35. Shifting though the gears like the pro he is, he quickly settles into cruising speed. After a few miles, traffic gets worse. "Must be getting near New Braunfels." Wall to wall trucks, pickups, and sport utility vehicles. "These Texas guys love their pickups and SUVs."

Construction on the left. Construction on the right. "I wonder why my arms and shoulders feel so tight."

Narrow lanes, narrower lanes. Concrete barriers on the left, concrete barriers on the right. Headlights coming up fast. "Can't change lanes now good buddy. Slow that rocket down. Now what's that fool doing, blinking his lights and honking his horn?"

Narrow lanes, narrower lanes. Concrete barriers on the left, concrete barriers on the right. Traffic on the left, traffic on the right. Can't change lanes. "Sorry good buddy, can't help you now." Stomach burning, arms and shoulders hurting.

"A gap ahead in the right lane? I think I can move this rig over so that fool behind me can go on and not kill us all."

"Where is he? I don't see him. That fool's in my no zone!"

About that time, a dual-wheeled, black crew-cab pickup roars past Bob, cuts back in front of him, and the driver slams on the brakes. Stomping his brakes, Bob fights to keep his rig in his lane.

As Bob's rig slides toward a crash, the pickup lurches forward with the driver holding his hand out the window, nominating Bob for "number one," and disappears into the night.

continues

THE DISPATCH BOARD *continued*

Fortunately because of Bob's professional driving skills and the other drivers around him, every one stayed upright and on the highway that night.

An isolated incident?

Unfortunately, no.

In a recent survey sponsored by the National Highway Traffic Safety Administration (NHTSA), over 60% of U.S. drivers said they consider unsafe driving practices to be a major threat to their personal safety.

Their fears are warranted.

Estimates indicate that drivers who tailgate, race down the road, run red lights, and zip from lane to lane without warning contribute significantly to the more than six million crashes that occur in the United States each year.

Another study by the NHTSA found that in 1997, two-thirds of the more than 41,000 traffic accident deaths that year were the result of road rage.

So what is causing all this road rage?

Jerry Smith, Chief of Police in a town north of San Antonio that straddles I-35, summed it up like this, "Stress, stress, and more stress. Stress about their jobs. Stress getting to and from their jobs. Sometimes because of an accident on I-35, the traffic has stopped for an hour or more. When some people have that much stress, day after day, something has to give."

"You are right," says Bob, "They are out there, and the heavier the traffic, the worse some four wheelers drive.

"So what can I do?"

There are basically two things Bob can do: one involves "them" and one involves him.

For them, in heavy traffic Bob can be more alert, be a good defensive driver, and leave more space between himself and other vehicles.

For him, as a professional driver Bob can keep his cool. If he gets caught up in horn honking, cursing, or hand gesturing, he is increasing his risk for having an accident.

If Bob gets involved with other drivers, not only is he increasing his risk for having an accident, but he is also increasing his stress level.

Bob knows being a professional driver is very stressful and that job stress can lead to stroke and heart attacks.

"So," Bob says, "I should keep my distance and keep my cool."

You got it Bob. I'll see you on down the road!

3 A Review of Federal Motor Carriers Safety Regulations Parts 383 and 391

The Commercial Driver's License is a special process by which professional drivers are certified to drive commercial vehicles. Studying is required for a test administered by the Department of Motor Vehicles in your state and tests are offered in most cities.

The CDL indicates that its holder has proved himself or herself capable of handling the responsibilities that come with driving a commercial vehicle on public streets and highways.

Passing the CDL also proves that you have knowledge of the law and observe certain regulations every time you climb into the cab of a truck or take the driver's seat in a van or a bus.

Professional drivers who operate commercial motor vehicles are covered by a series of regulations called the Federal Motor Carrier Safety Regulations, which are stated in several parts.

In this chapter, we will examine two main parts of the FMCSR that should be familiar to professional drivers. Notice we said "should be familiar." Do not memorize this information—just understand what these parts say and what they cover.

Hint: These regulations are quite lengthy. We have condensed much of the material found in these parts, but this chapter still runs fairly long . . . so *pace yourself.* Don't try to read this entire chapter in one sitting.

Now that we've gone over the road rules, let's get started on the regulations.

FMCSR Part 383—Commercial Driver's License Standards; Requirements and Penalties

The purpose of this part is to help reduce or prevent truck and bus accidents, fatalities, and injuries by requiring drivers to have a single commercial motor vehicle driver's license and by disqualifying drivers who operate commercial motor vehicles in an unsafe manner.

Q. What does the regulation mean by saying that a driver may "have a single commercial motor vehicle driver's license"?

A. Just what it says. Years ago, professional drivers often were licensed in several states, depending on where they drove, but the law has been changed. Drivers are now prohibited from having more than one commercial motor vehicle driver's license.

1. Professional drivers with a CDL are also required to notify their current employer and their state of domicile of certain convictions when or if they occur.

2. A driver is also required to provide previous employment information when applying for employment as an operator of a commercial motor vehicle. Most companies ask drivers for their past 10 years of work experience, with no gaps, so if you were unemployed for six months, you need to note that.
3. This part also prohibits an employer from allowing a person with a suspended license to operate a commercial motor vehicle.

Part 383 establishes disqualifications and penalties for CDL drivers if they commit certain offenses, establishes testing and licensing requirements, and requires states to administer knowledge and skills tests to all CDL applicants.

Part 383 also provides federal standards for procedures, methods, and minimum passing scores for states and others to use in testing and licensing commercial motor vehicle operators, and states requirements for the state-issued commercial license documentation.

Q. Do these regulations apply to everyone who drives a commercial motor vehicle?
A. Yes, for all commercial motor vehicle drivers, except military drivers, farmers, firefighters, emergency response vehicle drivers, and drivers of equipment removing ice or snow from the highways.

   For certain drivers in the state of Alaska, the state can waive certain requirements when issuing the CDL. Check with your Department of Motor Vehicles for specifics.

   There is also a restricted CDL for certain drivers in farm-related service industries: A State may, at its discretion, waive the required knowledge and skills tests and issue restricted CDLs to employees of these designated farm-related service industries. Restricted CDLs are also available for certain drivers in the pyrotechnic (fireworks) industry.

Q. May I continue to renew my automobile driver's license after I earn my CDL?
A. No person who operates a commercial motor vehicle shall at any time have more than one driver's license.

Q. How did the CDL come into being?
A. Effective April 1, 1992, no person shall operate a commercial motor vehicle unless they possess a CDL which meets the standards contained in Part 383, issued by his/her state or jurisdiction of domicile.

   If a commercial motor vehicle operator is domiciled in a foreign jurisdiction which, as determined by the Administrator, does not test drivers and issue a CDL, the person shall obtain a Nonresident CDL from a state which does comply with the testing and licensing standards.

Q. What is a learner's permit, and who is eligible for one?
A. Anyone preparing to take the CDL Knowledge, Skills, and Endorsement tests may be issued a learner's permit for a short period of time. It is considered a valid driver's license and is used while the new driver is training on public roads or highways.

Q. How do I get a learner's permit?
A. You must have a valid driver's license and have passed the vision and knowledge test. Then, a learner's permit can be used as long as the driver is accompanied by the holder of a valid CDL.

Q. What do I do if I get a ticket after I pass my CDL?

A. Everyone with a CDL who has violated any law in any type of motor vehicle must notify the officials in his or her home state of the conviction within 30 days of that conviction.

   If you are convicted of a violation, you must also notify your employer within 30 days. If you are not currently employed, notify the Department of Motor Vehicles in your state of residence.

Q. What is included in the notification?

A. The notification to the state official and employer must be made in writing and contain the following information:

1. Driver's full name
2. Driver's license number
3. Date of conviction
4. The specific criminal or other offense(s), serious traffic violation(s), and other violation(s) of state or local law relating to motor vehicle traffic control, for which the person was convicted and any suspension, revocation, or cancellation of certain driving privileges which resulted from such conviction(s)
5. Indication whether the violation was in a commercial motor vehicle
6. Location of offense
7. Driver's signature

Q. Whom do I notify if my license is suspended?

A. As a professional driver, a suspension of your license will end your paycheck, at least for the period of your suspension. Not a good thing!

   Each employee who has a driver's license suspended, revoked, or canceled by a state or jurisdiction, who loses the right to operate a commercial motor vehicle in a state or jurisdiction for any period, shall notify his/her employer by the end of the business day following notice of suspension or loss privilege.

Q. How much information should I provide about previous employment?

A. Any person applying for employment as an operator of a commercial motor vehicle shall provide at the time of application for employment, employment history information for the 10 years preceding the date the application is submitted shall be presented to the prospective employer by the applicant. The applicant shall also supply (1) a list of the names and addresses of the applicant's previous employers for which the applicant was an operator of a commercial motor vehicle; (2) The dates the applicant was employed by these employers; and (3) The reason for leaving such employment.

   The applicant shall certify that all information furnished is true and complete.

   An employer may require an applicant to provide additional information. The employer should also tell you that previous employers might be contacted.

Q. Are there special rules for hazardous materials and passenger offenses?

A. A driver is disqualified for a period of not less than 180 days nor more than two years if the driver is convicted of a first violation of an out-of-service order while transporting hazardous materials required to be placarded under the Hazardous Materials Transportation Act.

Q. What are the penalties for violations?

A. Any person who violates these rules may be subject to civil or criminal penalties.

Q. Are there special penalties when drivers violate out-of-service orders?

A. A driver who is convicted of violating an out-of-service order shall be subject to a civil penalty of not less than $1,000 nor more than $2,500, in addition to disqualification.

Q. How do I apply for a CDL?

A. Prior to obtaining a CDL, a person must meet the following requirements:

1. A person who operates or expects to operate in interstate or foreign commerce shall certify that he/she meets the qualification requirements.
2. Pass a knowledge test in accordance with these rules and regulations for the type of motor vehicle the person operates or expects to operate.
3. Pass a driving or skills test in accordance with the standards of Part 383 taken in a motor vehicle which is representative of the type of motor vehicle the person operates or expects to operate; or provide evidence that he/she has successfully passed a driving test administered by an authorized third party.
4. Certify that the motor vehicle in which the person takes the driving skills test is representative of the type of motor vehicle that person operates or expects to operate.
5. Provide to the state of issuance the information required to be included on the CDL.
6. Certify that he/she is not subject to any disqualification, suspension, revocation, or cancellation and that he/she does not have a driver's license from more than one state or jurisdiction.
7. The applicant shall surrender his/her non-CDL driver's licenses to the state.
8. License transfer. When applying to transfer a CDL from one state of domicile to a new state of domicile, an applicant shall apply for a CDL from the new state of domicile within no more than 30 days after establishing his/her new domicile.

Q. What is a Nonresident CDL?

A. When an applicant is domiciled in a foreign jurisdiction, where the commercial motor vehicle operator testing and licensing standards do not meet the standards of the U.S. CDL, the applicant shall obtain a Nonresident CDL from a state, which meets such standards.

Q. Do I have to consent to alcohol testing?

A. Any person who holds a CDL shall be deemed to have consented to such testing as is required of him/her by any state or jurisdiction in the enforcement. Consent is demonstrated by driving a commercial motor vehicle.

Initial licensure. Prior to issuing a CDL to a person, a state shall:

1. Require the driver applicant to certify, pass tests, and provide specific information about [himself/herself].

2. Check that the vehicle in which the applicant takes his/her test is representative of the vehicle group the applicant has certified that he/she operates or expects to operate.

3. Initiate and complete a check of the applicant's driving record to ensure that the person is not subject to any disqualification, suspensions, revocations, or cancellations and that the person does not have a driver's license from more than one state. The record check shall include but not be limited to the following:

   (a) A check of the applicant's driving record as maintained by his/her current state of licensure, if any.

   (b) A check with the Commercial Driver's License Information System (CDLIS) to determine whether the driver applicant already has a CDL, whether the applicant's license has been suspended, revoked, or canceled, or if the applicant has been disqualified from operating a commercial motor vehicle.

   (c) A check with the National Driver Register (NDR), when it is determined to be operational by the National Highway Traffic Safety Administrator, to determine whether the driver applicant has been disqualified from operating a motor vehicle (other than a commercial motor vehicle); had a license (other than a CDL) suspended, revoked, or canceled for cause in the three-year-period ending on the date of application; or been convicted of certain offenses.

If such applicant wishes to retain a hazardous materials endorsement, ensure that the driver has, within the two years preceding the transfer, either (1) Passed the test for such endorsement specified or (2) successfully completed a hazardous materials test or training that is given by a third party and that is deemed by the state to substantially cover the same knowledge base, and obtain the CDL issued by the applicant's previous state of domicile.

Q. What are the penalties for giving false information?
A. If a state determines, in its check of an applicant's license status and record prior to issuing a CDL, that false information has been given, the state shall at a minimum suspend, cancel, or revoke the person's CDL or his/her pending application, or disqualify the person from operating a commercial motor vehicle for a period of at least 60 consecutive days.

Q. Is a CDL issued in one state valid in another state?
A. A state shall allow any person who has a valid CDL, which is not suspended, revoked, or canceled, and who is not disqualified from operating a commercial motor vehicle, to operate a commercial motor vehicle in the state.

Q. What if my state doesn't provide CDL testing?
A. A state may authorize a person (including another state, an employer, a private driver training facility or other private institution, or a department, agency or instrumentality of a local government) to administer the skills tests.

Q. If I have a CDL from another state and apply for a CDL in my present home state, do I have to go through testing again?
A. At the discretion of a state, the driving skill test may be waived for a commercial motor vehicle operator who is currently licensed at the time of

his/her application for a CDL, and substituted with either an applicant's driving record and previous passage of an acceptable skills test, or an applicant's driving record in combination with certain driving experience. The state shall impose conditions and limitations to restrict the applicants from whom a state may accept alternative requirements for the skills test.

Commercial Vehicle Groups

Each driver applicant must possess and be tested on his/her knowledge and skills for the commercial motor vehicle group(s) for which he/she desires a CDL. The commercial motor vehicle groups are as follows:

1. Combination vehicle (Group A)—Any combination of vehicles with a gross combination weight rating (GCWR) of 11,794 kilograms or more (26,001 pounds or more) provided the gross vehicle weight rating (GVWR) of the vehicle(s) being towed is in excess of 4,536 kilograms (10,000 pounds).
2. Heavy Straight Vehicle (Group B)—Any single vehicle with a GVWR of 11,794 kilograms or more (26,001 pounds or more), or any such vehicle towing a vehicle not in excess of 4,536 kilograms (10,000 pounds) GVWR.
3. Small Vehicle (Group C)—Any single vehicle, or combination of vehicles, that meets neither the definition of Group A nor that of Group B as contained in this section, but that either is designed to transport 15 or more passengers, including the driver, or is used in the transportation of materials found to be hazardous for the purposes of the Hazardous Materials Transportation Act and which require the motor vehicle to be placarded under the Hazardous Materials Regulations.

Q. Should I take all the endorsement tests?
A. Some professional drivers take all the endorsement tests, but not all at one time. Some take only the endorsements they think they will need to begin their careers.

Q. What kinds of endorsements are there?
A. An operator must obtain state-issued endorsements to his/her CDL to operate commercial motor vehicles, which are:

- Double/triple trailers,
- Passenger vehicles,
- Tank vehicles, or
- Required to be placarded for hazardous materials.

Endorsement testing requirements. The following tests are required for the endorsements:

- Double/Triple Trailers—a knowledge test
- Passenger—a knowledge and a skills test
- Tank Vehicle—a knowledge test
- Hazardous Materials—a knowledge test

Q. What are the air brake restrictions?
A. If an applicant either fails the air brake component of the knowledge test, or performs the skills test in a vehicle not equipped with air brakes, the State shall indicate on the CDL, if issued, that the person is restricted from operating a commercial motor vehicle equipped with air brakes.

For the purposes of the skills test and the restriction, air brakes shall include any braking system operating fully or partially on the air brake principle.

Q. What are the general knowledge requirements?
A. All commercial motor vehicle operators must have knowledge of the following general areas:

Motor vehicle inspection, repair, and maintenance requirements. Procedures for safe vehicle operations; the effects of fatigue, poor vision, hearing, and general health upon safe commercial motor vehicle operation; the types of motor vehicles and cargoes subject to the requirements; and the effects of alcohol and drug use upon safe commercial motor vehicle operations.

Commercial motor vehicle safety control systems. Proper use of the motor vehicle's safety system (Figure 3-1), including lights, horns, side and rear view mirrors, proper mirror adjustments, fire extinguishers, symptoms of improper operation revealed through instruments, motor vehicle operation characteristics, and diagnosing malfunctions. Commercial motor vehicle drivers shall have knowledge on the correct procedures needed to use these safety systems in an emergency situation, such as skids, loss of brakes, or other emergencies.

Figure 3-1   Commercial motor vehicle control systems.

Safe vehicle control. The following areas should be familiar to anyone taking the CDL:

1. Control systems—The purpose and function of the controls and instruments commonly found on commercial motor vehicles
2. Basic control—The proper procedures for performing various basic maneuvers
3. Shifting—The basic shifting rules and terms, as well as shift patterns and procedures for common transmissions
4. Backing—The procedures and rules for various backing maneuvers
5. Visual search—The importance of proper visual search and proper visual search methods
6. Communication—The principles and procedures for proper communications and the hazards of failure to signal properly
7. Speed management—The importance of understanding the effects of speed
8. Space management—The procedures and techniques for controlling the space around the vehicle
9. Night operation—Preparations and procedures for night driving
10. Extreme driving conditions—The basic information on operating in extreme driving conditions and the hazards that are encountered in extreme conditions
11. Hazard perceptions—The basic information on hazard perception and clues for recognition of hazards
12. Emergency maneuvers—The basic information concerning when and how to make emergency maneuvers
13. Skid control and recovery—The information on the causes and major types of skids as well as the procedures for recovering from skids

Relationship of cargo to vehicle control. Drivers should know the principles and procedures for the proper handling of cargo.

Vehicle inspections. Drivers should know the objectives and proper procedures for performing vehicle safety inspections, such as:

1. The importance of periodic inspection and repair for vehicle safety
2. The effect of undiscovered malfunctions upon safety
3. What safety related parts to look for when inspecting vehicles
4. Pre-trip/enroute/post-trip inspection procedures
5. Reporting findings

Hazardous materials knowledge. Even if a driver is not taking the Hazardous Materials Endorsement tests, every professional driver needs to know what constitutes hazardous material requiring an endorsement to transport; classes of hazardous materials; labeling/placarding requirements; and what specialized training is needed as a prerequisite to receiving the endorsement and transporting hazardous cargoes.

Air brake knowledge. Even if a driver is not taking the Air Brake Endorsement test, every professional driver should know:

1. Air brake system nomenclature
2. The dangers of a contaminated air supply
3. The implications of severed or disconnected air lines between the power unit and the trailer(s)
4. The implications of low air-pressure readings

5. Procedures to conduct safe and accurate pre-trip inspections
6. Procedures for conducting enroute and post-trip inspections of air actuated brake systems, including ability to detect defects which may cause the system to fail

Operators for the combination vehicle group shall also have knowledge of the following:

1. *Coupling and uncoupling.*—The procedures for proper coupling and uncoupling a tractor to semi-trailer.
2. *Vehicle inspection.*—The objectives and proper procedures that are unique for performing vehicle safety inspections on combination vehicles.

Q. What are the required skills?

A. 1. *Basic vehicle control skills.* All applicants for a CDL must possess and demonstrate basic motor vehicle control skills for each vehicle group in which the driver operates or expects to operate. These skills should include the ability to start, to stop, and to move the vehicle forward and backward in a safe manner.
2. *Safe driving skills.* All applicants for a CDL must possess and demonstrate the safe driving skills for their vehicle group. These skills should include proper visual search methods, appropriate use of signals, speed control for weather and traffic conditions, and ability to position the motor vehicle correctly when changing lanes or turning.
3. *Air brake skills.* Applicants shall demonstrate skills with respect to inspection and operation of air brakes.
4. *Pre-trip inspection skills.* Applicants shall demonstrate the skills necessary to conduct a pre-trip inspection, which includes the ability to:
   (a) Locate and verbally identify air brake operating controls and monitoring devices.
   (b) Determine the motor vehicle's brake system condition for proper adjustments and ensure that air system connections between motor vehicles have been properly made and secured.
   (c) Inspect the low pressure warning device(s) to ensure that they will activate in emergency situations.
   (d) Determine with the engine running, that the system maintains an adequate supply of compressed air.
   (e) Determine that required minimum air pressure build-up time is within acceptable limits and that required alarms and emergency devices automatically deactivate at the proper pressure level.
   (f) Operationally check the brake system for proper performance.

Q. What driving skills are needed?

A. Applicants (in most states) are asked to successfully complete the skills tests in a vehicle they will be driving that is equipped with air brakes. Skills tests shall be conducted in on-street conditions or under a combination of on-street and off-street conditions. A state may utilize simulators to perform skills testing, but under no circumstances as a substitute for the required testing in on-street conditions.

Requirements for Double/Triple Trailers Endorsement. In order to obtain a Double/Triple Trailers Endorsement, each applicant must have knowledge covering:

- Procedures for assembly and hookup of the units.
- Proper placement of the heaviest trailer.

- Handling and stability characteristics including offtracking, response to steering, sensory feedback, braking, oscillatory sway, rollover in steady turns, and yaw stability in steady turns.
- Potential problems in traffic operations, including problems the motor vehicle creates for other motorists due to slower speeds on steep grades, longer passing times, possibility for blocking entry of other motor vehicles on freeways, splash and spray impacts, aerodynamic buffeting, view blockages, and lateral placement.

Requirements for Passenger Endorsement. An applicant for the Passenger Endorsement must satisfy both of the following additional knowledge and skills test requirements:

1. *Knowledge test*—All applicants for the Passenger Endorsement must have knowledge covering at least the following topics:
   (a) Proper procedures for loading/unloading passengers
   (b) Proper use of emergency exits, including push-out windows
   (c) Proper responses to such emergency situations as fires and unruly passengers
   (d) Proper procedures at railroad crossings and drawbridges
   (e) Proper braking procedures
2. *Skills test.* To obtain a Passenger Endorsement applicable to a specific vehicle group, an applicant must take his/her skills test in a passenger vehicle satisfying the requirements of that group.

Requirements for Tank Vehicle Endorsement. In order to obtain a Tank Vehicle Endorsement, each applicant must have knowledge covering the following:

1. Causes, prevention, and effects of cargo surge on motor vehicle handling.
2. Proper braking procedures for the motor vehicle when it is empty, full, and partially full.
3. Differences in handling of baffled/compartmental tank interiors versus nonbaffled motor vehicles.
4. Differences in tank vehicle type and construction.
5. Differences in cargo surge for liquids of various product densities.
6. Effects of road grade and curvature on motor vehicle handling with filled, half-filled, and empty tanks.
7. Proper use of emergency systems.
8. Retest and marking requirements (for drivers of Department of Transportation specification tank vehicles).

Requirements for Hazardous Materials Endorsement.

1. In order to obtain a Hazardous Materials Endorsement, each applicant must have such knowledge as is required of a driver of a hazardous materials-laden vehicle, and hazardous materials violations, including:
   (a) Hazardous materials table
   (b) Shipping paper requirements
   (c) Marking
   (d) Labeling
   (e) Placarding requirements
   (f) Hazardous materials packaging
   (g) Hazardous materials definitions and preparation
   (h) Other regulated materials (e.g., ORM–D)

     (i) Reporting hazardous materials accidents
     (j) Tunnels and railroad crossings

2. Passing the HazMat Endorsement also includes knowledge of the following:
     (a) Forbidden materials and packages
     (b) Loading and unloading materials
     (c) Cargo segregation
     (d) Passenger-carrying buses and hazardous materials
     (e) Attendance of motor vehicles
     (f) Parking
     (g) Routes
     (h) Cargo tanks
     (i) "Safe havens"

3. The HazMat Endorsement also includes testing over the operation of emergency equipment, including:
     (a) Use of equipment to protect the public
     (b) Special precautions for equipment to be used in fires
     (c) Special precautions for use of emergency equipment when loading or unloading a hazardous materials-laden motor vehicle
     (d) Use of emergency equipment for tank vehicles

4. The test will also cover emergency response procedures, including:
     (a) Special care and precautions for different types of accidents
     (b) Special precautions for driving near a fire and carrying hazardous materials, and smoking and carrying hazardous materials
     (c) Emergency procedures
     (d) Existence of special requirements for transporting Class A and Class B explosives

Q. What are some of the specifics asked on the Required Knowledge and Skills Tests?

A. The following is a sample of the specific types of items, which a state may wish to include in the knowledge and skills tests administered to CDL applicants.

Safe operations regulations. Driver-related elements of the following regulations:

1. Motor vehicle inspection, repair, and maintenance requirements
2. Procedures for safe vehicle operations as contained in Part 392
3. The effects of fatigue, poor vision, hearing, and general health on safe commercial motor vehicle operation
4. The types of motor vehicles and cargoes subject to the requirements contained in Part 397
5. The effects of alcohol and drug use on safe commercial motor vehicle operations

Commercial motor vehicle safety control systems. Proper use of the motor vehicle's safety system, including lights, horns, side and rear view mirrors, proper mirror adjustments, fire extinguishers, symptoms of improper operation revealed through instruments, motor vehicle operation characteristics, and diagnosing malfunctions. Commercial motor vehicle drivers shall have knowledge on the correct procedures needed to use these safety systems in an emergency situation (e.g., skids and loss of brakes).

Safe vehicle control.

Control systems—The purpose and function of the controls and instruments commonly found on commercial motor vehicles.

Basic control—The proper procedures for performing various basic maneuvers, including:

1. Starting, warming up, and shutting down the engine
2. Putting the vehicle in motion and stopping
3. Backing in a straight line
4. Turning the vehicle (e.g., basic rules, off tracking, right/left turns and right curves)

Shifting—The basic shifting rules and terms, as well as shift patterns and procedures for common transmissions, including:

1. Key elements of shifting, such as, controls, when to shift, and double clutching
2. Shift patterns and procedures
3. Consequences of improper shifting

Backing—The procedures and rules for various backing maneuvers, including:

1. Backing principles and rules
2. Basic backing maneuvers (e.g., straight line backing and backing on a curved path)

Visual search—The importance of proper visual search and proper visual search methods, including:

1. Seeing ahead and to the sides
2. Use of mirrors
3. Seeing to the rear

Communications—The principles and procedures for proper communications and the hazards of failure to signal properly, including:

1. Signaling intent, such as, signaling when changing speed or direction in traffic
2. Communicating presence, such as, using horn or lights to signal presence
3. Misuse of communications

Speed management—The importance of understanding the effects of speed, including:

1. Speed and stopping distance
2. Speed and surface conditions
3. Speed and the shape of the road
4. Speed and visibility
5. Speed and traffic flow

Space management—The procedures and techniques for controlling the space around the vehicle, including:

1. The importance of space management
2. Space cushions, such as, controlling space ahead and to the rear
3. Space to the sides
4. Space for traffic gaps

Night-time operation—Preparations and procedures for night driving, including:

1. Night driving factors, such as driver factors (vision, glare, fatigue, inexperience), roadway factors (low illumination, variation in illumination, familiarity with roads, other road users, especially drivers exhibiting erratic or improper driving), vehicle factors (headlights, auxiliary lights, turn signals, windshields, and mirrors)
2. Night-time driving procedures, such as preparing to drive at night and driving at night

Extreme driving conditions—The basic information on operating in extreme driving conditions and the hazards that are encountered in extreme conditions, including:

1. Adverse weather
2. Hot weather
3. Mountain driving

Hazard perception—The basic information on hazard perception and clues for the recognition of hazards, including:

1. Importance of hazard recognition
2. Road characteristics
3. Road user activities

Emergency maneuvers—The basic information concerning when and how to make emergency maneuvers, including:

1. Evasive steering
2. Emergency stopping
3. Off road recovery
4. Brake failure
5. Blowouts

Skid control and recovery—The information on the causes and major types of skids, as well as the procedures for recovering from skids.

Relationship of cargo to vehicle control—The principles and procedures for the proper handling of cargo, including:

1. The importance of proper cargo handling, such as consequences of improperly secured cargo, drivers' responsibilities, federal/state and local regulations
2. Principles of weight distribution
3. Principles and methods of cargo securement

Vehicle inspections—The objectives and proper procedures for performing vehicle safety inspections, as follows:

1. The importance of periodic inspection and repair to vehicle safety and to prevention of enroute breakdowns
2. The effect of undiscovered malfunctions on safety
3. What safety-related aspects to check when inspecting vehicles, such as fluid leaks, interference with visibility, bad tires, wheel and rim defects, braking system defects, steering system defects, suspension system defects, exhaust system defects, coupling system defects, and cargo problems

4. Pre-trip/enroute/post-trip inspection procedures
5. Reporting findings

Hazardous materials knowledge, as follows:

1. What constitutes hazardous material requiring an endorsement to transport
2. Classes of hazardous materials, labeling/placarding requirements, and the need for specialized training as a prerequisite to receiving the endorsement and transporting hazardous cargoes

Air brake knowledge as follows:

1. General air brake system nomenclature
2. The dangers of contaminated air (dirt, moisture, and oil) supply
3. Implications of severed or disconnected air lines between the power unit and the trailer(s)
4. Implications of low air pressure readings
5. Procedures to conduct safe and accurate pre-trip inspections, including knowledge of:
   (a) Automatic fail safe devices
   (b) System monitoring devices
   (c) Low pressure warning alarms
6. Procedures for conducting enroute and post-trip inspections of air actuated brake systems, and the ability to detect defects which may cause the system to fail, including:
   (a) Tests which indicate the amount of air loss from the braking system within a specified period, with and without the engine running
   (b) Tests which indicate the pressure levels at which the low air pressure warning devices and the tractor protection valve should activate

Operators for the combination vehicle group shall also have knowledge of:

1. Coupling and uncoupling—The procedures for proper coupling and uncoupling a tractor to semi-trailer
2. Vehicle inspection—The objectives and proper procedures that are unique for performing vehicle safety inspections on combination vehicles

Examples of Specific Skills Elements:

Basic vehicle control skills. All applicants for a CDL must possess and demonstrate the following basic motor vehicle control skills for each vehicle group, which the driver operates or expects to operate. These skills shall include:

1. Ability to start, warm up, and shut down the engine
2. Ability to put the motor vehicle in motion and accelerate smoothly, forward and backward
3. Ability to bring the motor vehicle to a smooth stop
4. Ability to back the motor vehicle in a straight line, and check path and clearance while backing
5. Ability to position the motor vehicle to negotiate, and then make left and right turns
6. Ability to shift as required and select the appropriate gear for speed and highway conditions

7. Ability to back along a curved path
8. Ability to observe the road and the behavior of other motor vehicles, particularly before changing speed and direction

Safe driving skills. All applicants for a CDL must possess and demonstrate the following safe driving skills for any vehicle group. These skills shall include:

1. Ability to use proper visual search methods
2. Ability to signal appropriately when changing speed or direction in traffic
3. Ability to adjust speed to the configuration and condition of the roadway, weather and visibility conditions, traffic conditions, and motor vehicles, cargo and driver conditions
4. Ability to choose a safe gap for changing lanes, passing other vehicles, and crossing or entering traffic
5. Ability to correctly position the motor vehicle before and during a turn to prevent other vehicles from passing on the wrong side as well as to prevent problems caused by offtracking
6. Ability to maintain a safe following distance depending on the condition of the road, on visibility, and on vehicle weight
7. Ability to adjust operation of the motor vehicle to prevailing weather conditions, including speed selection, braking, direction changes, and following distance to maintain control

Q. Tell me more about how the CDL tests are given.
A. Information on how to obtain a CDL and endorsements shall be included in manuals and made available by states to CDL applicants.

Q. What methods of testing are used?
A. • All tests shall be constructed in such a way as to determine if the applicant possesses the required knowledge and skills for the type of motor vehicle or endorsement the applicant wishes to obtain.
 • States shall develop their own specifications for the tests for each vehicle group and endorsement, which must be at least as stringent as the federal standards.
 • States shall determine specific methods for scoring the knowledge and skills tests.

Each basic knowledge test shall contain at least 30 items, exclusive of the number of items testing air brake knowledge. Each endorsement knowledge test, and the air brake component of the basic knowledge test shall contain a number of questions that is sufficient to test the driver applicant's knowledge of the required subject matter with validity and reliability.

Q. What are the minimum passing scores?
A. • The driver applicant must correctly answer at least 80 percent of the questions on each knowledge test in order to achieve a passing score on such knowledge test.
 • To achieve a passing score on the skills test, the driver applicant must demonstrate that he/she can successfully perform all of the skills required.

- If the driver applicant does not obey traffic laws, or causes an accident during the test, he/she shall automatically fail the test.

The scoring of the basic knowledge and skills test shall be adjusted as follows to allow for the air brake restriction:

- If the applicant scores less than 80 percent on the air brake component of the basic knowledge test, the driver will have failed the air brake component and, if the driver is issued a CDL, an air brake restriction shall be indicated on the license.
- If the applicant performs the skills test in a vehicle not equipped with air brakes, the driver will have omitted the air brake component and, if the driver is issued a CDL, the air brake restriction shall be indicated on the license.

Q. What does the CDL look like?

A. The CDL shall be a document that is easy to recognize as a CDL. All CDLs shall contain the following information:

- The prominent statement that the license is a "Commercial Driver's License" or "CDL"
- The full name, signature, and mailing address of the person to whom such license is issued
- Physical and other information to identify and describe such person, including date of birth (month, day, and year), sex, and height
- Color photograph of the driver
- The driver's state license number
- The name of the state which issued the license
- The date of issuance and the date of expiration of the license
- The group or groups of commercial motor vehicle(s) that the driver is authorized to operate, indicated as follows:
  - (a) A for combination vehicle
  - (b) B for heavy straight vehicle
  - (c) C for small vehicle

The endorsement(s) for which the driver has qualified, if any, indicated as follows:
  - (a) T for double/triple trailers
  - (b) P for passenger
  - (c) N for tank vehicle
  - (d) H for hazardous materials
  - (e) X for a combination of the tank vehicle and hazardous materials endorsements

At the discretion of the state, additional codes for additional groupings of endorsements, as long as each such discretionary code is fully explained on the front or back of the CDL document.

*   *   *   *   *

Okay, time to take a break, get up and stretch, and walk around. When you return, we'll go on to the next part of FMCSR.

Part 391: Qualifications of Drivers

The rules in this part establish minimum qualifications for persons who drive commercial motor vehicles as, for, or on behalf of motor carriers. These rules also establish minimum duties of motor carriers with respect to the qualifications of their drivers.

Q. What are the qualifications to become a driver?

A. A person shall not drive a commercial motor vehicle unless he/she is qualified to drive a commercial motor vehicle. A motor carrier shall not require or permit a person to drive a commercial motor vehicle unless that person is qualified to drive a commercial motor vehicle. These qualifications include:

- At least 21 years of age
- Can read and speak the English language sufficiently to converse with the general public, to understand highway traffic signs and signals in the English language, to respond to official inquiries, and to make entries on reports and records
- Can safely operate the type of commercial motor vehicle he/she drives
- Is physically qualified to drive a commercial motor vehicle
- Has a currently valid commercial motor vehicle operator's license issued by only one state or jurisdiction
- Has prepared and furnished the motor carrier that employs him/her with the list of violations or the certificate as required
- Is not disqualified to drive a commercial motor vehicle
- Has successfully completed a driver's road test and has been issued a certificate of driver's road test or has presented an operator's license or a certificate of road test which the motor carrier that employs him/her has accepted as equivalent to a road test.

Q. What are the responsibilities of drivers?

A. A motor carrier shall not require or permit a person to drive a commercial motor vehicle unless the person

1. Can, by experience, training, or both, determine whether the cargo he/she transports (including baggage in a passenger-carrying commercial motor vehicle) has been properly located, distributed, and secured in or on the commercial motor vehicle he/she drives.
2. Is familiar with methods and procedures for securing cargo in or on the commercial motor vehicle he/she drives.

Q. How can a driver be disqualified?

A. A driver who is disqualified shall not drive a commercial motor vehicle. A motor carrier shall not require or permit a driver who is disqualified to drive a commercial motor vehicle.

1. A driver is disqualified for the duration of the driver's loss of his/her privilege to operate a commercial motor vehicle on public highways, either temporarily or permanently, because of the revocation, suspension, withdrawal, or denial of an operator's license, permit, or privilege, until

that operator's license, permit, or privilege is restored by the authority that revoked, suspended, withdrew, or denied it.

2. A driver who receives a notice that his/her license, permit, or privilege to operate a commercial motor vehicle has been revoked, suspended, or withdrawn shall notify the motor carrier that employs him/her of the contents of the notice before the end of the business day following the day the driver received it.

A driver who is convicted of (or forfeits bond or collateral upon a charge of) a disqualifying offense can be disqualified from driving. The following offenses are disqualifying offenses:

1. Driving a commercial motor vehicle while under the influence of alcohol
2. Refusal to undergo such testing as is required by any state or jurisdiction
3. Driving a commercial motor vehicle under the influence of a 21 CFR 1308.11 Schedule I-identified controlled substance, an amphetamine, a narcotic drug, a formulation of an amphetamine, or a derivative of a narcotic drug
4. Transportation, possession, or unlawful use of a 21 CFR 1308.11 Schedule I-identified controlled substance, amphetamines, narcotic drugs, formulations of an amphetamine, or derivatives of narcotic drugs while the driver is on duty
5. Leaving the scene of an accident while operating a commercial motor vehicle
6. A felony involving the use of a commercial motor vehicle

Q. How long does the disqualification last?
A. A driver is disqualified for one year after the date of conviction if, during the three years preceding that date, the driver was not convicted of an offense that would disqualify the driver under the rules of this section.

If the driver is convicted during the preceding three years, he or she will be disqualified for three years.

Q. What if a driver is disqualified for violation of an out-of-service order?
A. A driver who is convicted of violating an out-of-service order for the first time will be disqualified for no less than 90 days or no more than one year. For the second violation, the disqualification is no less than one year and no more than five years. After that, subsequent violations are punished by disqualification of not less than three years and no more than five years during any 10-year period.

A driver is disqualified for a period of not less than 180 days nor more than two years if the driver is convicted of a first violation of an out-of-service order while transporting hazardous materials required to be placarded under the Hazardous Materials Transportation Act.

Q. Once I'm hired, does my employer check my records further?
A. Every 12 months, motor carriers shall review the driving record of each driver it employs. This review will determine if the driver meets minimum requirements for safe driving or is disqualified to drive a CMV.

Motor carriers will require each driver to furnish a list of all violations of motor vehicle traffic laws and ordinances (other than parking violations) of which the driver has been convicted over the past year.

DRIVER'S CERTIFICATION

I certify that the following is a true and complete list of traffic violations (other than parking violations) for which I have been convicted or forfeited bond or collateral during the past 12 months.	
Date of conviction	Offense
Location	Type of motor vehicle operated
If no violations are listed above, I certify that I have not been convicted or forfeited bond or collateral on account of any violation required to be listed during the past 12 months.	
(Date of certification)	(Driver's signature)
(Motor carrier's name)	
(Motor carrier's address)	
(Reviewed by: Signature)	(Title)

Figure 3-2   Sample driver's certification form.

The form of the driver's list or certification shall be prescribed by the motor carrier. The form shown in Figure 3-2 may be used to comply with this section.

Q. Does the carrier give a road test?

A. A person shall not drive a commercial motor vehicle unless he/she has first successfully completed a road test and has been issued a certificate of driver's road test in accordance with this section.

The motor carrier shall give the road test or a person designated by it. However, a driver who is also a motor carrier must be given the test by a person other than himself/herself. The test shall be given by a person who is competent to evaluate and determine whether the person who takes the test has demonstrated that he/she is capable of operating the commercial motor vehicle and associated equipment that the motor carrier intends to assign him/her.

The road test must give the driver opportunity to demonstrate skills, including:

1. Pre-trip inspection
2. Coupling and uncoupling combination units
3. Placing the motor vehicle in operation
4. Using the commercial motor vehicle's controls and emergency equipment
5. Operating the commercial motor vehicle in traffic and while passing other motor vehicles
6. Turning the commercial motor vehicle
7. Braking and slowing the commercial motor vehicle by means other than braking
8. Backing and parking the commercial vehicle

If the road test is successfully completed, the person who gave it shall complete a certificate of driver's road test in substantially the form prescribed. A copy of the certificate shall be given to the person who was examined. The motor carrier shall retain in the driver qualification file of the person who was examined during the road test.

Q. Who is qualified to drive a commercial motor vehicle?

A. A person is physically qualified to drive a commercial motor vehicle if that person:

- Has no loss of a foot, a leg, a hand, or an arm, or has been granted a waiver.
- Has no impairment of:
  (a) A hand or finger which interferes with power grasping;
  (b) An arm, a foot, or a leg which interferes with the ability to perform normal tasks associated with operating a commercial motor vehicle;
  (c) Any other significant limb defect or limitation which interferes with the ability to perform normal tasks associated with operating a commercial motor vehicle; or has been granted a waiver.
- Has no established medical history or clinical diagnosis of diabetes mellitus currently requiring insulin for control.
- Has no current clinical diagnosis of myocardial infarction (heart attack), angina pectoris, coronary insufficiency, thrombosis, or any other cardiovascular disease of a variety known to be accompanied by syncope (fainting), dyspnea (difficulty breathing), collapse, or congestive heart failure.
- Has no established medical history or clinical diagnosis of a breathing dysfunction likely to interfere with his/her ability to control and safely operate a commercial motor vehicle.
- Has no current clinical diagnosis of high blood pressure likely to interfere with his/her ability to safely operate a commercial motor vehicle.
- Has no established medical history or clinical diagnosis of rheumatic, arthritic, orthopedic, muscular, neuromuscular, or vascular disease which interferes with his/her ability to control and safely operate a commercial motor vehicle.

- Has no established medical history or clinical diagnosis of epilepsy or any other condition which is likely to cause loss of consciousness or any loss of ability to control a commercial motor vehicle.
- Has no mental, nervous, organic, or functional disease or psychiatric disorder likely to interfere with his/her ability to drive a commercial motor vehicle safely.
- Has distant visual acuity of at least 20/40 (Snellen) in each eye without corrective lenses or visual acuity separately corrected to 20/40 (Snellen) or better with corrective lenses and the ability to recognize the colors of traffic signals and devices showing standard red, green, and amber.
- First perceives a forced whispered voice in the better ear at not less than five feet with or without the use of a hearing aid or, if tested by use of an audiometric device, does not have an average hearing loss in the better ear greater than 40 decibels at 500 Hz, 1000 Hz, and 2000 Hz, with or without a hearing aid, when the audiometric device is calibrated to American National Standard.
- Does not use controlled substances or habit-forming drugs.
- Has no current clinical diagnosis of alcoholism.

A physical examination for all of the above is required by the Department of Transportation prior to employment and every year a professional driver is employed.

Let's Review

Read each question and all of the answers provided. Place the letter of the right answer in the space provided or, write your answers on a separate piece of paper so you can use these questions again as you review for the CDL. Once you have answered all the questions, check your answers against the answer key which follows.

_____ 1. True or False. A driver who is licensed for Group A vehicles may not drive Group B or Group C vehicles.

_____ 2. "Interstate" means between two states. "Intrastate" means
   (A) within the borders of a nation state,
   (B) within the borders of a single state,
   (C) within the borders of a province,
   (D) none of the above.

_____ 3. The first violation of an out-of-service order will subject the driver to
   (A) 90 days to one year disqualification,
   (B) 30 to 60 days disqualification,
   (C) one year to three years disqualification,
   (D) none of the above.

_____ 4. True or False. A road test is given by the motor carrier.

_____ 5. To begin the skills test, the applicant will
   (A) show that he/she can read and write English,
   (B) show that he/she knows where the ignition switch is located,
   (C) conduct a pre-trip inspection of the vehicle,
   (D) all of the above.

_____ 6. True or False. If a driver refuses to take a breath test when stopped for suspected driving under the influence, he/she is automatically disqualified from professional driving.

_____ 7. Which of the following is _not_ a requirement for the CDL?
   (A) at least 21 years of age,
   (B) can read and speak English,
   (C) meet physical qualifications,
   (D) hold a high school diploma or GED.

_____ 8. A driver who holds a CDL and is ticketed for a moving violation in his/her personal automobile
   (A) must report this to his/her employer,
   (B) must report this to his/her state of residence,
   (C) both of these,
   (D) none of the above.

_____ 9. The main knowledge areas for the CDL are
   (A) commercial motor vehicle safety control,
   (B) vehicle inspections,
   (C) hazardous materials knowledge,
   (D) all of the above.

_____10. When a driver applies for a job, the motor carrier will
   (A) ask for a 10-year past work history,
   (B) will ask for a list of past employers,
   (C) will call past employers,
   (D) all of the above.

Answers to Let's Review

1. False; 2. B; 3. A; 4. True; 5. C; 6. True; 7. D; 8. C; 9. D; 10. D

Terms You Should Know

The following terms have been taken from the contents of Chapter 3. Review them. If you see any you are unsure of, check the definition in the Glossary at the back of the book. If it helps you, keep a written list of the words and their definitions (or write in the definitions here) and review them several days prior to taking the CDL tests.

Administrator

Alcohol or "alcoholic beverage"

Alcohol concentration (AC)

Commerce

Commercial driver's license (CDL)

Commercial driver's license information system (CDLIS)

Commercial motor vehicle (CMV)

Controlled substance

Conviction

Disqualification

Driver applicant

Driver's license

Driving a commercial motor vehicle while under the influence of alcohol

Employee

Employer

Endorsement

Felony

Foreign

Gross combination weight rating (GCWR)

Gross vehicle weight rating (GVWR)

Hazardous materials (HazMat)

Motor vehicle

Nonresident CDL

Out of service order

Representative vehicle

Serious traffic violation

State

State of domicile (or residence)

Tank vehicle

United States

Vehicle

Vehicle group

THE DISPATCH BOARD
What Type of Truck Driver Are You Planning To Be?

Youngsters who announce they are going to be truck drivers when they grow up aren't usually asked, "Well, dear . . . what type of truck driver are you going to be?" But adults who are selecting professional driving as a career should at least ask this question of themselves.

According to the Professional Truck Driver Institute, Inc., there are several choices available.

Long-distance or over-the-road drivers are responsible for the operation of heavy trucks and move interstate or intrastate loads. Some of these long-distance, or long-haul, drivers travel routes that bring them home each night, logging a few hundred miles each day. Other over-the-road drivers travel thousands of miles per month and are away from home anywhere from a few nights a week to two or three weeks per month.

If you plan to be a specialized trucker, you'll be handling unusual, oversized, or sensitive loads. These drivers travel local, regional, and long distance routes. They are "specialized" because they have completed anywhere from a few days to a few weeks of additional training to operate their equipment.

The category of specialized trucking includes tank trucks, dump trucks, bulk carriers, and over-sized, over-weight loads, which are also called "permitted" loads.

Drivers responsible for transporting hazardous materials also complete extensive training in the handling of these specialized loads. This training is usually provided by the companies for which they work. HazMat drivers, as they are called, must be able to handle these loads safely and must know the content and the physical properties of these loads, as well as what to do if there is an emergency, such as an accident or damage to the cargo. These drivers are also required to earn the HazMat Endorsement, a special endorsement for handling and transporting hazardous materials, in addition to the CDL.

Independent contractors are those drivers who own his or her own equipment. This can be anything from a straight truck to a tractor-trailer rig. Some drivers lease this equipment—and their driving—to a larger company. Their job is to haul freight on a contractual basis for pay, usually a percentage of the revenue.

Husband-wife teams of independent contractors are becoming a larger part of the independent contractors population in the United States and many more drivers now work with a spouse, partner, or family member, usually on a long-haul basis. To enable more couples to work together, more companies are also offering training on automatic transmission rigs to entice more female participation.

Independent contractors, while sharing in revenues and usually doing very well as small businesses, do have a few additional expenses to cover, including truck payments, fuel costs, and insurance as well as tolls and some maintenance.

In most cases, independent contractors begin their careers as salaried drivers with a large or small motor carrier. Once they get to know the industry and have increased their driving skills, these drivers often make the decision to become lease operators.

4 FMCSR—Parts 392 and 393

FMCSR Part 392: Driving Commercial Motor Vehicles

Anyone involved in commercial motor transportation is responsible for knowing the contents of FMCSR Part 392, as amended July 28, 1995. It covers driving of vehicles, driver health and safety, driver schedules, safe equipment loading, and other general topics, including use of lights and reflectors, stopped vehicles, accidents and license revocations, safety while fueling, unauthorized passengers, and other prohibited practices.

FMCSR says drivers must obey local laws first and if the federal law is stricter, then the federal law must be obeyed instead. This is called "the higher standard of care," or, "the stricter rule always applies."

Q. What if I become ill or too fatigued to operate the vehicle safely?

A. Driver fatigue has been an ongoing concern of a number of agencies, including the American Trucking Associations and the Professional Drivers Training Institute. Research has been done and findings have been passed along to carriers and their drivers.

Federal regulations say no driver shall operate a motor vehicle if his or her ability or alertness is impaired due to illness, fatigue, or any other cause. However, in case of grave emergency where the hazard to occupants of the commercial motor vehicle or other users of the highway would be increased by compliance with this section, the driver may continue to operate the commercial motor vehicle to the nearest place at which that hazard is removed.

If you become so fatigued that you have difficulty staying alert, it is important to pull over and rest until you are able to drive. Studies have found that most people require at least seven to eight hours of restful sleep every 24 hours.

How do you avoid fatigue? Several suggestions are offered:

- Avoid medications—especially antihistamines—that can make you sleepy.
- Keep cool—make sure your cab is well-ventilated.
- Take breaks—walk around, inspect your vehicle, and get some fresh air.

Q. What do the rules say about drugs and other substances?

A. The misuse or abuse of drugs, alcohol or other substances is strictly forbidden. FMCSR says no driver shall be on duty and possess, be under the influence of, or use any of the following drugs or other substances:

1. Any 21 CFR 1308.11 Schedule I substance;
2. An amphetamine or any formulation thereof (including, but not limited, to "pep pills," and "bennies").

3. A narcotic drug or any derivative thereof, except as prescribed by a physician.
4. Any other substance, to a degree which renders the driver incapable of safely operating a motor vehicle.

Q. What are the rules regarding the use of alcohol?

A. The regulations say no driver should use alcohol within four hours of going on duty or having physical control of a vehicle. Neither should the driver have a measurable amount of alcohol in his or her system.

"Possession" of alcoholic beverages by the driver does not refer to alcoholic beverages or alcohol in the shipment or, in the case of a bus driver, alcoholic beverages in the possession of the passengers.

If a driver is found to be operating a commercial motor vehicle while under the influence of alcohol or has measurable alcohol in his or her system, the driver will be placed out of service for a period of 24 hours, which commences on issuance of the out-of-service order.

If an out-of-service order is issued, the driver must report this to his or her employer within 24 hours. The issuance of this out-of-service order must also be reported to the state issuing the driver's CDL within 30 days.

Q. If a driver receives an out-of-service order, is there anything he or she can do to get this erased from their driving record?

A. Any driver who is subject to an out-of-service order may submit a petition in writing within 10 days of the issuance of the order to the Regional Director of Motor Carriers for the Region in which the order was issued. The Regional Director of Motor Carriers may affirm or reverse the order. Any driver adversely affected by such order of the Regional Director of Motor Carriers may petition the Associate Administrator for review, in accordance with 49 CFR 386.13.

Q. Does a driver always have to drive the speed limit—even with a tough schedule?

A. No motor carrier shall schedule a run nor permit nor require the operation of any commercial motor vehicle between points in such period of time as would necessitate speeds greater than those legally allowed.

Q. Does my vehicle need to be up-to-date in order to operate?

A. No commercial motor vehicle shall be driven unless the driver is satisfied that the following parts and accessories are in good working order, nor shall any driver fail to use or make use of such parts and accessories when and as needed:

- Service brakes, including trailer brake connections
- Parking (hand) brake
- Steering mechanism
- Lighting devices and reflectors
- Tires
- Horn
- Windshield wiper or wipers
- Rear vision mirror or mirrors
- Coupling devices

Emergency equipment, such as spare fuses, fire extinguisher, warning devices (reflectors or flares), must also be in good working order.

Q. Is it necessary for a CMV to stop at every railroad crossing?

A. Drivers should stop—no closer than 15 feet and no farther than 50 feet—from a railroad track. The driver should then listen and look in each direction along the tracks for an approaching train, and determine that no train is approaching. When it is safe to do so, the driver may drive the commercial motor vehicle across the tracks in a gear that permits the commercial motor vehicle to complete the crossing without a change of gears. The driver must not shift gears while crossing the tracks.

A commercial motor vehicle does not need to stop at streetcar crossings or a railroad grade when a police officer or crossing flagman directs traffic to proceed.

Q. What are considered "hazardous" driving conditions?

A. Extreme caution in the operation of a commercial motor vehicle shall be exercised when hazardous conditions, such as those caused by snow, ice, sleet, fog, mist, rain, dust, or smoke, adversely affect visibility or traction. Speed shall be reduced when such conditions exist. If conditions become sufficiently dangerous, the operation of the commercial motor vehicle shall be discontinued and shall not be resumed until the commercial motor vehicle can be safely operated.

Q. Are seatbelts required by FMCSR?

A. If the commercial motor vehicle being driven has a seat belt assembly installed at the driver's seat, it is unlawful to drive it unless the seatbelt is used by the driver.

Q. What is required when I am forced to stop my vehicle?

A. Whenever a commercial motor vehicle is stopped on the traveled portion of a highway or the shoulder of a highway for any cause other than necessary traffic stops, the driver shall immediately turn on the signal flashers. They should continue flashing until the driver has placed warning devices in front of and behind the vehicle.

Whenever a CMV is stopped for more than 10 minutes, warning devices (reflector triangles or flares) should be placed in the following manner:

- One on the traffic side, 10 feet from the stopped CMV in the direction of approaching traffic
- One 100 feet from CMV in center of traffic lane or shoulder in the direction of approaching traffic
- One 100 feet from CMV away from approaching traffic
- There should be one lighted or liquid-burning flare at each of the prescribed locations. These flares should be extinguished when the vehicle is moved.

The placement of warning devices is not required within the business or residential district of a municipality, except during the time lighted lamps are required and when street or highway lighting is insufficient to make a commercial motor vehicle clearly visible at a distance of 500 feet to persons on the highway.

On a hill or a curve or where there is an obvious obstruction, the driver should place a warning signal 100 to 500 feet from the stopped vehicle to give approaching vehicles ample warning and time to stop.

Q. What if I find my cargo is leaking something flammable or otherwise dangerous?

A. In this case, no emergency warning signal producing a flame shall be lighted or placed except at such a distance from any such liquid or gas as will assure the prevention of a fire or explosion.

Q. What about lights and reflectors? Any special requirements?

A. No commercial motor vehicle shall be driven when any of the required lamps or reflectors are obscured by the tailboard, by any part of the load, by dirt, or otherwise.

Headlamps should be used beginning one-half hour after sunset until one-half hour before sunrise. Lights should be used any time it is too dark to see within 500 feet in front of the truck.

Q. Fueling a vehicle can be hazardous. What are the regulations?

A. FMCSR Part 393.50 says that a driver or any employee of a motor carrier shall not:

(a) Fuel a commercial motor vehicle with the engine running, except when it is necessary to run the engine to fuel the commercial motor vehicle;

(b) Smoke or expose any open flame in the vicinity of a commercial motor vehicle being fueled;

(c) Fuel a commercial motor vehicle unless the nozzle of the fuel hose is continuously in contact with the intake pipe of the fuel tank;

(d) Permit, insofar as practicable, any other person to engage in such activities as would be likely to result in fire or explosion.

Q. I've heard cases where drivers were fired for picking up hitchhikers or having other people along for the ride. Is there a federal regulation?

A. Unless specifically authorized in writing to do so by the motor carrier, no driver shall transport any person or permit any person to be transported on any commercial motor vehicle other than a bus. When such authorization is issued, it shall state the name of the person to be transported, the points where the transportation is to begin and end, and the date upon which such authority expires.

No written authorization is required in the case of:

1. Employees or other persons assigned to a commercial motor vehicle by a motor carrier;
2. Any person transported when aid is being rendered in case of an accident or other emergency;
3. An attendant delegated to care for livestock.

No person shall drive a bus, and a motor carrier shall not require or permit a person to drive a bus, unless

1. All standees on the bus are rearward of the standee line.
2. All aisle seats in the bus conform to the requirements

3. Baggage or freight on the bus is stowed and secured in a manner which assures
   (a) Unrestricted freedom of movement to the driver and proper operation of the bus
   (b) Unobstructed access to all exits by any occupant of the bus
   (c) Protection of occupants of the bus against injury resulting from the falling or displacement of articles transported in the bus

Q. Are there any rules about towing or pushing a commercial passenger vehicle?

A. No disabled bus with passengers aboard shall be towed or pushed; nor shall any person use, or permit to be used, a bus with passengers aboard for the purpose of towing or pushing any disabled motor vehicle, except in such circumstances where the hazard to passengers would be increased by observance of the foregoing provisions of this section, and then only in traveling to the nearest point where the safety of the passengers is assured.

In addition, it is illegal for anyone to ride inside a closed commercial motor vehicle unless there is an easily accessible exit.

Q. What do I do if carbon monoxide is detected?

A. No person shall dispatch or drive any commercial motor vehicle or permit any passengers thereon, when the following conditions are known to exist, until such conditions have been remedied or repaired:

1. Where an occupant has been affected by carbon monoxide;
2. Where carbon monoxide has been detected in the interior of the commercial motor vehicle; and
3. When a mechanical condition of the commercial motor vehicle is discovered which would be likely to produce a hazard to the occupants by reason of carbon monoxide.

Remember: *No open-flame heaters should be used in loading/unloading a commercial vehicle or when that vehicle is in motion.*

Q. Is it legal for a driver to use a radar detector on a commercial motor vehicle?

A. No!

FMCSR PART 393

This part of the FMCSR covers the parts and accessories necessary to operate all vehicles safely. This list includes:

- Lights, reflectors, and electrical equipment
- Brakes
- Windows
- Fuel systems
- Coupling devices
- Tires, windshield wipers, horn, and other parts

- Emergency equipment
- Cargo tie-downs
- Wheels, suspension systems, and other parts of the frame

As a professional driver, you need to know about these parts to know whether or not something is missing or broken.

FMSCR Part 393 says you can have other parts and accessories on your truck, but the required parts must be present on the vehicle in order for it to operate safely.

Q. What do I need to know about lights and reflectors?

A. FMCSR Part 393 contains thorough information about the required lights and reflectors required for many different types of commercial motor vehicles. There are also diagrams to match these descriptions.

Pay special attention to the lights and reflectors required on the vehicles you plan to drive, once you have earned your CDL.

Learn the number, type, color, and locations of all required lights and reflectors. Then, make note of all of them each time you do an inspection of your vehicle, taking time to make sure all are operational every time you take the vehicle out.

Q. What are the regulations regarding turn signals?

A. Some states still allow automobile drivers to use hand and arm signals when turning and stopping their vehicles. However, all trucks and buses must have operational signaling systems, as described in FMCSR Part 393. These lights work as turn signals as well as hazard lights.

Q. What about clearance lights?

A. All commercial motor vehicles must have clearance lamps to outline the length and width of the vehicle. These lights are found at the highest and widest part of the sides, back, and front of the vehicle.

Q. What are the regulations about the other lights?

A. Some vehicles have other lights and markers but they must not reduce how well the required lights work. Extra lighting that is brighter or larger than the required lighting is not permitted.

All lights must be electric. The exception would be liquid burning lights sometimes used to mark the end of loads protruding past the rear of the vehicle.

Q. What do the regulations say about headlights?

A. FMCSR Part 393 states that all vehicles must have headlights and fog lights on the front of the vehicle. According to regulations, these lights must be visible from a distance of 500 feet in clear weather to 50 feet away in foggy weather.

Q. What about the battery, wiring, and fuses?

A. As a driver, you want the battery as well as all wiring and fuses to work correctly and safely all the time. Regulations concerning this equipment concern manufacturers—but drivers should learn about the wiring system, battery, and fuses as part of the inspection process.

Detachable connections—electrical connections between towing and towed vehicles—are sometimes called the "pigtail" and it is made by simply twisting wires together with shielded cables. Wires and cables must be attached to terminals with the correct connectors.

Q. Brakes are always a concern. What do I need to know about the brakes?
A. Many drivers fail to do well on their CDL tests because they don't know enough about the braking systems on their vehicle.

Braking systems, of course, are very important because a faulty braking system threatens the life of the driver and others on the road, so drivers should know the braking system on their vehicle, backwards and forwards.

FMCSR Part 393 says your vehicle must have three types of brakes: service, parking, and emergency.

Emergency brake controls must be placed so the driver can reach them while sitting in the driver's seat with a seatbelt locked. The emergency brake control may be combined with the service brakes or the parking brakes. However, FMCSR 393 says the three controls may not be combined into one.

On a commercial motor vehicle, the controls must be designed so that one braking system will always work whatever the situation.

Q. What do I need to know about parking brakes?
A. Federal law states that all commercial motor vehicles manufactured after March 7, 1989, must have parking brakes. Farm vehicles and pole trailers are also required to have chocks, (blocks usually made of wood) used to hold tires in place to keep a vehicle from moving.

In some vehicles, the parking brake can be set by pulling a lever or knob. This controls the cable that pulls the brake into position. Such a system requires little effort, and should not require great strength to set or release.

Some other vehicles, however, do require parking brakes and in these vehicles, the parking brake is set with the help of air pressure. In these vehicles, the air supply to set the parking brake is separate from that of the service brake.

For any braking system, fluid pressure, air pressure, or electricity can be used to set the parking brakes but these elements cannot be used to keep the parking brakes set. When the brake is released, the system must be designed so that the parking brake can immediately be reapplied without any lag time.

As you might guess, air pressure does not meet these requirements because it takes time to build back up after each use. If the parking brake was applied using air pressure, released, and then immediately reapplied, nothing would happen because there would not have been enough time for the air pressure to rebuild.

The parking brakes on most commercial motor vehicles on the road today meet these requirements. Manufacturers must meet federal regulations or else the trucks would not be allowed into the market and on the road.

All professional drivers should understand the braking systems on the trucks they drive and know how to inspect and maintain these systems so the brakes are always in 100-percent working order.

FMCSR Part 393.42 requires that all wheels on all CMVs are equipped with working brakes. Exceptions to this regulation are vehicles manufactured before 1980 (and there are still plenty around). If the front brakes have been removed, the law requires that after February 26, 1988, all other CMVs must have working front brakes.

Q. What are the federal laws covering emergency brakes?

A. The law covering emergency brakes requires that if a driver is pulling a trailer with brakes and that trailer breaks away from the tractor, the service brakes on the tractor will still work.

If your vehicle has air brakes, there must be two ways of starting the trailer emergency brakes. One must work automatically if the air supply falls between 20 and 45 pounds per square inch (psi).

The second way of starting the emergency brakes must be with a manual control. This control should be within easy reach of the driver's seat and must be clearly marked and easy to operate.

Vehicles pulling trailers with vacuum brakes also must have two controls. One will be a single control that will operate all of the brakes of the total tractor-trailer combination. The second must be a trailer emergency brake, operated with a manual control and independent of the brake air, hydraulic, and other pressure supplies. It must also be separate from the other controls.

The one exception to this regulation is that if there is a failure of the pressure that the second control depends on, the trailer brakes will activate automatically.

Trailers required to have brakes must have automatic brakes. If the trailer breaks away from the tractor, these brakes must remain activated for at least 15 minutes.

The air supply for tractor braking must be protected from air back-flow if the tractor air pressure falls. If there is a problem with the tractor's air supply, the system must prevent the trailer's air supply from flowing back to the tractor.

Why would this be a problem? Because both the tractor and the trailer would be left without a supply of air. A relay or check valve would prevent this from happening.

As mentioned earlier, these regulations generally concern the manufacturer only, but it is also the professional driver's responsibility to know how these systems are designed so he or she will be able to inspect and maintain the braking system—and know when the brakes are not functioning at 100 percent so the problem can be corrected.

Note: These requirements don't apply if the vehicle is being towed.

Q. Do these same federal regulations apply to brake tubing and hoses?

A. FMCSR Part 393 provides the requirements for hoses and tubing used in the brake lines. These must meet manufacturing standards. However, after months and miles of use, these components of the braking system can become worn or even damaged. As a professional driver, it is your job to check the tubing and hoses on your vehicle to make sure the brake lines meet federal requirements.

Q. What if one part of the vehicle's braking system stops working?

A. First of all, hope this never happens. You can ensure this to some point by always conducting a thorough pre-trip inspection. However, if any braking system stops working, have it corrected before taking the vehicle on the highway—if you drive a vehicle manufactured before March 1, 1975, you should read the sections on braking again.

Q. What are the brake reservoirs?

A. The brake reservoirs, (pronounced rez-uh-vars), or tanks are described in FMCSR Part 393.

For air or vacuum braking systems, the reservoirs must be large enough to ensure a full-service brake application, even with the engine stopped. ("Full service brake application" means pushing the brake pedal to the limit.) This situation must lower the air pressure or vacuum to below 70 percent of the pressure on the gauge just before the brakes were applied.

Brake reservoirs must be protected from leaks and if the connection to the air or vacuum supply is broken, a device called a check valve must be used to seal off the tank so the entire supply isn't lost.

Each time you inspect your rig, check the check valve to make sure it is working.

Some braking systems have a wet tank and a dry tank. In these cases, the check valve is located between these two tanks. There is also a manually operated drain cock on the wet tank which can be used to inspect the check valve.

When checking the system, test the check valve operation of vacuum systems when the engine is off. The vacuum gauge should show that the system is still holding the vacuum. If the gauge indicates that the pressure is rising, the check valve is malfunctioning and should be repaired.

Q. Is there any type of warning system to signal a problem with the brakes?

A. FMCSR Part 393 covers warning devices on service brake systems—and there are several warning systems available.

Hydraulic and vacuum brakes have warning devices that can be seen and heard. Air brakes have warning systems consisting of a low air pressure warning device.

Braking systems must also have gauges. On air brakes, gauges signal how many psi of pressure are available for braking.

This section of FMCSR requires that all warning mechanisms on brake systems must be kept in working order.

Some hydraulic braking systems are assisted by air or by vacuum and these systems must also have warning devices and gauges as well as gauges and warning devices for the hydraulic mechanism.

Q. What are the FMCSR standards for brake performance?

A. According to FMCSR Part 393, there are standards of performance for both emergency brakes and service brakes. There is even a standard braking force as a percentage of the GVWR or the GCWR. You are not expected to memorize this table because these are actually manufacturing specifications, but it is included for you to scan.

This performance table, (Table 4-1), also states how quickly the vehicle must slow and how far it should travel while slowing down.

Q. Are there any regulations regarding the windows and windshield of a commercial motor vehicle?

A. Yes. According to FMCSR, there must be a certain amount of glass in your vehicle to ensure good visibility while you're driving down the highway.

Table 4-1
Vehicle Brake Performance

Type of motor vehicle	Service brake	Systems	Emergency	Brake systems
(2) Vehicles with a seating capacity of more than 10 persons, including driver, and built on a passenger car chassis; vehicles built on a truck or bus chassis and having a manufacturer's GVWR of 10,000 pounds or less	52.8	17		
(3) All other passenger carrying vehicles	43.5	14	35	85
B. *Property carrying vehicles.*	52.8	17	25	66
(1) Single unit vehicles having a manufacturer's GVWR of 10,000 pounds or less				
(2) Single unit vehicles having a manufacturer's GVWR of more than 10,000 pounds, except truck tractors. Combinations of a 2-axle towing vehicle and trailer having a GVWR of 3,000 pounds or less. All combinations of 2 or less vehicles in driveaway or towaway operation	43.4	14	35	85
(3) All other property carrying vehicles and combinations of property carrying vehicles	43.5	14	40	90

Note: There is a definite mathematical relationship between the figures in columns 2 and 3, if the decelerations set forth in column 3 are divided by 32.2 feet per second, the figures in column 2 will be obtained. (For example, 21 divided by 32.2 equals 65.2 percent.) Column 2 is included in the tabulation because certain brake testing devices utilize this factor.

The decelerations specified in column 3 are an indication of the effectiveness of the basic brakes, and as measured in practical brake testing are the maximum decelerations attained at some time during the stop.

These decelerations as measured in brake tests cannot be used to compute the values in column 4 because the deceleration is not sustained at the same rate over the entire period of the stop. The deceleration increases from zero to a maximum during a period of brake system application and brake force buildup. Also, other factors may cause the deceleration to decrease after reaching a maximum. The added distance which results because maximum deceleration is not sustained is included in the figures in column 4 but is not indicated by the usual brake testing devices for checking deceleration.

The distances in column 4 and the decelerations in column 3 are not directly related. "Brake system application and braking distance in feet" (column 4) is a definite measure of the overall effectiveness of the braking system, being the distance traveled between the point at which the driver starts to move the braking controls and the point at which the vehicle comes to rest. It includes distance traveled while the brakes are being applied and distance traveled while they are retarding the vehicle.

The distance traveled during the period of brake system application and brake force buildup varies with vehicle type, being negligible for many passenger cars and greatest for combinations of commercial vehicles. This fact accounts for the variation from 20 to 40 feet in the values in column 4 for the various classes of vehicles.

The terms "GVWR" and "GVW" refer to the manufacturer's gross vehicle rating and the actual gross vehicle weight, respectively.

(From the United States Department of Transportation Federal Motor Carrier Safety Administration 36 FR 20298, Oct. 20, 1971, as amended at 37 FR 5251, Mar. 11, 1972; 37 FR 11336, June 7, 1972.)

The glass must be clear, clean, and undamaged. FMCSR Part 393 sets the standards for windshields and their condition. This is one of the things you'll check when you perform your pre-trip inspection.

FMCSR Part 393 says you may not have any labels, stickers, decals, or other decorations on your windshield or on your side windows. (This does not prohibit placing a wreath on your front bumper during the holidays!)

The only stickers allowed are those required by law and these must be placed at the bottom of the windshield, no higher than 4.5 inches from the bottom of the windshield.

FMCSR Part 393 says your truck must have a windshield and windows on each side of the cab. This ruling does not apply if you drive a truck equipped with folding doors or doors with clear openings in place of windows.

Q. What about windshield wipers?

A. Commercial motor vehicles *must* have windshield wipers in working order. In some cases, one wiper will do as long as it clears your windshield to within one inch of your field of vision on either side.

In a towing operation, only the vehicle being driven must meet this standard, so the towed vehicle does not have to have working wipers.

Q. What about defrosters?

A. If you drive in snow, ice, or frost—and that means almost everywhere in the country at one time of the year or another—your vehicle must have a windshield defroster in working order. As with wipers, if your vehicle is being towed, the defrosters don't need to be in working order.

Q. What are the regulations about rear-view mirrors?

A. If you drive an automobile or small truck, you know how much you use the rear-view mirror. Now double or triple that use when you're driving a commercial motor vehicle.

According to FMCSR Part 393, all trucks built after 1980 must have rear-view mirrors, one on each side. In older trucks, there may be only one outside rear-view mirror and another that gives full view of the rear of the truck. Mirrors should be positioned to show the highway behind the vehicle as well as both sides of the vehicle.

More Regulations for Your Safety

Q. What about fuel systems and fuel storage?

A. The fuel that powers your truck must be handled and stored carefully and safely at all times. The regulations set forward in FMCSR Part 393 state that the fuel system must be installed specifically on the vehicle and also provide specifications about how fuel tanks are mounted. Leakage tests are specified and must be passed on the fuel tanks. The manufacturers conduct these tests.

FMCSR Part 393 covers the handling and storage of liquid petroleum gas (LPG) systems. Some CMVs use LPG for fuel or to power auxiliary equipment, including refrigerated units.

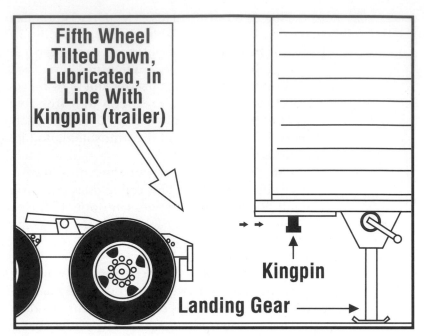

Figure 4-1   Coupling system.

Q. What about coupling devices and towing?

A. This portion of FMCSR Part 393 covers descriptions and definitions of the fifth wheel or coupling system (Figure 4-1), something the driver inspects both on pre-trip and post-trip inspections.

The regulations provide limits on coupling and towing tractors together and hauling them as cargo. When one tractor tows another as cargo, a special fifth wheel device, called a saddle mount, is used. Only three saddle mounts can be used in any combination. No more than one tow-bar can be used.

When towing vehicles with saddle mounts or tow-bars, the towed vehicles must have brakes and their brake lines must run all through the combination to the towing tractor.

The driver towing other vehicles must be able to apply the brakes of all vehicles in the combination from the tractor. If all the vehicles in the combination have brakes, then the stopping ability improves.

A driver may not use the tractor's bumper as a tow-bar. Towed vehicles must face forward and, in some cases, their front wheels must be controlled so they won't turn past the widest part of the tractor.

Tow-bars must provide some control over the towed vehicles' steering and the towed vehicles must track the towing vehicle.

This section has many specifications, mainly for manufacturers, about how tow-bars must be constructed, as well as the construction specifications for saddle-mounts and U-bolts.

Any driver driving in a driveaway-towaway operation must know how to operate and inspect all equipment involved.

Q. What about tires?

A. This part of the FMCSR 393 says that you cannot drive on tires worn so the belts show through. Also prohibited are the following:

TIRE COMPONENTS

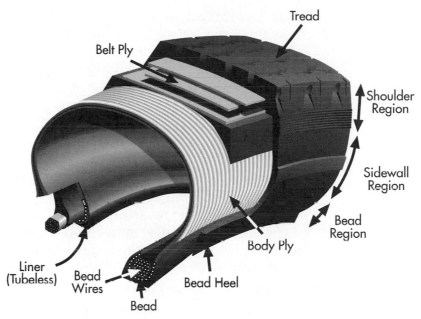

Figure 4-2   Parts of a tire.

- Tires that have sidewall or tread separation
- Tires that are flat or have audible (can be heard) leaks
- Tires that have a tread groove pattern of less than 2/32 of an inch (4/32 of an inch for front tires where more traction is required)

Regrooved tires are not to be used on the front wheels of a truck or tractor that has more than an 8000-pound front axle rating.

With few exceptions, tires cannot be used to support weights heavier than the tire itself is rated to handle. In addition, tires must be inflated to the pressure specified for the load they are hauling. Figure 4-2 shows tire components.

Check the Federal Motor Vehicle Safety Standards for more information—if these are not included in the FMCSR, look in the Code of Federal Regulations Title 49.

Q. What about sleeper berths?
A. FMCSR Part 393 specifies the size, shape, and structure of the sleeper berth. Most specifications are geared to the safety and comfort of the professional driver. The specifications offered in this part are for the manufacturer, but drivers should be aware of these specifications if they plan to customize their sleepers.

Q. What about heaters?
A. Every commercial motor vehicle must be equipped with a heater. FMCSR Part 393 prohibits heaters that give off exhaust gases in the cab. Heaters must be securely mounted and, in the case of combustion heaters, it must be vented to the outside.

Q. What about horns?

A. All trucks and buses must be equipped with a horn.

Q. What does FMCSR say about speedometers?

A. Every truck and bus must have an operational speedometer. If a vehicle is being driven in a driveaway-towaway operation, it does not need a speedometer if its speed is limited to 45 miles per hour. A truck being towed as cargo is not required to have an operational speedometer.

Q. What about the exhaust system?

A. All commercial motor vehicles must have an exhaust system, which must be installed so hot gases or surfaces don't damage the wiring, fuel supply, or any flammable or combustible part of the vehicle.

   FMCSR Part 393 specifies that an exhaust gases must be discharged in a certain manner and that an exhaust system must be installed and maintained to meet these requirements.

   The professional driver must ensure that the exhaust system continues to function in the specified manner. This section also specifies that an exhaust system may not be repaired with wrap or patches.

Q. What about the floor?

A. FMCSR Part 393 even has a standard for the floor of every commercial motor vehicle on the road. This standard guards against floors which have been damaged or in which holes have been made. This section of FMCSR specifies that floors must be free of holes, oil, and grease, which would make them slippery. The holes could cause harm to the driver by allowing exhaust fumes to accumulate in the cab.

Q. Are television receivers allowed?

A. A television receiver is allowed in a truck but it should not be visible to the driver when the truck is in operation. FMCSR states that a television must be installed behind the driver's seat or otherwise outside of the driver's line of vision while he or she is driving. The regulations further state that the television must be placed in such a manner than the driver will have to leave the driver's seat to watch it.

Q. What about rear end protection and projecting loads?

A. Any part of the vehicle or load that extends beyond the rear or sides of the truck must be marked by tying on a red flag. To be flagged, the load must extend more than four inches from the sides of the truck or four feet beyond the rear of the truck. Flags used to mark projecting loads must be at least 12 inches square and must be red.

Q. What about seatbelts?

A. Most trucks are now equipped with some sort of seatbelt and, in most states, the law requires that a seatbelt be worn anytime the vehicle is in operation. Tractors with incomplete cabs must also have seatbelts when they are being towed as cargo.

Q. What about noise levels coming from the truck?

A. The cab of your truck is a limited and enclosed space. The concentration of noise in this area may be distracting enough to cause problems in operating the truck. This is discussed in FMCSR Part 393—and drivers are encouraged to report unusually high levels of noise. But other than being detrimental to the driver's own well-being, a lot of noise in the cab could signal a problem

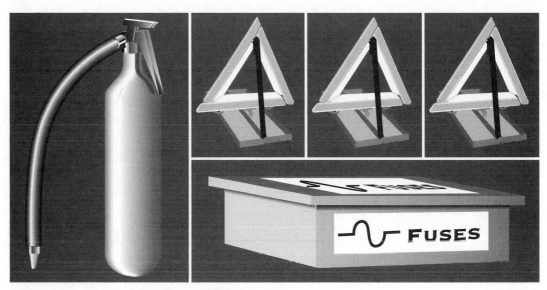

Figure 4-3 Emergency and safety equipment.

in the mechanical area of the truck. Repair could bring relief—but ongoing high levels of noise not only impairs a driver's ability to operate the vehicle but also could impair hearing or cause high levels of anxiety and stress. So, don't ignore all that noise—inspect closely and make any repairs necessary to quiet the cab.

Q. What about emergency equipment?

A. According to federal regulations, most vehicles are equipped with a fire extinguisher, spare fuses, and warning devices for use when your vehicle is parked for emergency reasons (Figure 4-3). The only trucks without this equipment may be light vehicles or vehicles towed as cargo.

FMCSR Part 393 states that the fire extinguisher must be mounted and within easy reach. The driver is responsible for having the extinguisher checked, filled, and ready to use at all times.

Before using a vehicle, make sure there is at least one spare fuse on board. However, there is no need for spare fuses if all overload protective devices are circuit breakers that can be reset.

Warning devices are needed for use during an emergency stop. Each truck manufactured after 1974 must have three reflective triangles. In trucks manufactured before 1974, there must be three electric lamps or three red emergency reflectors and two red flags, instead of the reflective triangles. Flares can be substituted for any of this equipment—except when the truck is hauling flammable liquids or gas or explosive materials.

Read FMCSR Part 393 for specifications for reflective triangles or other warning devices that are acceptable for use.

Q. What about cargo securement?

A. According to FMCSR Part 393, there are four ways to keep cargo from shifting or falling. All vehicles must use one of these four options to safely haul every load:

  • Option A—vehicles must have sides, sideboards, or stakes and a rear endgate, endboard, or stakes. There need not be solid pieces, but there should not be spaces large enough for cargo to escape. These items should be installed so they are stable and will not fall off of the vehicle.

- Option B—vehicles must have tiedowns for every 10 feet of cargo and extra tiedowns should be available if they are needed. Only two tiedowns are needed for pole trailers, with one used at each end.
- Option C—FMCSR Part 393 describes securement of metal cargo.
- Option D—there is allowance for other securement devices as long as they are as efficient at securement as those described in Options A, B, or C.

This part of FMCSR also discusses how to secure coils of metal on a flatbed and discusses how to tie down other metal cargo.

It also discusses intermodal cargo containers, which are some of the fastest growing aspects of the transportation industry. Drivers should read this part carefully so they can fasten these containers securely to the trailer.

Containers should not be allowed to shift too much with the motion of the trailer. FMCSR specify that containers may not move more than one-half inch in any direction and should not rise up off the trailer more than one inch.

Specifications for chains, straps, cables, binders, webbing, hardware, and other securement devices are also described in this part. No driver should use any securement device that does not meet these specifications.

FMCSR also state that the trailer must have a front-end structure, such as a headerboard. Without this structure, the cargo could shift and crush the tractor's cab with a quick stop.

If there is no headerboard in the vehicle, cargo must be braced or blocked.

Most vehicles used to carry cargo must have headerboards, but for vehicles used only to tow other vehicles, no headerboard is necessary on the trailer if the tractor has a cab guard.

Q. What about body components?

A. In this last section of FMCSR Part 393, standards and specifications are given for body parts, such as the frame, cab, wheels, steering, and suspension. These areas will be covered in other chapters.

The last part of the FMCSR covers accident reporting. This won't appear on the CDL Knowledge Tests because most of the responsibility for accident reporting lies with the motor carrier. However, as a professional driver, you are a witness to the incident and will need to help the carrier make the required reports.

In some cases, motor carriers have a routine to follow if an accident should occur.

Be sure to get a copy of FMCSR Part 394 and read it thoroughly. You can find it on the Internet under Federal Motor Carrier Safety Regulations on the Department of Transportation's website.

Let's Review

Read each question and all of the answers provided. Place the letter of the correct answer in the space provided, or write your answers on a separate piece of paper so you can use these questions again as you review for the CDL. Once you have answered all the questions, check your answers against the answer key which follows.

____ 1. In a driveaway-towaway situation, the vehicle is
(A) cargo,
(B) required to have a speedometer,
(C) required to have four new tires,
(D) all of the above.

____ 2. True or False. Clearance lights are optional on any commercial motor vehicle.

____ 3. The emergency brake control must be
(A) marked in red letters,
(B) within reach of the driver's seat,
(C) should be operated with the right hand,
(D) all of the above.

____ 4. When setting the parking brake requires tremendous strength, the truck is usually equipped with
(A) a permanent assistant,   (C) air pressure to set the brake,
(B) "cheater bars,"   (D) all of the above.

____ 5. Vehicles that pull trailers with vacuum brakes must have how many controls?
(A) Two,   (C) Four,
(B) Three,   (D) One.

____ 6. A brake reservoir is a
(A) knob control,   (C) tank,
(B) lever control,   (D) none of the above.

____ 7. True or False. Hydraulic and vacuum brake system warning devices can be seen but not heard.

____ 8. True or False. Braking force is a manufacturer's specification.

____ 9. True or False. Braking standards assume the vehicle is braking on a downgrade in rainy weather.

____ 10. If your tractor has a television, it must be installed
(A) so passenger can see it while going down the road,
(B) just to the right of the driver,
(C) in a position such that the driver would have to leave the driver's seat to view it,
(D) none of the above.

Answers to Let's Review

1. A; 2. False; 3. B; 4. C; 5. A; 6. C; 7. False; 8. True; 9. False; 10. C.

Terms You Should Know

The following terms have been taken from the contents of Chapter 4. Review them. If you see any you are unsure of, check the definition in the Glossary at the back of the book. If it helps you, keep a written list of the words and their definitions (or write in the definitions here) and review them several days prior to taking the CDL tests.

Air backflow

Air pressure

Bobtail tractor

Brake reservoirs

Braking distance

Braking force

Braking performance

Braking rate

Cargo securement

Clearance lights

Deceleration

Defrosting device

Driveaway-towaway

Emergency brakes

Field of vision

Fluid pressure

Fuel system

Groove pattern

Headerboard

Heater

Hydraulic braking system

Intermodal containers (fishyback/piggyback)

Noise levels

Parking brakes

"Pigtail"

Pole trailers/pulpwood trailers

Projecting loads

Pounds per square inch (psi)

Rear-end projection

Service brakes

Spring brakes

Steering wheel lash

Television receiver

Tie-downs

Vacuum brakes

THE DISPATCH BOARD
Taking Time to Enjoy the Beauty of Each Day

All too often, professional drivers are so busy trying to deliver loads on time, they may not always take time to actually experience the marvels that surround them every mile of the route.

The following story may help you remember.

I had a teacher in high school many years ago whose husband unexpectedly died of a sudden heart attack.

About a week after his death, and as the late afternoon sunlight came streaming in through the classroom windows, she moved a few things aside on the edge of her desk and sat down. "Before class is over, I would like to share with all of you a thought that is unrelated to class, but which I feel is very important," she said.

"Each of us is put here on earth to learn, share, love, appreciate, and give of ourselves. No one knows when this fantastic experience will end. So I would like you all to make me a promise.

"From now on, on your way to school, or on your way home, find something beautiful to notice. It doesn't have to be something you see. It could be a scent, perhaps of freshly baked bread, or it could be the sound of the breeze slightly rustling the leaves in the trees, or the way the morning light catches one autumn leaf as it falls gently to the ground.

"Please look for these things and cherish them. For, although it may sound trite to some, these things are 'the stuff' of life . . . the little things we are put here on earth to enjoy. The things we often take for granted."

The class was completely quiet. We picked up our books and filed out of the room silently. That afternoon, on my way home from school, I found more beauty in that one day than I had that whole semester.

Every once in awhile, I think of that teacher and remember what an impression she made on all of us. That reminds me to appreciate all those things that sometimes we all overlook.

Take notice of something special today. Enjoy watching the fingers of sunset bring down the curtain at night. Marvel at the passing landscape. Stop off to get a double-dip ice cream cone.

Remember! Life is not measured by the number of breaths we take, but by the moments that take our breath away.

5

FMCSR—Parts 395, 396 and 397

FMCSR Part 395

This section of the Federal Motor Carriers Safety Regulations defines "Hours of Service" and requires all drivers to keep a Record of Duty Status. Included in this section are descriptions of adverse driving conditions, emergency conditions, and relief from regulations, and covers drivers who have been taken "out of service." These regulations apply to all motor carriers and drivers, with few exceptions.

Unlike most other professions, driving has its own schedule. The workday does not end at 5 PM. Oftentimes you won't start working at 8 AM.

Professional drivers are governed by what is known as "hours of service," and FMCSR Part 395 sets the limits of these hours.

The number of hours and the kind of work you perform during this time depends on the hours you worked the day before.

Every hour and every type of duty you do is recorded in a logbook, the "record of duty status." This record helps drivers stay within the legal limits.

If a driver encounters adverse driving conditions and cannot safely complete the run within the 10-hour maximum driving time permitted, the driver is permitted or required to drive a commercial motor vehicle for not more than two additional hours in order to complete that run or to reach a place offering safety for the occupants of the commercial motor vehicle and security for that vehicle and its cargo.

However, the driver may not drive or be permitted to drive

- For more than 12 hours in the aggregate following eight consecutive hours off duty; or
- After he or she has been on duty 15 hours following eight consecutive hours off duty.

In case of any emergency, a driver may complete his/her run without being in violation of the provisions of the regulations in this part, if such a run reasonably could have been completed absent the emergency.

Definitions to Remember

Adverse driving conditions are snow, sleet, fog, other adverse weather conditions, a highway covered with snow or ice, or unusual road and traffic conditions, none of which were apparent based on information known to the person dispatching the run at the time it was begun.

Automatic on-board recording device is an electric, electronic, electromechanical, or mechanical device capable of recording driver's duty status information accurately and automatically. The device must be integrally synchronized with specific

73

operations of the commercial motor vehicle in which it is installed. At minimum, the device must record engine use, road speed, miles driven, date, and time of day.

Driver salesperson is any employee who is employed solely as such by a private carrier of property by commercial motor vehicle, who is engaged both in selling goods, services, or the use of goods, and in delivering by commercial motor vehicle the goods sold or provided or upon which the services are performed, who does so entirely within a radius of 100 miles of the point at which he/she reports for duty, and who devotes not more than 50 percent of his or her hours on duty to driving time.

Selling goods, for purposes of this section, shall include in all cases of solicitation or obtaining of reorders or new accounts, and may also include other selling or merchandising activities designed to retain the customer or to increase the sale of goods or services, in addition to solicitation or obtaining of reorders or new accounts.

Driving time is all time spent at the driving controls of a commercial motor vehicle.

Eight consecutive days means the period of eight consecutive days beginning on any day at the time designated by the motor carrier for a 24-hour period.

Multiple stops means that all stops made in any one village, town, or city may be computed as one.

On-duty time means all time from the time a driver begins to work or is required to be in readiness to work until the time the driver is relieved from work. On-duty time includes:

1. All time at a plant, terminal, facility, or other property of a motor carrier or shipper, or on any public property, waiting to be dispatched, unless the driver has been relieved from duty by the motor carrier.
2. All time inspecting, servicing, or conditioning any commercial motor vehicle at any time.
3. All driving time.
4. All time, other than driving time, in or upon any commercial motor vehicle, except time spent resting in a sleeper berth.
5. All time loading or unloading a commercial motor vehicle, supervising, or assisting in the loading or unloading, attending a commercial motor vehicle being loaded or unloaded, remaining in readiness to operate the commercial motor vehicle, or in giving or receiving receipts for shipments loaded or unloaded.
6. All time repairing, obtaining assistance, or remaining in attendance upon a disabled commercial motor vehicle.
7. All time spent providing a breath sample or urine specimen, including travel time to and from the collection site, in order to comply with the random, reasonable suspicion, post-accident, or follow-up testing required by a motor carrier.
8. Performing any other work in the capacity, employ, or service of a motor carrier and performing any compensated work for a person who is not a motor carrier.

Seven consecutive days means the period of seven consecutive days beginning on any day at the time designated by the motor carrier for a 24-hour period.

Sleeper berth is a berth conforming to the requirements of FMCSR §393.76.

Transportation of construction materials and equipment means the transportation of construction and pavement materials, construction equipment, and construction maintenance vehicles by a driver to or from an active construction site (a construction site between mobilization of equipment and materials to the site to the final completion of the construction project) within a 50 air-mile radius of the normal work reporting location of the driver.

Twenty-four-hour period means any 24 consecutive hour period beginning at the time designated by the motor carrier for the terminal from which the driver is normally dispatched.

Utility service vehicle is any commercial motor vehicle used or designed to facilitate the work or transportation of utility workers.

FMCSR §395.3: Maximum Driving Times

This portion of FMCSR Part 395 gives the limits for how long a driver is allowed to drive. These limits are sometimes called "the 10-hour rule" and "the 15-hour rule."

If a driver has been off duty for eight straight hours, then he or she may drive no more than 10 hours, the 10-hour rule. After eight straight hours off-duty, a driver may be "on-duty" for no more than 15 hours. Then the driver may not drive again until he or she has had some off-duty time, the 15-hour rule. As you read more of this section, you will find some exceptions to these rules.

No motor carrier shall permit or require any driver used by it to drive nor shall any such driver drive:

1. More than 10 hours following eight consecutive hours off duty; or
2. For any period after having been on duty 15 hours following eight consecutive hours off duty.

No motor carrier shall permit or require a driver of a commercial motor vehicle to drive, nor shall any driver drive, regardless of the number of motor carriers using the driver's services, for any period after having been on duty:

1. 60 hours in any seven consecutive days if the employing motor carrier does not operate commercial motor vehicles every day of the week; or
2. 70 hours in any period of eight consecutive days if the employing motor carrier operates commercial motor vehicles every day of the week.

FMCSR §395.8: Driver's Record of Duty Status

Every driver must keep a "record of duty status" or "log book," which is a record of how you spent your time during each 24-hour period.

If you keep a handwritten log, you must make two copies and use a form—called a grid—that meets requirements of FMCSR Part 395 (see examples below).

1. Every driver who operates a commercial motor vehicle shall record his or her duty status, in duplicate, for each 24-hour period. The duty status time shall be recorded on a specified grid.

    The grid may be combined with any company forms. The previously approved format of the Daily Log, Form MCS 59, or the Multi-day Log (Figure 5-1), Form MCS 139 and 139A, which meets the requirements of this section, may continue to be used.
2. Every driver who operates a commercial motor vehicle shall record his or her duty status by using an automatic on-board recording device that meets the requirements.

```
                    HOURS OF SERVICE RECORD FOR FIRST TIME
                            OR INTERMITTENT DRIVERS

        Name (Print) _____
                             First        Middle         Last


                    DAY                 TOTAL TIME ON DUTY
                     1                       _____
                     2                       _____
                     3                       _____
                     4                       _____
                     5                       _____
                     6                       _____
                     7                       _____
        _____
                            TOTAL _____

        I hereby certify that the information contained herein is true to the best of my
        knowledge and belief, and that my last period of release from duty was from

        _____        to     _____
            (Hour/Date)                     (Hour/Date)


        Signature _____        Date _____
```

Figure 5-1   Driver's Daily Log (for first time or intermittent drivers).

The duty status shall be recorded as follows:

(a) "Off duty" or "OFF."
(b) "Sleeper berth" or "SB" (only if a sleeper berth used).
(c) "Driving" or "D."
(d) "On duty not driving" or "ON."

For each change of duty status (e.g., the place of reporting for work, starting to drive, on duty not driving and where released from work), the name of the city, town or village, with state abbreviation, shall be recorded.

Note: If a change of duty status occurs at a location other than a city, town, or village, show one of the following: (1) the highway number and nearest milepost followed by the name of the nearest city, town, or village and state abbreviation, (2) the highway number and the name of the service plaza followed by the name of the nearest city, town, or village, and state abbreviation, or (3) the highway numbers of the nearest two intersecting roadways followed by the name of the nearest city, town, or village and state abbreviation.

The following information must be included on the form in addition to the grid:

1. Date
2. Total miles driving today
3. Truck or tractor and trailer number
4. Name of carrier

5. Driver's signature/certification
6. 24 hour period starting time (e.g., midnight, 9:00 AM, noon, 3:00 PM)
7. Main office address
8. Remarks
9. Name of co-driver
10. Total hours (far right edge of grid)
11. Shipping document number(s), or name of shipper and commodity

Failure to complete the record of duty activities, failure to preserve a record of such duty activities, or making of false reports in connection with such duty activities shall make the driver and/or the carrier liable to prosecution.

The driver's activities shall be recorded in accordance with the following provisions:

1. Entries to be current. Drivers shall keep their record of duty status current to the time shown for the last change of duty status.
2. Entries to be made by driver only. All entries relating to driver's duty status must be legible and in the driver's own handwriting.
3. Date. The month, day, and year for the beginning of each 24-hour period shall be shown on the form containing the driver's duty status record.
4. Total miles driving today. Total mileage driven during the 24-hour period shall be recorded on the form containing the driver's duty status record.
5. Commercial motor vehicle identification. The driver shall show the number assigned by the motor carrier or state and the license number of each commercial motor vehicle operated during each 24-hour period on his or her record of duty status. The driver of an articulated (combination) commercial motor vehicle shall show the number assigned by the motor carrier or the state and the license number of each motor vehicle used in each commercial motor vehicle combination operated during that 24-hour period on his or her record of duty status.
6. Name of motor carrier. The name(s) of the motor carrier(s) for which work is performed shall be shown on the form containing the driver's record of duty status. When work is performed for more than one motor carrier during the same 24-hour period, the beginning and finishing time, showing AM or PM, worked for each motor carrier shall be shown after each motor carrier's name. Drivers of leased commercial motor vehicles shall show the name of the motor carrier performing the transportation.
7. Signature/certification. The driver shall certify to the correctness of all entries by signing the form containing the driver's duty status record with his or her legal name or name of record. The driver's signature certifies that all entries required by this section made by the driver are true and correct.
8. Time base to be used. The driver's duty status record shall be prepared, maintained, and submitted using the time standard in effect at the driver's home terminal, for a 24-hour period beginning with the time specified by the motor carrier for that driver's home terminal.

    The term "seven or eight consecutive days" means the seven or eight consecutive 24-hour periods as designated by the carrier for the driver's home terminal.
9. The 24-hour period starting time must be identified on the driver's duty status record. One-hour increments must appear on the graph, be identified, and preprinted. The words "Midnight" and "Noon" must appear above or beside the appropriate one-hour increment.

10. Main office address. The motor carrier's main office address shall be shown on the form containing the driver's duty status record.
11. Recording days off duty. Two or more consecutive 24-hour periods off duty may be recorded on one duty status record.
12. Total hours. The total hours in each duty status: off duty other than in a sleeper berth; off duty in a sleeper berth; driving; and on duty not driving shall be entered to the right of the grid. The total of such entries shall equal 24 hours.
13. Shipping document number(s), or name of shipper and commodity shall be shown on the driver's record of duty status.

Graph Grid. The graph grid must be incorporated into a motor carrier record-keeping system, which must also contain the information required.

Graph Grid Preparation. The graph grid may be used horizontally or vertically and shall be completed as follows:

1. Off duty—Except for time spent resting in a sleeper berth, a continuous line shall be drawn between the appropriate time markers to record the period(s) of time when the driver is not on duty, is not required to be in readiness to work, or is not under any responsibility for performing work.
2. Sleeper berth—A continuous line shall be drawn between the appropriate time markers to record the period(s) of time off duty resting in a sleeper berth, as defined in §395.2. (If a non-sleeper berth operation, sleeper berth need not be shown on the grid.)
3. Driving—A continuous line shall be drawn between the appropriate time markers to record the period(s) of driving time.
4. On duty–not driving—A continuous line shall be drawn between the appropriate time markers to record the period(s) of time on duty not driving specified in §395.2.
5. Location–Remarks—The name of the city, town, or village, with state abbreviation where each change of duty status occurs shall be recorded.

Note: If a change of duty status occurs at a location other than a city, town, or village, show one of the following: (1) the highway number and nearest milepost followed by the name of the nearest city, town, or village and state abbreviation, (2) the highway number and the name of the service plaza followed by the name of the nearest city, town, or village and state abbreviation, or (3) the highway numbers of the nearest two intersecting roadways followed by the name of the nearest city, town, or village and state abbreviation.

Filing driver's record of duty status. The driver shall submit or forward by mail the original driver's record of duty status to the regular employing motor carrier within 13 days following the completion of the form.

Drivers used by more than one motor carrier. (1) When the services of a driver are used by more than one motor carrier during any 24-hour period in effect at the driver's home terminal, the driver shall submit a copy of the record of duty status to each motor carrier.

The record shall include:

1. All duty time for the entire 24-hour period;
2. The name of each motor carrier served by the driver during that period; and the beginning and finishing time, including AM or PM, worked for each carrier.

Motor carriers, when using a driver for the first time or intermittently, shall obtain from the driver a signed statement giving the total time on duty during the immediately preceding seven days and the time at which the driver was last relieved from duty prior to beginning work for the motor carrier.

Retention of driver's record of duty status. (1) Each motor carrier shall maintain records of duty status and all supporting documents for each driver it employs for a period of six months from the date of receipt.

The driver shall retain a copy of each record of duty status for the previous seven consecutive days which shall be in his or her possession and available for inspection while on duty.

Q. When is a driver declared out of service?

A. Every special agent of the Federal Highway Administration is authorized to declare a driver out of service and to notify the motor carrier of that declaration, upon finding at the time and place of examination that the driver has violated the out-of-service criteria.

Out-of-service criteria include:

1. No driver shall drive after being on duty in excess of the maximum periods permitted by this part.
2. No driver required to maintain a record of duty status under §395.8 or §395.15 shall fail to have a record of duty status current on the day of examination and for the prior seven consecutive days.
3. A driver failing only to have possession of a record of duty status current on the day of examination and the prior day, but has completed records of duty status up to that time (previous six days), will be given the opportunity to make the duty status record current.

Q. What are the motor carriers' responsibilities about this area of the regulations?

A. No motor carrier shall:

1. Require or permit a driver who has been declared out-of-service to operate a commercial motor vehicle until that driver may lawfully do so under the rules in this part.
2. Require a driver who has been declared out of service for failure to prepare a record of duty status to operate a commercial motor vehicle until that driver has been off duty for eight consecutive hours and is in compliance with this section. The consecutive eight-hour off duty period may include sleeper berth time.

Q. What is the Motor Carrier Certification of Action?

A. It is a part of the form MCS 63 (Driver Vehicle Examination Report). The motor carrier should deliver the copy of the form either personally or by mail to the Regional Director of Motor Carriers, Federal Highway Administration, at the address specified upon the form within 15 days following the date of examination. If the motor carrier mails the form, delivery is made on the date it is postmarked.

Q. What are the driver's responsibilities?

A. 1. No driver who has been declared out-of-service shall operate a commercial motor vehicle until that driver may lawfully do so under the rules of this Part.

2. No driver who has been declared out-of-service for failing to prepare a record of duty status shall operate a commercial motor vehicle until the driver has been off duty for eight consecutive hours and is in compliance with this section.

3. A driver to whom a form has been tendered declaring the driver out of service shall within 24 hours thereafter deliver or mail the copy to a person or place designated by motor carrier to receive it.

4. FMCSR §395.13 does not alter the hazardous materials requirements pertaining to attendance and surveillance of commercial motor vehicles.

Q. Are there rules governing automatic on-board recording devices?

A. A motor carrier may require a driver to use an automatic on-board recording device to record the driver's hours of service in lieu of complying with the requirements of FMCSR 395.

Every driver required by a motor carrier to use an automatic on-board recording device shall use such a device to record the driver's hours of service.

Q. What information is required when using on-board recording devices?

A. Automatic on-board recording devices shall show a driver's hours of service chart, electronic display, or printout showing the time and sequence of duty status changes, including the drivers' starting time at the beginning of each day.

This device shall provide a means whereby authorized federal, state, or local officials can immediately check the status of a driver's hours of service. This information may be used in conjunction with handwritten or printed records of duty status for the previous seven days.

The driver shall have in his or her possession records of duty status for the previous seven consecutive days available for inspection while on duty. These records shall consist of information stored in and retrievable from the automatic on-board recording device, handwritten records, computer generated records, or any combination thereof.

All hard copies of the driver's record of duty status must be signed by the driver. The driver's signature certifies that the information contained thereon is true and correct.

The duty status and additional information shall be recorded as follows:

1. "Off duty" or "OFF," or by an identifiable code or character
2. "Sleeper berth" or "SB," or by an identifiable code or character (only if the sleeper berth is used)
3. "Driving" or "D," or by an identifiable code or character
4. "On duty not driving" or "ON," or by an identifiable code or character.
5. Date
6. Total miles driving today
7. Truck or tractor and trailer number
8. Name of carrier
9. Main office address
10. 24-hour period starting time (e.g., midnight, 9:00 AM, noon, 3:00 PM)
11. Name of co-driver
12. Total hours
13. Shipping document number(s), or name of shipper and commodity
14. Location of duty status change

For each change of duty status (e.g., the place and time of reporting for work, starting to drive, on duty–not driving, and where released from work), the name of the city, town, or village, with state abbreviation, shall be recorded.

Motor carriers are permitted to use location codes. A list of such codes showing all possible location identifiers shall be carried in the cab of the commercial motor vehicle and available at the motor carrier's principal place of business. Such lists shall be made available to an enforcement official on request.

Entries made by driver only. If a driver is required to make written entries relating to the driver's duty status, such entries must be legible and in the driver's own handwriting.

The driver is required to note any failure of automatic on-board recording devices, and to reconstruct the driver's record of duty status for the current day, and the past seven days, less any days for which the driver has records, and to continue to prepare a handwritten record of all subsequent duty status until the device is again operational.

Q. If the carrier uses on-board recording systems, what else is required?

A. Each commercial motor vehicle must have on-board the commercial motor vehicle an information packet containing the following items:

1. An instruction sheet describing in detail how data may be stored and retrieved from an automatic on-board recording system; and
2. A supply of blank driver's records of duty status graph grids sufficient to record the driver's duty status and other related information for the duration of the current trip.

The driver shall submit, electronically or by mail, to the employing motor carrier, each record of the driver's duty status within 13 days following the completion of each record.

Q. What else should drivers know about submitting an electronic log?

A. Motor carriers that use automatic on-board recording devices for recording their drivers' records of duty status in lieu of the handwritten record shall ensure that:

1. A certificate is obtained from the manufacturer certifying that the design of the automatic on-board recorder has been sufficiently tested to meet the requirements of this section and under the conditions it will be used;
2. The automatic on-board recording device permits duty status to be updated only when the commercial motor vehicle is at rest, except when registering the time a commercial motor vehicle crosses a State boundary;
3. The automatic on-board recording device and associated support systems are, to the maximum extent practicable, tamperproof and do not permit altering of the information collected concerning the driver's hours of service;
4. The automatic on-board recording device warns the driver visually and/or audibly that the device has ceased to function. Devices installed and operational as of October 31, 1988, and authorized to be used in lieu of the handwritten record of duty status by the Federal Highway Administration, (FHWA), are exempted from this requirement;

5. Automatic on-board recording devices with electronic displays shall have the capability of displaying the following:
   (a) Driver's total hours of driving today
   (b) The total hours on duty today
   (c) Total miles driving today
   (d) Total hours on duty for the seven consecutive-day period, including today
   (e) Total hours on duty for the prior eight consecutive-day period, including the present day
   (f) The sequential changes in duty status and the times the changes occurred for each driver using the device
6. The on-board recorder is capable of recording separately each driver's duty status when there is a multiple driver operation;
7. The on-board recording device/system identifies sensor failures and edited data when reproduced in printed form. Devices installed and operational as of October 31, 1988, and authorized to be used in lieu of the handwritten record of duty status by the FHWA are exempted from this requirement;
8. The on-board recording device is maintained and recalibrated in accordance with the manufacturer's specifications;
9. The motor carrier's drivers are adequately trained regarding the proper operation of the device; and
10. The motor carrier must maintain a second copy (backup copy) of the electronic hours of service files, by month, in a different physical location than where the original data is stored.

FMCSR Part 396: Inspection, Repair, and Maintenance

This section of FMCSR focuses on when to inspect commercial motor vehicles. It doesn't point out what to inspect because, as a professional driver, you will know that anyway. But it will cover inspections, lubrication, and unsafe operations.

This section makes it the responsibility of the carrier, drivers, and employees involved in maintenance or inspection to be knowledgeable of the regulations and to comply with the rules listed in this section.

It also says that every motor carrier shall systematically inspect, repair, and maintain, or cause to be systematically inspected, repaired, and maintained, all motor vehicles subject to its control. (See Figure 5-2.)

Q. What do these inspections accomplish?
A. Because drivers conduct pre-trip and post-trip inspections for every shift, the inspections necessary to be in compliance with FMCSR 396 will determine the following:

1. Parts and accessories shall be in safe and proper operating condition at all times. These include those specified in Part 393 of this subchapter and any additional parts and accessories which may affect safety of operation, including, but not limited to, frame and frame assemblies, suspension systems, axles and attaching parts, wheels and rims, and steering systems.

GOAL OF INSPECTION

- **Goals**
  - To Identify
    - A Part or System That Is Malfunctioning or Has Already Failed (or Is Missing)
    - A Part or System That Is in Imminent Danger of Failing or Malfunctioning
    - A Part or System That is All Right or Is Functioning Properly
    - The Legal Requirements for Various Parts or System Conditions
- **Driver Responsibility**
  - Safety of Vehicle and Cargo
  - Vehicle Inspection
- **Types of Inspection**
  - Pre-Trip
  - Enroute
  - Post-Trip
- **Basic Reasons**
  - Safety
  - Economy
  - Public Relations
  - Legality
- **Three Elements of a Good Inspection**
  - Knowing What to Look for
  - Having a Consistent Way of Looking for It
  - Being Able to Report Findings in a Technically Accurate Way So That the Mechanics Will Be Able to Identify and Repair the Problems

Figure 5-2 Vehicle Inspection Guide.

2. Pushout windows, emergency doors, and emergency door marking lights in buses shall be inspected at least every 90 days.

Q. Are records kept of these inspections?

A. Motor carriers shall maintain, or cause to be maintained, the following record for each vehicle for a period of one year and for six months after they no longer control the vehicle:

1. An identification of the vehicle including company number, if so marked, make, serial number, year, and tire size. In addition, if the motor vehicle is not owned by the motor carrier, the record shall identify the name of the person furnishing the vehicle;
2. A means to indicate the nature and due date of the various inspections and maintenance operations to be performed;
3. A record of inspections, repairs, and maintenance, indicating their dates and nature; and
4. A record of tests conducted on pushout windows, emergency doors, and emergency door marking lights on buses.

Q. How often are vehicles lubricated?

A. Every motor carrier shall ensure that each motor vehicle subject to its control is properly lubricated and free of oil and grease leaks.

Q. What are "unsafe" operations?

A. FMCSR §396.7 says a motor vehicle shall not be operated in such a condition as to likely cause an accident or a breakdown of the vehicle. The only exemption would be any motor vehicle that is discovered to be in an unsafe condition while being operated on the highway may be continued in operation only to the nearest place where repairs can safely be made. Such operation shall be conducted only if it is less hazardous to the public than to permit the vehicle to remain on the highway.

Q. When are authorized inspections permitted and who can do them?

A. Every special agent of the Federal Highway Administration is authorized to enter and perform inspections of motor carrier vehicles in operation.

The result of this inspection is "The Driver Equipment Compliance Check," which is used by authorized FHWA personnel. If the vehicle does not pass inspection, the FHWA personnel may declare the vehicle "out of service."

A vehicle may also be declared "out of service" because of its mechanical condition or if it is loaded in a way that would likely cause an accident or breakdown. FHWA personnel will use an "out of service vehicle" sticker to mark vehicles they declare "out of service."

No motor carrier shall require or permit any person to operate nor shall any person operate any motor vehicle declared and marked "out of service" until all repairs required by the "out-of-service notice" have been satisfactorily completed. The term "operate" as used in this section shall include towing the vehicle, except that vehicles marked "out of service" may be towed away by means of a vehicle using a crane or hoist. A vehicle combination consisting of an emergency towing vehicle and an "out of service" vehicle shall not be operated unless such combination meets the performance requirements of this subchapter, except for those conditions noted on the Driver Equipment Compliance Check.

No person shall remove the "out-of-service vehicle" sticker from any motor vehicle prior to completion of all repairs, required by the "out of service notice."

Q. What happens if the vehicle I'm driving is declared "out of service"?

A. The driver of any motor vehicle receiving an out-of-service inspection report shall deliver it to the motor carrier operating the vehicle upon his or her arrival at the next terminal or facility. If the driver is not scheduled to arrive at a terminal or facility of the motor carrier operating the vehicle within 24 hours, the driver shall immediately mail the report to the motor carrier.

Violations or defects noted thereon shall be corrected within 15 days following the date of the inspection. Then the motor carrier will certify that all violations noted have been corrected by completing the "Signature of Carrier Official, Title, and Date Signed" portions of the form.

Then they will return the completed roadside inspection form to the issuing agency at the address indicated on the form and retain a copy at the motor carrier's principal place of business or where the vehicle is housed for 12 months from the date of the inspection.

Q. What are Vehicle Condition Reports and what should be done?

A. Every driver shall prepare a report in writing at the completion of each day's work on each vehicle operated and the report shall cover at least the following parts and accessories:

- Service brakes including trailer brake connections
- Parking (hand) brake

- Steering mechanism
- Lighting devices and reflectors
- Tires
- Horn
- Windshield wipers
- Rear vision mirrors
- Coupling devices
- Wheels and rims
- Emergency equipment

The report shall identify the vehicle and list any defect or deficiency which would affect the safety of operation of the vehicle or result in its mechanical breakdown. If no defect or deficiency is discovered, the report shall so indicate. In all instances, the driver shall sign the report.

On two-driver operations, only one driver needs to sign the Vehicle Condition Report, provided both drivers agree as to the defects or deficiencies identified. If a driver operates more than one vehicle during the day, a report shall be prepared for each vehicle operated.

Q. What if problems are found?

A. Every motor carrier or its agent shall repair any defect or deficiency listed on the Vehicle Condition Report and shall certify that the defect or deficiency has been repaired or that repair is unnecessary before the vehicle is operated again.

Every motor carrier shall maintain the original Vehicle Condition Report, the certification of repairs, and the certification of the driver's review for three months from the date the written report was prepared.

Q. After problems have been corrected, does the driver have to do anything else?

A. Before driving a motor vehicle, the driver should make sure that the motor vehicle is in safe operating condition, should review the last Vehicle Condition Report, and then sign the report only if there is a certification that the required repairs have been performed.

Driver Tow-Away Operations

When a vehicle is being towed as cargo, no inspection is required but the saddle mount or tow bar must be checked. The tow-truck driver must also make certain that the towed vehicles are tracking as required by FMCSR Part 393.

If the vehicle is being driven to point of delivery, the driver must ensure that it is safe to operate, roadworthy, and capable of reaching the destination.

Periodic (Every 12 Months) Inspections

Every commercial motor vehicle shall be inspected every 12 months and this includes each vehicle in a combination vehicle. For example, for a tractor semitrailer, fulltrailer combination, the tractor, the semitrailer, and the fulltrailer (including the converter dolly if so equipped) shall each be inspected.

Where the motor carrier operating the commercial motor vehicles did not perform the commercial motor vehicle's last annual inspection, the motor carrier shall be responsible for obtaining the original or a copy of the last annual inspection report upon demand of an authorized federal, state, or local official.

FMCSR Part 397

The last part of FMCSR professional drivers are required to know is Part 397, which covers transportation of hazardous materials. This part covers:

- Attendance of motor vehicles
- Parking
- Routes
- Fires
- Smoking
- Fueling
- Tires instructions
- Documents and instruction

Q. What do I need to know about hazardous materials (HazMat)?
A. Basic information will do unless you plan to actually haul hazardous materials. At that point, you'll need a HazMat Endorsement on your CDL.

Until then, you need to know that you must use placards when you haul hazardous materials.

You also need to know that some materials are not hazardous until they are transported in specific amounts.

FMCSR Part 383 says there are some things all drivers must know about HazMat—which is why this section is included—even if you do not plan to haul HazMat. Look at the shipping papers, manifest listings, labels, and any other cargo information. It is also important for drivers to be able to recognize other vehicles hauling HazMat along the same highways.

First of all, you must know when you need placards, what is hazardous, and what part of the law applies to hazardous materials.

Q. So, what materials are hazardous?
A. The Federal Hazardous Materials Regulations define hazardous materials as those judged by the secretary of transportation to be "a risk to health, safety and property when transported."

This list includes hazardous wastes and any by-products of any chemical processes. The official list also includes:

- **Radioactive materials**—materials or a combination of materials that will give off radiation.
- **Poison gases or liquids**—Class A poisons will harm or kill in small amounts when mixed with air. Class B poisons will be harmful in contact with skin but are not as hazardous as Class A poisons.
- **Flammable gases**—compressed gas is gas under pressure which is flammable.
- **Nonflammable gases**—compressed gas (gas under pressure) which will not burn.

- **Flammable liquids**—a liquid that gives off vapors which will ignite. Gasoline is a good example of a flammable liquid.
- **Oxidizers**—substances which cause other materials to react with oxygen with possible dangerous results. These oxidizers often cause other materials to burn.
- **Flammable solids**—not an explosive but will burn as a result of friction or a chemical change that involves heat. It could start burning on its own due to a chemical change occurring in processing. When some materials get wet, they can burn or emit toxic gases.
- **Corrosive materials**—substances able to dissolve or wear away other materials. Materials are considered "corrosive" if they can destroy human tissue or can eat away steel.
- **Irritating materials**—a liquid or solid producing dangerous fumes when it comes in contact with air or fire.
- **Combustible liquids**—a liquid giving off vapors capable of igniting between 100 and 200 degrees Fahrenheit is considered a combustible liquid.
- **Explosives**—can be chemical compounds, mixtures, or devices that explode. Class A explosives are the most dangerous. Class B explosives don't explode but burn rapidly. Class C explosives are materials that contain small amounts of Class A or Class B explosives. Blasting agents are explosive.
- **Any agent capable of causing disease**—any agent that causes human disease.
- **Other Regulated Materials (ORM)**—any material that, in some way, will risk public health, safety, or property while being transported.

Q. What are HazMat labels and what do they look like?

A. HazMat labels are diamond shapes, four inches square. They show the class of hazardous materials and any numbers on the labels are part of the worldwide system used to identify hazardous materials. Every number signifies a different hazardous material.

Labels are not used on compressed gas cylinders—but they are placed on a hangtag around the neck of a cylinder. In some cases, a decal is used.

Q. What are shipping papers and how are HazMat shipping papers different?

A. Shipping papers must be carried with every shipment and will certify that certain cargo is dangerous. The papers must also certify that the materials are handled and packaged according to Department of Transportation regulations.

Q. Where are shipping papers kept?

A. When the driver is in the cab, the HazMat shipping papers are placed on top of all shipping papers for regular cargo. Regulations state the papers must be within easy reach of the driver while he or she is wearing a seatbelt.

If the driver leaves the cab, the shipping papers must be kept in a pouch inside the driver's door or on the driver's seat in plain view. This ensures that if the driver is injured or away from the vehicle, safety workers and emergency crews will know exactly where to find the papers that detail the contents of the cargo.

Q. What about placards? Where do they go?

A. HazMat placards are required to be attached to the outside of the vehicle. If there is more than one type of hazardous material included in the cargo, regulations say one placard marked "Dangerous" is ample.

   The vehicles must be marked on all sides and tank vehicles used to haul HazMat must have placards at all times, even if empty.

Q. What about leaving a vehicle loaded with HazMat?

A. If your cargo is explosives, you should never leave a vehicle—and there should be a qualified person in attendance at all times. If you leave a vehicle loaded with explosives, it should be parked in a "safe haven," which is a special parking area set aside for HazMat-loaded vehicles.

Q. Are HazMat loads usually transported on special routes?

A. HazMat loads should avoid routes through heavily populated areas unless there is no other possible route to the destination.

   For loads containing Class A or Class B explosives, the carrier/driver must have a written route plan, including curfews and permits from cities that require permits.

   The written plan includes certain hours when the vehicle may travel through the city. Some cities determine what time of day hazardous materials may pass through. Other cities require permits, which must be obtained in advance. Check cities along the route if you find yourself carrying explosives—each will have different laws.

Q. What do I do in case of fire?

A. It goes without saying—with a HazMat load, stay away from fires, from cigarettes to open flames. Also check tires frequently to make sure the rubber doesn't get too hot.

   Even without a HazMat endorsement, a driver may haul certain dangerous materials that don't require HazMat placards. There are also special situations where a HazMat vehicle may move materials without placards—when escorted by state or local government officials, when the carrier has permission from the Department of Transportation, or when the vehicle must be moved to protect health, property, or people.

Let's Review

Read each question and all of the answers provided. Place the letter of the correct answer in the space provided or write your answers on a separate piece of paper so you can use these questions again as you review for the CDL. Once you have answered all the questions, check your answers against the answer key which follows.

_____ 1. True or False. When hauling explosives, you may only leave your vehicle for rest stops, dinner breaks, and eight-hour rests in hotels or motels.

_____ 2. You may exceed maximum driving time—by two hours—only when driving under adverse conditions, which include
(A) snow,   (C) fog,
(B) sleet,   (D) all of the above.

_____ 3. When a Federal Highway Administration official conducts a roadside inspection and declares a vehicle "out of service," the driver may drive the vehicle
(A) to his or her destination,
(B) to the closest terminal owned by the carrier,
(C) to the closest repair center,
(D) none of the above.

_____ 4. When hauling hazardous materials, the driver must keep shipping papers
(A) on his or her person,   (C) in the glove box,
(B) on the driver's seat,   (D) none of the above.

_____ 5. True or False. If any agent of the Federal Highway Administration conducts an inspection and finds a driver's log not up to date, he or she may be declared "out of service."

_____ 6. True or False. If a vehicle is being towed as cargo, it must still meet inspection standards.

_____ 7. When you prepare to drive a vehicle, you must check inspection reports as well as make certain
(A) the cab has been swept out,
(B) the reported problems have been corrected,
(C) you fix any problems,
(D) none of the above.

_____ 8. If you are driving a vehicle and it develops a problem, you can drive it only
(A) to your destination,
(B) to the nearest terminal for repair,
(C) only so long as it takes to get it to the nearest place to be repaired,
(D) none of the above.

_____ 9. If your vehicle does not pass a roadside inspection, you must
(A) deliver this report to the carrier at the next terminal,
(B) mail the report to the home office if you will not reach the next terminal within 24 hours,
(C) all of the above,
(D) none of the above.

_____10. True or False. If your on-board trip recorder fails, you can blame it on the carrier.

Answers to Let's Review

1. False; 2. D; 3. D; 4. D; 5. True; 6. False; 7. B; 8. C; 9. C; 10. False.

Terms You Need to Know

The following terms have been taken from the contents of Chapter 5. Review them. If you see any you're unsure of, check the definition in the Glossary at the back of the book. If it helps you, keep a written list of the words and their definitions (or write in the definitions here) and review them several days prior to taking the CDL tests.

Adverse driving conditions

Automatic on-board recording device

Drivers declared "Out of Service"

Driver's Record of Duty Status

Driver-salesman

Eight consecutive days

Emergency conditions

Etiologic agents

Grid preparation

Hazardous materials (HazMat)

Labels

Log books

Maximum driving time

Multiple stops

On-duty time

Placards

Relief from regulations

Safe haven

Seven consecutive days

Shipping papers

Sleeper berth

Trip recorders

Total mileage driven

Travel time

Twenty-four hour period

Written route plan

Vehicle Condition Report

THE DISPATCH BOARD
It's Not What Happens . . . It's What You Tell Yourself

Ron Adams, Ph.D.

After driving hard for six hours, Ann maneuvers her rig though the noontime traffic and into the terminal. "Been gone for three weeks. Now, I have to get home and find out what's wrong with Billy. Here lately he won't say much to me."

Billy, Ann's son, stays with Ann's mom when Ann is on the road.

"Three weeks. I hate to be gone that long. I know my child needs me at home but I have to make a living."

Ann is so tired she can hardly keep her eyes open as she pulls her dusty Ford pickup into the driveway of the home she shares with her mother. She stops sharply to avoid a bicycle in the driveway. As Billy emerges from the house, Ann sternly shouts, "Billy how many times do I have to tell you not to leave your bicycle in the driveway?"

The youngster turns and runs towards the woods behind the house, shouting over his shoulder, "What do you care? You're never here anyway. You're not my mom, Maw-maw is my mom!"

*****

Roberto is a ten-year veteran of long-distance driving. He expertly ushers his rig from the interstate into the rest area. "Gotta call home again. Wonder why Mary didn't return my call?"

His job requires three weeks on the road and one week at home.

"I know she is running around on me," says the nagging voice in the back of his mind.

*****

Isolated cases? Family experts don't think so.

Professional truck driving isn't always easy. Being away from home, the driver often misses rich family experiences.

continues

THE DISPATCH BOARD *continued*

After a few years of driving, the driver is often on the outside looking in as his or her family shares more and more experiences. This sometimes leads to a blurring of family roles, with no one knowing for sure who to ask for permission, who to confide in.

This confusion in the family leads to misunderstandings and stress, which is unhealthy for all the family members and a safety hazard for the driver.

So what is going on with our drivers?

Ann is tired after pushing hard to get home. She has feelings of guilt because she isn't always there for her kids. She is frustrated because her children go to her mother with their problems rather than to her. She was angry when she saw the bicycle in the driveway. All of this leads to stress.

Roberto feels guilty about being gone so much. He loves his job, but is very insecure in his relationship with Mary. This guilt and insecurity also leads to . . . you guessed it . . . stress.

In reality, Ann and Roberto are disturbed with themselves, others, or the world around them. They express these feelings in many different ways. Some persons get depressed, worry, or feel inferior or worthless. Others use drugs, develop ulcers, or worse.

So what can Ann and Roberto do?

As a first step, they can change what they see. In other words, they can change what they think is going on their lives.

Two thousand years ago a famous Greek teacher said, "It's not what happens in your life that is upsetting, it's what you tell yourself about it."

In other words, it is your opinion about something, not the situation, that is upsetting to you.

There is no other person, situation, or event that can make you feel angry, depressed, guilty, worthless, or inferior—except you. And, *you* are responsible for your own emotional reactions.

Things, therefore, do not disturb people. People are disturbed by how they see a situation.

Let's see how this works. Suppose Ann has to go to the doctor's office. Ann gets on a crowded elevator and someone behind her starts poking her.

Because the elevator is crowded, Ann cannot turn around to see what is going on. Instead she begins to get angry. As the elevator lets her off on her floor, she decides to give the "poker" a piece of her mind.

Just as Ann is about to begin, she suddenly realizes the person is blind and has unknowingly been poking her with his cane.

What happened to her anger and her proposed tongue-lashing?

Probably she was much less upset. She might feel pity or even guilty for almost criticizing a person who is physically challenged.

So, what caused this sudden change? Ann looked at the situation differently.

A change in mind caused a change in feelings.

How can Ann and Roberto use this information to make themselves feel better about their family relations—and, therefore, make their family relations better?

THE DISPATCH BOARD *continued*

First let's look at three basic principles of human beings developed by Dr. Albert Ellis of the Rational Emotive Thinking Institute, the source for much of this information:

1. **Human beings have the unique ability to think and reason.**
   No matter the situation, we always have an opinion. We may not always come up with the right opinion, but we always think something about our experiences.
2. **We feel the way we think.**
   Our emotions depend on how we see things. Usually the more extreme our point of view, the more intense our emotions.
3. **Actions usually, although not always, follow our feelings.**
   What we will often do next depends on how we see a particular situation.

Ann and Roberto agree that *thinking* produces *feelings*, which in turn generates *actions*.

The A-B-C of Emotions. In his Rational Emotive Thinking theory, Dr. Ellis developed the A-B-C of Emotions which goes something like this: **A,** an event happens; **B,** you tell yourself about the event; **C,** you have a feeling about the event.

Let's see how A-B-C works. There is an old family story that Ann heard many times from her father, who was also a truck driver.

It seems Ann's father Paul was driving one summer in Nebraska, hauling grain during the wheat harvest. After driving in the dust of the fields and unpaved farm roads, it was finally time for lunch.

As Paul pulled his rig into the parking lot of the local café, he was thinking of how good his lunch would be with a good cup of coffee and a piece of good old pecan pie, just like his mother use to make.

Paul eased his tired body into a booth worn smooth by the countless overalls that had slid in and out of it over the years. Behind the counter directly across from Paul, he saw a pecan pie.

"That's what I want for dessert," he thought.

He savored every bite of his fried chicken, mashed potatoes covered with cream gravy, and green beans flavored with bacon grease. As he finished off the last bite of chicken with a big hunk of cornbread oozing butter, he thought, "Now I'll have that pecan pie."

The waitress from behind the counter looked at Paul and asked if he would like anything else. Paul could almost taste the pecan pie as he told the waitress he would like a piece of that pecan pie behind her.

"What pecan pie?" asked the waitress, turning toward the shelf that held the pies. As the waitress moved toward the shelf, the pecans on the pie began to fly away. It was then Paul realized that what he thought were pecans on top of the pie were really bugs.

Gulping down the last bit of his coffee, Paul slid out of the booth and headed toward the door mumbling something about not caring for any pie after all. Needless to say, Paul didn't stop at that café again.

Let's see how the A-B-Cs worked with Paul:

When Paul thought he saw pecan pie,

A. He saw the pie.
B. He thought about how good the pie would be.
C. He wanted a piece of the pie.

continues

THE DISPATCH BOARD *continued*

After Paul saw the bugs fly away,

A. He saw the bugs fly off the pie.
B. He thought about how gross the pie was.
C. He did not want any pie.

Now let's see how Ann and Roberto can apply this theory to improve their situations.

First, Ann and Roberto need to realize that they have very stressful jobs.

Additionally, Ann and Roberto need to talk to their families about the time demands of their job that keeps them away so much. A frank discussion with their families about the advantages and disadvantages of their jobs will go a long way in dispelling any anger and guilt that they or their families may have.

Here are some actions Ann can take to make her life better:

A. Because she is tired and sleepy when she gets home, Ann might arrange her schedule so she can get some rest before she gets home.
B. To lesson the frustration she experiences when her child goes to her mother rather than her, Ann can discuss the situation with her mother and child, pointing out why she is gone from home so much. During the discussion Ann can point out that it takes a village to raise children and that she is grateful that her mother is there to help with her child.
C. To prevent anger about the bicycle in the driveway: During the family meeting, there should be a discussion regarding expectations. If Ann feels strongly about the bicycle in the driveway, she should tell her son specifically what she expects. Ann needs to realize that if she is home only one week out of four, her son may forget and leave the bicycle in the driveway. Ann and her son will feel a lot better if she will overlook the bicycle and give her son a big hug and tell him how much she's missed him.

Now, here are some actions Roberto can take:

A. Roberto and his family need to discuss the good and bad points of his job. Roberto should tell his family why he is an over-the-road driver (probably finances has a lot to do with it), that he is sorry he is gone so much, and that he loves them. A solution should be found for any problems his absence causes. This discussion will give Roberto an opportunity to think some positive thoughts about his job, which will reduce his feeling of guilt.
B. Roberto and Mary need to have a frank discussion about their relationship. Roberto should tell Mary how he feels when he can't contact her while he is on the road. He can tell her when he can't contact her, he is very stressed and that the stress can lead to a dangerous situation while he is driving. Roberto could suggest to Mary that she keep him informed of her schedule. If Mary is cooperative regarding Roberto's suggestions, this will make Roberto feel more secure about their relationship.

So remember that during your driving career, you will have some good times and some bad times. You'll be dealing with some really nice people and some not-so-nice people.

But always keep in mind what that famous Greek teacher said over two thousand years ago, "It's not what happens in your life that is upsetting, it's what you tell yourself."

And, when you order pecan pie, take a good look before you take your first bite!

PART II

Professional Driver Skills

6 Vehicle Inspections

As a professional driver, safety is your number one priority. It is your priority when your rig is being loaded, during your pre-trip inspection, on the road, and when you are delivering your cargo.

No one in America has a more dangerous job than a professional driver. Much like the men and women who work in America's oil fields, a professional driver is aware of safety precautions from the minute he or she steps into the vehicle to the minute he or she steps out of the vehicle—for any reason.

A vehicle inspection is the first step toward safe operations.

State and federal law requires that you, the driver, conduct a thorough vehicle inspection each time you take your vehicle onto the highway. FMCSR Part 383 states that professional drivers must be familiar with FMCSR Part 396—and this includes the vehicle inspection.

Further, the FMCSR Part 392.7 states:

> *No motor vehicle shall be driven unless the driver thereof shall have satisfied himself or herself that the following parts and accessories are in good working order, nor shall any driver fail to use or make use of such parts and accessories when and as needed:*
> - *Service brakes, including trailer brake connections*
> - *Parking (hand) brake*
> - *Steering mechanism*
> - *Lighting devices and reflectors*
> - *Tires*
> - *Horn*
> - *Windshield wiper or wipers*
> - *Rear-vision mirror or mirrors*
> - *Coupling devices*

Knowing that the "parts and accessories are in good working order" comes from a thorough vehicle inspection—before going on the road.

These guidelines are used by most states on their CDL tests, and the guidelines also ask that professional drivers must be able to demonstrate that they can conduct a thorough vehicle inspection. Most examiners will request that you conduct an inspection as part of the CDL Skills Test.

In this segment of the Skills Test, you may be requested to describe the different systems and parts on your vehicle as you conduct your inspection. Or, the examiner may choose to stop your inspection periodically to ask questions about the equipment.

You should know the required equipment for your vehicle, how the systems work, how certain damage or defects keep the vehicle from operating properly, and how to load cargo properly.

You should be able to make certain repairs and conduct some maintenance, and it is also important that you be able to determine when problems occur while you are operating the vehicle.

Note: *One more hint for the inspection portion of the CDL Skills Test: Have an inspection routine so you won't miss anything. With a routine, you won't forget or overlook something and you won't get confused. Get a routine and keep the same routine each time you inspect your vehicle.*

The 'Who' and 'When' of Inspections

Who Inspects?

Generally, the main inspection responsibility is assigned to the motor carrier. The carrier must also perform periodic inspections of their vehicles, called an "annual inspection."

But, in most cases, it is the driver's responsibility to inspect the vehicle before and after each trip. Would you want to drive a vehicle loaded with 80,000 pounds of hazardous materials that you had not inspected? The answer, of course, is "no".

There is one other group that inspects a commercial vehicle—these are federal and state inspectors who can conduct an inspection at any time. It may be at a weigh station or it may be while you are driving down the road. For these inspections, you either (1) have to stop at an inspection point or (2) the inspector pulls you over to conduct a roadside inspection . . . anywhere in the country.

When these inspections occur, if the vehicle is found to be unsafe in any area, it can be put "out of service," which means you don't go anywhere until the vehicle is repaired and is safe to go back on to the highway.

When Are Inspections Conducted?

As the name tells you, pre-trip inspections are conducted *before* each trip. These inspections are so important that you should record them in your log book. During these inspections, you look for problems and damage to the vehicle that could cause a breakdown or an accident. Any damage you find must be repaired before the vehicle heads for the highway.

A post-trip inspection, as the name tells you, is conducted at the *end* of the trip— or if the trip lasts several days, at the end of each day or at the end of each shift.

The post-trip inspection may include filling out a Vehicle Condition Report, listing any damage or other problems you find. This helps the carrier know when something needs to be fixed on specific pieces of equipment.

But any veteran driver will also tell you that you ensure your personal safety and the safety of others by inspecting your vehicle *during* the trip, watching gauges for trouble and using your senses—sight, hearing, smell and feel—to check for any problems that may occur when you're on the road.

While driving, you should plan to stop every 150 miles or every three hours for an "enroute" inspection (Figure 6-1). Loads do shift and bindings do loosen, so it is important to make sure that your cargo is still safe. Remember to do a complete walk-around every time you stop the vehicle.

Figure 6-1   Enroute inspections save time and lives.

A veteran driver will also encourage you to check critical systems every time you stop. These are systems found on most all vehicles that ensure the safe operation of the vehicle. They are:

- Lights and wiring
- Brakes
- Windows
- Fuel and fuel system
- Coupling devices (on combinations)
- Tires
- Windshield wipers and defrosters
- Rear-view mirrors
- Horn
- Speedometer
- Floor
- Rear bumper
- Flags on over-sized or projecting loads
- Seatbelts
- Emergency equipment
- Cargo straps, webbing, and other devices used to secure the load
- Frame
- Cab
- Wheels, rims, and tires
- Steering
- Suspension

Some states may require vehicles to have more equipment than is listed above. This chapter will cover the commonly required items by most states. Before taking the CDL, you should find out about the requirements in the state where your headquarters is located and any state you'll be running in.

Note: It is possible to be put "out of service" in one state for a condition on your vehicle that is acceptable in the next three states.

Vehicle Inspection—Let's Take It One Sector at a Time!

Lights and reflectors

- Make sure all required lights and reflectors are in place.
- Make sure they are all clean and in working order.

Electrical system

- Check for wiring problems:
  - ——Loose wires—should be reattached
  - ——Broken and worn wires—should be replaced
  - ——Corrosion around attachments—should be cleaned with wire brush
- Check fuses—replace any that have blown
- Inspect the battery:
  - ——Check that each cell has a vent cap
  - ——Clean clogged vent caps
  - ——Check fluids in wet-charged battery
  - ——Check battery mount/make sure hold-down bars fit well
  - ——Check battery box—it should be in place and free of cracks or leaks
  - ——Check cables for wearing or fraying
  - ——Check connections—they should be tight
- In the cab:
  - ——Check voltmeter and ammeter—readings should be in normal range

Brake system (excluding air brakes)

- Inspect all four wheels:
  - ——At each wheel, check for cracks and hubs for any leaking fluid (Figure 6-2).
  - ——Check brake drums for cracks.
  - ——Check brake shoes for fluid or fluid on pads—and for missing or broken shoes. Any problems? They should be replaced or repaired immediately!
  - ——Check brake lines for worn or weak spots.
  - ——Make sure lines aren't kinked or twisted.
  - ——Check hydraulic fluid level in master cylinder (when inspecting engine area). Use sight glass or visual—check the vehicle manual for proper inspection method. Make sure fluid level reaches mark indicated. Leaks in this area mean trouble.
- In the cab, check hydraulic brake system:
  - ——Turn engine on (transmission is in neutral)
  - ——Pump brake pedal three times.
  - ——Then, press firmly on brake pedal—no less than five seconds (some manufacturers specify longer). The pedal should not move.

TO TEST THE PARKING BRAKES MOVE FORWARD SLOWLY

Figure 6-2   Careful inspection means safer operations.

——If pedal does move, or is not firm, there is air in the lines.
——If pedal sinks toward the floor—that's a sign of a leak—it must be fixed.
- Check vacuum brakes (if available)
  ——Push on brakes—if you have to push hard, there may be defects in the vacuum system.
  ——If you experience brake fade, that's also a sign of a problem.
- Check parking brakes:
  ——Put your seatbelt on.
  ——Put vehicle in gear and let it move slowly forward.
  ——Apply parking brake. Vehicle should stop. If it doesn't, get parking brake repaired before your trip.
- Check service brake:
  ——Go forward—about five miles per hour.
  ——Push pedal firmly—if vehicle veers left or right, this could mean brake trouble.
  ——Any pause before brakes "catch?"—another sign of a problem.
  ——If the brake pedal "feels" weird—takes too much time to catch or requires too much effort to push—have brakes checked and repaired before going anywhere.

Cab

- Cab should be neat, orderly, and clean.
  ——Doors should open and close easily and securely.
  ——Check for loose, sagging, or broken parts.
  ——Hood is securely fastened.

——Seats are secured firmly in place.
——Required front bumpers are secure.
——Rear bumpers are required for vehicles higher than 30 inches from the ground (empty). If bumper is in place, check to see it is firmly in place.

Steering system

Steering column is securely mounted and steering wheel must be secure, must move easily, and be free of cracked spokes (Figure 6-3).

- "Steering wheel lash" or "free play" (the number of turns steering wheel makes before wheels move) should be no more than 10 degrees or two-inches on the rim of a 20-inch steering wheel, according to FMCSR Part 393. If free play exceeds limits, vehicle will be difficult to steer.
- Check U-joints for wear, slack, damage, or signs of welding repair (not acceptable for U-joint repair).
- Gearbox is free of damage, and bolts and brackets are in place and secure.
- Pitman arm is secure.

For vehicles with power steering:

- All parts free of damage and in good operating order.
- Belts that are frayed, cracked, or slipping should be replaced or adjusted.
- Look for leaks in lines and tank and make sure tank contains ample power steering fluid.
- If you see missing nuts, bolts, cotter keys, or other damaged parts, replace immediately. The same goes for damaged, loose, or broken steering column, gear box, or tie rod.

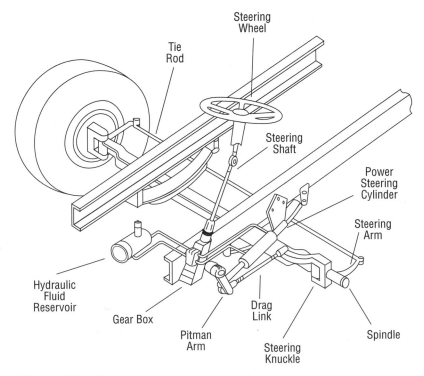

Figure 6-3 Steering system.

Windows and glass

Check out all window glass and windshield. Viewing area must be free of stickers and clean—no dirt, no discolorations. And remember, only factory tints to reduce glare are allowed!

- Only required stickers, please—at the bottom of the windshield, no more than 4.5 inches into viewing area.
- No cracks (longer than an inch) or dings in the glass

Wipers and defrosters

All vehicles with windshields must have one or two windshield wiper blades and a windshield defroster.

- Blades must be on each side of centerline of windshield.
- Wipers must be automatic and in working condition.
- Make sure rubber blades do the job. Loose rubber blades don't work.
- Old blades—stiff, loose, crumbling—must be replaced.
- Turn defroster on and off at every inspection, putting hand over vent to confirm warm air.
- Washers are optional—if you have them, test them and check fluid level. If they don't work, make sure lines aren't kinked, broken, or leaking.

Rear-view and side-view mirrors

Rear-view mirrors on each side of cab should be adjusted when you're in the driver's seat. You should be able to see down both sides to the rear of the vehicle. Mirrors should also be clean and free of damage.

Horn

Make sure horn is working. All vehicles are required to have one. A note to the wise: Watch blowing or sounding your horn in a truck stop! Some drivers may be sleeping.

Seatbelts

Make sure seatbelt is well-anchored and in good condition. When taking the CDL skills tests, put seatbelt on before starting the truck.

Floor

Floorboards are clean and free of holes.

Frame

On every inspection, check for looseness, cracks, sagging, or damage over the frame.

- Check for missing bolts.
- Replace any broken bolts on the frame.
- Check that all bolts and rivets are tight and in place.

Fuel System

Check your tank or tanks:

- They should be securely mounted.
- Check for damage or leaks.

- Fuel crossover line should be secure and high enough off roadway to be free of possible damage. Your truck may or may not have crossover lines.
- Fuel caps are in place.
- Neoprene gaskets in place.
- Tanks should be 95 percent full (fuel expands when it heats).

Exhaust system

A malfunctioning exhaust system could cost you your life.

- Check for broken, loose, or missing exhaust pipes, mufflers, tailpipes, or stacks.
- Look for loose or broken mountings, missing brackets, bent clamps, or missing or broken nuts and bolts.
- Check to make sure no parts of the exhaust system are rubbing against parts of the fuel system.
- Check for broken, worn, or frayed hoses, lines, and wires.
- With your hand close (not on it—you'll burn yourself) to the exhaust manifold, check for leaks—you'll feel them.
- Never patch or wrap the exhaust system. Note any such repair work on your inspection as a defect and have it fixed.

Coupling devices

This includes saddle mounts, tow bars, pintle hooks, and safety chains used in tow-away situations.

- Visually check—for bends or warping—all parts used to couple vehicles.
- Safety chains should not have broken or twisted links.
- Check to assure that lights, reflectors, steering, and brakes work on all vehicles—for the towed vehicle as well as the towing vehicle.

Tires

Whether you've driven for two or 20 years, you already know that it is dangerous to drive with bad tires.

- Look for worn treads and body ply or belts showing through the tread.
- Look for separation of tread or sidewall.
- Look for deep cuts or cracks that reveal ply or belt beneath.
- Look for damaged or cracked valve stems—or missing stems and valve caps.
- If tire is low or flat—or any of the above—get it repaired.
- Listen for air leaks—and look for bulges (could mean blowout).
- Check inflation pressure with tire gauge (especially during CDL test).
- Check for wear—need no less than 4/32 inch tread depth in every major groove on the front and 2/32 inch tread depth on other wheels (Figure 6-4).
- Dual tires—make sure they're not touching each other or another part of the vehicle.
- All tires should be the same size—and the same type. Radial and bias-ply tires should not be used on the same axle—this is forbidden in most states.
- No regrooved tires on the front of the tractor or tractors with 8,000-plus pounds front axle rating.

When checking your tires, remember this acronym ICD: inflation, condition, depth.

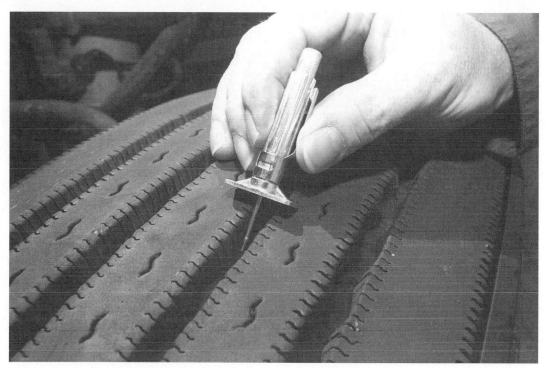

Figure 6-4 Checking tire tread depth.
(Photo courtesy of ATA Associates, Inc.)

Wheels and rims

Check for cracks or damaged wheels or rims:

- Look for missing spacers, studs, lugs, and clamps.
- Look for damaged or mismatched lock rings.
- If welding has been used to repair wheels or rims, note as a defect.
- If you see rust around wheel nuts, check for looseness with wrench.
- Out-of-round (oval or egg-shaped) stud or bolt holes on rims indicate problems.
- Check hub oil supply—and make sure there are no leaks.

Mud flaps or splash guards

A common state requirement is that mud flaps must be as wide or wider than the tires.

- Mud flaps should be no more than six inches from the ground with the vehicle fully loaded. States vary, so be sure to check your state's restrictions.
- Flaps should be mounted as far to the rear of the wheel as possible.

Tire chains

Another state-by-state requirement concerns driving in snow and ice: Include tire chains in your equipment. Be able to mount and remove them if asked to by the CDL examiner. Check home state regulations and regulations in every state in which you'll be operating. Tire chains are usually required in the mountain regions.

Suspension system

Don't drive a rig with suspension problems, such as broken or cracked parts. Figure 6-5 shows the suspension system.

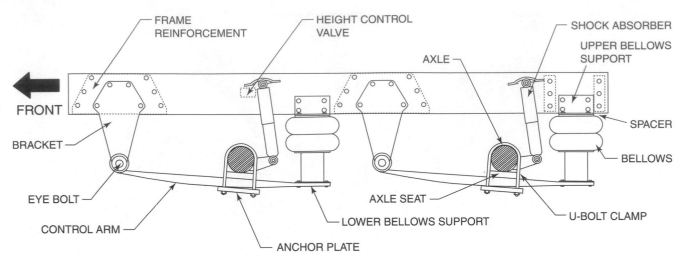

Figure 6-5   Suspension system.

- Check for damaged spring hangers, U-bolts, and axle positioning parts.
- Steering problems mean loose or bent spring hangers.
- Drive axles should be free of leaks.
- Look for missing or broken parts of the leaf spring. If 25 percent is missing, this will put a vehicle out of service, but any defect in this area is dangerous—life-threatening to the driver and others on the road.
- Check all springs for cracks, breaks, or other damage.
- Check shock absorbers for leaks and damage.
- With air suspension system, check for leaks and make sure air pressure regulator valve is operational by checking vehicle's air pressure gauge.
- Check to ensure air suspension isn't leaking more than 3 psi in five minutes. If leak exceeds this, repair it.

Emergency equipment

- Fire extinguisher is securely mounted with easy access—should be checked as part of the inspection. Most vehicles require that the extinguisher have a 10 B:C rating from Underwriters Laboratory (UL) located near the UL certification. Is nozzle clear? Is tip of ring pin in place? Check pressure gauge to ensure needle is in the green area.
- Know how to use the fire extinguisher.
- Three reflective emergency triangles (see FMCSR Part 393.95 for full description and options).
- Make sure you have spare fuses and know how to install them—unless your vehicle has circuit breakers.
- Tire changing kit.
- Accident notification kit (Idea: Keep a disposable camera in the accident kit to visually record damages).
- Emergency phone numbers.

Cargo securement

Safely loaded cargo (no room for shifting or falling) should be inspected and the following should be in good working condition:

- Tailgate
- Doors
- Cab guard or header board (headache rack) free of damage and securely in place.
- Stakes/sideboards—if necessary—in good condition
- Tarps—tied down and tight
- Spare tire
- Binders
- Chains
- Winches
- Braces and support
- Curbside doors secured and locked

Cargo loaded without blocking view or impeding driver's arms and legs.

- Hauling sealed loads? Need security seals on doors.
- Hauling hazardous materials? Need placards, proper paperwork—and the HazMat Endorsement on your CDL.

Remember: Anything you find on the pre-trip inspection that is broken or not functioning properly, must be repaired before you take the vehicle on the road. Federal and state laws forbid operating an unsafe vehicle.

Your Inspection Routine

Every driver should have an inspection routine, a way of checking all necessary items on straight trucks or vehicle combinations—the same way of checking every time you make an inspection. Learn it well—and perform it better.

*Note: **Important!** For the CDL test, check with the examiner to find out if you will be permitted to use a checklist for your inspection. Then, as you perform the inspection, tell the examiner what you're inspecting and tell about the problems and/or defects that are most common at each site.*

Ready for the routine? Here it is!

- Approach the vehicle.
- Look underneath for leaking fluids.
- Look around for any obstacles.
- Raise the hood or tilt the cab to check engine compartment. If you tilt the cab, make sure that everything in it is secured inside the cab.
- Start the engine/inspect inside cab.
- Check the lights and reflectors.
- Walk around the vehicle, inspecting each section.
- Check the signal lights.
- Check the brakes.

The Seven-step Pre-trip Inspection is, by far, the most commonly used routine. Here is what you look at during each step of the routine:

1. **Vehicle overview**—Begin inspection by approaching the vehicle and noting the general condition.

- Look for damage, whether the vehicle is leaning (flat tire, shifted cargo, or overloaded—or a suspension problem).
- Look down on the ground—any fresh leakage of coolant, fuel, grease or oil?
- Check area for people and hazards (low wires, low limbs, etc).
- Look at most recent inspection reports, both pre-trip and post-trip. If items listed affect safety, check to ensure that mechanic's certification indicates repairs were made or that no repair was needed.
- Inspect these areas yourself to find out what was done about problems noted on last inspection.

2. **Engine compartment** (Figure 6-6)—Parking brakes should be on and/or wheels are chocked. Check this.
- Raise hood, open engine compartment door, or tilt cab (after stowing any loose items in the cab).
- Check engine oil level (should be above "Low" or "Add" marks) on dipstick.
- Check coolant level—should be above "Low" mark.
- Check radiator shutters (if you still have them)—remove any ice and check to ensure winter front isn't closed. Inspect fan—make sure blades are undamaged and hoses and wires are out of the way.
- Power steering? Check fluid level with dipstick on oil tank. Level should be above "Low" or "Add" marks. Check condition of hoses.
- If windshield washers, check fluid level.
- Battery in this compartment? Perform check now.
- Automatic transmission? Check fluid level (may do this with engine running).

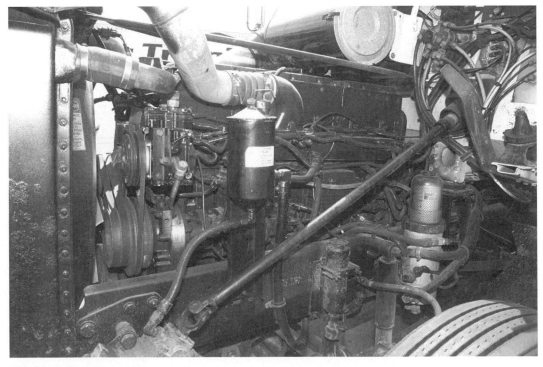

Figure 6-6   View of an engine.

(Photo courtesy of ATA Associates, Inc.)

- Check drive belts for damage, wear, and tightness. Check owner's manual for how much slack is allowed. If belts slide easily over a pulley, it's too loose or too worn.
- Look over engine compartment for any leaks—fuel, oil, power steering fluid, battery fluid, hydraulic fluid, and coolant.
- Check wiring for any wear, breaks, or other problems.
- Lower and/or latch hood or cab or engine compartment door.
- Check and clear debris or obstacles from any hand holds, steps, or deck plates leading to cab.

3. **Inside the cab**—As you get into the cab, look around and inspect inside of cab. Put your seatbelt on. Make sure parking brake is on and vehicle is in "neutral" or "park."
   - Start engine and listen for a few seconds to hear any unusual noises.
   - Check gauges—oil pressure goes to normal in seconds.
   - Ammeter and voltmeter—normal readings.
   - Coolant temperature—should start "Cold" and gradually go to normal.
   - Engine oil temp—slowly goes to normal.
   - Oil, coolant, and charging circuit warning lights come on and should go off almost immediately (unless a problem exists).
   - All controls in working order—check loose or sticking controls, any damage or improper readings or settings to the following:
     - ——Steering wheel
     - ——Accelerator
     - ——Foot brake
     - ——Parking brake
     - ——Retarder controls (If available)
     - ——Transmission controls
     - ——Interaxle differential lock (if available)
     - ——Horn
     - ——Windshield wipers/washers (if available)
     - ——Headlights
     - ——Dimmer switch
     - ——Turn signals
     - ——Four-way flashers
     - ——Clearance, identification, and marker light switch(es)
   - If there's a clutch, test it by pushing it in until there's slight resistance. More than one or two inches to get to the resistance means there's a problem. If there is no free play before getting to resistance, have clutch adjusted immediately.
   - Check mirrors and windshield for defects or problems.
   - Check to confirm you have required emergency equipment in good working order.
   - Check optionals, such as tire changing kit, and items required by state laws, such as mud flaps and tire chains.

4. **Turn off engine and check lights**—Make sure engine is off (take key with you—very important) and parking brake is set.
   - Turn on headlights (low beams) and four-way flashers. Go to front of vehicle to check that all are working.
   - Get back into cab—turn on high beams—check to see that they work.
   - Turn off headlights and four-way flashers.

- Turn on parking, clearance, side-marker, and identification lights.
- Turn on right turn signal—then get out of cab and begin walk-around.
- The key may need to be in the ignition and in the on position to check the turn indicators.

5. **Walk-around inspection**—Start with the driver's side of the cab—cover the front and then work down the opposite side. Go over the rear of the vehicle and back to the driver's side of the cab.

- General
  - ——Walk around, inspecting as you go.
  - ——Clean all lights, reflectors, and glass as you walk around.
- Check left front
  - ——Driver's door glass should be clean.
  - ——Locks in working order.
  - ——Condition of wheels, rims, and tires—no missing, bent or broken studs, clamps or lugs. (A) Tires properly inflated, valve stem and cap in place. No serious cuts, slashes, bulges or signs of tread wear. (B) Test lug nuts for looseness (rust streaks coming from the lug nuts also indicate looseness). (C) Hub oil level good with no leaks.
  - ——Left front suspension—good condition of spring, spring hangers, shackles, U-bolts, and shock absorbers.
  - ——Left front brake drum and hoses in good condition.
  - ——Check brake chambers and slack adjusters.
- Check front
  - ——Check front axle for cracks or other problems.
  - ——Check for loose, worn, bent, damaged, or missing parts of the steering system and test for looseness.
  - ——Windshield should be free of damage and clean. Wipers should be in good working order—check for proper spring tension in wiper arm. Check blades for stiff rubber and ensure that they are secure.
  - ——Parking, clearance, and identification lights are clean, operational, and proper color—amber in front.
  - ——Right turn signal light must be clean, operating, and proper color—amber or white.
- Check right front
  - ——Check all items on right front as for left front.
  - ——If cab-over-engine model, all primary and safety locks engaged and working.
  - ——Right fuel tank—securely mounted, no leaks. Fuel crossover lines secure, adequate fuel in tank for trip, and caps and gaskets on and secure.
  - ——Condition of visible parts—rear of engine has no leaks, transmission not leaking, exhaust system secure and not leaking or touching wires or lines. No cracks or bends in frame and cross members.
  - ——Airlines and electrical wiring—no snagging, rubbing, or wearing.
  - ——Spare tire carrier not damaged and spare tire/wheel right size at proper inflation.
  - ——Cargo secure—cargo blocked, braced, tied, and chained. Header board secure, sideboards and stakes free of damage and properly placed. Canvas or tarp secured to prevent tearing, billowing, or blocking mirrors.

———Oversized loads have required signs properly mounted and all required permits in driver's pouch.

———Curbside cargo compartment doors closed and latched with all required security seals in place.

- Check right rear
———Condition of wheels, rims and tires—no missing, bent, or broken spacers, studs, clamps, or lugs. Tires evenly matched, are of same type (no mixing of radial and bias types), properly inflated with valve stems and caps in place. No cuts, bulges, or tread wear. Tires are not rubbing and are clear of debris.

———Wheel bearing/seals not leaking.

———Suspension—condition of springs, spring hangers, shackles, and U-bolts good, axle secure, and drive axle(s) not leaking gear oil.

———Check condition of torque rod arms and bushings.

———Check condition of shock absorber(s).

———If retractable axle, check lift mechanism. If air-powered, check for leaks.

———Brakes—brake drums in good condition and hoses checked for wear, rubbing, etc.

———Check brake chambers and slack adjusters.

———Lights and reflectors—side-marker lights clean, operating, and red at rear—others amber. Same for side markers.

- Check rear
———Rear clearance and identification lights clean, operating, and red at rear. Reflectors clean and red at rear. Taillights clean, operating, and red at rear. Right turn signal operating and proper color—red, yellow, or amber at rear.

———License plates present, clean, and secure.

———Splash guards properly fastened, undamaged, and not dragging or rubbing tires.

———Cargo secure—properly blocked and braced, tied, and chained. Tailboards up and secure. End gates free of damage and secured in stake sockets.

———Canvas or tarp secured to avoid billowing, tearing, blocking rear-view mirror, or covering rear lights.

———For over-length or over-width loads, have all signs and additional flags and lights in proper position and have all required permits.

———Rear doors closed and locked.

- Check left side
Check everything you checked on the right side, as well as:

———Batteries (if not located in the engine compartment), battery box (securely attached and cover also secure).

———Batteries not damaged or leaking and no movement.

———Check battery fluid levels—except maintenance-free types.

———Cell caps and vents in place, free of debris, and secure.

6. **Check signal lights**
- Get in and turn off all lights.
- Turn on stop lights (apply trailer hand brake).
- Turn on left turn signals.
Get out and check lights

- Left front turn signal—light is clean, operating, and proper amber or white color on signals facing the front.
- Left rear turn signal and stoplights—lights are clean, operating and proper red, yellow, or amber color.

7. **Start engine and check brake system**
   - Before starting the engine and brake system check, fasten your seatbelt!
   - Get in, turn off lights not needed for driving.
   - Check all required papers, trip manifests, permits, etc.
   - Secure all loose articles in the cab.
   - Start the engine.
   - Test for hydraulic leaks—if hydraulic brakes, pump them three times. Then apply pressure to the pedal and hold five seconds. The pedal should not move. If it does, there may be a leak or other problem. Fix it before beginning your trip.
   - Test air brakes.
   - Test parking brake—fasten seatbelt, allow vehicle to move forward slowly, and apply parking brake. If it doesn't stop the vehicle, get it fixed.
   - Test service brake stopping action—move vehicle at about five miles per hour, push brake pedal firmly. If vehicle pulls to one side, this means possible brake trouble. Any unusual feel of the pedal or delayed stopping action could signal a problem.

Check air brakes on doubles and triples like any other combination vehicle.

Some Final Notes about Vehicle Inspection

Make out your written inspection report each day. Report anything you find on inspection that will have an impact on the vehicle's safety or may lead to a breakdown.

Keep a copy of your inspection report for 24 hours or as long as your company specifies.

When driving in extreme weather—winter or summer—or for mountain driving, you'll add steps to the inspection.

Let's Review

Read each question and all of the answers provided. Place the letter of the correct answer in the space provided or, write your answers on a separate piece of paper so you can use these questions again as you review for the CDL. Once you have answered all the questions, check your answers against the answer key which follows.

_____ 1. When you're conducting a pre-trip inspection, your fuel tank should be
    (A) full and topped off,   (C) almost full,
    (B) at "add",   (D) at "low."

_____ 2. When inspecting tires, a bulge means
    (A) tire pressure is at capacity,
    (B) tires can go across rough terrain,
    (C) tire could blow out,
    (D) all of the above.

_____ 3. To test your service brakes
    (A) go forward at five miles per hour and push the brake pedal firmly,
    (B) pump brakes and pull emergency brake lever,
    (C) roll backward and push in clutch,
    (D) none of the above.

_____ 4. When you inspect your brakes, check
    (A) discs for ripples,
    (B) hubcaps for lubrication,
    (C) drums, shoes, and linings for leaks, cracks, or wear,
    (D) none of the above.

_____ 5. When checking hydraulic brakes, the engine should be
    (A) off and the transmission in reverse,
    (B) on and the transmission in neutral,
    (C) off and the transmission in neutral,
    (D) none of the above.

_____ 6. True or False. It is federal law that your vehicle has mud flaps.

_____ 7. When inspecting an air suspension system, leaking air means
    (A) too much air has been injected,
    (B) not enough air is in the tank,
    (C) a defect has occurred,
    (D) all of the above.

_____ 8. The best way to check tire inflation pressure is to
    (A) use a tire gauge,   (C) kick the tire,
    (B) use a tire billy,   (D) all of the above.

_____ 9. Vehicle inspections should be done
    (A) before the trip,   (C) on the road,
    (B) after the trip,   (D) all of the above.

_____ 10. When inspecting wiring and electrical systems, look for
    (A) broken or loose wires,
    (B) worn insulation,
    (C) bare wires making contact with each other,
    (D) all of the above.

Answers to Let's Review

1. C; 2. C; 3. A; 4. C; 5. B; 6. False; 7. C; 8. A; 9. D; 10. D.

Terms You Should Know

The following terms have been taken from the contents of Chapter 6. Review them. If you see any you're unsure of, check the definition in the Glossary at the back of the book. If it helps you, keep a written list of the words and their definitions (or write in the definitions here) and review them several days prior to taking the CDL tests.

Accelerator

Binders

Braces and supports

Brakes

Cab

Cargo doors

Cargo securement devices

Chains

Checklist

Coupling devices

Defrosters

Dimmer switch

Emergency equipment

Engine compartment

Exhaust system

Flags

Four-way flashers

Frame

Fuel and fuel system

Winches

Windshield wipers

Wheels

THE DISPATCH BOARD
What Professional Drivers Should Know about NAFTA
by Kristin Berthelsen

The North America Free Trade Agreement (NAFTA), signed on January 1, 1994, is a contract between Canada, the United States, and Mexico to remove tariffs and to open trade between the three countries. The goal of the trade agreement was to increase trading in North America.

According to 2001 statistics, importing and exporting has increased in North America, which has been a great boost to all three economies.

Most of the goods transported between each country are carried by trucks. The trucking industry has seen an increase in jobs due to NAFTA, and the American Trucking Association has reported that more than 70 percent of trading freight is carried by trucks.

Initially, NAFTA stipulated that international borders would open between the countries in December 1995. In keeping with the agreement, trucks began freely moving between the United States and Canada to make deliveries and pick up shipments. But, this was not the case between Mexico and the United States.

The Department of Transportation (DOT) refused to grant access to Mexican truckers due to safety reasons. Because of this, there has been a barrier between the United States' and Mexico's trucking borders. Ultimately, it will be removed.

President George W. Bush indicated his desire to lift this barrier in 2002, allowing cross-border trucking between the United States and Mexico.

The trucking industry has welcomed any improvements to these barriers. The American Trucking Association believes that allowing cross-border trading only increases trucking deliveries made between the three countries.

So what does this mean for you as a truck driver? It is possible that motor carriers will begin extending routes into Mexico much as they have done in Canada. And eventually Mexican trucks will travel freely through the United States as Canadian carriers have done since the free trade treaty was signed.

What new skills will you need if you travel into Canada and Mexico? You will need to understand the requirements, restrictions, and standards of driving in these countries. This may include an International Commercial Driver's License. And for carriers traveling into Mexico from the United States, drivers will need a general understanding of the Spanish language.

Also, with safety as a continuing concern for cross-border trucking, defensive driving and familiarity with new routes will be necessary. As in any driving situation, your job will be to not only watch out for yourself but also for those driving around you.

NAFTA has definitely opened new opportunities for motor carriers across the United States and, with the opening of the Mexican border, it may also be possible for drivers to experience the new adventure of traveling "South of the Border."

7 Basic Vehicle Control

Basic Driving Skills

As a professional driver, you'll be spending most of your working hours operating a vehicle. As a professional driver, you also will be expected to have excellent skills in handling this vehicle in any number of situations.

This chapter will provide you with information necessary not only to pass the CDL Knowledge Test but also the CDL Skills Test.

Once again, it's your responsibility to read closely and carefully, take good notes, and review what you've learned before setting a time to take the tests leading to the CDL.

It also will be helpful to take a copy of the Federal Motor Carrier Safety Regulations (you can get one from the local Department of Motor Vehicles or look at the FMCSR web pages on the Internet). Look at Subpart G and you'll find a list of driving skills necessary to earn a CDL.

So, let's get started—you'll learn a lot in this chapter.

Be Prepared!

When you climb into that cab, you take on many new responsibilities, including your own well-being and the well-being of fellow motorists. But you also take on the responsibility for your vehicle, its safe operation, its maintenance, and its performance of the task it was built to do.

When someone talks about operating a vehicle safely—much like your personal vehicle—several things come to mind. These may include (a) steering along the highway, (b) shifting gears to go up and down hills, (c) accelerating when necessary, and (d) braking when necessary.

As you swing up in the cab, you should be reviewing some of these basic driving skills so that you will be in complete command of the vehicle and its systems and controls. If you're driving this vehicle for the first time, take time to inspect it. A professional driver never starts an engine without first thoroughly going over a vehicle to make certain it will respond to his or her every command.

Before taking the driver's seat, look at the details of the cab—the handholds, the steps—and make sure they are free of greasy substances or dirt.

As you sit in the driver's seat of a new vehicle, adjust the seat as much as you can to fit your height and your comfort. But the most important thing about the height of the seat is whether or not you can *comfortably* reach the controls.

Check out the control panel . . . what do you see?

Become familiar with the panel and then check out the shift lever to determine the kind of transmission and the shifting pattern. Next, find all the controls and gauges you'll need to operate the vehicle safely.

Ladies and Gentlemen, Start Your Engines!

Ready to turn on the ignition? If you're running a gasoline engine, depress the gas pedal at least once, all the way to the floor, and then turn the ignition key. After the engine turns over, press the accelerator to increase the revolutions per minute (rpms). This supplies gas to the engine.

If you're starting a diesel engine, don't depress the gas pedal. Fuel injectors will inject metered diesel fuel into the cylinders to get the engine started and keep it running, so just press the clutch to the floor and hold it while you turn the key.

By doing this, you'll cause electricity to flow from the batteries to the starter motor—this turns the flywheel and cranks the engine, and the air and fuel ignite in each cylinder. When this happens, the pistons are pushed down and that turns the crankshaft. As soon as a diesel engine fires, release the key.

Any questions? If so, read these few paragraphs again.

One other point: When you start the gasoline engine, keep your clutch pedal down to the floor—this will assist you in starting the engine safely and it will also place less wear and tear on the engine.

Q. Do I need to warm up a truck engine like I do my personal vehicle?

A. There are mixed ideas about this, but most mechanics will tell you that engines work more efficiently when they've had a chance to warm up. Gasoline engines need about five minutes. A diesel engine should warm up to about 120 degrees Fahrenheit before you engage the clutch. Normal operating temperature for a diesel is between 165 and 185 degrees Fahrenheit.

Warming up the engine heats most of the liquids needed to run the engine. But check the owner's manual to make sure you're doing the right thing for your vehicle.

A safety reminder: Don't allow the vehicle to roll back when it's being started and warmed up. You might hit somebody . . . or something. Start the truck with the parking brake on— and release it when you've got enough engine power to keep from rolling back.

Q. Hear the motor running? Headed for the highway?

A. Once you're in gear and ready to go, increase your speed gradually to keep from damaging the vehicle and the engine. Rough acceleration can also damage the coupling, especially in poor traction, such as rain or snow. Too much power too fast may cause the wheels to spin. If that happens, don't lose control. Take your foot off the accelerator.

Q. Any other suggestions?

A. Let's talk about steering. Like driving any other vehicle, the old-fashioned 10 o'clock and 2 o'clock positions for the hands are best for controlling the steering wheel. Pretend the steering wheel is a clock face. Place your left hand at 10 o'clock and your right hand at 2 o'clock. Rest the thumbs on top of the wheel. And when turning, don't cross your arms over the wheel. Instead, pick up your hands, one at a time, and reposition them.

What You Need to Know about Shifting

For most new drivers, shifting gears on a truck is the biggest concern. In fact, in some companies who have programs where spouses can learn to drive so they can team with their significant others, women learn to drive with automatic transmissions so they won't have to deal with the fear of shifting.

But, let's take it step by step:

1. First of all, it's a good idea to read the owner's manual for the vehicle and then use your tachometer as a guide for shifting ranges.
2. The rpm where you shift becomes higher as you move up through the gears. Find out what's right for each vehicle you drive.
3. You can also use road speed—and what speeds each gear is good for. Then, by using the speedometer, you'll know when to shift up.
4. Experienced drivers can tell by engine sounds when it's time to shift.

Q. What's "double-clutching" and why do I need to know about it?
A. If your vehicle has a manual transmission, changing gears will require double-clutching—a basic upshifting method where you (1) release the accelerator and (2) push in the clutch and shift to neutral at the same time.
   Now, release the clutch, let the engine slow down to the rpm required for the next gear, then simultaneously (at the same time) push in the clutch and shift to the higher gear. Release the clutch and press accelerator at same time.

Warning: If you stay in neutral too long, it may be hard to get into the next gear. So, don't force it! *Remain in neutral, increase engine speed to match road speed and try again.*

To downshift:

1. Release the accelerator, push in the clutch and shift to neutral at same time.
2. Release the clutch and press the accelerator. Increase engine and gear speed to the rpm required for the next lowest gear.
3. Push in the clutch and shift to the lower gear.
4. Release the clutch and press on the accelerator at the same time.

Hint: Watch the speedometer or tachometer and downshift at the correct rpm or road speed.

When starting down a hill: Downshift before going down the hill. Slow down and shift *down* to a speed you can control without slamming on your brakes.

Warning: If your brakes overheat, you may lose braking power, just when you need it most. One rule of thumb—shift to a gear lower than one you'd use to climb this same hill.

Q. What about situations where I need to slow down quickly, such as driving around a curve or entering a freeway ramp?
A. Downshift before entering the curve—that would be the wisest move. Then slow down to safe speed and downshift to the right gear for that speed. This leaves you with some power to make it through the curve and keeps the vehicle stable.

Q. What about vehicles with auxiliary transmissions and multi-speed rear axles?
A. These usually give you extra gears and can be operated with a knob or switch on the gearshift lever for the main transmission.
   Check your owner's manual for the vehicle's shift pattern.

Q. What about automatic transmissions?
A. With some transmissions, the lower ranges can prevent the transmission from shifting beyond the selected gear—unless the governor rpm is exceeded. Using a lower gear is an important braking strategy to use when driving a downgrade.

Q. How hard is it to back a rig?

A. First, an interesting fact—most backing accidents cause damage to the top of the vehicle. That's right! Low-hanging branches or wires can damage the top of the vehicle or tear off an exhaust stack, so before backing, make sure the area is clear of wires, low branches, the eaves of a building, etc.

The next most common damage occurs to the rear of the trailer, so check that area before you start backing.

Most damage and most accidents occur on the right side of the vehicle, because the "blind spot" is there—from the rear axle to midway up the trailer and from midway down the door to the ground.

Think your spotter mirror will help? Not always—it won't show you everything you need to see at once.

Q. How do I back this vehicle?

A. Here are some easy steps for straight line backing (Figure 7-1):

1. Turn off any distractions—your CB, your radio, your CD player—and focus totally on what you're doing.
2. Get out of the truck and check the area under the truck, at the rear, and the area around where you're backing for low limbs, wires, or anything that would damage your rig.

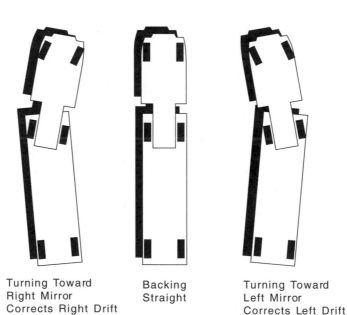

Turning Toward Right Mirror Corrects Right Drift	Backing Straight	Turning Toward Left Mirror Corrects Left Drift

1. Position Vehicle Properly
2. Back as Slowly as Possible
3. Constantly Check Behind with Mirrors
4. Use Push-Pull Method of Steering
   • When the Trailer Gets Bigger in One Mirror, Turn the Steering Wheel Toward that Mirror to Correct the Drift

Figure 7-1   Steps in straight line backing.

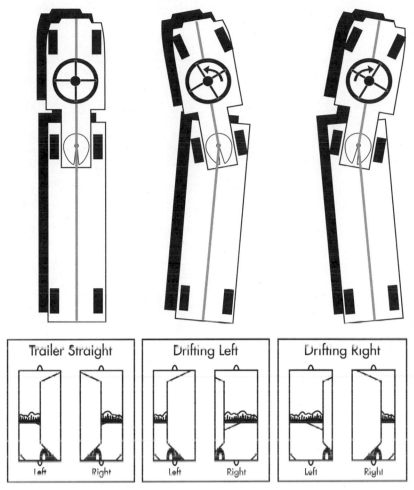

Figure 7-2 Watch both sides of the vehicle when backing.

3. Put on your flashers—never back without them. They warn others about what you're doing so they'll watch out and stay out of your way.
4. Using your mirrors, watch both sides (Figure 7-2)—but don't open your door and lean out.
5. When backing a trailer, turn the steering wheel in the opposite direction of where you want the trailer to go (Figure 7-3). If you want it to go right, turn the steering wheel left. If you want it to go left, turn the wheel right. This is called "jacking the trailer."
6. Once the trailer starts to turn, turn the wheel the other way—to follow the trailer. This is called "following the trailer."

Okay let's review. To turn the trailer, turn the steering wheel in the opposite direction you want the trailer to go. Once the trailer has begun turning, "follow the trailer" by turning the wheel the other way.

Q. What are "retarders" and what will they do?
A. You can slow your vehicle by using the brakes or, in some situations, by downshifting. But there's another option—some vehicles have "retarders" that help slow the vehicle without using the brake. So, retarders reduce wear on your brakes.

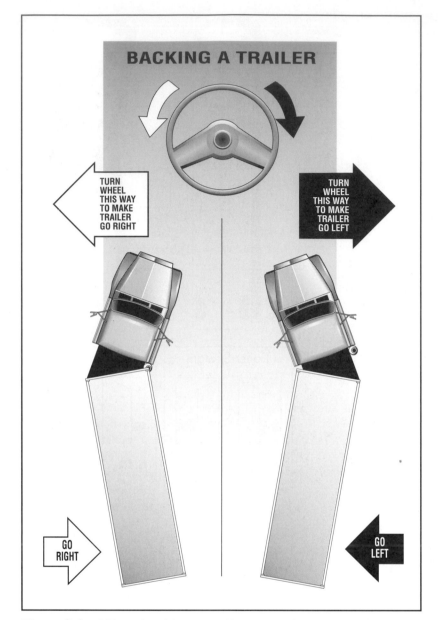

Figure 7-3   When backing a trailer, turn the steering wheel in the opposite direction of where you want to go. This is called "jacking the trailer."

Retarders come in several varieties—all can be turned on or off by the driver. Some retarders offer power adjustments. When the driver turns on the retarders, their braking power is applied to the drive wheel when you let up on the accelerator.

Warning: When driving on wet, icy, or snowy roads, turn the retarders off. If left on, the retarders could cause you to skid.

Q. Time to shut down the engine? What steps are necessary?
A. The engine has been running for a few hours and now it's time to shut it down. Here are the steps:

1. Let it idle for about three minutes. Why? This keeps the lubricant flowing while the hot engine starts to cool.
2. When you stop the engine, be sure to take your foot off the accelerator.
3. Set the parking brake before leaving your vehicle.

Keeping Your Eyes 'Glued' to the Road

This may sound basic, but to be a professional driver and keep a clean driving record, you need to train yourself to be aware of what's happening around your vehicle at all times. This means in front, to the sides, and behind.

If you are not aware—or visually alert at all times—you leave yourself open to accidents.

Q. How far ahead should I look?

A. Remember that you are handling a vehicle three or four times the length of a four-wheeler, so your forward vision must be at least 12 to 15 seconds ahead of where the vehicle is on the highway.

It takes longer for a tractor-trailer rig to change lanes. It takes longer for the rig to stop. And it takes a little time for your brain to translate what you want to do and then send this signal to your hands and feet.

So, looking ahead a quarter mile is necessary. If you're driving city streets—and at lower speeds than highway driving—then you should look (and plan) ahead at least one block.

And as you're looking a quarter-mile down the road, your eyes still need to take in what's going on around you. Much like checking both mirrors, shift your eyes from near to far vision and watch for:

- Vehicles coming into your lane
- Vehicles entering the highway
- Vehicle brake lights and slowing traffic

Also, look at the road and its condition. Look for traffic lights and signs. Approaching an intersection? Slow down. The same goes for stop signs or amber warning lights.

Q. I've heard truckers talking about using their mirrors—What for?

A. Driving down the highway, your main focus must be the road ahead, but quickly check each mirror from time to time to know what's happening around you. However, don't spend a lot of time doing so. Train yourself to glance quickly into each mirror. Then, focus on what's happening ahead of you.

Some truckers like using a curved mirror—these show a wider view than flat mirrors—but everything looks smaller and farther away. Make allowances if you want to use a "bug-eye" or "fish-eye" or "spotter" mirror.

Letting Drivers Know You're There—And What You're Planning to Do

As we have mentioned earlier, the vehicle you're driving offers several ways of communicating with other drivers. These include turn signals, brake lights, reflectors, and vehicle lights.

When I drive my personal vehicle, it drives me nuts to see people who leave their turn signal on, even after they turn!

Beyond irritating other drivers, there's also a safety hazard involved. There's no question: When you're turning or changing lanes, cancel your turn signal immediately after you've completed the turn or lane change.

Also, remember to put on your turn signal well before you plan to turn.

Q. What about using the brake lights as a signal?

A. Use your brake lights for the following situations:

1. Tap the brake a few times to let other drivers know you're slowing down.
2. Use the flashers when you're driving slowly or when you've stopped your rig.
3. If you're driving a van or a bus and are stopping to let passengers disembark, let other drivers know you're planning to stop by flashing your brake lights. Don't stop without giving notice.

Note: Several states have laws about when to use emergency flashers—be sure you know these before entering into a new state.

Q. What else do I need to know about communicating with other vehicles?

A. Think about your personal experience driving on the highway or on city streets. Many times you have passed another automobile or a pedestrian or a bicyclist and they probably didn't know you were there.

There are some theories that say, "If you don't think that they know you are there, tap on the horn lightly so they won't suddenly move in front of you while you're passing them." But you also don't want to blast your horn to startle them and make them lose control. It is a fine line between warning and startling, so use caution.

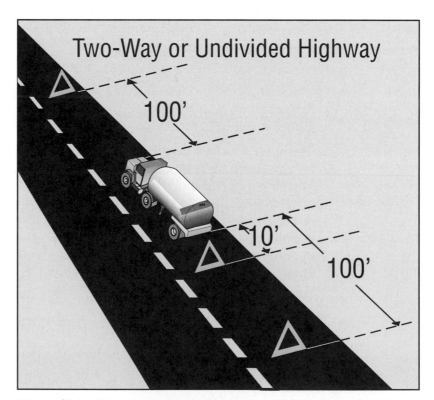

Figure 7-4 Place reflective triangles on the traffic side of your vehicle as shown.

At night, flashing your lights from low beam to high beam and back is a good way to let someone in front of you know you're coming ahead.

In hazy weather, your vehicle's lights make it easier to see. The same is true for rain or snow. Use your headlights on low beam and your identification lights. And if you need to pull off the road in any weather, your flashers will make you more visible and will let other drivers know you've stopped.

Warning: If you plan to be stopped on the shoulder for more than 10 minutes, regulations say you must put out your reflective triangles—on the traffic side within 10 feet of the front and rear of your vehicle. You should also place triangles about 100 feet behind your vehicle and 100 feet ahead if you stop on a curve or a hill. (See Figure 7-4.)

On a hill—Place markers within 500 feet so oncoming traffic will be looking for you as they come up the hill (Figure 7-5).

On a one-way or divided highway—Your markers should be placed at 10, 100, and 200 feet toward approaching traffic (Figure 7-6). The whole point is to *make yourself visible if your vehicle is stopped anywhere on the roadway.*

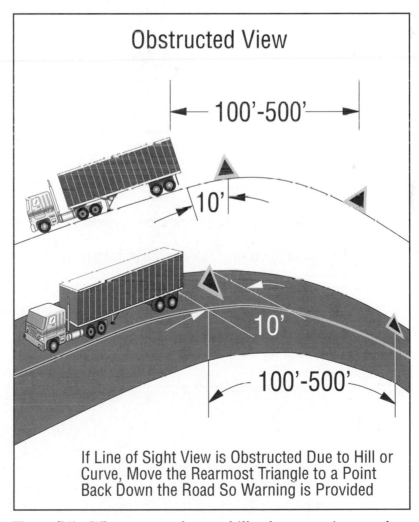

Figure 7-5   When stopped on a hill, place warning markers within 500 feet of your vehicle.

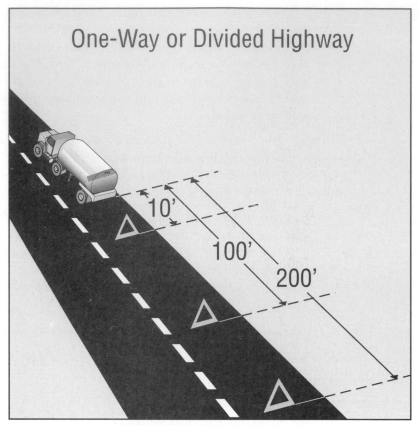

Figure 7-6 On a divided highway, place markers at 10, 100, and 200 feet toward oncoming traffic.

Speed—On Various Types of Highway in Various Conditions

You've been on the highway as trucks zoomed past. It may have appeared that those drivers were breaking the speed limit—and some were.

How fast you should drive is your decision, but before you make it, you should understand the factors that go into deciding what speed you should travel.

Some of those factors are:

1. Weather
2. Visibility
3. Road conditions
4. Traffic
5. Hills
6. Traction

Another question you need to consider when setting your speed: How much time will it take me to stop if I have to?

Stopping distance is calculated by:

- **Perception time**—how long it takes your brain to interpret what your eyes see as a hazard up ahead. If you are an alert driver, looking 3/4 of a mile up the road, it will take you about 3/4 of a second to see and interpret an upcoming hazard. In that time, if you're traveling 55 mph, your vehicle will travel 60 feet.

- **Reaction time**—how long it takes your brain to make your body react to the upcoming hazard. That involves your brain deciding what to do and your foot easing off the accelerator and pushing the brake. The average reaction time for most drivers is 3/4 of a second—so add another 60 feet your vehicle's stopping distance.
- **Braking time**—If you have good reaction time and good brakes, if you are traveling 55 mph on good roads and dry conditions, it will take a loaded rig about 170 feet—and 4 to 5 seconds—to stop.
- **Total stopping distance**—from the time you see the hazard until your rig has stopped—about the length of a football field. If you're traveling faster than 55 mph, the distance it takes to stop increases. Here's the equation: If you double your speed, it will take you four times the distance to stop.

And don't forget about the weight factor. If your vehicle is fully loaded, it will require more braking power to stop, but an empty vehicle requires more distance to stop because it will have less traction and could cause you to go into a skid more easily.

Road Conditions—An Important Factor in Determining Speed

As you gain professional driving experience, you'll become familiar with the states that offer well-maintained highways and those that do not. Some states offer well-paved roads with roomy shoulders. Some states are notorious for roads full of chuckholes, no shoulders, and terrible upkeep.

It is common sense that the roads that are well-maintained are those where you can travel at higher—but safe—speeds.

Remember: You cannot steer or brake your vehicle without traction, which is friction between the vehicle's tires and the road.

Some road conditions make traction difficult, some make it easier. Slippery roads and roads with lots of curves reduce traction.

When a road is wet, icy, or snow-covered, traction is more difficult, so you must travel at slower speeds. It is more difficult to stop and easier to skid on these surfaces.

One rule of thumb: When roads are wet, your stopping distance doubles. Most drivers recommend reducing your traveling speed by one-third when roads are wet, icy, or snowy. On packed snow, reduce speeds by one-half or more. And an experienced driver will tell you, when snow is packed—*stop driving as soon as possible.*

Here are some other terms to remember:

- Icy bridges—in cold weather, roadways on bridges will freeze before the roads themselves ice over. Drive carefully when the temperature drops into the freezing range (32 degrees Fahrenheit or lower).
- Wet ice—when melting occurs, wet ice is more slippery than normal icy conditions.
- Black ice—a thin coating of ice that is usually invisible because you can see the roadway through it. Many drivers, thinking there is no ice on a road, have had problems—sometimes fatal—with black ice. Anytime temperatures are in the freezing range (32 degrees Fahrenheit or lower) and the road appears to be wet—be alert for black ice.

- Ice checks—to find out about the road conditions, roll down your window and check for ice on the mirror or mirror support. If you find ice on these, that's a sign there's probably ice on the highway.

Driving in the Rain

Whether it's pouring rain or only misting, those first few drops will mix with the oil on the road to make the road very slick. If it continues to rain for awhile, this mixture washes away, but be aware: *roads are more slippery at the beginning of a rainstorm.*

Q. What is hydroplaning—and what do I do if this happens?
A. If water or slush collects on the roadway, your vehicle could ride on top of the water—much like you do on water skis. If you're riding on top of the water instead of on top of the roadway, your vehicle will have no traction—and when there's no traction, you'll have problems steering and braking your vehicle.

Note: Even if you're traveling 30 mph, your vehicle could hydroplane. And watch for puddles—if water is deep enough, your vehicle can hydroplane here, too.

Q. If my vehicle is hydroplaning, how do I regain control?
A. First, release the accelerator. Then, push in the clutch to slow your vehicle and let the wheels turn on their own. If you start to skid, don't use the brake to slow down. Instead, push in the clutch to let the wheels turn.

And remember—hydroplaning is more likely to occur if tire pressure is low or if the treads are worn on the tires. If the treads aren't deep enough, they won't carry the water away from the tires.

Other Road Conditions

Q. What about driving curves in the road?
A. When the road curves, adjust your speed downward. If you take a curve too fast, you can lose traction and your vehicle will continue forward in a straight line—and that's not good.

If you enter a curve too fast and the wheels maintain traction, you may have a rollover—and the same goes for the short curves of a freeway ramp. If you're driving a tanker or any vehicle with a high center of gravity, the chances for rollover are even greater, even traveling at the posted speed.

So, to avoid rollovers—slow before you begin the curve. Slow enough so you don't have to use your brakes. *Never exceed the speed limit for the curve. Your speed needs to be much slower!*

Q. What about speeds the rest of the time?
A. Whatever the weather or the road conditions, you should always travel at a speed that allows you to stop within the distance you can see ahead. For example, driving in fog you cannot see as far down the highway as you normally could. Slow your speed so that you can stop within the distance you can see down the road.

At night, of course, your visual field is also limited. Some of the time, you can use your high beams, but when low beams are required, decrease your speed so you can stop within the area you can see with your low beams.

Driving in traffic? The best speed is the speed of the vehicles around you—if it is safe and if it is the legal speed.

Remember: Trying to save time by going faster is a bad idea. Trying to maintain a faster speed is fatiguing and this increases also your chances for an accident.

Q. What about speeds when driving on a downgrade?

A. The most important thing to remember about driving on a downgrade—a long, steep hill—is to enter the hill at a speed slow enough to prevent hard braking. If you have to brake heavily, you risk making your brakes too hot to slow you down. Follow these steps for a downgrade:

1. Check brakes before starting downhill.
2. Downshift to the gear that's one gear lower than you would use to climb the hill.
3. Use retarders if you have them.
4. If you need to use your brakes, use a light, steady pressure.

Allowing Enough Space to Drive Safely

If you think about it, driving safely is simply a matter of allowing enough space around your vehicle—to move forward, to change lanes, and to make maneuvers necessary to drive safely.

Here's how much space you need:

Ahead—Make sure you're not following the vehicle in front of you too closely. If you are, slow down and back off. A good rule of thumb: Keep one second of space between you and the vehicle in front of you for every 10 feet of vehicle length you have. So, if you've got a 40-foot vehicle and you're traveling 40 mph, you'll need four seconds between you and the vehicle in front of you. Add another second for bad weather or slippery road conditions and one more second for night driving. In the worst conditions—leave at least seven seconds of space between you and the next vehicle.

How do you calculate seconds? Watch the front vehicle pass a certain marker alongside the road—it may be a billboard or a mile marker. Then count—one-thousand-and-one, one-thousand-and-two—until you've counted at least four seconds before you pass that same marker. If you can't count four seconds between that vehicle and yours, slow down!

Behind—You have no control on how closely other vehicles follow you, but one rule to follow is always keep to the right. If you're heavily loaded and can't keep up with the speed of the rest of the traffic, stay to the right.

You'll find, during bad weather, that many other drivers tend to follow 18-wheelers, because they rely on professional drivers to get them through a rough part of the driving. So, when other vehicles follow closely, avoid any quick changes, and if you have to reduce your speed, do so as gradually as possible. If you are making a turn, signal early.

Note: If you're being followed too closely, never speed up! *If another driver is tailgating, it is much safer to do so at a slower speed!*

Sides—The best way to keep safe distances on the sides of your vehicle is to *never* drive side-by-side with another vehicle. Also, be aware that you have certain "blind spots," so make certain you don't change lanes or turn without checking to make sure there's no obstruction here.

If you do have to travel next to another vehicle, make certain there is enough space for the two of you. And be aware of wind conditions—high winds can make it hard to stay in your lane and gusts do strange things, so it is important to have enough space around your vehicle.

Above—You've seen bridge markings that display the height of the bridge. These markings tell truckers how much clearance there is between the bridge and the top of the truck. But here's the kicker—sometimes these posted heights are not accurate due to a variety of reasons, perhaps because of road resurfacing that has caused the roadway to be higher, or packed snow, or other situations.

Remember, too, that a loaded trailer rides lower than an empty trailer which rides higher. If you're in doubt about whether you have enough clearance to pass safely under a bridge, go slowly. If you're not sure you can make it, take another route.

And also remember—before backing, get out of your cab and check overhead clearance, watching for branches and wires.

Below—There are several obstacles here. First, when crossing a railroad track, don't get hung on the track if the dirt approach has worn away. Second, always check under your truck before backing. Finally, if you see something on the roadway that may get hung up under your rig, try to avoid the obstacle, but don't make any sudden and unsafe maneuvers out of your lane.

Mastering the Turning Maneuver

When driving your personal vehicle, you probably think nothing of making a right or left turn. In a larger vehicle, however, turning can be a complex maneuver—and you need ample space to make turns successfully.

Professional drivers will tell you that right turns are more difficult to make than left turns. Why? Because in a right turn, you can't always see what's happening on the right of your vehicle as well as you can see on the left side.

Q. How do I make a successful right turn—every time?
A. It takes practice, but following these steps will help:

1. Turn the vehicle slowly and surely to give yourself time to avoid problems.
2. If there's no room to turn wide at the beginning of the maneuver, swing wide as you complete the turn.
3. Don't go into the oncoming lane to turn widely as you start the turn. Why? Because people behind you may think you're going to make a left turn.
4. Keep the rear of your vehicle close to the curb. This helps you turn and keeps others from trying to pass on the right. (See Figure 7-7.)
5. If crossing over into the next lane is necessary, give oncoming vehicles ample time to stop or go by. Don't back up for them because you run the risk of hitting someone behind you.

To make a left turn:

1. Roll to the center of the intersection before starting your turn.
2. Remember off-tracking and don't start your turn too soon.

TRACTOR-TRAILER TRACKING CHARACTERISTICS

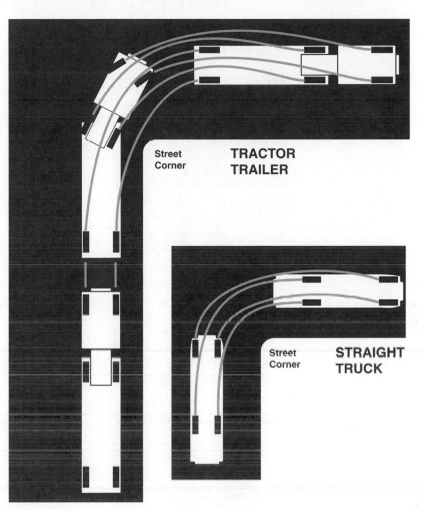

Figure 7-7 Making a successful right turn.

3. If there are two turn lanes, always start a left turn from the outer turn lane (see Figure 7-8).
4. Don't start your turn in the inside lane because you may have to swing right to make the turn.

Making Night Driving Safer and Easier

What makes night driving more challenging? Is it because drivers can't see as far down the road at night as they can during the day? Is it because hazards can't be seen as readily and reaction times must be rapid-fire? Sometimes vision is less keen at night than during daylight hours—or it may be that the driver is tired and simply is not as alert as usual. All of these reasons make night driving more difficult.

MAKING A LEFT TURN

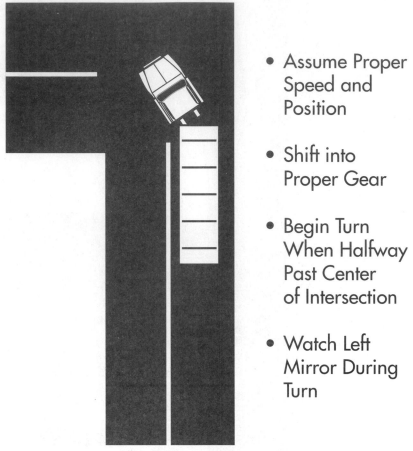

- Assume Proper Speed and Position

- Shift into Proper Gear

- Begin Turn When Halfway Past Center of Intersection

- Watch Left Mirror During Turn

Figure 7-8   Making a successful left turn.

Here are some suggestions to make night driving safer:

1. Clean headlights mean better night vision—your headlights become your main light source at night.
2. If headlights are out of adjustment, have this corrected before going on the road at night.
3. Make sure reflectors, marker lights, tail lights, clearance lights, and identification lights are all clean and in working order.
4. Clean windshields can also make a difference in your night vision—so make certain your windshield and mirrors are clean on the inside and outside before you start driving.
5. It goes without saying—avoid drugs that tend to take the edge off of your alertness or make you drowsy. The same goes for drinking—when you're driving at night (or any other time), there's no room for alcohol or other chemical use.
6. When driving at night, eat a light evening meal—a heavy meal will make you groggy and will compromise your alertness.

7. If you think coffee will keep you going a few more miles, think again! Coffee will only make you jittery and bug-eyed.
8. The only cure for sleepiness or fatigue is sleep.

Bad Weather Driving Techniques

We've talked about black ice and driving in cold, rainy weather—but what about hot weather driving?

1. Watch for bleeding tar—in very hot weather, tar bleeds to the surface and can be very slippery.
2. Make certain you slow down enough to keep the engine and tires from overheating. Keep your vehicle as cool as possible—this lessens the chance for tire failure, fire, or engine failure.
3. Driving the desert? Make certain you have enough coolant and good tires before you start your day.
4. Check the water gauge and temperature gauge in your coolant from time to time. If the gauge goes above normal, there may be a chance of engine failure and possibly fire—so stop driving and try to find out what is wrong.
5. Check your engine belts—make sure they're not too loose or too worn.
6. If the engine fan doesn't work properly, it won't keep your engine cool.
7. Make sure your hoses can handle the heat. If they're worn or frayed, have them replaced.

Special Tactics for Road Hazards

There are a variety of road hazards—there always have been, always will be. Be prepared—train yourself about what to do. Being prepared reduces chances for accidents or putting your life in danger.

Here are some of the various road hazards you will find and the suggested tactics for overcoming these hazards:

- Work zones—Some states are assigning heavy fines for dangerous driving around work zones. Be alert—drive at the recommended speed limit or below. Use your four-way flashers or brake lights to warn others behind you that you are taking this strip of the highway slowly and carefully.
- Sometimes when the road is being resurfaced, there may be narrower lanes and uneven road between lanes—so don't drive too near the edge. You'll also find it harder to steer in a drop-off area.
- Is there something in the road ahead—perhaps a box or a piece of tire? Do everything possible to miss it, but if you are unable to maneuver around it, go over it as slowly as possible.
- Are other drivers taking stupid risks? Give them plenty of room. And be suspicious of drivers who are weaving, leaving the road, stopping at the wrong time or waiting too long for a stop, driving with the windows down in cold weather, or speeding up and then slowing down suddenly.
- Be alert for sleepy drivers—especially in the early mornings.
- Watch rental trucks carefully—these drivers probably have little experience driving vans of this size.

- Remember: Anywhere vehicles are present, there is danger and accidents just waiting to happen. Keep your mind on your driving and your eyes on the road at all times.

What to Do in an Emergency: Driving Defensively

Anything can happen anytime in traffic. The professional driver is aware of this possibility and can, in most cases, avoid accidents. However, sometimes the driver has no ability to control the situation.

The following are some tips for the professional driver when making emergency maneuvers:

- If you see an obstacle in your path, often the best maneuver is to steer around it—to turn to miss it. Stopping is not always the best option for these reasons: (1) you may not have enough room to stop, and (2) sometimes a quick stop may cause the tractor-trailer rig to flip over.
- Countersteering—Once you've steered around the obstacle, you will turn the wheel back in the other direction. This is called "countersteering" and you must be prepared to steer in the opposite direction. A speedy reaction time is important in this maneuver.
- When turning to miss an obstacle, do it quickly and don't apply your brakes, because this could lock your brakes, causing you to skid out of control.
- In most situations, steering to the right will move you and your rig out of harm's way. If you are blocked on both sides, moving to the right is the best choice—because you won't move into the oncoming traffic or cause anyone to move into the opposite lane.
- If you have to leave the paved roadway to avoid an accident, try to keep one set of wheels on the pavement for better traction.
- If your brakes fail, downshift to lowest gear possible and try to pump the brakes. With hydraulic brakes, you can often build enough pressure to stop the vehicle. The emergency brake is another option—but be sure to press the release button or pull the release lever at the same time you pull the emergency brake. If nothing works, find an escape ramp or turn uphill. This will sometimes slow your vehicle.
- If your tires fail (thumping, vibration, or steering feels tight), stop as soon as possible. To maintain control of your vehicle, hold the steering wheel firmly, and stay off the brake until vehicle has slowed. Then pull off the road and stop.

Q. What if my rig starts to skid?
A. Whenever your tires lose traction, a skid can result. The obvious move is to apply the brakes, but braking too hard may lock up your wheels.

Oversteering can also cause skidding, so don't turn the wheels more than the vehicle itself can turn.

Driving too fast is one of the most common reasons a vehicle goes into a skid. Manage your speed, matching it with road and weather conditions.

Other common reasons a rig will skid when the rear wheels lose traction—over-braking or over-accelerating. When the rear wheels skid, it is usually a result of overbraking and the wheels locking.

When you skid because of ice or snow on the road, simply take your foot off the accelerator and push in the clutch.

To correct a drive wheel braking skid, take your foot off the brake, allow the wheels on the rear to roll and—if you are on icy roads—push in the clutch to let the wheels turn freely.

If the vehicle begins to slide sideways, steer in the direction you want the vehicle to go—and turn the wheel quickly. As a vehicle corrects its course, the tendency is to keep on turning, so unless you turn your wheel the other way quickly, you may start skidding again.

Q. What do I do in case of a front wheel skid?
A. A front wheel skid usually occurs because you're driving too fast, the front tires are worn, or you're carrying too much weight on the front axle.

In a front wheel skid, the best maneuver is to let the vehicle slow down. Stop turning or hard braking. Slow as quickly as possible without skidding.

Let's Review

Read each question and all of the answers provided. Place the letter of the correct answer in the space provided or write your answers on a separate piece of paper so you can use these questions again as you review for the CDL. Once you have answered all the questions, check your answers against the answer key which follows.

_____ 1. Hydroplaning occurs when the tires
    (A) fly through the air,
    (B) ride on top of water on the pavement,
    (C) ride atop soft tar on hot pavements,
    (D) none of the above.

_____ 2. Many more accidents occur at night because of
    (A) driver fatigue,   (C) less light,
    (B) lower field of vision,   (D) all of the above.

_____ 3. True or False. Left turns are more difficult than right turns.

_____ 4. In backing a rig, most damage occurs to the
    (A) right front tire,   (C) top right of the trailer,
    (B) back of the trailer,   (D) none of the above.

_____ 5. In driving defensively, the best way to avoid a road hazard is to
    (A) steer to the right,   (C) steer to the outside lane,
    (B) steer to the left,   (D) none of the above.

_____ 6. The best way to brake a vehicle on a downgrade is to
    (A) stomp brakes to the floor,   (C) brake lightly and gradually,
    (B) continually pump brakes,   (D) none of the above.

_____ 7. True or False. In an emergency, stopping is the safest maneuver for your rig and for other motorists.

_____ 8. If you find the best maneuver is to drive your rig off the highway, it is always good to
    (A) keep one set of wheels on the pavement,
    (B) phone home,
    (C) roll down the driver's window,
    (D) all of the above.

_____ 9. Countersteering is used
    (A) after you've started your engine,
    (B) after you've steered around an obstacle,
    (C) when you want to turn your truck around,
    (D) none of the above.

_____10. The most common skid happens when
    (A) the tires lose traction,
    (B) the drive wheels lose traction,
    (C) the rear wheels lose traction,
    (D) all of the above.

Answers to Let's Review

1. B; 2. D; 3. False; 4. C; 5. C; 6. A; 7. C; 8. False; 9. A; 10. C.

Terms You Need to Know

The following terms have been taken from the contents of Chapter 7. Review them. If you see any you're unsure of, check the definition in the Glossary at the back of the book. If it helps you, keep a written list of the words and their definitions (or write in the definitions here) and review them several days prior to taking the CDL tests.

Backing

Black ice

Bleeding tar

Blind spot

Braking

Braking distance

Brake failure

Bridge icing

Cancelling the turn signal

Clutch pedal

Communicating with others

Coolant

Countersteering

Drop-off

Escape ramp

"Fish-eye" mirror

Front wheel skids

Gear

Gearshift

Glare

Hazard

High beams

Hydraulic brakes

Hydroplaning

Low beams

Night driving

On ramp/off ramp

Oversteering

Perception distance

Radiator shutters

Reaction distance

Rear-wheel skids

Revolutions per minute (rpm)

Selector knob

Shutting down the engine

Skid control

Spotting mirror

Steering

Stopping distance

Tachometer

10 o'clock and 2 o'clock

Tire failure

Total stopping distance

Traction

Turn to the right

Turning space

Visual awareness

Warm up

Weaving

Work zones

THE DISPATCH BOARD
Break Room and Beauty Parlor Horror Stories

Here are some helpful hints to keep your relationship going strong, even when you're out on the road.

It never fails. When a driver goes to work for an over-the-road company, one of the first things a spouse or significant other may hear at the beauty shop is that drivers have so much time on their hands, they tend to be unfaithful.

"I get tearful calls from spouses who've heard these horror stories, sitting in the beauty shop—how their husband is probably fooling around at that very minute," said Melody Bronson, a driver counselor for Stevens Transport. "But faithfulness is a double-edged sword. If a couple has built trust into the relationship, when a driver goes over the road, that trust must continue. It's the trust factor that allows you to believe or discard gossip in the break room or the beauty parlor—and trust is an important glue in any relationship."

Some younger drivers—those married for a short time and with a new baby—think they can handle being gone three to five weeks at a time, but some marriages are just not ready, just not strong enough to handle the challenges that go along with professional driving. "Sometimes these young drivers report their lives are in a whirlwind, that they need help to resolve some of the problems that keep coming up. That's why some carriers make counselors available—to help them smooth out the rough spots—whether it's a personal problem, a payroll or insurance problem, or a conflict with a dispatcher or fleet manager."

Bronson has also worked with trainees who begin their driving careers when their marriages are on the verge of breaking up. "We tell them that driving is a tough job and if they've got a weak relationship, driving probably won't make it better," she said. "And we also tell them that if the trust factor in their marriage has been broken before they start driving, things probably won't get any better."

Aside from the counseling—by phone and in person at Stevens—drivers may also be referred to psychologists at a counseling center that the company works with on a regular basis. And the company store also provides help, such as *Marriage and the Long Run,* a book by Ellen C. Voie for drivers and their spouses that addresses over-the-road issues, such as trust, fidelity, spending time together, and other issues.

And then there's the element of surprise. Too many times a driver has decided to "surprise" his or her family by coming home unexpectedly. And while the driver may enjoy pulling off the surprise, Bronson has seen examples where the "surprise" can backfire. "When the driver comes home just in time to see his or her spouse walking out the door to go bowling or to a movie with friends, the 'surprise' becomes another point of contention," the counselor said, "and the spouse is put into the position of choosing between his or her ongoing life and spending time with the significant other."

The choice is not easy—the consequences of the "surprise" may be more painful than positive. "Surprises—we would counsel a driver to avoid surprises," Bronson said. "It may be a great idea at the time, but too many times it only adds to the stress that's already on the relationship."

The bottom line: When a spouse decides to become a professional driver, this decision involves the entire family. Why? Because when one family member is away from home, the responsibilities of those remaining will definitely change.

Working together, giving as well as taking, and making a team effort to make things work in a relationship is necessary, whatever your career choice. With professional drivers, there must be support at home for their careers to be successful.

8 Safety Control Systems

This chapter is about just what it says—knowing what equipment is included in your vehicle's safety control systems.

After you finish reading this chapter, you will know where these systems are and how they work, plus when to use them.

We'll look at all aspects of the system, so you'll understand why they're there and how they help.

Let's get started.

Lights

FMCSR Part 393 describes the types of lights and reflectors that must be used on commercial motor vehicles. This part of the FMCSR also describes the lights and reflectors needed during every situation—from road operations to tow-away operations.

Lights have numerous purposes:

* To help others see you
* To help you see others
* To signal intentions, such as lane changes, slow down, or stop
* To communicate with other vehicles

Laws require that you have your lights on one-half hour before sunset and continuously to one-half hour after sunrise.

The following are the lights and reflectors required on commercial motor vehicles:

* **Headlights**—two white headlights, one to the right and one to the left, on the front of the tractor. Required on buses, trucks and truck tractors. Headlights must have a high-beam and low-beam setting.
* **Fog lamps and other bad weather lights**—required in addition to, but not instead of, headlights.

Required for buses, trucks, semitrailers, full trailers and pole trailers.

* **Front side marker lamp**—two amber lights, one on each side of the front of buses and trucks, tractors, semitrailers, and full trailers.
* **Side marker lamps**—two amber lights to each side or near the center between the front and rear side marker lamps. Required for buses, trucks, semitrailers, full trailers, and pole trailers.
* **Front side reflectors**—two amber reflectors on each side toward the front of buses and trucks, tractors, semitrailers, full trailers, and pole trailers.

- **Side reflectors**—two amber reflectors on each side or near the midpoint between the front and rear side reflectors of buses and trucks, large semitrailers, large full trailers, and pole trailers.
- **Front turn signals**—two amber signals to the left and right front of the tractor. These signals can be above or below the headlights. Required on buses, trucks, and truck tractors.
- **Front identification lamps**—three amber lights at the center of the vehicle or cab. Required on large buses, trucks, and truck tractors.
- **Front clearance lamps**—two amber lamps at each side of the front of large buses, trucks, truck tractors, large semitrailers, full trailers, pole trailers, and projecting loads.
- **Rear side marker lamps**—one red light on each side of the lower left and lower right rear of the side of buses and trucks, semitrailers and full trailers, and pole trailers.
- **Rear side reflectors**—red reflectors located just below the rear side marker lamps, required on buses, trucks, semitrailers, full trailers, and pole trailers.
- **Rear identification lamps**—three red lights centered in the top rear of large buses and trucks, large semitrailers, full trailers, and pole trailers. Not required on smaller vehicles.
- **Rear clearance lamps**—two red lights at the top right and left of the rear of large trucks and buses, tractors, semitrailers, full trailers, pole trailers, and projecting loads. These lamps outline the overall width. Not required on smaller vehicles.
- **Rear reflectors**—two red reflectors on the lower right and lower left of the rear of small and large buses and truck trailers, full trailers, and pole trailers.
- **Stop lamps**—two red lights, one at the lower right and one at lower left of the rear of the vehicle. All vehicles are required to have these. Not required on projecting loads.
- **License plate lamp**—one white light at center rear on buses, trucks, tractors, semitrailers, full trailers, and pole trailers.
- **Backup lamp**—one white light at rear of buses, trucks, and truck tractors.
- **Rear turn signal lamps**—two amber or red lights, each located at lower right and lower left of the rear of trucks and buses, tractors, semitrailers, full trailers, pole trailers, and converter dollies.
- **Parking lamps**—two amber or white lights located just below the headlights on small buses and trucks.
- **Four-way flashers**—two amber lights at the front and two amber lights or red lights at the rear of vehicle. These are usually the front and rear turn signal lights, equipped to do double duty as warning lights. They can be set to flash simultaneously. Required on buses and trucks, tractors, semitrailers, full trailers, pole trailers, and converter dollies.

Horn

Every vehicle must have a horn and, like the lights, it is used to communicate with other motorists. The horn often distracts or alarms other drivers, so don't use it without a good reason. When you inspect your vehicle, make certain your horn works—if it doesn't, look for a blown fuse or faulty or broken wire.

Mirrors

Most commercial motor vehicles have rear-view mirrors on each side of the cab. A few vehicles may have an outside mirror on the driver's side. A mirror inside the vehicle gives a view of the rear of the rig.

In the large, flat mirror, you should be able to see traffic and the sides of your trailer. You should also be able to see the road behind you from mid-trailer and back.

Adjust mirrors so you can see the ground, starting in front of the trailer wheels and all of both lanes. In the small convex mirror, you should be able to see traffic. Convex mirrors also help you see the "blind spots" along the middle of your vehicle.

Vehicle Fires

All professional drivers have the responsibility of knowing how to put out a vehicle fire. The first priority in this situation is to protect your life and the lives of others. Then try to save the vehicle and its cargo. To accomplish this, you will need to know about fires and have a working fire extinguisher.

Q. What causes vehicle fires?

A. Fires can start after accidents, as a result of a fuel spill, or from the improper use of flares.

There's also the possibility of a tire fire. Underinflated tires and dual tires that touch create enough friction to cause fires.

On some trucks, there's a strong possibility of electrical fires, usually due to short circuits caused by damaged insulation or loose wires.

Carelessness is a major cause of vehicle fires, including behaviors such as smoking around the fuel pump, improper fueling, and loose fuel connections. In addition, fires can be caused by flammable cargo or cargo that is improperly sealed, ventilated, or loaded.

All of these reasons make it very important to make a complete pre-trip inspection of your vehicle's electrical, fuel, and exhaust systems, plus tires and cargo.

Q. Do I need to check all along the way?

A. It's always a good idea to check the tires, wheels, and truck body for signs of heat—whenever you stop during the trip.

Always fuel the vehicle safely and be careful with any part of the vehicle that usually creates heat or flame.

Check gauges and other instruments often while driving. Use mirrors to look for signs of smoke, and if any system is overheating, fix it before you have a bigger problem.

Q. What if there is a fire in or around my vehicle?

A. Keep in mind that caution is most important. Drivers who don't know what to do during a fire have made the situation worse. Don't be one of them!

In case of a fire, follow these steps:

1. Get the vehicle off the road and stop. Park in an open area, away from buildings, trees, brush, and other vehicles. *Don't pull into a service station!*

2. Use your CB or cell phone to notify police, highway patrol, or 911. Be sure to give them your location.
3. Keep the fire from spreading. Before trying to put out the fire, do what you can to keep it from traveling elsewhere.
4. For engine fires, turn off the engine. Don't open the hood if you don't have to. Aim the fire extinguisher through the radiator louvers or from beneath the vehicle.
5. In case of a cargo fire, keep the doors shut! Opening the doors will feed the fire with air from outside.
6. Use water on burning wood, paper, or cloth—but not electrical because you could get shocked. Don't use water on a gasoline fire. It'll feed and spread the flames.
7. A burning tire should be cooled, so you'll need to bathe it with a lot of water. If no water is in the area, throw sand or dirt on the flames.
8. Use the correct kind of fire extinguisher.

Fire Extinguishers

Remember FMCSR Part 393? It talks about carrying a fire extinguisher in your truck—*always*. And it talks about having the extinguisher inspected every two years.

When fighting fires, it is important to know that types of fires are grouped according to class. Fires involving wood, paper, cloth, trash and other ordinary material are Class A fires.

When the fire is fueled by gasoline, grease, oil, paint, or other flammable liquids, the fire is a Class B fire. Electrical fires are Class C fires.

Most trucks carry a five-pound fire extinguisher—it's the law. These can put out Class B and C fires.

If the vehicle is hauling hazardous materials that are placarded, you must have a 10-pound B:C fire extinguisher filled with a dry chemical. When squeezing the handle on this kind of extinguisher, a needle punctures an air pressure cartridge inside the tank, releasing air pressure that forces the powder out of the tank. This powder travels through the hose, out the nozzle, and onto the fire.

In this case, the fire is extinguished by smothering it.

How do you use the extinguisher? You aim it at the base of the fire—that's the problem, not the flames.

If you don't already know, find out how the fire extinguisher works in your truck. When using the extinguisher, stay as far from the fire and flames as possible. Position yourself with your back to the wind.

Continue dousing the fire until whatever is burning has cooled—regardless of whether there's visible smoke or flames. Make sure the fire is completely out so it won't start again.

Instruments and Gauges

Now, this is an easy one. The instrumental panel of a truck is called "the dashboard" or "the dash." Some of the gauges you'll find on the dashboard monitor the operation of the engine. Others monitor other systems, reporting on their conditions at all times.

VOLTMETER

Starting
- Green — Well Charged Battery
- Yellow — Low Battery Charge
- Red — Very Low Charge

Operating
- Green — Okay
- Red — Voltage Output Too High!

AMMETER
- Normal is ZERO
- Continuous High Charge +
  or Discharge –
  Means Problems With
  the Electrical System

Figure 8-1   Gauges used to measure the electrical system.

Besides gauges and warning lights, the dashboard also contains switches and controls that are used to operate the vehicle or its systems. A simple example is the air conditioning. There's a switch and when you move it, it turns on the air-conditioning system.

Starting at the far left on most dashboards, you'll see the air-conditioning vent. Next to it, there are five gauges:

- The voltmeter (Figure 8-1) shows whether or not the battery is charging properly.

    This gauge can be identified by the word "Volts" on the lower portion of the gauge and there may be a picture of the battery.

    There are three segments of this gauge, each showing a different condition. The far left segment (red) shows undercharging. The middle (green) segment shows normal battery condition. The far right hand (red) segment indicates overcharge. A pointer shows the condition of the battery at the moment.

    If the voltmeter shows a continuous undercharging or overcharging condition, there's a problem in the charging system.

- The ammeter (Figure 8-1) may also be located on the dashboard and is used to indicate the amount of charge or discharge the battery is receiving from the generator. It should read "zero" when the engine and the electrical system are off. Starting the engine will move the needle from "zero" to the charge side. Once the engine is on and warm, the needle should drop back to "zero." It is also normal for it to read slightly on the charging side.

- The engine temperature gauge is usually marked "Temp" or "Water Temp." This gauge indicates the temperature of the engine's cooling system in degrees. The typical gauge has a range from 100 to 250 degrees Fahrenheit. Normal temperature is between 165 and 185 degrees Fahrenheit. If you are driving in hot weather, the temperature will read higher, so don't be alarmed.

- The oil pressure gauge (Figure 8-2) indicates how the engine is being lubricated, measured in pounds per square inch (psi).

    When the engine is running and the oil is cold, the gauge will show a high reading. When the engine has been running for awhile and the oil is warmer, the reading will go back to normal. When the engine is running at normal temperatures and the oil is hot, the normal idle pressure runs from five to 15 psi. In normal operation, pressure runs from 30 to 75 psi.

Remember! *Always check this instrument after starting the engine. If no pressure is indicated, stop the engine at once because you can damage the engine by running it with no oil pressure.*

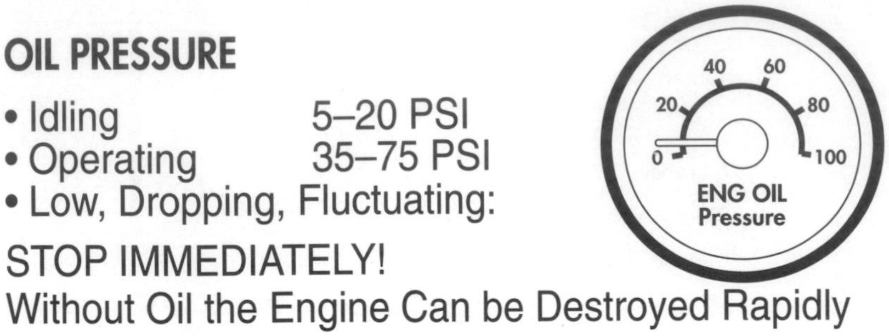

OIL PRESSURE

- Idling   5–20 PSI
- Operating   35–75 PSI
- Low, Dropping, Fluctuating:

STOP IMMEDIATELY!
Without Oil the Engine Can be Destroyed Rapidly

Figure 8-2   Oil pressure gauge.

A low reading may mean that oil level is low. There may be a leak or the filter could be clogged.

If you have an oil temperature gauge, make sure the temperature is within the normal range while you are driving.

- The pyrometer displays the engine exhaust temperature. The safe range will be indicated next to the gauge on the dashboard. High exhaust temperatures could be trouble—a leak or clog in the air intake or the exhaust system. Or there could be problems with the fuel ignition. Or the vehicle could be in the wrong gear ratio for the load, grade, or altitude.

On most dashboards, below these instruments are gauges that indicate the temperature of various parts of the vehicle during operation. These are:

- The transmission temperature gauge—oil temperatures range from 180 to 250 degrees Fahrenheit. These are only guidelines.
- Rear rear axle and forward rear axle temperature gauges—normal temperature range for axles is from 160 to 220 degrees Fahrenheit. These are only guidelines.

The range of some transmissions—like the Fuller Transmission—may be 180 to 225 degrees Fahrenheit. If the temperature gauge on this transmission reads 250 degrees Fahrenheit, you're almost to a critical range. Check the owner's manual to find out what's normal.

Like the engine temperature gauge described above, these gauges display information in degrees. A high reading will tell you there are problems in that particular part of the vehicle. If the temperature is high, stop the vehicle before more damage occurs.

Continuing our tour around the dashboard, the next set of lights are the warning lights:

- Left-hand turn signal (LH)
- Water level warning light (WATER)
- Oil level warning light (OIL)
- High beam (HB)
- Low air light (AIR)
- Differential lock warning lights (DL)
- Right-hand turn signal (RH)
- Cab lock light, not on all trucks, only on tilt-up cabs

There may also be warning buzzers, depending on the vehicle's manufacturer.

This cluster of lights is sometimes called the "telltale" panel because some of these warning lights will tell you if a control's working and some tell you if a gauge or control is not working. Still others tell you there is a big problem that demands your attention *now!*

Q. Are turning indicators really important?

A. Turn signal warning lights come on whenever the right or left turn signal is used. If they don't come on, something's wrong. Either the warning light is defective or the signal is not working. Turn signals are a safety tool for all professional drivers because they let other motorists know what you plan to do. It is illegal to drive without them.

Q. What's happening when the water temperature, oil level, and low air lights come on?

A. That means that something is wrong. If the water temperature in the coolant plant gets too high, the water temperature light will come on. If the oil pressure is too low, the oil pressure light will come on. And if the air pressure in the braking system drops below 60 psi, the low air lights will come on. Some of these warning lights are also equipped with buzzers when something goes wrong.

Q. What do the high beam and differential lock lights do?

A. The high beam light tells you your high beams are on. The differential lock light tells you the differential lock is in the locked position.

Q. What does the charging circuit warning light indicate?

A. This light is standard on some vehicles and not on others. This light comes on if your battery isn't charging. It's usually lit when the starter switch is turned on and tells you the light is working. It goes out as soon as the engine starts—unless there is a problem.

Q. What does the low vacuum warning light indicate?

A. When this light comes on, it means the vacuum in the brake booster is below safety limits and it may be that you are low on braking power. What do you do next? You don't drive the vehicle until the brake problem is checked out and repaired.

On some cabs, there is a cab lock warning light that tells you when the cab tilt lock isn't secure—not a good thing!

Let's Start the Engine

- The cluster lights should come on for a few moments to indicate that they are working properly.
- If a light doesn't come on, check to see whether it is broken or a problem exists.

Q. What's behind the steering wheel?

A. Behind the steering wheel you'll find:

- **Tachometer** (Figure 8-3)—usually called "the tach," shows how many revolutions the engine crankshaft makes per minute (rpm) This tells you when it's time to shift gears. To read engine rpm, multiply the number on the tach by 100. So, if you see 15 on the tach and multiply by 100, you have the rpm—1500.

TACHOMETER

- Measures engine speed in RPMs

- Tells you when to shift

Figure 8-3   The tachometer.

The average diesel engine horsepower goes to a maximum of 2100 rpm. The engine's range may be from 500 rpm at idle to 2100 rpm.

The recommended operating range can be found in the owner's manual.

- **Speedometer/odometer** (Figure 8-4)—the speedometer shows the vehicle's road speed in miles per hour (mph). The odometer (located inside the speedometer) keeps track of the total miles the vehicle has traveled. Mileage is shown in one-tenth of a mile increments.
- **Throttle**—you may want to think of the throttle as the accelerator pedal on the dashboard. You pull it out to set engine speed and you would use the throttle in cold climates to keep the engine warm during idle.
- **Ignition switch**—(or starter) supplies electricity to the engine and other systems. When the key is turned, it turns on the accessory circuits. As soon as the engine starts, release the key. If you have a "false start," let the engine cool for 30 seconds before giving it another try.

The next part of the dashboard contains the fuel gauge, fuel filter gauge, and the air brakes control.

- **Fuel gauge** (Figure 8-5)—shows the fuel level in the fuel supply tanks. Some vehicles have more than one tank—if your vehicle does, be sure to check the fuel level in all tanks before deciding that you're out of fuel.

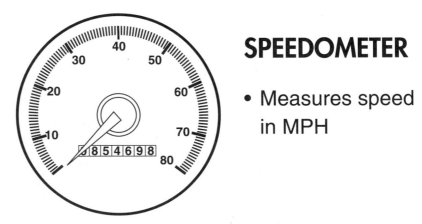

SPEEDOMETER

- Measures speed in MPH

Figure 8-4   The speedometer/odometer.

FUEL GAUGE

- Not always accurate! Inspect the fuel tank

- May have separate gauge for each tank

Figure 8-5 The fuel gauge.

- **Fuel filter gauge**—has a colored band divided into two segments to indicate the condition of the fuel filter. It has numbered markings as well as a white segment on the left, and red segments for the middle and the right. If the needle reads "red," you have a clogged fuel filter.
- **Air brake controls**—if your vehicle is equipped with air brakes. (Information about air brakes is covered in the "air brakes endorsement.")

After this cluster of fuel gauges and indicators, you'll find the light switches. This panel controls all the lights, except the dimmer switch for the high beams (which is on the floor and is operated by your foot).

Some vehicles display their light switches on a stalk to the left of the steering wheel. You may find your switches here, including the dimmer switch, turn signals, and flashers.

Below the light switches, you'll find other controls:

- **Inter-axle differential controls**—for vehicles with dual rear axles that have inter-axle differentials. In the unlocked position, these controls allow each axle shaft to turn at different speeds. The control should be set at "Unlocked" or "Off" unless the road is slippery. For these conditions, set the control to "Locked" or "On" to supply power to all wheels.
- **Windshield wipers**—on tilt cabs, electric wipers have two controls—one for each wiper. Some air wiper systems use one control knob, located on the dash, for both wipers. The position of the knob controls wiper speed and there is a separate control for the windshield washers.
- **Air-conditioning controls**—air speed controls determine the temperature in the cab, usually with low, medium, and high settings. There are controls for heating, cooling, and defrosting—much like automobiles.
- **Cold start and warm-up switch**—this switch is used in cold weather when the engine is hard to start. The switch will light to tell you it is on—but check the operator's manual for the engine and starting aid on your vehicle.
- **Exhaust brake switch**—if your vehicle has one, turn the exhaust brake switch "On." This provides extra slowing power, which comes in handy for steep downgrades or when you're pulling an extra-heavy load.

We're not quite through talking about the cab controls. If you will turn your attention to the floor, you'll find:

- **The accelerator pedal**—located just under the steering wheel, you can operate this pedal with your right foot to control engine speed. When you push this pedal, the vehicle will speed up. As you let your foot off, the vehicle slows down.

- **The brake pedal**—just to the left of the accelerator and also operated with your right foot. When you press down on the pedal, the brakes are applied and the vehicle slows down.
- **The clutch pedal**—located to the left of the brake pedal, the clutch pedal is operated with your left foot. You press the clutch pedal to disengage the clutch and when you release the pedal, you engage the clutch.
- **The dimmer switch**—located on the floor to the left of the brake pedal (if it isn't on the dashboard). This switch allows you to move headlights from low beams to high beams. Low beams are best when driving in traffic. High beams help on dark, open roads where there is little traffic and no street lights.
- **The transmission control lever**—some vehicles have a power take-off lever (PTO), which is really two knobs. Pull up on the first knob—it connects the PTO to the transmission. Pull up on the second knob to use the PTO.
- **The trailer brake hand-control valve**—usually found on the steering column and allows you to apply the trailer's service brakes without applying the tractor's service brakes.

FMCSR Part 383

This part tells you that you must be able to do a certain amount of mechanical troubleshooting while driving a truck. The gauges and instruments may indicate a problem. You must know how to read them and what needs to be done when a light comes on, indicating a problem. This is called "problem-solving" and much of your skill at troubleshooting will come with time and with experience.

To give you a foundation for troubleshooting, it is important that you understand what the major systems do when the truck is running. This review will also help you get ready for the CDL tests.

> **Q. How do I show that I can "troubleshoot" when I take the CDL?**
> **A.** One of the first ways is when the examiner asks questions about vehicle parts and systems as you are doing the pre-trip inspection. You must know what makes each system work and show knowledge about repairing small problems, should they arise.

The systems and parts you will cover over the next few pages are also listed in the FMCSR Part 393. To learn about systems and parts:

- Read FMCSR Part 393
- Read the owner's manual for your truck. If you can't find one, perhaps you can obtain a copy from the truck dealership nearest you or you may find information on the Internet.
- If you have specific questions, ask the carrier's maintenance personnel.
- You may also find books in the bookstore or at the library on diesel mechanics, electricity, hydraulics, motor vehicles, and other related topics.

Wiring and Electrical Systems

Let's start at the beginning.

Your commercial motor vehicle gets its power from an engine, and that power is electrical power.

Without electricity, you couldn't start your engine, you couldn't run your lights, and your instruments and gauges wouldn't work—so electricity is important to understand because it serves many purposes.

Here are some of the basics:

1. An electron is a tiny particle carrying a negative charge of electricity.
2. Electrical flow produces electrical current—and some materials carry this electrical current to its purpose better than others.
3. A good electricity conductor is a material whose electrons can be easily moved. Copper wire is such a conductor and it is frequently used to move electrical charge from its source to its point of use. Because rubber is not a good conductor of electrical current, copper wire is usually surrounded with rubber insulation.
4. Insulated wires bring electrical current where electricity is needed.
5. Terminals are the connecting devices between the electrical wires and the part where electricity is needed. Terminals connect wires to the components.
6. There is also a main terminal where the wires start. This same main terminal contains the system circuit breakers and fuses.

Q. **What is a "closed" or "continuous" circuit?**

A. A circuit is a continuous path made up of a conductor (wire) and a source of power that moves the current around the circuit (batteries and alternator or generator).

The components that use electricity (the vehicle's starter and lights, for example) are a part of the path. This type of circuit is called a "complete" or "closed" circuit, because the current can flow only if all parts of the circuit are grounded.

What we're saying here is that there must be a wire (conductor) to bring the electrons back to where they started.

There are two kinds of circuits where electricity will not flow:

- **Open circuit**—occurs when the normal flow of electrical current is stopped. One of the reasons for this stoppage could be corroded connections or broken wires.
- **Short circuit**—occurs when electrical current bypasses part of the normal circuit. So instead of going to the light bulb, for example, the current stops before it gets to the bulb and flows back to the source (the battery). This happens because the insulation has come off a section of wire and it touches another wire, allowing the electrical current to take the shortest route back to the source of power.

The following conditions may cause a short circuit:

- The wires on an electrical coil lose their insulation and touch each other.
- A wire rubs against the frame or other metal part of the vehicle until that bare wire touches another piece of metal.

This should encourage us all to take a close look at the wiring for rubbing or fraying or breaks each time we do a pre-trip inspection! Replace broken wires and any insulation that is worn.

Regulations require that wiring be installed and insulated so shorts won't occur.

Q. What does grounding mean?
A. A grounding circuit works for your safety:

- When electrical wires burn or break, the normal path or circuit is broken. But instead of stopping, the current looks for a way to complete the trip. If you saw the broken wires and picked them up with both hands, your body would complete the circuit, and that wouldn't be good.
- If wires had rubbed to the point that the insulation was worn off and a short circuit occurred, and the wire was touching the metal of the vehicle's frame, if you touched the frame, you would again become part of the circuit—and strong current could kill you.

A ground provides an alternate safe path for the current if the normal path is accidentally broken.

Batteries

These little black boxes work very hard, converting chemical energy into electrical energy. Once this is done, they supply power to the rest of the vehicle's electrical system.

The parts of the battery include:

- **The case**—to neatly hold all the parts together.
- **The vent caps**—located on top of the battery. They allow gas build-up to escape. Remove the vent caps to check the battery—you may find them clogged and in need of cleaning from time to time.
- **Individual cells**—there are dry-charged, wet-charged, and maintenance-free batteries. A dry-charged battery has no fluids in it when it leaves the factory and the dealer adds water to the battery when it is sold. A wet-charged battery has fluid in it when it leaves the factory. These two types must be checked for fluid levels when you do a pre-trip inspection. Maintenance-free batteries require no additional liquid.
- **Cell connectors**—these transport the electricity from the cell to the power supply.
- **Two terminal posts**—located on top of the battery. There is a positive post (the larger one) and a negative post.

Electricity can be dangerous if you do not exercise extreme caution when you are working around it.

Here are some tips for working around batteries safely:

- Disconnect the battery ground strap before you begin any electrical or engine work.

- Connect the ground strap last when you install a new battery.
- Never lay metal tools or other objects on the battery.
- Never hook up the battery backwards—make sure to connect the positive cable to the positive terminal post. Connect the negative cable to the negative post. (The positive cable clamp and terminal usually are larger than the negative cable clamp and terminal.)
- Be careful when handling batteries. Battery acid is corrosive.
- Don't lean too closely to the battery when adding water—any splash could get into your eyes.
- Keep fires away from batteries. If you're a smoker, save your cigarette until after you've finished working under the hood.

Circuit Breakers and Fuses

To protect the circuit from short circuits and current overloads, circuit breakers and fuses are built-in protection.

- A current overload happens when a circuit gets more current than it can handle.
- Wires are rated according to how much load they can handle. If they become overloaded, they may burn.

A short circuit usually causes the overload. When you turn on the lights, the radio, and the starter, the flow of the electricity actually slows down. If there is a short circuit, these systems won't work. This means the current coming in the wire is more than the wire can handle, so it overheats and burns. Fuses and circuit breakers prevent this from happening.

Q. How do fuses work?
A. Like wires, fuses are rated on their ability to handle a quantity of current. To protect the circuit, use a fuse that's rated lower than the wiring.

When an overload happens, if it is larger than the fuse's rating, the fuse will blow before the current builds to the point of damaging the wire.

Q. What do I do if a fuse blows?
A. You may think the answer is obvious, but some people don't know that the fuse must be replaced before the circuit can be completed again. But if an overload has occurred, you also need to find the cause of the overload, or you'll immediately blow another fuse.

Circuit breakers are also rated by their capacity to carry current. The circuit breaker used in a circuit must match the circuit's current capacity.

Q. Does a circuit breaker work like a fuse?
A. If there's an overload of current in the circuit, the circuit breaker opens so current won't build up and burn the circuit. Once the circuit breaker has opened, it has to be reset before it operates again—this is a good time to figure out what overloaded the circuit in the first place.

One More Important Electrical Part

The detachable electrical connection—working in combination between the tractor and the trailer—supplies power from the tractor's power plant to the trailer, where it powers the trailer's lights.

Straight trucks don't have detachable electrical connections.

The Electrical System

The last several paragraphs have been devoted to wires, circuit breakers, fuses, terminals and current-using parts that create the circuits in a commercial motor vehicle.

One main terminal block contains all the circuit breakers and fuses—and from this terminal block, wires run to connectors, where they split and go to other connectors or other parts of the vehicle that require electricity.

Most CMVs contain a basic 12-volt electrical system. And if you look closely, you'll see many of the same parts you would find in your personal vehicle. All depend on the battery for electrical power—to start the engine and for other functions.

Once the engine starts, the alternator or generator supplies the power that keeps the battery charged and runs the truck's systems. Older vehicles rely on generators, whereas newer vehicles rely on alternators.

A belt from the engine's crankshaft drives the generator when the engine is running. That generator is then responsible for producing electricity to run all other electrical circuits—and at the same time, keep the battery charged.

When the engine is turned off, the stored energy in the battery provides the electrical "juice" to run the horn, lights, and other instruments.

The alternator does the same job that the generator is responsible for doing, but alternators are lighter, cheaper to build, and produce more current at low speeds.

Brakes

Even a novice mechanic knows the brakes stop the vehicle. The engine makes it go, the brakes make it stop, right?

Q. What makes the brakes work?

A. Friction. In drum brakes, the brake shoes move toward the brake drums. The shoes have a lining or pad of coarse material, and when this is pushed into the drum, it creates friction—which stops the truck.

In another kind of brakes—disc brakes—the friction pad moves toward a metal disc. When these parts connect, friction results—and the vehicle stops.

The amount of pressure applied to the brakes creates the amount of force the shoes apply to the drum. In your personal vehicle, if you stomp on the brakes with a lot of force, the vehicle stops quickly. If you just tap the brakes and allow the vehicle to slow to a stop, this light, smooth technique stops the car more slowly.

Q. What about the brakes needed to stop a truck?

A. On larger commercial motor vehicles, the brake shoes and linings are pushed toward the drum or disc, thanks to pressure—which can be one of three types:

- **Hydraulic pressure**—usually on straight trucks and buses; hydraulic brakes use fluid pressure.
- **Vacuum pressure**—vacuum brakes have a cylinder with a moving piston, much like hydraulic brakes. In vacuum brakes, atmospheric pressure is on one side and the vacuum is on the other. The pressure of the atmosphere trying to fill the vacuum pushes the piston into the vacuum.
- **Air pressure**—see Chapter 10 on air brakes.

Q. How do hydraulic brakes work?

A. As mentioned earlier, hydraulic brakes use fluid pressure. There are three other facts about fluids you also need to know:

1. Fluids flow—it's their nature. If they're not allowed to flow, they create pressure—like a volcano.
2. Oil is a fluid that cannot be compressed or squeezed to be made smaller.
3. In a closed system, the pressure on the fluid inside that system is equal in every part of the system.

These facts explain how the pressure you put on the brake to stop the truck can be transmitted to the brakes located on the wheels.

If there are breaks or leaks in the system, the fluid pressure varies all over the system and your brakes fail. But more frequently, if there's no fluid, there is nothing to transmit the pressure when the driver puts a foot on the brake.

Remember the emphasis placed on checking for leaks, breaks, cracks, or other damage. This is one of the main reasons why pre-trip and post-trip inspections are so important!

Q. What if my vehicle has vacuum brakes . . . how do they work?

A. The vacuum contains a control valve with four chambers. One chamber contains atmospheric air. The second combines atmospheric air and a vacuum to create different levels of pressure. The third has a vacuum. The fourth contains hydraulic fluid.

When the driver puts on the brakes by pressing the pedal, hydraulic pressure from the master cylinder closes the vacuum valve and opens the atmospheric valve. Then, the atmospheric air enters the mixing chamber and the result is lowered pressure—which closes the atmospheric valve. But it can be re-opened by stepping on the brake pedal again.

When you let up on the brake pedal, you open the vacuum valve. So, pressing and releasing the brake pedal changes air pressure in the mixing chamber.

Pressure from the master hydraulic cylinder also affects the vacuum cylinder and pushes the piston forward—which pushes the hydraulic fluid beyond it into the brake lines.

Then, pressure from the control valve will add to or boost the pressure from the master cylinder. In this situation, pressure from the main hydraulic braking system and the vacuum booster works to apply the brakes. In fact, with a vacuum booster, the effort to stop the vehicle is reduced by 30 to 70 percent.

Q. Where does the vacuum come from?

A. It comes from the engine's intake manifold. But diesel engines do not operate in the same manner. They don't create a vacuum on their intake strokes. Therefore, when the engine doesn't produce a vacuum, a pump creates one.

However, if there's a break or crack in the vacuum lines, nothing works. Why? Because the break or crack in the line will allow the vacuum to leak out. No vacuum—no brakes!

Parking Brakes

This part is not rocket science. The parking brakes are used when you park. All commercial motor vehicles manufactured after 1989 are required to have parking brakes.

Q. How do I apply the parking brakes?

A. It's pretty straightforward. Simply pull the parking brake control. All braking systems use this kind of control, but on some vehicles, pulling a lever or knob controls the cable that pulls the parking brakes into position.

To release the brakes: Push the control back in. When you push in the knob, that releases the cable and the brakes. In most trucks, it takes a little effort to pull the brakes on—sort of like the parking brake in your personal vehicle. It takes an extra pull to set the parking brakes.

On some vehicles, setting the parking brakes requires more strength than the average driver may have—and that's when the parking brake mechanism is set with the help of air pressure. See Chapter 10 on air brakes.

FMCSR Part 393 requires that you be able to set and release the manual parking brake as often as needed.

Fuel Systems

Almost all fuel systems are alike and have similar parts:

- **The fuel tank** holds the fuel.
- **The primary and secondary fuel filters** clean the fuel before it reaches the fuel pump.
- **The fuel pump** delivers the fuel to the engine.
- **The fuel lines** carry the fuel from the pump to the cylinders.
- **The fuel injectors** spray the fuel into the combustion chambers.

Fuel is highly flammable and must be handled with care in all situations. Like the engineers going out to the site of the oil rig or pump jack, once they step out of their trucks, they are on alert—not careless, always cautious. You should conduct yourself the same way around any form of fuel.

Fuel lines must not come in contact with hot surfaces. They must be supported and not allowed to drag on the ground.

While driving, remember that the fuel lines should be protected from debris on the highway, but there should be enough slack in the lines so they won't break as the vehicle moves. Also, check to make sure the fuel tanks are mounted and secure.

Look for leaks when you do your pre-trip and mid-trip inspections. A leaking fuel system wastes precious and costly fuel, but it can also be a hazard. Dripping fuel on a hot surface could cause it to ignite.

Coupling and Towing Devices

FMCSR Part 393 provides full details of the requirements for commercial motor vehicles used to tow other vehicles. According to these federal regulations, there are two main methods for towing vehicles: (1) when the tractor is pulling the trailer, and (2) when a tractor or other towing vehicle is being towed as cargo—called a tow-away operation.

The following are brief descriptions of parts used to pull trailers.

Fifth Wheel

Some people know the term *fifth wheel* because it is used to describe a recreational vehicle with four wheels that hitches in the back of a pick-up (which serves as the "fifth wheel" for the trailer). In commercial motor vehicles, the fifth wheel is a device that allows the trailer to be connected or uncoupled from the tractor (Figure 8-6). It's mounted on the rear of the tractor frame with brackets and fasteners. The lower half of the fifth wheel (called the mounting assembly) must be kept free of bent parts or loose bolts.

The fifth wheel controls how much weight is distributed on each axle of the tractor. If weight distribution is not equal, it can impact steering and can also cause tires to wear unevenly.

Figure 8-6   The fifth wheel.
(Photo courtesy of ATA Associates, Inc.)

Fifth wheels can also be found on converter dollies as well as tractor frames. A converter dolly converts a semitrailer to a full trailer—which is how it got its name.

Locking Device

The fifth wheel has a locking device that keeps the towed trailer and towing tractor together until you're ready to uncouple them. This locking device is called the "locking jaws" and it locks around the shaft of the trailer's kingpin. This makes the connection secure for the trip.

Tow Bars

Trailers must have tow bars—and there must be locking devices on the towing vehicles. This is how two trailers coupled with a converter dolly are kept from separating. Aside from tow bars, safety chains, or a cable with the tow bar connection to the towing vehicle are also used.

Saddle Mounts

A saddle mount is a steel assembly that couples a towed vehicle (trailer or semitrailer) with the towing vehicle. The saddle mount has a kingpin that fits into the locking jaws of the fifth wheel of the vehicle towing the trailer. Then, a set of U-bolts or clamps secures the coupling to the front axle of the trailer.

Tires

Although they're often taken for granted, tires are an essential part of the rig because they provide traction, reduce vibration, and absorb shock.

Q. **How important is it to have good tires?**
A. First of all, they have to be good enough to provide traction—in all kinds of weather. But they also have to be able to transfer braking and driving force to the road.

As you know, today's market offers numerous different tire designs. But the fact is, all tires are made about the same. All tires have:

- **Plies**—separate layers of rubber-cushioned cord. Plies make up the body of the tire and are tied into bundles of wire called bead coils.

    Plies can be bias, belted bias, or radial. **Bias plies** (Figure 8-7) are placed at a criss-crossed angle. This makes the sidewall and the tread very rigid. **Belted bias plies** (Figure 8-8) cross at an angle and there's an added layered belt of fabric between the plies and the tread. Belts make the tread more rigid than on bias ply tires and the tread will last longer. Why? Because the belts reduce tread motion when the tire is rolling. **Radial** tires (Figure 8-9) have plies that do not cross at an angle but are laid from bead to bead, across the tire. Radial tires have a number of belts and their construction means the sidewalls have less flex and less friction—which

BIAS PLY
Body Cords Run
Diagonally Across the
Tread.

Figure 8-7 Bias ply.

BELTED BIAS
Body Cords Run
Diagonally Across the
Tread. Bolt Plies Run
Circumferentially
Around the Tire Under
the Tread.

Figure 8-8 Belted bias ply.

RADIAL
Body Cords Run
Perpendicular Across
the Tread. Belt Plies Run
Circumferentially
Around the Tire Under
the Tread.

Figure 8-9 Radial ply.

requires less horsepower and saves fuel. Plus, radial tires also hold the road, resist skidding, and give a smoother ride than the bias types.

- **Bead coils and beads**—bead coils form the bead—the part of the tire that fits into the rim. Bead coils provide the hoop strength for the bead sections, so the tire will hold its shape when being mounted on a wheel.
- **Sidewalls**—layers of rubber covering that connect the bead to the tread. Sidewalls also protect the plies.
- **Tread**—the part of the tire that hits the road. Treads are designed for specific jobs, such as extra traction and high speed. Tires on steering axles should be able to roll and provide good traction. Drive tires must provide good traction for braking and acceleration. Tires for trailers should roll well. Drive wheel position tires need maximum traction—in all conditions.
- **Inner liner**—the sealing material that keeps air in the tire.

Q. What should I know about tire size?

A. Tire size is usually shown by a number or a series design designation on the sidewall of the tires. For example, in the number 10.00 × 22, the first number is the tire's width. This means an inflated tire of this size will measure 10 inches from the farthest point outside on one sidewall to the farthest point outside the other sidewall.

The second number is the rim size. In 10.00 × 22, the tire will fit a 22-inch-diameter rim.

The series design designation came about because of the low-profile tire—a tire wider than its height. These tires are measured in millimeters rather than inches.

If the sidewall reads 295/75 R 22.5, it means (1) the section width is 295 millimeters, (2) the aspect ratio (height compared with width) is 75, (3) the "R" tells the type of tire—a radial, and (4) the rim is 22.5 inches in diameter.

Government regulations require tire manufacturers to label all tires with several items of information. Some of these items include: (1) the brand, (2) the manufacturer, (3) the load rating, and (4) the maximum load pressure.

Load rating refers to the strength of the tire. This can be rated from A to Z—with Z being the strongest. The maximum load rating is shown in pounds.

FMCSR Part 393 does not permit the use of a tire that cannot support the load, and the load rating makes certain you have the right tire for the job.

Maximum pressure is designated in pounds per square inch (psi). This measurement is given for cold tires that have been driven less than one mile. This is why you should check tire pressure *before* you drive—and don't check tire pressure by kicking them! Tires have come a long way since your great-grandpa's day, when kicking actually told you something.

Use a tire gauge instead. And measure tread depth with the proper instrument, not your fingernail.

FMCSR Part 393 provides information about the legal minimum tread depth on a tire. According to this portion of the law, a motor vehicle cannot use tires that:

- Have fabric exposed through tread or sidewalls.
- Have less than $\frac{4}{32}$ of an inch of tread measured at any point in a major tread groove on the front axle.
- Have less than $\frac{2}{32}$ of an inch of tread measured at any point in a major tread groove on all other axles.
- Have front tires that have been regrooved, if tires have load capacity equal to or greater than an 8.25-20 eight-ply tire.

Regrooved tires are not allowed in most states. Be aware of any local regulations regarding these tires.

A few more tire terms will help you do a good job each time you do a pre-trip inspection.

When measuring depth of tread, don't measure at the tie bar, hump or fillet. The best place to measure is on a major tread groove. Use a tread depth gauge or a Lincoln penny. To use the penny, insert it in the groove with Lincoln's head upside down. The edge of the penny should touch the body of the tire and the tread should come to the top of Lincoln's head—or $\frac{2}{32}$ of an inch. To measure $\frac{4}{32}$ of an inch, the tread depth should reach Lincoln's eyebrow.

The hump is a pattern of tire wear that has the same appearance as a cupped hand—the hump is at the edge or higher part of the cup.

Tie bars and fillets are design factors—not wear patterns. So is a sipe—which is a cut across the tread to improve traction.

You may use regrooved tires, recaps and retreads on drive wheels and trailer wheels. They *cannot* be used on steering—or front—wheels on most trucks or tractors.

Note: If you've just had a tire changed, stop after you've driven it for awhile and make sure nuts have not loosened.

Wheels and Rims, Hubs and Lugs

Tires are mounted on wheels and the wheel connects the tire to the axle. There are spoke wheels and disc wheels.

> **Q. What's the main difference between spoke wheels and disc wheels?**
> **A.** Spoke wheels clamp onto wheels with wheel clamps and if these are not installed properly, the wheel will soon be out of round. That means it will wobble when it rolls.
>
> On a disc wheel, the rim and center portions are a single piece. The rim is part of the wheel and the wheel is bolted to the assembly for the hub and brake drum. With a disc wheel, there is less chance for the wheel to be out of round.

> **Q. What purpose does the rim serve?**
> **A.** The rim supports the tire bead and supports the lower sidewall.
>
> When inspecting this area, make certain that the wheel and the rim are not damaged—cracked or broken—in any way. A cracked or broken wheel or rim can cause an accident. If a rim is damaged, there's a chance the tire could lose pressure or even come off.
>
> The bolt holes and the studs should be perfectly round. If they're egg-shaped, they are out of round and are signs of defects.
>
> All nuts and bolts should be in place, tightened, and free of rust. Use a wrench to check tightness. Never use your hands—it's not a good test.
>
> Missing clamps, spacers, studs, and lugs could cause problems. So could mismatched, bent, or cracked lock rings—they're dangerous, too.
>
> When inspecting, if you see evidence that wheels or rims have been welded in the past, note these welds as defects.
>
> One more thing to check on the tires and wheels—make sure there are no leaks around the hubs and make sure the hubs have a good supply of oil. You can check the oil level mark on the window of the hubcap.

Suspension System

What You Need to Know

Every wheeled vehicle's weight is supported by the suspension system. You are probably familiar with the suspension system—struts and shocks—in personal vehicles. It keeps the ride, smooth, right?

The same applies in a commercial motor vehicle. The suspension system prevents the frame of the vehicle from riding right on the axles and it provides a smoother ride for the driver and the cargo.

Ask old-timers about the early suspension systems and they'll complain for hours. Today's suspension systems are better designed to absorb road shocks and protect the driver and the load.

Today's suspension systems come in four major types:

- **Leaf spring**—in this design, layers of pliable metal are bolted together and the axle is located on the middle of the spring. The front and rear of the spring are attached to the frame.

- **Coil spring**—a spiral of heavy-duty metal is placed at each wheel and the top of the spiral is attached to the frame. The bottom is indirectly connected onto each wheel.
- **Torsion bar**—made of heavy-duty metal that returns to its original shape after it has been twisted, torsion bars absorb shock by twisting. On the highway, the metal contracts, extends, or twists in response to the various levels of the road. The torsion bar allows the wheel to move in and out of low places and over high places while the frame remains stable and level.
- **Air bag**—made of rubber fabric and supplied with compressed air. The supply of air allows the bag to expand or shrink—much like springs contract and expand in response to road shocks.

Q. What do shock absorbers do?

A. They are attached to the springs and are partially filled with hydraulic fluid. When the piston moves up and down in the cylinder as the spring moves over high and low places, the shock absorber minimizes the spring's motion that's eventually transmitted to the driver.

To maintain the suspension system, keep the springs in good condition, because any cracks, rust, breaks, or other damage often reduce the driver's ability to control the vehicle.

If you have an air bag suspension system—watch for leaks and valve problems. You should also know that the braking system should get charged with air before the air bag suspension system—and the braking system must have at least 55 psi before the air pressure valve on the air bag lets air in. The air bags should also fill all the way around or the vehicle will not be level.

Note: There should be no air leakage more than three psi over five minutes when the vehicle's air pressure gauge reads "normal." If there's more than three psi over five minutes, get the system fixed before going on the road.

Steering

Most people think that a professional driver is a good driver if he or she can steer the rig down the road within the lane markings. But there's so much more skill to driving than this . . . as you're learning.

A good driver understands the steering mechanism of his or her truck, the parts of the mechanism, and how it all works.

The steering system allows the driver to make the necessary maneuvers to move the truck from Point A to Point B. That may include turning corners, moving around barriers, and entering and exiting highway ramps—without slipping, sliding, or rolling over.

The steering system begins with the steering wheel—the hand control of the wheels connected to the steering axle. Between the steering wheel and the steering axle are the parts that make steering possible.

Let's begin at the beginning:

1. The **steering wheel** is connected to the **steering column** with a nut. The steering wheel translates the driver's movements to the steering system. When the steering wheel turns, the steering column turns in the same direction.

2. This motion continues through the **U-joint** to the **steering gear shaft**. From there, the driver's motion continues through another U-joint to the steering gear box.

3. The **steering gear box** is also called the "**steering sector**." It changes the rotating motion of the steering column to a back-and-forth motion on the Pitman arm.

4. The **Pitman arm** is a lever attached to the steering gear box and a **drag link** joins the Pitman arm and the steering lever.

5. The **steering lever** is the first part of the **steering (or front) axle** and it performs two separate jobs—it carries a load and it steers the vehicle.

6. The steering lever turns the front wheels left and right when the Pitman arm pulls it back and forth.

7. The steering lever connects to the **steering knuckle** (the moveable connection between the axle and the wheel that allows the wheels to turn left or right).

   There is a **steering knuckle** at the end of each axle. They contain the **seals**, **bushings**, and **bearings** that support the vehicle's weight.

8. The steering knuckles translate the motion from the driver to the **cross-steering lever** and the **cross-steering tube** (the tie rod).

9. **Spindles**, which are parts of the **steering axle knuckles**, are inserted through the wheels. Spindles are also called **stub axles** and are attached to the kingpin.

10. The **tie-rod** holds both wheels in the same position. As the left wheel turns, the right wheel follows in the same direction. A **kingpin** in the steering knuckle gives each wheel its own pivot point.

A vehicle with a power steering system uses hydraulic pressure or air pressure to assist in making the turn—this requires less strength on the part of the driver.

When hydraulic pressure assists steering a vehicle, a hydraulic unit replaces the steering gear box and a hydraulic pump is added to the engine to supply the pressure used to help turn the wheels.

With hydraulic pressure to help turn the wheels, when the steering wheel is turned to the right, the hydraulic valve senses it, opens, and fluid pressure helps turn the wheels to the right.

Okay, time to take a few deep breaths.

You've just completed reviewing the major systems found in most commercial motor vehicles—the wiring and electrical systems, braking systems, fuel systems, coupling devices, tires, emergency equipment, body components, suspension, and steering.

Each of these systems and all of this equipment have been deemed "necessary for safe operation" of a commercial motor vehicle, according to the Federal Motor Carrier Safety Regulations.

When you take the CDL test, the examiner may ask you questions about any or all of these systems.

He or she may ask you to identify the parts on your truck. You may be asked to tell how they work.

You will be expected to recognize defects and tell how they impact safe operations.

We suggest you go back over the information in this chapter in a few days. Give it time to settle in, go over the diagrams. Read over the areas that are least familiar to you.

Review the test questions a couple of times—or make up some of your own. The point: This chapter is *important*. The more familiar you are with this information—and the vehicle you'll use for the test—the better your score will be!

Let's Review

Read each question and all of the answers provided. Place the letter of the correct answer in the space provided or write your answers on a separate piece of paper so you can use these questions again as you review for the CDL. Once you have answered all the questions, simply refer to the answer key that follows and check your work.

_____ 1. True or False. Fog lights and other bad weather lights are not required by FMCSR standards.

_____ 2. A major cause of truck fires is
   (A) carelessness,   (C) dirty headlights,
   (B) mechanical malfunction,   (D) misfiring pistons.

_____ 3. In the case of a cargo fire,
   (A) open the hood,   (C) open the cargo doors,
   (B) open the cab doors,   (D) none of the above.

_____ 4. True or False. Some trucks have more than one fuel tank.

_____ 5. Electricity is the power source used to
   (A) start the truck's engine,   (C) operate instruments and gauges,
   (B) light the vehicle,   (D) all of the above.

_____ 6. Battery cell connectors
   (A) cause ignition to occur,
   (B) transport electricity from the cell to the power supply,
   (C) transport voltage from the power supply to the cell,
   (D) all of the above.

_____ 7. The "fifth wheel" controls
   (A) how fast the truck can travel,
   (B) how much weight is distributed on each axle of the trailer,
   (C) skidding,
   (D) all of the above.

_____ 8. During a pre-trip inspection, if you see evidence of welding used to repair a wheel or a rim,
   (A) make a note of your pre-trip check list,
   (B) consider welds a defect,
   (C) report welds to the maintenance department,
   (D) all of the above.

_____ 9. Every wheeled vehicle's weight is supported by
   (A) the suspension system,   (C) the fifth wheel,
   (B) the tractor front wheels,   (D) all of the above.

_____10. Shock absorbers
   (A) absorb extra oil from the wheel hubs,
   (B) absorb jolts from uneven or rough roads,
   (C) absorb the weight of the cargo,
   (D) none of the above.

Answers to Let's Review

1. False; 2. A; 3. D; 4. True; 5. D; 6. B; 7. B; 8. D; 9. A; 10. B.

Terms You Need to Know

The following terms have been taken from the contents of Chapter 8. Review them. If you see any you're unsure of, check the definition in the Glossary at the back of the book. If it helps you, keep a written list of the words and their definitions (or write in the definitions here) and review them several days prior to taking the CDL tests.

Accelerator

Air bag suspension

Alternator

Amperage

Backup lamp

Battery

Belted bias

Bias

Brake pedal

Closed circuit

Clutch pedal

Coil spring suspension

Cold start and warm-up switch

Converter dolly

Coupling devices

Dashboard

Dimmer switch

Electron

Engine temperature gauge

Fifth wheel

Fire extinguisher

Flammable cargo

Four-way flashers

Front clearance lamps

Front identification lamps

Front side marker lamp

Front side reflectors

Front turn signals

Fuel injectors

Fuel lines

Fuel pump

Fuel tank

Generator

Grounding

Headlights

Horn

Hydraulic brakes

Ignition switch

Insulation

Kingpin

Leaf spring suspension

License plate lamp

Lights

Load rating

Locking device

Locking jaws

Mirrors

Odometer

Oil temperature gauge

Parking brakes

Parking lamps

Pitman arm

Plies

Power take-off (PTO) lever

Pyrometer

Radial

Rear clearance lamps

Rear identification lamps

Rear reflectors

Rear side marker lamps

Rear side reflectors

Rear tail lamps

Rear turn signal lamps

Saddle mounts

Shaft of the kingpin

Side marker lamps

Side reflectors

Speedometer

Spindles

Steering axle

Steering column

Steering gear box

Steering gear shaft

Steering lever

Steering wheel

Steering wheel knuckles

Stop lamps

Tachometer

Throttle

Tie-rod

Tires

Torsion bar suspension

Tow-away operation

Tow bars

Transmission control lever

Tread

U-bolts

Vacuum brakes

Voltmeter

THE DISPATCH BOARD
Beware of Bullies—On and Off the Road

Everyone remembers the boys and girls in grade school who were loud, hateful, and focused on making life miserable for you or your friends. Their main talent was finding your "soft spot" and then digging in with both barrels.

And as you've worked in your adult life, you have spotted some of these same bullies on the job—because, sadly, there are bullies in the workplace. They are older, they dress in uniforms or business suits, but they are just as mean, just as manipulative, and just as hateful as those younger bullies on the playground.

In the workplace, bullies work on their victims quietly, sometimes through racial or sexual harassment or sometimes by working to make people feel inadequate, inferior, and worthless. Victims of bullying often feel guilty and don't think they are of much value to the company.

A study reported by Wayne State University found that 21.5 percent of the American workforce had been bullied in one way or another in the past year. That means nearly one-fourth of American workers are bullied by someone on the job.

What is a bully? A bully is an individual who persistently snaps at fellow employees, is abusive, and works to intimidate anyone he or she feels is weak or vulnerable. Bullies want their victims to feel upset, humiliated, and threatened . . . all the time.

Bullies cause inefficiency in the workplace and, according to studies, make up 1 percent of the population.

In the workplace bullies will:
- Blame co-workers when errors are found
- Criticize the work of others
- Enforce rules only when it helps them or hurts others
- Exclude the weak and vulnerable from activities
- Communicate through yelling or screaming
- Downplay the accomplishments of others
- Take credit for the efforts of others
- Insult people in front of others, put down fellow employees, and threaten job loss

The Wayne State University study found that about 70 percent of all bullies are men, but the remaining 30 percent who are women usually target other women. The most surprising statistic is that 82 percent of all bullies are bosses.

Here's another fact worth mentioning: 52 percent of all bully victims spent company time worrying rather than working and 28 percent of these victims admitted they actually missed work because of a bully. One in five admitted their quality of work went down and almost 12 percent of the victims said they had changed jobs because of a bully.

In the case of supervisors or managers who are bullies, the study found that bully bosses use fear to motivate their victims. They use scare tactics, finger pointing, back biting, and firing to make their victims squirm.

Bullies become managers because they know the business and have great technical skills. Because intimidated employees rarely complain, bullying managers generally have their jobs for a long time.

What can you do if you have a boss or co-worker who uses bullying tactics?

The main thing is to understand that bullies will use shouting, berating, criticism, or other tactics to try to make you feel bad. Try not to take this personally. Know that you're doing a good job and keep up the good work. Don't mistake the "humor" of cutting remarks as a bully trying to be friends.

Avoid bullies at all costs. If you allow them to make you feel bad, they definitely will. Be consistent, work hard, and don't wear your feelings on your sleeve. If you don't react, if you keep working hard to do a good job, eventually the bully will find someone else to bother.

Loading, Securing, and Hauling Cargo

As a professional driver, you are not only skilled in operating a commercial vehicle but you are also knowledgeable about loading, securing, and moving cargo from Point A to Point B. Nobody in the business knows this area of the industry better than you, the driver.

That's what this chapter is about. You will learn about how to inspect cargo, how to secure a load, and how to handle specific cargo, as well as weight and balance guidelines.

But, before we begin, here are some quick tips about moving cargo safely and efficiently:

- Never take another person's word for the condition of your cargo, how it's loaded, how it's balanced, and/or how it's tied down.
- Always check the load—even if you're just stopping to take a break (Figure 9-1).
- Remember—getting the cargo there in good shape is your job.
- Loading a device—such as tires, wheels, and suspension—beyond its manufacturer's weight rating is illegal and unsafe.
- Remember—legal size and weight limits are based on perfect weather and road conditions. In bad weather or on bad roads, it may not be safe to operate at the legal speed. In bad weather, it may be necessary to slow down, to increase following distance, and to increase the distance you perceive it will take you to stop.
- When hauling cargo, adjust your driving to avoid cargo shift. That means avoid making sudden moves, don't swerve, and don't stop suddenly.
- In poor conditions drive under the "safe speed" limits, keep a safe distance from the vehicle in front of you, and give yourself space and time to maneuver.
- Don't pull off onto an uneven surface.
- Avoid parking on inclines.

Figure 9-1 Inspect your cargo and make necessary adjustments.

Loose cargo is dangerous:

- It could fall off the truck and injure another driver on the road.
- It could fall off the truck, causing an accident.
- It could injure or even kill you during a quick stop.

And what if your vehicle is overloaded?

- If you are overloaded, it will affect how you steer or control the rig.
- If you are overloaded, you could damage your vehicle.
- If you are overloaded, your vehicle could damage the road.
- If you are overloaded, it is more difficult to stop and stopping distance increases.
- If you are overloaded, brake failure is more likely to occur—the additional weight makes brakes work harder because it exceeds their limits.
- If you are overloaded, you'll have to take upgrades slower and be ready to control faster speeds on downgrades.

Step One: Inspecting Cargo

When should you inspect your cargo and how it is secured? (Figure 9-1)

1. The inspection process begins while cargo is being loaded.
2. It continues as part of your pre-trip inspection—checking for overloads, poorly distributed and balanced weight, and cargo that is not properly secured.
3. Check again after you've driven 25 miles from the originating dock or terminal. It's a federal regulation—so make any adjustments needed.
4. Check again about every three hours or every 150 miles that you drive.
5. Check every time you take a break during your trip.

Remember to protect yourself, your carrier, and your customer. Ask yourself, "Is the cargo in good order?"

Federal, state, and local regulations governing weight, securing cargo, covering of cargo, and truck routes vary across the country. Know the rules and regulations in the states where you will be operating your vehicle. If you're a cross-country driver, find out about all these regulations. It will be to your advantage.

Step Two: Loading Cargo

Before loading, look at the floor of the trailer and make certain there are no nails, splinters, or other obstacles that could damage the cargo. In vans, make certain the floor and walls are clean and dry.

When cargo is loaded onto a trailer, the weight of the total cargo must be evenly distributed between all the axles.

It is the driver's responsibility to make sure that the vehicle is *not* overloaded.

Q. What is the legal weight limit?

A. That depends where you are—all states have maximums for gross vehicle weights and for axle weights (Figure 9-2). As you review legal cargo weights for the states you'll be running (find them in trucker's map books), it is important to know the following terms:

- **Gross vehicle weight** (GVW)—total weight of a single vehicle and its load.
- **Gross combination weight** (GCW)—total weight of a powered unit, its trailer, and its load, such as a loaded tractor-trailer.
- **Gross combination vehicle weight rating** (GCVWR)—maximum weight specified by the manufacturer for a specific combination of vehicles and their loads.
- **Center of gravity**—the point where weight acts as a force. A vehicle's center of gravity affects its stability.
- **Axle weight**—weight transmitted to the ground by one axle or one set of axles. Axle weight is not how much the axles themselves weigh! Axles support the vehicle and its load.
- **Tire load**—the maximum weight a tire can carry safely at a certain tire pressure. This information is stamped on the side of the tire. If tires are overinflated or underinflated, this rating may no longer apply—thus, an underinflated or overinflated tire may not safely carry the same load that it could with the correct inflation pressure.
- **Suspension systems**—all such systems have a manufacturer's weight/capacity rating. The manufacturer states how much weight these parts can carry safely.
- **Coupling device capacity**—all coupling devices are rated by the manufacturer for the weight they can safely carry.
- **Bridge weight**—because bridges can handle only so much weight at any one point, some states have bridge laws—a formula used to determine how much weight is put on any point of the bridge by any group of axles, such as one set of tandems. If the vehicle has more than one set of tandems, the formula takes into account how close the sets of axles are to each other. The resulting maximum axle weight for axles that are closer together may be lower for each axle in the group.

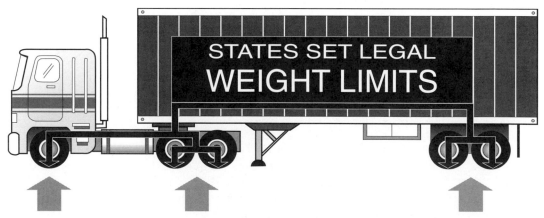

Figure 9-2 It is the driver's responsibility to make sure the vehicle is not overloaded.

Balancing the Load

Some people in the trucking business have a sixth sense about how to achieve a balanced load. Others learn from experience. Figure 9-3 shows a well balanced load.

Point One: Distribute the weight of the cargo over all axles and remember the center of gravity. You should put the load's center of gravity where it has the most support.

The height of the vehicle's center of gravity is important for safe handling of that vehicle. If cargo is piled up high on the trailer or in the trailer, or if heavy cargo is on top, this high center of gravity will cause the rig to tip over.

This is especially true on curves or if you have to swerve suddenly to avoid an accident or a hazard.

It is best to distribute the weight of the load over all axles and keep the center of gravity as low as possible. Load the heaviest parts of the cargo under the lightest parts.

Here's another illustration. Picture your empty vehicle sitting on level ground. Remember—the weight should be distributed over all the axles, including the front axles under the cab. Draw a line from wheel to wheel. When the center of gravity falls over the center of this rectangle, the vehicle will be most stable.

WEIGHT DISTRIBUTION
ON TRACTOR AND TRAILER

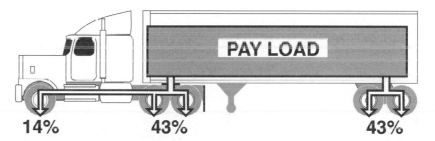

PAY LOAD

14%   43%   43%

EXAMPLE OF A WELL BALANCED LOAD
TRACTOR
- Distribute Weight Properly Over Axles
- Weight Distribution Depends on Position of Fifth Wheel
  - Single Axle - Slightly Forward of Centerline
  - Tandem Axle
    - Stationary - Just Ahead of Centerline
    - Sliding - Last Notch of Slider Adjustment
    - Fifth Wheel Moved Forward
      - MORE of LOAD Shifted to Front Axle

TRAILER
- Divide Load Evenly Between Front and Rear
- Adjust Load to Meet Axle Weight Limitations
  - Heavy Freight on Bottom
  - Properly Distributed

Figure 9-3   Experienced drivers assure cargo is loaded in a balanced manner.

It's important to balance the weight because:

- A poorly balanced load will make the vehicle tough to handle and unsafe. Also, damage to suspension and axle are possible.
- Too much weight on the steering axle makes the vehicle difficult to steer— and can cause damage to the steering axle and tires.
- Underloaded front axles can make the steering axle weight too light—making it difficult to steer safely.
- Too little weight on the driving axles means poor traction (in bad weather it will be difficult for the truck to keep going).
- If the center of gravity is too high, the possibility of rollover increases.
- If the center of gravity is too high on a flatbed load, it will shift to the side and may fall off.

Q. What about length and width?
A. All states have length and width regulations as well as weight regulations.

If you are overloaded or if your cargo has been loaded unsafely, it is possible that you may be put out of service until the cargo has been reloaded in a safe configuration if you are inspected.

Oversized loads usually require special permits, may be allowed on certain roads only at certain times, and may be asked to take "irregular" routes rather than the usual interstate routes. Some oversized loads are required to have escorts—either those provided by the carrier (a pilot car) or the police.

Step Three: Securing Cargo

Proper loading is an important part of moving freight safely and efficiently from one point to another. Securing the cargo is equally important for the same reasons: safety and efficiency.

The following are step-by-step guidelines for properly securing all types of loads.

In the Cargo Compartment

Bracing is a method that prevents movement of the cargo in the trailer or any other cargo compartment. When you brace a load, you use various elements to steady the load, from the upper part of the cargo to the floor. You also place braces on the walls of the compartment to minimize movement.

Blocking is another method, used in front, in back, and/or on the sides of a piece of cargo to keep it from sliding in the trailer (Figure 9-4). Blocking is usually shaped to fit tightly against and around the cargo and then is secured to the deck of the trailer to prevent the cargo from moving.

"Load locks" are long poles that stretch from wall to wall in a trailer. These should be at the rear of the load to prevent cargo from falling. Place one at the top—and another halfway down.

Loading pallets, make certain the pallets don't lean. Each should be placed tightly against the one ahead or in front of it. Leave space between rows of pallets and between the pallets and the walls of the trailer. However, leave as little space as possible between pallets and walls to prevent the cargo from shifting.

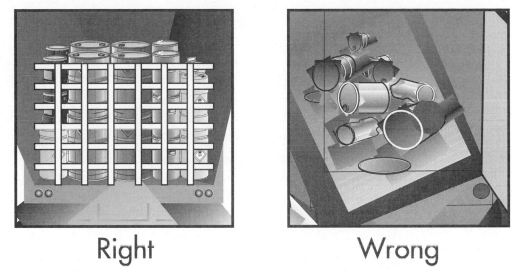

Figure 9-4 Blocking and bracing cargo protects it for the duration of the trip.

On the Flatbed Trailer

Tiedowns are used to keep cargo from moving in closed trailers as well as on flatbed trailers without sides (Figure 9-5). This secures the cargo, preventing it from shifting and/or eventually falling off the trailer.

When using tiedowns to secure cargo, they must be of the correct type and strength. Obviously, tying down a mammoth turbine with kite string will not secure the cargo.

Note: As a general rule, the combined strength of all cargo tiedowns must be strong enough to lift one-and-one-half times the weight of the cargo that is to be tied down.

Cargo should have at least one tie-down for each 10 feet of cargo. Make sure you have enough tie-downs to meet this need. No matter how small the cargo is, there should be at least two tie-downs holding it.

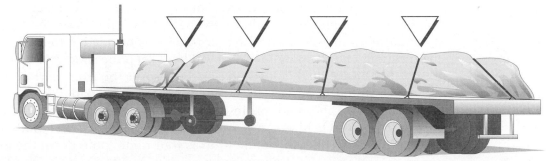

Figure 9-5 Adequate tie-downs keep cargo from shifting.

Proper tiedown equipment includes ropes, straps, and chains.

Tension devices used in tiedowns include winches, ratchets, and cinching components.

All tiedowns—regardless of material—should be attached correctly to the vehicle using hooks, bolts, rails, and rings.

Note: *All cargo must be secured by tiedowns, every 10 feet. It is important to have enough tiedowns to meet these requirements.*

Don't damage the cargo by securing it too tightly!

No matter how small, the cargo must be secured to the trailer by *at least two tiedowns.* Various pieces of metal have special tiedown requirements. If you haul this kind of cargo, find out the specific requirements to tie down this special cargo.

What's a "Header Board?"

Header boards at the front end of the load are called "headache racks"—they protect the driver from the freight shifting or crushing the cab in an accident or a sudden stop. Headache racks are attached to the tractor frame between the rear of cab and the fifth wheel. Front-end header boards protect the driver when the vehicle is carrying loads capable of shifting.

Covered Cargo: What You Should Know

In the past, when you've seen an 18-wheeler pulling big cargo pieces on a flatbed trailer, you probably thought it was covered to keep it clean.

According to regulations, cargo is covered for two reasons: (1) to protect people from spilled cargo, and (2) to protect the cargo from the weather.

In some states, the cargo must be covered to prevent spills—find out what the covering rules are in the states where you will be running.

Tarps (tarpaulins) are used to cover most freight and are tied down with rope, webbing, or elastic hooks (Figure 9-6).

How to 'Tarp' a Load

Lift the rolled up tarp to the top of the front racks. Then, unroll it over the bars to the back of the truck bed. Pull it tight. Tie it to cross bars on the rack. If the tarp is placed over the cargo tightly and evenly, it will not flap.

To tarp a load that is uneven or of irregular shape, place the tarp on the cargo after the tiedown assemblies are tight. Then tie down the tarp so the wind and weather don't get inside. Longer ropes may be needed to tie down irregular configuration. Overlapping the front will help keep the wind and weather out.

To "smoke tarp" a load on a flatbed, cover the front part of the load to keep exhaust from the smokestacks from discoloring the load.

While on the road, professional drivers check the covering on a load every 150 miles or three hours, whichever comes first. If a cover pulls free, uncovers the cargo, and is flapping in the wind as your trailer pulls down the highway, you should stop and reattach it immediately so that the cover won't fly off and block your vision—or someone else's. In addition, a flapping tarp will eventually tear itself to pieces, and tarps are very expensive.

CARGO COVERS

SPILL PROTECTION
•TO PROTECT PUBLIC
•TO MEET STATE LAW REQUIREMENTS

CARGO PROTECTION
•TO PREVENT CORROSION OR OTHER WEATHER DAMAGE
•COMPANY CAN BE LIABLE FOR RUINED CARGO
•USE TARP WHEN NEEDED
•MAKE SURE TARP DOES NOT LEAK
•MAKE SURE TARP IS TIED PROPERLY SO IT WILL NOT TEAR OR LEAK

Figure 9-6 To protect cargo from spilling, covers should be tied down and secure throughout the trip.

Loading Flatbed Loads

If a crane or forklift is to be used in placing or unloading a heavy piece of freight, place loose packing material (called "dunnage") for the load to ride on. This will allow the forklift at the receiving dock or destination to get under the load without a problem.

What about Sealed and Containerized Loads?

Note: You can't inspect a sealed load but you should check to see that you are not exceeding the gross weight or axle weight limits.

Container traffic—cargo that is placed in a container and sealed to be carried part of its journey by rail or ship—is one of the fastest growing components of the freight business in the country.

Some shippers prefer containerized shipments because they are easier to handle and more secure, especially if the cargo is traveling by ship or rail.

Containers—once they reach port—are loaded onto trucks and are on their way to the end-user. Containers may also be transported from the manufacturer or shipper from the shipper's location to the loading dock for rail or transoceanic movement.

Some containers have their own tiedowns that attach to a special frame for container loads.

Others are loaded onto flatbed trailers and are secured with tiedowns every two feet, just like any other cargo.

Cargo That Requires Special Handling

1. **Dry bulk tanks**—like liquid tankers, dry bulk tankers (Figure 9-7) have a high center of gravity, which means the driver must use special care, particularly when rounding curves and when entering or exiting a freeway ramp. When hauling a dry bulk tanker or any tanker, always drive at a speed well under the posted speed limit on curves, ramps, and in any kind of bad weather.
2. **Swinging meat**—a side of beef or any other meat can be extremely unstable, when hanging in a refrigerated trailer (reefer). This type of load also has a high center of gravity. Drive under the speed limit and use care on curves, turns, ramps, and in bad weather.
3. **Livestock**—hauling live animals, such as beef, hogs, horses, sheep, goats, etc., creates the same problems as liquid loads. And these animals add a few additional challenges. Livestock trailers always have a high center of gravity. Live animals also have a tendency to lean while going around a curve—and this creates a problem similar to the liquid surge found in liquid tanks.

Note: If you don't have a full load, use portable bulkheads to keep the animals from moving around. The tighter the animals are packed, the less movement there will be.

Remember the "nose factor." When you are parked in a truck stop or roadside rest area, park downwind. Otherwise, you will accumulate legions of enemies.

SPECIAL PURPOSE VEHICLES

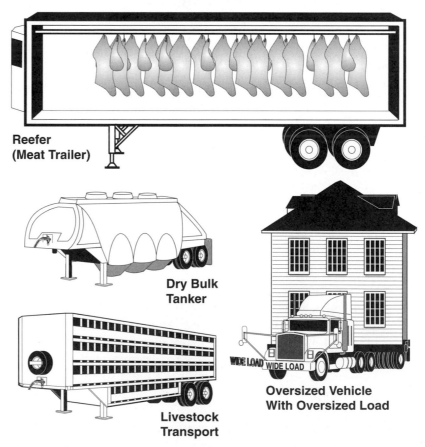

Reefer
(Meat Trailer)

Dry Bulk
Tanker

Livestock
Transport

Oversized Vehicle
With Oversized Load

Figure 9-7 Each special purpose vehicle has its own requirements for operation.

Step Four: Driving with a Load

The high center of gravity associated with some trailers and the way cargo is loaded has already been covered. Just remember, when you're loaded and have a high center of gravity, give yourself plenty of time and room to stop, and drive slowly on curves, entrance ramps, exit ramps, and into turns. A loose load will "surge" whether it's liquid in a smooth bore tank or swinging meat. This causes the center of gravity to change from moment to moment while the vehicle is in motion.

When you are loaded, remember that:

- A heavy load gives you better traction—which means you can stop faster and more safely.
- A light load or empty vehicle does not give good traction. You may be able to move faster but it also takes more distance to stop this type of vehicle.
- Poor distribution of cargo weight makes axles too light—this makes it easier to skid (Figure 9-8).

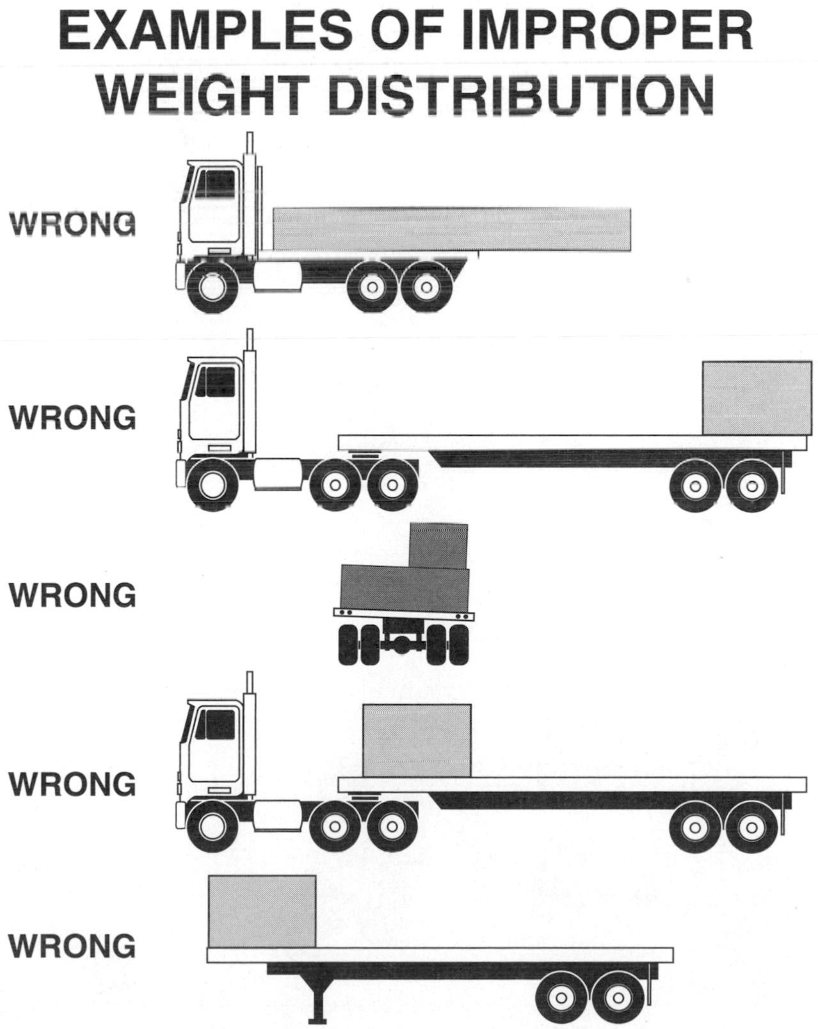

EXAMPLES OF IMPROPER WEIGHT DISTRIBUTION

WRONG

WRONG

WRONG

WRONG

WRONG

Figure 9-8   Weight should be distributed evenly over all axles.

When you are turning, remember that:

- A loaded trailer puts more weight on the axles, including the steering axle. The heavier the weight on the steering axle, the more difficult the rig will be to steer.
- Too much weight on the rear axles means there is not enough weight on the steering axle. This decreases steering control.

Driving Banks and Curves

A load with a high center of gravity will make driving banks and curves more hazardous. If the cargo is loaded incorrectly with a high center of gravity, the vehicle will tip when taking a steep bank or curve (Figure 9-9). The same will happen if cargo is unbalanced when it is loaded.

If you're driving a flatbed on a bank or curve and your cargo is not secure, it may shift or fall off.

If you're hauling hanging sides of meat suspended from rails in the trailer, the swinging caused by the motion of the trailer may cause a problem. As the meat swings more and more, the load builds momentum, which can make the vehicle very unstable, especially on curves and ramps.

If you're hauling dry bulk, you'll be driving a tanker—which has a high center of gravity because of its design. Sometimes—on curves and sharp turns or ramps—the load will shift, creating a very dangerous situation.

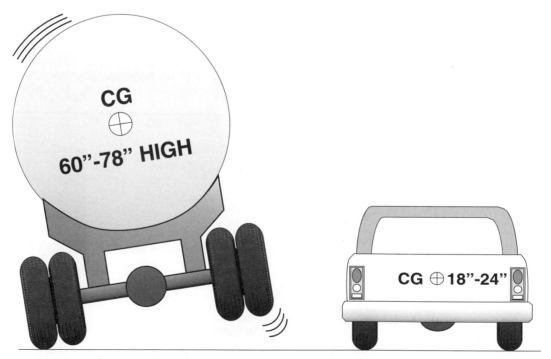

Figure 9-9   Tankers have a high center of gravity, which makes rollovers easier.

Driving Upgrades and Downgrades

A properly secured load will not cause any problems, but the way that a vehicle is loaded will affect how it performs on upgrades and downgrades.

If the truck is overloaded, it will navigate a hill very slowly. Always use a climbing lane. Otherwise, be aware of traffic behind you and other drivers who may be apt to tailgate your vehicle.

On a downgrade, the loaded vehicle will pick up momentum at a greater rate than the same unloaded vehicle. If your speed on the downgrade becomes excessive, use your brakes. But remember: Trying to slow or stop a loaded vehicle while traveling at a high rate of speed on a downgrade may cause brake failure—a common accident, but one that is easily preventable.

A common rule of thumb is to go down the hill or grade one gear lower than the gear used to climb the hill or grade.

Let's Review

Read each question and all of the answers provided. Place the letter of the correct answer in the space provided or write your answers on a separate piece of paper so you can use these questions again as you review for the CDL. Once you have answered all the questions, check your answers against the answer key which follows.

_____ 1. While driving, the first time you inspect your load is
    (A) 500 miles from origination,   (C) when you feel like it,
    (B) 25 miles from origination,   (D) none of the above.

_____ 2. If your vehicle is overloaded, you will
    (A) have trouble steering,   (C) damage the road,
    (B) damage the vehicle,   (D) all of the above.

_____ 3. Axle weight is
    (A) the actual weight of each axle,
    (B) the weight of the axle minus 10 percent,
    (C) how much weight the axle transmits to the ground,
    (D) none of the above.

_____ 4. The gross vehicle weight (GVW) is the total weight of
    (A) the cargo,   (C) the vehicle minus the tractor,
    (B) the vehicle and its load,   (D) all of the above.

_____ 5. For stability, the center of gravity should always be located
    (A) in the center of the cargo compartment,
    (B) toward the back of the van or trailer,
    (C) just behind the tractor,
    (D) none of the above.

_____ 6. True or False. A professional driver is required to know only the length and weight limits in the state in which he or she is licensed.

_____ 7. In order to safely transport a heavy cargo, the driver should
    (A) take only half the load at one time,
    (B) slow down on turns, curves, and ramps,
    (C) drive in a team,
    (D) all of the above.

_____ 8. If cargo is loaded incorrectly, the result will be
    (A) shifting of the load,   (C) difficulty in steering the vehicle,
    (B) damage to the vehicle,   (D) all of the above.

_____ 9. When your vehicle is loaded,
    (A) a heavy load gives you better traction—which means you can stop better,
    (B) a light load does not give good traction,
    (C) you may be able to move faster with a light load, but it also takes more distance to stop this type of vehicle,
    (D) all of the above.

_____10. You can't inspect a sealed load, but you are still responsible for
    (A) not exceeding load weight limits or axle weight limits,
    (B) tarping the load,
    (C) making a diagram of the load,
    (D) none of the above.

Answers to Let's Review

1. B; 2. D; 3. C; 4. B; 5. A; 6. False; 7. B; 8. D; 9. D; 10. A.

Terms You Need to Know

The following terms have been taken from the contents of Chapter 9. Review them. If you see any you're unsure of, check the definition in the Glossary at the back of the book. If it helps you, keep a written list of the words and their definitions (or write in the definitions here) and review them several days prior to taking the CDL tests.

Axle weight

Balanced load

Banks

Blocks

Bracing

Cables

Cargo securement devices

Cargo shift

Center of gravity

Chains

Climbing lane

Curves

Downgrade

Dry bulk tanks

Dunnage

Flatbed

FMCSR Part 393

Gross vehicle weight (GVW)

Gross vehicle weight rating (GVWR)

Headache rack or header board

Length and width limits

Livestock

"Nose factor"

Overload

Pallets

Portable bulkheads

Reefers (refrigerated units)

Straps

Swinging meat

Tarp or tarpaulin

Upgrade

Webbing

Wide load

Winches

THE DISPATCH BOARD
Food for Fitness and Safety

By Ron Adams, Ph.D.

While in high school, where he played basketball and ran track, Bob was 6 ft. tall and wore size 30 jeans. After a three-year stint in the U.S. Army where he was assigned to the motor pool, Bob decided to make transportation his life's work. One year after his discharge from the service, Bob had finished his CDL training and had a good job with a national carrier.

Six years later Bob has put together a great safety record and is one of the best over-the-road drivers in his company. Bob feels good about his life. He likes his job; he is saving some money for retirement and a boat. Things are going pretty well for old Bob, except he sometimes has trouble sleeping while on the road. His blood pressure, like his dad's and his granddad's before him, is slowly creeping up. He now wears size 38 jeans and his back hurts after sitting for a couple of hours.

So what is happening to Bob? Like so many drivers, Bob has spent too much time sitting, visited too many all-you-can eat buffets, and had too many burgers. He is overweight and starting a downward spiral in his health which, according to research, makes him a less safe driver. For any driver of any age, this mid-life downward spiral is a double whammy. Having poor health, which is bad enough, may also make Bob a safety risk to himself and others.

What can being overweight do to Bob's health? Medical authorities believe that being overweight contributes to stroke, cardiovascular diseases, hypertension, and diabetes. It also makes such conditions as arthritis or back pain worse.

Is being overweight a problem in the trucking industry?

A 1993 study of 2,945 drivers attending a trade show noted that 73 percent of respondents to a survey were overweight.

A 1993 study examining the prevalence of sleep apnea in 125 drivers working for one company revealed that 71 percent of the drivers were overweight.

A 1994 study of a cross-sectional population of 90 long haul commercial truck drivers revealed that overweight drivers had an accident involvement rate that was double that of non-overweight drivers.

What can Bob do to turn things around? He has to make better choices. As a driver, Bob makes thousands of choices each day. He chooses when to drive, when to shift gears, when to change lanes, at what speed to drive, when to sleep, and what to eat. Bob must make better choices in what he eats.

Here are some healthy eating guidelines from the U.S. Department of Agriculture for Bob to consider:

Eat a variety of foods:
Not only is variety the spice of life, but also variety in food choices is basic to good nutrition. Each day Bob's body needs the nutrients that a variety of foods provide. Most foods have several nutrients, but none has all of them.

Balance the food you eat with physical activity:
Bob like most Americans gains weight each year. A good choice for Bob is to manage his weight with a combination approach. Balancing calories in his eating plan with at least 30 minutes of walking or some other type of exercise each day.

continues

THE DISPATCH BOARD *continued*

Choose a diet with plenty of grain products, vegetables and fruits:
Grain products, vegetables (including legumes) and fruits should make up most of Bob's food consumption. These types of foods are excellent sources of vitamins, minerals, and complex carbohydrates, as well as fiber and other healthful food substances. Legumes are also high in protein. An added attraction to these foods is they are low in fat content. Bob should be careful and not add high fat sauces or dressings to these foods. Most of his food choices should come from this group of foods. If he were to divide his plate into pie-shaped sections, 75 percent of his plate should be filled with grains, fruits, or vegetables (without cheese, gravy, or other rich sauces).

Choose a diet low in fat, saturated fat, and cholesterol.
Fat is a nutrient that is essential for good health. Besides supplying energy, it carries vitamins A, D, E, and K into the blood stream. Yet too much fat, and too much cholesterol can negatively affect health. High-fat diets are linked to many health problems, including high blood cholesterol and obesity, as well as heart disease and some cancers.

Cutting down on fat and saturated fat, but not cutting it out entirely, is a sensible choice for Bob's daily diet.

Choose a diet moderate in sugars.
Sugar, a form of carbohydrate, is present in many foods. Sugars in food come from two sources: naturally occurring, such as sugars found in fruits and dairy foods, and added sugars, used for flavoring in a variety of foods.

Carbohydrates, including sugars, are the body's main source of energy. For sugars, moderation is the best guideline, especially if the energy needs are low.

Choose a diet moderate in salt and sodium.
Sodium is a nutrient and a natural part of many foods. Salt is made of sodium and chloride. As nutrients, sodium and chloride help the body maintain fluid balance and regulate blood pressure.

For some persons, extra sodium passes right through the body. However, others have blood pressure that's sodium-sensitive; for these people, a high sodium intake, along with obesity, heredity, or getting older, contributes to high blood pressure. Moderation is a wise guideline in the use of sodium.

Bob can continue to enjoy his professional life and improve his health by making wise choices about the foods he eats and taking time to balance his food intake with exercise. It's not as bad as it may sound—and, truth be told, five servings of fresh fruits and vegetables a day actually improves most meals while it also improves your health. Not a bad result for a little effort, is it?

(Information for this article was provided by the American Dietetic Association's "Complete Foods & Nutrition Guide," 1998, Chromimed Publishing, Minneapolis, MN.)

10 Air Brake Endorsement

This chapter contains information for all CDL candidates who drive or who will be driving commercial motor vehicles equipped with an air brake system. Those individuals will be required to pass the CDL Air Brake Endorsement, which includes all Class A CDL candidates and many Class B CDL candidates.

Those who do not take the Air Brake Endorsement will receive a CDL marked with the words, "Air Brake Restriction," and will not be permitted to operate vehicles equipped with air brakes.

To pass the Air Brake Endorsement, candidates will need to know the parts of the air brake system and how it works. Why? The federal government believes that in order to safely operate a vehicle with air brakes, a driver must have—at the very least—a working knowledge of how air brakes function.

Available information about air brakes is extensive, so we will cover only the key parts of the system and how it works in this chapter. If you want additional information, consult the Internet, the public library, or veteran drivers.

Air Brakes—Three Systems

All air brake systems have three major braking systems (Figure 10-1):

- **Service brake system**—this is the system that applies and releases the brakes as you apply and release pressure on the service brake. You'll use it every day. The service brake system works by applying pressure with your foot to the brake pedal.
- **Parking brake system**—this is the system used when applying the parking brake.
- **Emergency brake system**—this is the system that stops the commercial motor vehicle in an emergency situation—usually caused by failure of the braking system. The emergency brake system uses parts of the service and parking brake systems.

Parts of the Air Brake System You Should Know

Air Compressor

Air brakes use compressed air to brake the vehicle. The air compressor compresses air and pumps it into the air tanks (also known as the storage tanks or reservoirs).

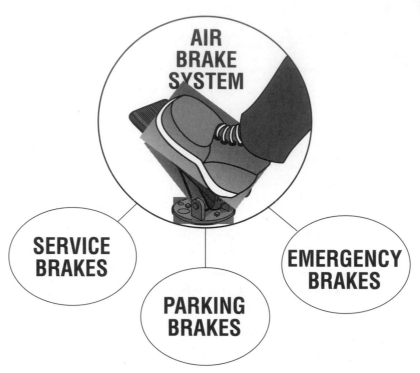

Figure 10-1 Three major braking components of air brake
systems.

There are several types of air compressors in use today. Some are air-cooled,
while others are cooled by the engine's cooling system. Some are connected to the
engine with gears. Some use V-belts—and if you use this system, check the condition of the belts during the inspection. If these belts are not in good condition, the
air compressor will fail, which means there will be no air for the braking system.

*Remember: During the pre-trip inspection, always check the air compressor belts. Some are
lubricated by engine oil. If the air compressor has its own oil, check it during this inspection.*

Air Compressor Governor

This maintains constant air pressure in the air tanks—between 100 psi and 125 psi.
The governor keeps air in the air tanks and regulates air pressure. The governor
also makes sure the braking system has enough air for proper braking. This is done
with the **cut-in level** (which turns the air compressor on) and **cut-out level** (which
turns the air compressor off).

*This is important! When the air pressure in the tanks is below a certain level—usually 100
psi—the cut-in turns on the air compressor so the air pressure is built back up. When the air
pressure in the tank reaches about 125 psi, the cut-out level is achieved and the compressor
turns off.*

Air Storage Tanks

These tanks are also called "air tanks" or "air reservoirs" (Figure 10-2). These tanks
hold compressed air produced by the air compressor. They have enough air to stop

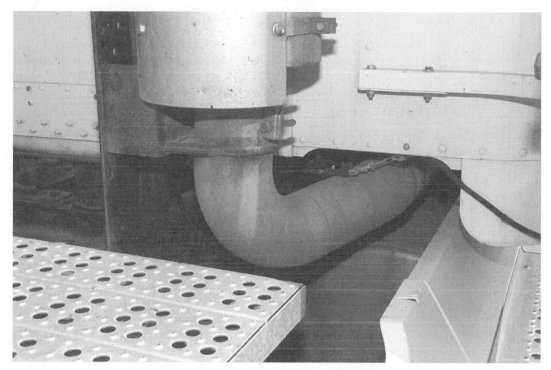

Figure 10-2 Air storage tanks.
(Photo courtesy of ATA Associates, Inc.)

the vehicle several times, even if the air compressor stops working. The size and number of air tanks in a system vary among vehicles.

Air Tank Drains

Air tanks are equipped with drains, which are usually located at the bottom of the tank. Oil and water accumulate in the tanks and must be drained daily.

- **Manual drain**—is operated by turning a knob (or petcock) a quarter turn—or by pulling a cable.
- **Automatic drain**—is activated automatically. You will hear these drains blow out the air and any accumulated oil and water from time to time.

Why is it important that these air tank drains be drained daily, especially in winter? Because freezing temperatures will cause any moisture in the lines to freeze, causing serious braking system problems.

Also, the government recommends that tanks be drained at the beginning of each day, so it makes sense to drain the tanks when you perform your pre-trip inspection and then again during your post-trip inspection.

Alcohol Evaporators

Some air brake systems have these—they are designed to automatically inject alcohol into the system to reduce the chance that water in the system will freeze. However, even if the truck has an alcohol evaporator, you must still drain the air tanks daily. And during cold weather, you must check and fill the alcohol level daily.

Safety Valve (or Pop-Off Valve)

Located in the first tank into which the air compressor pumps, this valve will release excess air and protect the air system from exceeding psi limitations (and possibly damaging the system.) Most safety valves will release if the pressure reaches 150 psi. If the safety valve pops off, most likely something is wrong with the air compressor. Or the problem could be with the safety valve. Have a mechanic check it out as soon as possible!

Brake Pedal

A part of the service brake system, the brake pedal is also called "the foot valve" or the "foot brake" or the "treadle valve." When you press the brake pedal with your foot, you apply the brakes. How? By forcing air through the lines to the brakes. The more pressure you apply with your foot, the harder the brakes will be applied—and the more air will be used.

Take your foot off the pedal and the air that has been used will be released and the air in the air tanks is reduced. The more times you press and release the pedal, the less air you will have in the system. When air pressure reaches about 100 psi— the cut-in level—the air compressor's governor will allow the air compressor to turn on and pump air into the system to replace the air that has been used.

If you use too much air (because you repeatedly applied and released the brake pedal), you could use enough air to make your brakes useless.

Note: You must have adequate air in the air tanks in order for the service brake system to work properly. Use your brake pedal only when needed!

Low Air Pressure Warning Devices

All vehicles equipped with air brakes must have a "low air pressure" warning device. These devices come on before air pressure goes below 60 psi. Warnings are usually red lights, which are sometimes accompanied by a loud buzzer. If you see the red light or hear the buzzer, you've got a problem. If this occurs while you're driving, stop immediately when you find a safe spot. Don't attempt to drive the vehicle until the problem has been identified and repaired.

The **wig-wag** is another type of low air pressure warning device. This is a metal arm located above the driver's sight-line—attached at the top of the windshield near the visor. When air pressure reaches around 60 psi, the wig-wag will swing in front of the driver's face. Again, if this happens while you're driving down the highway, stop immediately. The wig-wag can't be reset until the air pressure in the system is above 60 psi.

Foundation Brakes

Each wheel has a foundation brake. The foundation brake most often used is the S-cam brake. To pass the CDL test, you must know the parts of the S-cam brake and the major parts of the braking system.

- **Brake drums**—located at ends of the axle. The drum contains the braking mechanism and the wheels are bolted to the drums.

- **Brake shoes and brake linings**—the brake shoes and brake linings press against the drum, creating enough friction to slow or stop the vehicle. Friction causes heat and the longer and harder the shoes and linings are held against the brake drum, the more heat is generated. If this heat becomes too intense, the brakes will begin to "fade" or lose their ability to stop the vehicle. Too much heat will also eventually warp or crack the drum.
- **Brake chamber**—when the driver applies the brake and air is applied to the braking system, air is pumped into the brake chamber and pushes out the push rod—which is attached to the "slack adjuster." When the driver takes his or her foot off the brake pedal, the air is released out of the brake chamber and the return spring pulls the brake shoes away from the drum.
- **Slack adjuster**—is attached to one end of the push rod and on the other to the brake cam shaft. When it is pushed out, it causes the brake cam shaft to twist, which will cause the S-cam to turn. This forces the brake shoes away from each other and presses them inside the drum, causing the vehicle to stop.
- **Push rod**—is attached to one end of the slack adjuster.
- **Return spring**—pulls the brake shoes away from the drum when the brake pedal is released.
- **Brake cam shaft**—when the slack adjuster is pushed out, the brake cam shaft twists, causing the S-cam to turn, forcing the brake shoes away from each other to press against the brake drum.

Wedge Brakes and Disc Brakes

These are additional braking systems, although the S-cam brake is most often used today. The **wedge system** works similarly to the S-cam brake, except that the wedge is pushed by a push-rod between the ends of the brake shoes. The push-rod shoves the shoes apart and presses them against the brake drum. Wedge brakes have one or two brake chambers. The **disc system** works the same as the S-cam, except that the disc brake has a power screw, which is turned when air pressure is applied. This causes the power screw to clamp the disc between the caliper's brake lining pads.

Supply Pressure Gauge

All air brake systems must have an air pressure supply gauge (Figure 10-3) to tell the driver the amount of air pressure (measured in pounds per square inch—psi) in the system. If the vehicle has dual air brakes, there will either be one gauge with two needles or two separate gauges.

Application Pressure Gauge

This lets the driver know how much air pressure is being applied to the brakes. The amount of air being applied is determined by the amount of pressure placed on the brake pedal. Be sure to know the difference between the supply pressure gauge and the application pressure gauge.

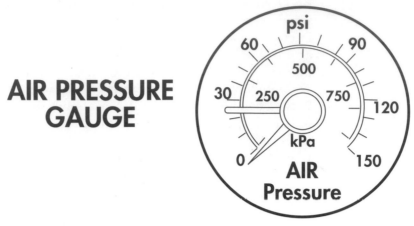

Figure 10-3 Air pressure supply gauge.

Stop Lamp Switch

Stop lights come on when the brake pedal is applied. The electrical switch that turns on the stop lights is activated by air pressure.

Front Brake Limiting Valve

Vehicles built before 1975 have a front brake limiting valve control switch on the dash. The valve has two positions—normal and slippery. Putting the valve in the "slippery" position reduces normal air pressure to front brakes by 50 percent—and in doing so, reduces the braking power of front brakes by 50 percent.

That was the understanding 25 or more years ago. Today, we know that whenever the braking power to the front wheels is reduced, the only result is increased stopping distance. Front wheel braking is good under all conditions. Under no circumstances should the "slippery" position of the front brake limiting valve ever be used. Keep the front brake limiting valve in the normal position—*always!*

Spring Brakes ("Fail Safe Brakes")

Spring brakes are the most commonly used emergency brake and/or parking brake system on tractors and buses. These brakes must be mechanical because air can leak out.

When the parking brakes are applied, air is released from the brake chamber. This releases the springs and applies the brakes.

In an emergency—when air pressure has fallen to around 20 psi—the spring brakes will be automatically applied. When this happens, things can get a little more exciting than you planned! This is the reason for the low air pressure warning light/buzzer or wig-wag. Warning signals come on at about 60 psi—so you are only 30 to 40 psi away from the spring brakes locking up. When warnings come on, find a safe place to stop—quickly!

The spring brakes are effective only when the brakes are properly adjusted. The same goes for the service brake system.

When the vehicle is parked and the parking brakes are applied, never apply pressure to the brake pedal—damage could result! The combined force of the spring brake and the brake pedal could create a real problem!

Parking Brake Controls

In older vehicles, the parking brake will be controlled by a lever. In newer models, the driver applies the parking brakes (spring brakes) using a yellow, diamond-shaped push-pull knob. You pull the knob out to apply the parking brakes and push it in to release.

When you park, always use the parking brakes—that guarantees you'll never have a roll-off.

Most tractors have a handle attached to (or near) the steering column called a "Johnson bar" or "trolley valve." It is used to apply the trailer brakes. Some drivers park their vehicles using this handle and locking trailer brakes only. *Don't do it!* It's a dangerous habit. Always park your vehicle using the parking brake.

Modulating Control Valve

This valve is available on some vehicles. It is controlled by a handle located on the dashboard and is used to apply the spring brakes gradually. The more the handle is moved, the more the brakes are applied. This valve is designed to use in case the service brakes fail while driving. Once you have stopped the vehicle, lock the handle in the "down" position with the locking device. Do not move your vehicle until the service brake problem is repaired.

Dual Parking Control Valves

Some vehicles (mainly buses) have auxiliary air tanks that can be used to release the spring brakes so the vehicle can be moved to a safe place. Vehicles with dual parking control valves have two control knobs on the dash—one is a push-pull knob used to apply the spring brakes for normal parking. The other is spring-loaded in the "out" position. When you push it in, it releases air from the auxiliary tank and releases the air brakes. Because this is a spring-loaded knob, it must be held in while moving the vehicle. When you let go, it pops back out and reapplies the spring brakes. It can be used for only a few times before running out of air.

Dual Air Brake Systems

These systems are available on most newer models. Dual air brake systems offer more protection against brake failure. With these systems, the truck has two separate air brake systems but only one set of controls—primary and secondary.

One system usually operates the brakes on the rear axle or axles. The second system usually operates the brakes on the front axle and maybe on one rear axle. Both systems supply air to the trailer or trailers.

Before driving a vehicle with a dual air brake system, you must wait until the air pressure builds up to at least 100 psi. Normally, there is an air gauge for each system, but there may be only one gauge with two needles—one for each system.

With a dual air brake system, if the low air warning buzzer and light go on, you must stop as quickly and as safely as possible. Don't drive the vehicle again until you get the system fixed.

Inspecting Air Brake Systems

No professional driver would ever get into a vehicle without first checking its brakes—it's common sense. And it's your life you're putting on the line if you don't. Here are 10 steps for checking the brake system. Learn them well:

1. **Check air compressor belt and oil**—Check the belt for tightness, glazing, or any signs of wear, like fraying and cracks. If a compressor has its own lubrication, check to see that the oil level is full.
2. **Check manual slack adjusters on S-cam brakes**—To do this, park the vehicle on level ground, put it in gear, turn off the engine, release the brakes, and chock the wheels (this will prevent the truck from moving). Take your keys with you. Locate the slack adjusters and pull them as hard as you can. If they move more than one inch where the push rod is connected, they are out of adjustment and will need to be adjusted before you begin your trip.

Note: Out-of-adjustment brakes are the most common problem found during state and DOT inspections—and they will cost you time and money if inspectors find this problem.

3. **Check the brake drums (discs), linings, and hoses**—If brake drums or discs have cracks longer than one-half the width of the friction area, they are out of service and the truck shall not be driven until they are repaired.

    Check the brake linings. They should not be loose or soaked with oil or grease. They also should not be too thin—this is dangerous. Mechanical parts must be in place—not broken or missing. Hoses connected to the brake chambers should not be cracked, worn, or rubbing other hoses.
4. **Test the low pressure warning signal**—With air pressure built up to the point that the buzzer or warning light has turned off, turn off the engine, and then turn key to "On" but do not start the engine. Begin applying and releasing brakes until the low air buzzer warning light comes on. This should happen at about 60 psi. If it doesn't come on, get it repaired before beginning your trip.
5. **Check to make sure spring brakes come on automatically**—Use the same procedure as you did to test the low pressure warning signal, except put the unit in gear or chock the wheels and release the parking brake. Continue pumping the brakes until the parking brake control knob pops out—between 20 and 40 psi. This indicates that the spring brakes have been applied.
6. **Check the rate of pressure build-up**—With the dual air system and engine idling, air pressure should build to between 84 to 100 psi within 45 seconds. With single air systems, it could take three minutes to build pressure to between 50 to 90 psi. If the air pressure does not build up within these time limits, there must be a problem. Get it checked before driving.

7. **Test the air leakage rate**—With the air system fully charged and the gauge showing around 125 psi, turn off the engine. Then release the service brakes and allow time for the air pressure drop. For a straight truck, the loss rate should be less than 2 psi in one minute. For a combination vehicle, the loss rate should be less than 3 psi in one minute.

   Apply 90 psi or more with the brake pedal. After the initial drop (don't count it), the air loss for straight trucks should not be more than 3 psi in one minute. In combination vehicles, air loss should not exceed 4 psi in one minute (Figure 10-4).

   If you are losing more than 3 psi for a straight truck or 4 psi for a combination, check the vehicle for air leaks and get them repaired before starting your trip.

8. **Check the air compressor governor cut-in and cut-out pressure**—The governor should have the compressor cut-in when the air pressure gets to about 100 psi and should cut out at about 125 psi.

   With the engine idling and air gauge at about 125 psi, begin pumping the brake pedal. When the pressure is pumped down to about 100 psi, the compressor should start. When it does, the needle on the gauge will begin rising, indicating a building of air pressure. When the gauge reaches 125 psi, the needle should stop rising, indicating that the governor has turned off the air compressor.

   If the governor is not working properly, get it checked before starting your trip.

9. **Test the parking brake**—With the vehicle stopped, apply the parking brakes and *gently* attempt to move the vehicle in first gear. The parking brake must hold the vehicle in place.

10. **Test the service brakes**—After air pressure has built up completely, release parking brakes and *slowly* begin to move forward. At 5 mph, apply the brakes using only the brake pedal. Brakes should stop the vehicle firmly. If the vehicle pulls to one side, if the brakes feel spongy, or if there is a delayed stop action, get the brakes checked before going on the road.

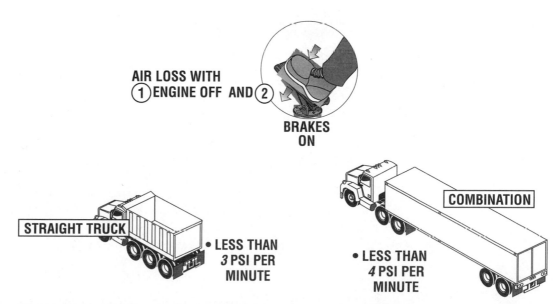

Figure 10-4   Always test the air leakage rate before starting a trip.

If you are driving a combination vehicle (pulling a trailer), check the brakes on the trailer by *slowly* moving forward. At about 5 mph, pull the trailer hand valve down. The trailer brakes should lock firmly. If they don't, get them checked.

Using the Air Brakes

There are three situations in which the use of air brakes must be learned and understood. You must also learn the differences between each situation. These situations are:

- **Normal stopping**—in a normal stopping situation, you apply pressure to the brake pedal until the vehicle comes to a stop. Pressure is applied smoothly and steadily.
- **Controlled braking** (also called "squeeze braking")—accomplished by squeezing brakes firmly *without locking the wheels* (Figure 10-5). While squeezing the brakes, don't attempt to turn the wheels, because they may lock and you will lose all steering control. If you need to turn the wheel or if the wheels start to lock up, release the brakes. Make the necessary adjustments in steering and then reapply the brakes.
- **Stab braking**—used in emergency situations only, (Figure 10-6) is done in three steps:
  1. Apply the brakes as hard as possible.
  2. Release the brakes when the wheels lock up.

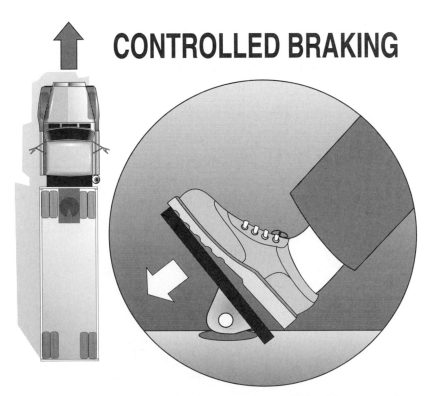

CONTROLLED BRAKING

Figure 10-5   Controlled braking is accomplished by squeezing brakes firmly without locking the wheels.

STAB BRAKING

RELEASE AFTER WHEELS LOCK UP

Figure 10-6   Use 'stab braking' only in an emergency.

3. When the wheels start rolling again, reapply the brakes hard—and repeat these steps as often as you have to.

Note: If your truck is equipped with anti-lock brakes, this section may not apply. Read the vehicle manual for proper emergency procedures.

The purpose of stab braking is to lock the wheels.
You should also remember that:

1. When the wheels are locked, there's no steering control.
2. When you take your foot off the brake, it will take one second before the wheels begin rolling again.
3. Keeping the wheels locked for too long could make the vehicle slide sideways or begin to jackknife *be careful when you perform stab braking!*

Q. What should I know about stopping distance when using air brakes?
A. The stopping distance for a vehicle with air brakes is different than the stopping distance for a vehicle with hydraulic brakes.

   With air brakes, there is an added time delay because of the time it takes for the air to travel to the brakes once the brake pedal has been pushed. It doesn't take a lot of extra time, but it's enough to make a difference.

   There are four factors in the stopping distance of a vehicle equipped with air brakes—and you should know them for the CDL test!

1. **Perception distance**—The distance the vehicle will travel from the time the driver sees a hazard and the time the driver reacts (presses the brake pedal). Average perception time is ¾ of a second—time enough for the vehicle to travel approximately 60 feet.

2. **Reaction distance**—The time it takes for the driver's foot to move off the accelerator and stomp on the brake. Average driver reaction time is ¾ second—time for the vehicle to travel another 60 feet—and the driver will just be beginning to brake at this point.

3. **Brake lag distance**—The distance the vehicle travels once the brakes have been applied and begin to work. This takes another ½ second. Traveling at 55 mph, the vehicle will travel another 40 feet in ½ second.

4. **Effective braking distance**—The distance the vehicle travels once the brakes make contact with the drum. With good braking technique and perfectly adjusted brakes on good, dry pavement, the vehicle going 55 mph will travel 150 additional feet until it comes to a complete stop.

Taking all these distances into account, to stop a vehicle traveling 55 mph, it will require 310 feet—that's about the length of a football field!

Q. How do I brake properly on a downhill grade (Figure 10-7)?

A. Brakes get hot when they're used. This heat comes from the friction between the shoes and the drum—just like on an automobile. The trick is to use the brakes so they don't get too hot—so they don't begin to "fade" or lose their ability to stop your vehicle.

Q. How do I know if my brakes are "fading?"

A. The answer is simple: When the brakes take more pressure to maintain the same speed, they are fading. If this happens, the best thing to do is pull over

Figure 10-7   Be prepared to shift to proper gear and break carefully on downhill grades.

and let the brakes cool. Once they cool down, they will regain some of their ability to stop your vehicle—and they may need to be adjusted, depending on how heated they became.

If they need to be adjusted, and if you are qualified, go ahead and adjust them. If you are not able to adjust them, get a mechanic to adjust them before continuing down the road.

Q. How can I avoid brake "fade?"

A. There are several ways to avoid this problem:

1. If possible, before driving a long downgrade, pull over and make sure the brakes are adjusted and in good working condition.
2. When beginning the downhill run, get into a gear that will allow you to maintain a safe speed by using the braking effect of the engine. This effect is greatest when it is close to the governed rpm of the gear you have chosen—usually one or more gears lower than the climbing gear.
3. The "safe speed" is posted as the speed limit. Never exceed the posted speed.
4. Apply the brakes when you reach the "safe speed." Apply them enough to activate all brakes—you'll feel the vehicle slowing down. You'll need at least 20 psi braking pressure to accomplish this.
5. Keep the brakes applied until the vehicle speed is down to 5 mph under the "safe speed" and then release the brakes. If you're in the correct gear, brake application should last three seconds.

Q. What gear will help maintain the vehicle at the "safe speed" on a downgrade?

A. Today's engines are so powerful they can go up a steep grade without downshifting. For this reason, you should choose a gear that is several gears lower than the one you used to climb the hill to go down the hill.

Here's an example: On a particular road, the "safe speed" is 30 mph. You climbed the hill in ninth gear. But, to keep close to the governed rpm's at 30 mph, you will need to use sixth gear to go downhill. When the vehicle reaches 30 mph, you apply approximately 20 psi to the brake pedal and feel the vehicle slowing. You continue to apply the brakes until the vehicle reaches 25 mph, or 5 mph below the safe speed. At that point, release the brakes. When your vehicle speeds up to 30 mph again, repeat the process until you get to the bottom of the hill.

Q. What happens if my vehicle loses air pressure?

A. First, stop the vehicle as soon as possible—as safely as possible!

When the low air pressure warning comes on, it usually means there is a leak in the air system. When the pressure drops to approximately 60 psi, the warning buzzer and light will come on.

The brakes will lock when the air pressure drops to between 20 and 45 psi.

The time between the low air warning signals until the brakes lock is very short.

What should you do? Pull over and stop as soon as possible after the low air warning comes on.

If you don't stop, the brakes may lock while you are traveling down the road—*not a good thing!* Why? Because it may lead to loss of control of the vehicle!

Note: If a major rupture occurs (like a trailer separating from the tractor and ripping off the air hoses) in your air system, the one-way check valve prevents air from escaping from the air system.

Parking Brakes

Whenever you park, never use the trolley valve or trailer handbrake. *Always* use the parking brake!

There are certain times when you should not use the parking brake—like right after coming down a long grade and the brakes are very hot. In this case, excessive heat can damage the brakes. You should also not use the parking brake when you are operating in cold weather—using the parking brakes may cause them to freeze and lock.

If the brakes freeze up, do this: With the engine off, the transmission in gear, and the wheels chocked, release the parking brake. Get your tire-checker or small metal bar or pipe and lightly tap the brakes. This may break the ice and release the brakes.

Always park using *only* your parking brakes. If that's not possible—because your brakes are hot after a downgrade or the temperature is freezing or below—use chocks.

Never use the trailer hand brake!

Let's Review

Read each question and all of the answers provided. Place the letter of the correct answer in the space provided or write your answers on a separate piece of paper so you can use these questions again as you review for the CDL. Once you have answered all the questions, check your answers against the answer key which follows.

_____ 1. The low air pressure warning will light or buzz at approximately
(A) 60 psi, (C) 45 psi,
(B) 30 psi, (D) 25 psi.

_____ 2. Air tanks should be drained
(A) on pre-trip and post-trip inspections, (C) every 150 miles,
(B) every four hours, (D) none of the above.

_____ 3. "Stab braking" is when you
(A) brake hard until the wheels lock, then release until the wheels begin to roll and repeat the process;
(B) brake hard but not enough to lock wheels;
(C) brake gently and steadily by pumping action;
(D) none of the above.

_____ 4. On a long downhill grade, it is recommended that you
(A) gear down and keep your speed at 55 mph,
(B) gear down three gears from climbing gear and keep your speed at 60 mph,
(C) gear down and keep your speed 5 mph below the "safe speed,"
(D) all of the above.

_____ 5. The service brake system
(A) stops the vehicle in an emergency,
(B) is the system used when you apply the parking brake,
(C) applies and releases the brakes when you apply and release pressure on the service brake,
(D) none of the above.

_____ 6. When air pressure in the tanks falls below a certain level, the cut-in
(A) notifies the dispatcher at the carrier's headquarters,
(B) turns on the air compressor,
(C) turns off the compressor,
(D) reads the gauge and gives you a digital read-out.

_____ 7. True or False. Air tanks collect oil and water when the air brakes are being used.

_____ 8. The application pressure gauge tells you to
(A) stop and take a drug test, (C) stop the wig-wag,
(B) let up on the brake pedal, (D) none of the above.

_____ 9. "Brake fade" is where
(A) it takes more and more pressure on the brake pedal to slow the vehicle,
(B) it takes less and less pressure on the brake pedal to slow the vehicle,
(C) it takes more and more pressure on the accelerator to move the vehicle,
(D) none of the above.

_____10. True or False. Disc brakes are the most widely used brakes on commercial vehicles today.

Answers to Let's Review

1. A; 2. A; 3. A; 4. C; 5. C; 6. B; 7. True; 8. D; 9. A; 10. False.

Terms You Need to Know

The following terms have been taken from the contents of Chapter 10. Review them. If you see any you're unsure of, check the definition in the Glossary at the back of the book. If it helps you, keep a written list of the words and their definitions (or write in the definitions here) and review them several days prior to taking the CDL tests.

Air compressor

Air compressor governor

Air leakage rate

Air storage tanks

Air tank drains

Alcohol evaporators

Application pressure gauge

Automatic drain

Brake cam shaft

Brake chamber

Brake drums

Brake fade

Brake lag distance

Brake linings

Brake shoes

Controlled braking

Cut-in and cut-out levels

Disc brakes

Downhill grade

Dual air brake systems

Dual parking control valves

Effective braking distance

Emergency brake system

Fail-safe brakes

Foundation brakes

Front brake limiting valve

Johnson bar

Low air pressure warning signal

Manual drains

Modulating control valve

Normal stopping

Parking brake controls

Parking brake system

Perception distance

Push rod

Reaction distance

Reservoirs

Return spring

S-cam brakes

Safe speed

Safety valve

Service brake system

Slack adjuster

Spring brakes

Stab braking

Stop lamp switch

Stopping distance

Storage tanks

Supply pressure gauge

Trolley valve

Wedge brakes

Wig-wag

THE DISPATCH BOARD
Why Pre-Trip Inspections Are Important

By Martin Garsee, Instructor
Houston Community College Professional Driving Program

The pre-trip inspection (or pre-trip) is very important to the safety of the driver and to the longevity of the vehicle.

First, the pre-trip is the law, so performing the inspection is not an option. But, let's look at the benefits of the pre-trip.

Safety depends on the driver and the condition of the vehicle. When we do a complete pre-trip, we can start with a safe truck. Then, when we do our jobs as safe drivers, we will have a safe trip.

The pre-trip identifies problems and allows drivers to deal with these problems before the trip begins. Repairs at the terminal should be faster and less costly and ensure a safe truck at the starting point of any trip.

Here's an example of what could happen if you did not do a thorough pre-trip:

You have a flat tire that you don't see during an incomplete pre-trip inspection. You leave the terminal without it being repaired.

Driving down the road, the tire becomes hot and begins to come apart. Pieces of the tire fly into a passing motorist's windshield, cracking it in the process.

A report is called in on you and a claim is filed against your company by the four-wheeler's insurance company, which could lead to increased premiums for your employer.

You continue and the tire catches fire, damaging the trailer and its cargo. The shipper is unhappy that you've damaged the product. The receiver is equally unhappy because they don't get the product they ordered on time nor is what they end up with usable.

You, as a driver have lost time because most companies pay only for miles driven, not sitting on the side of the road waiting for a tow-truck. If you're not going down the road, you're not making any money.

It is costly to replace the cargo and to repair the trailer.

But, what about the safety issues? Here's another example of an inadequate pre-trip inspection:

You did not check the front end of your truck. The U-bolts are not tight on the leaf springs. As you enter the freeway and go down the road a few miles, the U-bolt comes loose and the leaf springs come off, causing you to start to lose control of your steering . . . and wham! You're involved in an accident—where you or others could be injured or even killed—all because you didn't take the time to do a thorough pre-trip inspection.

As you can see, whether you drive a different truck or the same truck each day, a proper and thorough pre-trip is a must.

Note: *The minimum standards for a pre-trip are found in FMCSR Part 392.7. Many companies will have their own forms for doing a pre-trip, which must be filled out for company compliance.*

11 Hazardous Materials and the HazMat Endorsement

Who Should Read This Chapter?

If you plan to transport hazardous materials in quantities that require hazardous materials placards on your vehicle, then you should read this chapter—and read it carefully, because you will need to pass the Hazardous Materials (HazMat) Endorsement for your CDL.

The Commercial Motor Vehicle Safety Act of 1986 requires all persons with a HazMat Endorsement on their CDL to retake the HazMat Endorsement test each time they renew their CDL.

Sound like a lot of work? Maybe, but think about it this way. Hazardous materials are becoming more and more frequent cargo. There are changes in how such materials are handled and changes in how they should be hauled. And if you regularly haul HazMat cargoes, you will want to know the latest and safest way to handle these loads.

Some states now require drivers to retake the HazMat Endorsement every two years, others do not—so check with your local Department of Motor Vehicles to find out what you will be required to do.

Should you learn everything in this chapter to pass the test? Probably not everything, but to be informed and knowledgeable about how to handle HazMat loads, read through this chapter carefully—reading it more than once will help bring the total picture into focus for you.

So, let's get started.

Training Guidelines

Federal law requires all drivers who transport hazardous materials to receive HazMat training. This regulation further requires that a record of the driver's training in hazardous materials be kept on file while that driver is employed with the company and for 90 days after the driver leaves employment.

The record must have (1) the driver's name, (2) most recent training date, (3) description of the training materials used to meet the requirements of the section, (4) name and address of the person providing training, and (5) certification that the employee was trained and tested according to regulations.

Federal law also requires that all drivers involved in transporting hazardous materials receive (1) general awareness training, (2) function specific training, (3) safety training, and (4) driver training.

This study manual meets the requirements for general awareness training, safety training, and driver training for HazMat drivers, including a test at the end of each chapter. These can be placed in the driver's files and serves as testing the drivers in accordance with the HazMat regulations.

In order to certify that training and testing were conducted, the trainer must teach the general awareness portion of the training from this chapter. The Safety Training and Driver Training certification can be obtained by reviewing Chapters 7, 10, 11, and 12 in this manual, along with the appropriate test.

The Hazardous Material Regulations (HMR) can be found in parts 171–180 of Title 49 of the Code of Federal Regulations—49 CFR 171–180.

Frequently Asked Questions (FAQ) about Hazardous Materials

Q. Who needs HazMat training and testing?

A. According to regulations, all drivers involved in transporting hazardous materials must receive training and testing. Your employer is required to provide this training for you and is required to keep a log (record) of this training as long as you work for the company and for 90 days after you leave.

Regulations also require that employees receive updated HazMat training every two years.

Drivers who haul flammable cryogenic liquids and certain route-controlled quantities of radioactive material are required to receive training every two years. These drivers must also, at all times, carry a dated certificate showing the date of training.

If you haul cargo tanks and portable tanks, you must also have training in HazMat every two years.

Q. What is special routing?

A. Sometimes HazMat loads are required to take certain routes (Figure 11-1) and some states require a special permit before certain hazardous materials are moved. Make sure you know about any special rules regarding hazardous materials in your state and in the areas in which you will be driving. You can find out from your company's safety official or the local Department of Motor Vehicles to make certain you comply with all federal and state HazMat regulations.

Q. Why so many regulations? Isn't this just freight or cargo?

A. Yes and no. Yes, it is freight and yes, it is cargo, but many hazardous materials can injure or kill people if allowed into the environment. So, the reason for the regulations is to lessen the danger.

HazMat rules exist for drivers as well as for shippers and the general public. These rules are very clear about how a material is packaged, loaded, hauled, and unloaded.

These are called **Containment Rules.** They are procedures to ensure that hazardous materials are contained and handled properly and to ensure that no leaking and no spillage occur.

Anyone dealing with hazardous materials—shippers and carriers—must tell drivers and others about the hazardous qualities and drivers must warn motorists about the risk. Drivers must also warn others in case of an accident or spill.

Figure 11-1   HazMat regulations lessen any dangers to the public.

Q. How do I warn motorists about hazardous materials and communicate the risks of these materials?

A. You use placards on all four sides of your vehicle to let drivers know the risk and also ensure the proper placement of shipping papers while HazMat cargo is being moved.

   If you are hauling HazMat cargo and you don't have the HazMat Endorsement on your CDL, you will be fined and possibly jailed for noncompliance. So, *don't break the rules*. These rules are here for your safety and the safety of others.

Q. Who is responsible for proper and lawful handling of HazMat cargo?

A. This is a big responsibility and it is usually divided equally among the shipper, carrier, and driver.

Q. What is the shipper's role?

A. Anyone sending hazardous materials from Point A to Point B must understand and use HazMat regulations in order to decide the following for each HazMat product:

- Proper shipping name
- Hazardous class

- Identification numbers
- Correct type of packing
- Correct label and marking on the package
- Correct placard(s)

The shipper is also responsible for packing the HazMat cargo properly, labeling it properly, and identifying it properly on the package. The shipper is also responsible for supplying the proper placards and preparing the shipping papers.

The shipper must also certify on the shipping papers that the shipment has been prepared according to regulations. (The only exception is when the shipper is a private carrier, transporting its own products.)

Q. What's the carrier's responsibility when it comes to HazMat cargo?
A. The carrier plays a smaller but equally important role. The carrier must:

- Transport the shipment to the proper destination.
- Ensure that the shipper has correctly named, labeled, and marked the HazMat shipment.
- Report any accident or incident involving the HazMat cargo to the proper government agency.

Q. What is the driver's responsibility?
A. It is the driver's responsibility to:

- Double-check with both the shipper and carrier—make sure the load is properly identified, marked, and labeled.
- *Refuse* any leaking cartons or shipments.
- Communicate the risk by attaching proper placards to the vehicle.
- Deliver products as safely and quickly as possible and obey federal and state HazMat regulations.
- Keep all HazMat shipping papers in proper place—a *requirement*.

Q. What is meant by the "Hazard Class?"
A. The "Hazard Class" of materials indicates the degree of risk associated with that material. The Hazard Class has nine classes or categories. They are found in Part 173 of the HMC and the provisions of Section 172.101.

Q. What do these class numbers mean?
A. The first number indicates the class of the hazardous material (i.e., explosive, gases, flammable liquids, flammable solids, oxidizing substances, poisons, radioactive materials, corrosive material and miscellaneous material).

The second number indicates the division. In the number 1.3, the 1 tells you it's an explosive and the 3 tells you the division—which is explosive B. Table 11-1 lists the hazard classes and the divisions.

Q. What exactly do the different classes of explosives mean?
A. An explosive is any material or substance or item (like an explosive device) designed to operate through an explosive action or through a chemical reaction. Or this material may function in a similar manner, even though it was not designed to explode.

Table 11–1
HM-181 Classes and Divisions

New Classes and Divisions	Old Classes
Class 1 (Explosives)	**Explosives**
1.1	Explosive Class A
1.2	Explosive A or B
1.3	Explosive B
1.4	Explosive C
1.5	Blasting Agent
1.6	
Class 2 (Gases)	**Gases**
2.1	Flammable Gas
2.2	Non-Flammable Gas
2.3	Poison Gas
Class 3 (Flammable Liquids)	**Flammable Combustible Liquids**
3.1	Flammable Liquid
3.2	Combustible Liquid
Class 4 (Flammable Solids)	**Flammable Solids**
4.1	Flammable Solid
4.2	Flammable Solid/Liquid
4.3	Flammable Solid—dangerous when wet
Class 5 (Oxidizing Substances)	**Oxidizing Substances**
5.1	Oxidizer
5.2	Organic Peroxide
Class 6 (Poisons)	**Poisons**
6.1	Poison B
6.2	Etiologic Agents (infectious substances)
Class 7 (Radioactive Materials)	**Radioactive Material**
Class 8 (Corrosive Material)	**Corrosive Material**
Class 9 (Miscellaneous Material)	**ORM (Other Regulated Material)**

Class 1—Explosives

- Division 1.1—Explosives that are a mass explosion hazard—if one goes, they all go—which makes for a bad situation. It's dangerous, to say the least.
- Division 1.2—Explosives that are not a mass explosion hazard but are a projection hazard.

- Division 1.3—Explosives that have a fire or minor blast or minor projection hazard—or both—but not a mass explosion hazard.
- Division 1.4—Explosive devices with a minor explosion hazard (can contain more than 25 grams of detonating material).
- Division 1.5—Insensitive explosives—they usually carry a mass explosion hazard but chances are remote. Under normal conditions, they would make the transition of being on fire and then exploding.
- Division 1.6—Items without mass explosion hazard—only very insensitive detonating substances and demonstrate little chance of accidental fire or explosion.

Class 2—Gases

- Division 2.1—This class of gases is any material which will ignite at 68 degrees Fahrenheit (20 degrees Celcius) and 14.7 psi pressure when mixed with air.
- Division 2.2—Nonflammable and nonpoisonous compressed gases. This includes compressed gas, liquefied gas, pressurized cryonic gas, and compressed gas, which is in solution. Any material in this division does not meet the definition of Division 2.1 or 2.3.
- Division 2.3—Known to be poisonous and to be toxic enough to be a hazard to human health—even if adequate data do not currently exist—but have been toxic to laboratory animals.

Class 3—Flammable Liquids

Class three has no divisions. A flammable liquid is one with a flash point of not more 140 degrees Fahrenheit. This is true except for materials meeting the definition of any Class 2 material. And this class also includes a mixture having components that have a flash point greater than 141 degrees Fahrenheit or higher—if it makes up at least 99 percent of the total volume of the mix. Or it could also be a distilled spirit of 140 proof or lower, considered to have a flash point of lower than 73 degrees Fahrenheit.

Class 4—Flammable Solids

- Division 4.1—Includes three types of flammable solids. First, there are wetted explosives that when dry are explosives of Class 1; there are some exceptions. Second, there are self-reactive materials that may undergo—at normal or elevated temperatures—a decomposition that could make them ignite. This can happen in high transport temperatures or through contamination.

  Any solids that are readily combustible can create fire through friction. This material shows a burning rate faster than 2.2 millimeters per second. The third type of flammable solid in this division includes metal powder that can ignite and react over the test area in 10 minutes or less.
- Division 4.2—These are solid materials which, even in small quantities, ignite within five minutes of exposure to air under certain test procedures.

- Division 4.3—These materials that can become spontaneously flammable on contact with water. This division also contains material that can emit (give off) flammable or toxic gases at a rate of 1 liter per kilogram per hour or greater.

Class 5—Oxidizing Substances

- Division 5.1—Because they emit oxygen, these materials can cause or increase the combustion of other materials.
- Division 5.2—This division includes organic peroxide—a derivative of hydrogen peroxide.

Class 6—Poisons

- Division 6.1—This division includes materials that are toxic to humans or so toxic that they pose a health hazard during transportation. The division also includes materials presumed hazardous to humans because of results in laboratory tests. This division also includes irritants, such as tear gas.
- Division 6.2—Infectious substances which may cause disease or death in animals or humans. This includes human or animal excretions, secretions, blood tissue and tissue components.

Class 7—Radioactive Material

This class includes any radioactive material with a specific activity greater than 0.002 microcuries per gram.

Class 8—Corrosive Material

Includes materials—liquid or solid—that cause destruction/irreversible damage to human skin tissue on contact. Also has high corrosion rate on steel and/or aluminum.

Class 9—Other Regulated Material (ORM)

Any material which presents a hazard during transport but is not included by any of the other classes—and is subject to HazMat regulations.

Q. **Exactly what is the "shipping paper?"**
A. This is a form—a document describing the HazMat cargo you are transporting (Figure 11-2). Every item listed on the shipping paper must show the hazardous materials hazard class. Shipping papers may include bills of lading and manifests.

Q. **What else should be shown on the shipping paper?**
A. Each copy of the shipping paper should have numbered pages, with the first page indicating the total number of papers for the shipment.

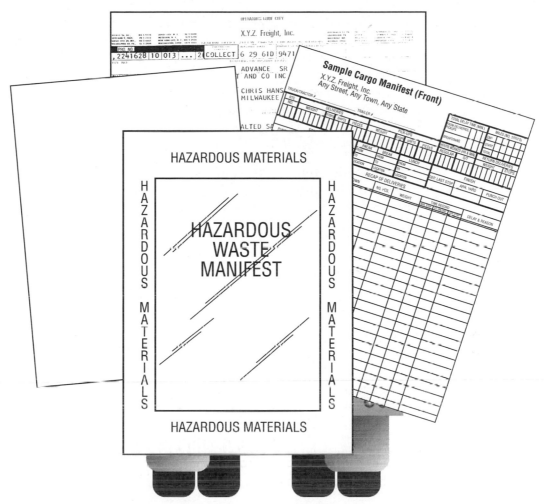

Figure 11-2 Every item of hazardous material must have a HazMat hazard class on all shipping papers.

The shipping paper should have the proper description of any hazardous material.

The shipper's certificate—signed by the shipper's representative—must also be included. This certificate verifies that the shipment has been prepared according to all applicable regulations.

Q. Are there any exceptions to the shipping paper rules?

A. Yes—if the shipper is a private carrier that is transporting its own freight, the shipper does not need to sign a shipper's certificate.

Q. What if the shipment has a mix of nonhazardous and hazardous materials?

A. In this case, if the shipping papers show a mix of hazardous and nonhazardous materials, those items that are hazardous must be marked by:

- Describing the item first, or
- Highlighting or printing in a different color, or
- An "X" before the shipping name in the column marked HM, or
- The letters RQ if the shipment is a reportable quantity.

Remember: *The description of the hazardous product must include the proper shipping name. It must also include the HazMat class or division and the Identification (ID) number and must be written in that order—shipping name, hazard class and ID number. No abbreviations!*

The only abbreviations permitted are for the packaging type and the unit of measure—and these can appear on the shipping paper before or after the description.

If the shipment is hazardous waste, then the word "waste" must appear before the name of the material being shipped.

Also included must be the total quality and unit of measure (i.e., drums, cylinders, cartons). And if the HazMat shipment is a reportable quantity, the letters RQ must be marked on the shipping paper under HM.

Q. Why is the shipping paper so important?

A. The shipping paper is used for several purposes, but the primary purpose is to communicate what's being shipped and if there's any risk involved (Figure 11-3). If, for some reason, the driver is injured or is taken ill and

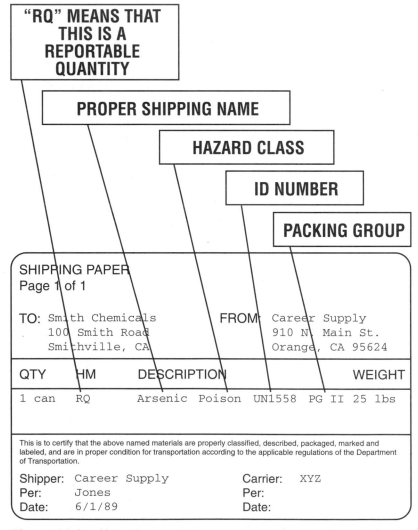

Figure 11-3 Shipping papers communicate items being shipped and any possible risk.

unable to speak, then the shipping paper would inform the authorities if hazardous materials are included in the cargo.

After the attending officials obtain information regarding the shipment, they can take appropriate action to protect the safety of everyone.

This makes the shipping paper a very important part of the shipment and emphasizes why it should be filled out correctly. Your life or the lives of others may be at stake and fast action may be required—an emergency is no time to try and decipher what the cargo holds.

Q. What happens if a truck carrying HazMat cargo is involved in an accident (Figure 11-4)?

A. It may be necessary for law enforcement officials to obtain information quickly and for this reason, the following regulations also apply to the shipping papers:

- They must be tagged or tabbed and placed on top of all other shipping papers—this is the responsibility of the carrier and the driver.
- When driver is out of the truck, the shipping papers must be placed on the driver's seat or in a pouch in the driver's door.
- While driving, the driver must place the shipping papers in a pouch in the driver's door or in clear view of the driver when the seatbelt is being used.

Q. Are there any other responsibilities—for the shipper or driver—regarding HazMat cargo?

A. The shipper must label the package properly, applying diamond-shaped labels indicating the hazardous materials within the package.

If the label cannot be placed on the package, the shipper must attach a tag or decal, indicating the hazard involved.

Figure 11-4 In case of accident, HazMat shipping papers provide law enforcement officials with necessary information.

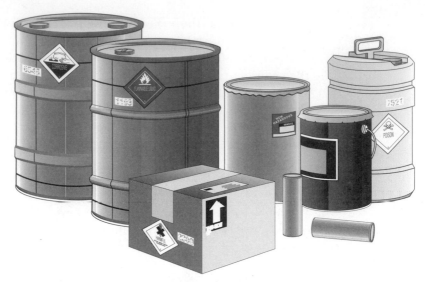

Figure 11-5   Paper labels are required for all HazMat items.

Q. What is the difference between a HazMat placard and a HazMat label?
A. Both are diamond-shaped and both are used to communicate the contents
and the hazards they involve.

   The HazMat label is the responsibility of the shipper and goes on the
shipment itself—whether it is a box, cylinder, etc (Figure 11-5).

   The HazMat placard is the responsibility of the driver and is a diamond-
shaped sign that is placed on all four sides of the tractor-trailer carrying the
hazardous materials. The placards must be readable in all four directions.
The placards must be placed on the rear of the trailer, both sides, and either
the front of the trailer or the front of the tractor (Figure 11-6).

   Placards must read from left to right and must be located at least three
inches away from other markings. And they must be placed "on point."

   If a tanker is being used, the ID number of the HazMat shipment must be
shown inside the placard or on an orange panel.

*Note: Once the HazMat cargo has been unloaded, it is the driver's responsibility to remove
the placards! In most cases, HazMat placards are not allowed on empty trailers.*

Q. Are there any other protections offered when hauling a HazMat load?
A. There are three main HazMat Lists for shippers, carriers, and drivers to use.
These lists help each party involved determine the proper handling of any
HazMat load.

   These lists are:

1. The Hazardous Materials Table (Table 11-2)
2. The List of Hazardous Substances and Reportable Quantities
3. The List of Marine Pollutants

*Remember: Before transporting any unfamiliar products or items, look for its name on each
list. Each list will have the proper shipping name, hazardous class, identification number,
and proper labeling required.*

PLACARD LOCATIONS

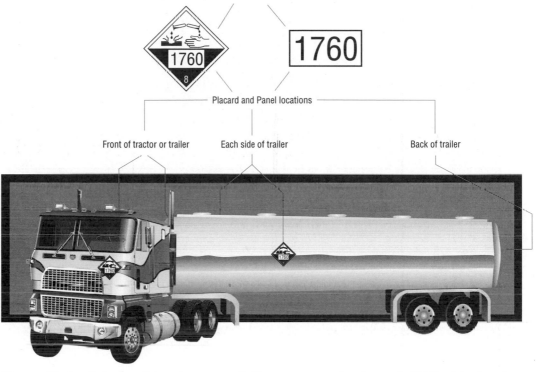

Figure 11-6 It is the driver's responsibility to properly placard all HazMat loads.

Information about the Hazardous Materials Table

Column one has symbols that have a specific meaning. These include:

- + The designated proper shipping name and hazardous materials class must always be shown, even if product doesn't match a hazard class definition.
- D The proper shipping name is appropriate for describing materials for domestic transportation but may not be proper for international transport.
- A Cargo is subject to the regulations only when transported by air, unless materials are hazardous substances and hazardous waste.
- W Cargo is subject to regulations only when transported by water, unless material is a hazardous substance, hazardous waste, or marine pollutant.
- G Technical names of the hazardous materials must be listed in parentheses after the proper shipping name.
- I Proper shipping name is appropriate for use in international transportation.

Column 2 shows the name of regulated materials in alphabetical order. On this table, the proper shipping names are always shown in regular type. The names shown in italics are not proper shipping names and can only be used along with the proper shipping name.

Table 11–2
Part of the Hazardous Materials Table

(1) Symbols	(2) Hazardous materials descriptions and proper shipping names	(3) Hazard class or Division	(4) Identification Numbers	(5) PG	(6) Label Codes	(7) Special provisions	(8) Packaging (§173.***)			(9) Quantity limitations		(10) Vessel stowage	
							(8A) Exceptions	(8B) Non-bulk	(8C) Bulk	(9A) Passenger aircraft/rail	(9B) Cargo aircraft only	(10A) Location	(10B) Other
	Air bag inflators, compressed gas or Air bag modules, compressed gas or Seat-belt pretensioners, compressed gas.	2.2	UN3353		2.2	133	166	166	166	75 kg	150 kg	A	
	Air bag inflators, pyrotechnic or Air bag modules, pyrotechnic or Seat-belt pretensioner, pyrotechnic.	9	UN3268	III	9		166	166	166	25 kg	100 kg	A	
	Air, compressed	2.2	UN1002		2.2	78	306	302	302	75 kg	150 kg	A	
	Air, refrigerated liquid, (cryogenic liquid).	2.2	UN1003		2.2, 5.1		320	316	318, 319.	Forbidden	150 kg	D	51
	Air, refrigerated liquid, (cryogenic liquid) non-pressurized.	2.2	UN1003		2.2, 5.1		320	316	318, 319.	Forbidden	Forbidden	D	51
	Aircraft evacuation slides, see Life saving appliances etc.												
	Aircraft hydraulic power unit fuel tank *(containing a mixture of anhydrous hydrazine and monomethyl hydrazine) (M86 fuel)*	3	UN3165	I	3, 6.1, 8		None	172	None	Forbidden	42 L	E	
	Aircraft survival kits, see Life saving appliances etc.												
G	Alcoholates solution, n.o.s., *in alcohol.*	3	UN3274	II	3, 8		None	202	243	1 L	5 L	B	
	Alcoholic beverages	3	UN3065	II	3	24, B1, T1	150	202	242	5 L	60 L	A	
				III	3	24, B1, N11, T1	150	203	242	60 L	220 L	A	
	Alcohols, n.o.s	3	UN1987	I	3	T8, T31	None	201	243	1 L	30 L	E	
				II	3	T8, T31	150	202	242	5 L	60 L	B	
				III	3	B1, T7, T30	150	203	242	60 L	220 L	A	
G	Alcohols, flammable, toxic, n.o.s	3	UN1986	I	3, 6.1	T8, T31	None	201	243	Forbidden	30 L	E	40
				II	3, 6.1	T8, T31	None	202	243	1 L	60 L	B	40
				III	3, 6.1	B1, T8, T31	None	203	242	60 L	220 L	A	
	Aldehydes, n.o.s	3	UN1989	I	3	T8, T31	None	201	243	1 L	30 L	E	
				II	3	T8, T31	150	202	242	5 L	60 L	B	
				III	3	B1, T7, T30	150	203	242	60 L	220 L	A	
G	Aldehydes, flammable, toxic, n.o.s	3	UN1988	I	3, 6.1	T8, T31	None	201	243	Forbidden	30 L	E	40
				II	3, 6.1	T8, T31	None	202	243	1 L	60 L	B	40

From 49CFR172—Part 172—Hazardous Materials Table. Available: www.access.gpo.gov/nara/cfr

Column 3 shows the hazard class or division—or it may have the word "forbidden." When you see "forbidden," *never* transport this material.

The hazard class for the material is the indicator of what placards to use. To choose the proper placard, you must have three pieces of information:

1. The hazard class for the cargo
2. The amount being shipped
3. The amount of all hazardous materials in all classes on the vehicle

If the words "inhalation hazard" appear on the shipping papers, you must use a poison placard in addition to the others that are required.

Column 4 shows the ID number for each proper shipping name. These ID numbers are preceded by the initials "UN" or "NA." The letters "NA" are used only in shipments between the United States and Canada.

The ID number must also appear on the shipping paper, the package, and the cargo tanks and all other bulk packages.

Column 5 identifies packing group, which is assigned to material.

Column 6 shows the hazard label, which shippers must put on packages of hazardous materials. Some products require more than one label. If the word "none" appears, then no label is required.

Column 7 includes any additional provisions for this material—if you see a Column 7 entry, refer to federal regulations for specific information.

Column 8 is a three-part column which shows section numbers covering packaging for HazMat cargo.

Columns 9 and 10 do not apply to highway transport.

Q. Are there any more responsibilities for the driver regarding HazMat loads?
A. Glad you asked!

The Department of Transportation (DOT) and the Environmental Protection Agency (EPA) must be notified in the event of a leak or spill of certain hazardous materials.

The **Hazardous Substances and Reportable Quantities List** will tell you if the cargo is a reportable quantity. The product and the amount spilled determines whether or not it is reportable.

An asterisk (*) next to the name indicates the product also appears on the HazMat table.

If any size spill of any hazardous materials occurs, the driver must report the spill to his or her employer.

Q. How much more do I need to know about HazMat?
A. As a driver, you must know the following information:

1. You must be able to recognize that you are loading and will be hauling hazardous materials. How do you do that? First, look at the shipping papers. Then, determine if hazardous materials are being shipped.
2. If hazardous materials are part or all of the cargo, check to make sure the shipping papers are properly filled out with the proper shipping name, hazard class, and ID number, listed in that exact order.
3. You must also look for highlighted products or the letters "X" or "RQ" in the HM column.
4. When accepting a delivery for shipment, the driver must be 100-percent sure the shipping papers are correct, the packages are properly labeled, and the vehicle is properly loaded and is displaying the appropriate placards.

Note: If you are not 100-percent certain that the process has been followed TO THE LETTER, you should contact the terminal dispatcher and make certain that the proper process has been followed.

Never accept damaged or leaking HazMat shipments. If you have any questions, contact the dispatcher. Dispatchers know everything!

HazMat Placards

Q. Is there any time it is legal to drive an improperly placarded vehicle?
A. Only in an emergency to save or protect life or property.

Q. How will I know what placards are the correct ones to use?
A. This isn't always the easiest task, but following these three steps can help:

1. Check the shipping papers for the hazard class, amount shipped, and total weight of all hazardous materials in this shipment.
2. Check the shipment and make certain the packages match the hazard class listed on the shipping papers.
3. Once the labels have been matched to the shipping papers, check the placard tables to determine which placards should be used.

There are two placard tables—one requires placards for any amount of hazardous material being shipped.

The other placard table requires placards if the amount being shipped is more than 1000 pounds.

Note: If you pick up hazardous materials from more than one location, add the weight of product you picked up to the product already loaded.

If weight of the combined shipment is 1001 pounds or more, then you'll be required to display the proper placard.

Hazardous Waste Manifest

Any cargo containing hazardous waste must be accompanied by a hazardous waste manifest—and this must be signed by the driver.

Q. Who is responsible for preparing the manifest?
A. This manifest is the responsibility of the shipper. And the driver will treat the hazardous waste manifest as any other shipping paper.

The carrier who accepts the hazardous waste cargo must make certain that the hazardous waste manifest is properly completed and a shipment labeled as hazardous waste may only be delivered to another registered carrier or to a facility that is authorized to receive and handle hazardous waste.

The carrier must maintain a copy of the hazardous waste manifest for three years following transport. And once the cargo is delivered to the authorized hazardous waste facility, the facility's operator must sign for the shipment.

Q. When can the "Dangerous" placard be used?

A. You can use the "Dangerous" placard if you have a load requiring a flammable placard and then pick up 1000 pounds of combustible material, instead of using two separate placards—like "flammable" or "combustible."

There are two exceptions (1) if you have loaded 5000 pounds of HazMat cargo at one location, you must use the placard for that material, and (2) if the words "Inhalation Hazard" appear on the shipping papers, you must use the material's specific placard AND a "Poison" placard.

Blasting agents (1.6), Oxidizer (5.1), and Dangerous placards are not required if the vehicle contains Class 1 explosives and you're using Division 1.1, 1.2, or 1.3 placards.

When the vehicle displays a Division 2.1 Flammable Gas or an Oxygen placard, you do not need to display a Nonflammable Gas placard if you pick up that material and add it to your load.

Remember: *Displaying the wrong placard is just as wrong as not displaying any placard.*

Placards are used to communicate with and inform others. Incorrect information is just as harmful as no information.

Note: *If a vehicle carrying hazardous materials spills or leaks an RQ (reportable quantity), it must be reported to the carrier.*

The carrier reports it to the National Response Center (NRC), which has the ability to contact the proper law enforcement agency and the proper containment or clean-up personnel (Figure 11-7).

The carrier is required to call the NRC (800-424-8802) if an incident of leakage or spill occurs and if:

- Someone is killed
- Someone is injured and requires hospitalization
- Estimated property damage exceeds $50,000
- One or more major roadways is closed for one hour or more
- Fire, breakage, spillage, or suspected radioactive contamination occurs
- Fire, breakage, spillage, or suspected contamination of etiologic agents occurs

When calling the NRC, give the following information:

- Name
- Name and address of carrier
- Phone number where carrier can be reached
- Date, time, and location of event
- The extent of injuries—if any
- The class, name, and quantity of the hazardous materials involved
- The type of incident and the nature of hazardous material involvement
- If a reportable quantity of hazardous substance is involved, the caller should also give the name of the shipper and the quantity of the hazardous materials discharged.

Q. What is CHEMTREC?

A. CHEMTREC is the acronym for the Chemical Transportation Emergency Center in Washington, DC. It has a 24-hour toll-free line and has evolved to provide emergency personnel with technical information and expertise

**NATIONAL RESPONSE CENTER
(800) 424-8802**

**CHEMTREC
(800) 424-9300**

CHEMICAL EMERGENCY

You need to know and understand what these agencies do and what they cannot do.

Figure 11-7 Agencies to call in case of accident or chemical involving a HazMat load.

about the physical properties of hazardous products. The NRC and CHEMTREC work closely together. If you call either CHEMTREC at 800-424-9300 or the NRC at 800-424-8802, whichever agency you call will notify the other about the problem.

In addition to calling the NRC or CHEMTREC, drivers are responsible for helping the carriers make a detailed written report. The driver is particularly valuable in completing these reports, so it is a good idea for the driver to write out a report, detailing what took place, as soon as possible.

Q. What should I know about loading, unloading, and hauling hazardous materials?

A. There are a few rules to always keep in mind when handling hazardous materials:

- No smoking—at any time, but particularly when loading explosives, oxidizers, or flammables. Never handle these materials around a heat source.
- Never load damaged or leaking packages or containers.
- Never open any packages during transport. If a package breaks open, call your dispatcher immediately.
- No overhangs or tailgate loads for explosives, oxidizing materials, or flammable solids.
- Rules forbid using cargo heaters or air-conditioning unless you know the rules for the cargo you're hauling. If in doubt, check with your company.
- When you park, set the brakes and chock the wheels.
- Do everything possible to protect the public.

Q. Are there any specific rules for loading HazMat cargo?

A. Unless otherwise stated, these materials must be loaded in a closed cargo space unless packages are fire- and water-resistant or covered with a fire- or water-resistant tarp:

Class 1 Explosives

1. Before loading or unloading, turn off the engine.
2. Disconnect heat power for cargo heaters and drain heater fuel tanks.
3. Check the trailer or truck for any sharp points that could damage the cargo.
4. Check the floorboards and sidewalls; you must use floor lining with Divisions 1.1, 1.2, or 1.3 explosives. The liner may not contain steel or iron.
5. Never transfer explosives from one vehicle to another on a public highway. The only exception is an emergency situation.
6. Never accept damaged packages or packages stained with oil or dampness.
7. Never transport Division 1.1 explosives in triples.
8. Never transport Division 1.2 and 1.3 explosives in the combination if there's a placarded cargo tank in the combination or if you're hauling initiating explosives, radioactive materials (Class 7) or Class 6 poisons or hazardous materials in a portable tank.

Q. What do I need to know about corrosive liquids?

A. If you're loading by hand, handle containers one at a time—don't drop, turn over, or top load them unless the weight can be stabilized by freight on the bottom of the stack. Keep containers right side up—no if's, and's or but's. Never load nitric acid above anything else—and never more than two stacks high.

Never load corrosives with explosives, flammable solids, or oxidizing materials.

If you are loading cylinders (compressed gases or cryogenic liquids) and the vehicle doesn't have built-in racks, then the cylinders must be kept upright or braced lying down or in boxes to prevent them from turning over.

If you are handling poisons, never mix loads with foodstuffs and never load these materials in the driver's cab or sleeper.

Q. What about radioactive materials—are they handled any differently?

A. No matter how well radioactive materials are packaged, radiation escapes from each package. Look at Class 7 HazMat for the number of packages that can be transported. This is the "transport index." This tells the degree of control necessary during transportation—the total transport index of all packages in a single vehicle cannot exceed 50.

Q. How should mixed loads be handled?

A. Federal regulations—the Segregation and Separation Chart—demand that certain hazardous materials be loaded separately (see Table 11–3).

Q. Are there any rules for a actually hauling HazMat cargo?

A. As soon as the shipping papers have been checked and the truck has been properly placarded, there are a few reminders for drivers:

- Never park within five feet of the traveled part of the road if you're hauling explosives.
- Never park within 300 feet of a bridge, tunnel, or building; places where people gather; or an open fire when hauling explosives.
- Someone—the shipper, the carrier, or the consignee—should be in attendance of the vehicle at all times when hauling explosives.
- The vehicle can be left unattended on a government-approved safe haven—a location approved for parking unattended vehicles loaded with explosives.

Table 11–3
Segregation and Separation Chart

Don't Load . . .	In the Same Vehicle With . . .
Poison—Class 6	Animal or human foodstuff, unless the poison package is over-packed in an approved way. (Foodstuff can be anything you swallow—except mouthwash, toothpastes, and skin cream, which are not foodstuffs.)
Poison—Division 2.3	Oxidizers, flammables, corrosives, organic peroxides.
Charged Storage Batteries—Division 1.1	Explosives.
Detonating Primers	Any other explosives, unless in authorized containers or packages.
Cyanides or Mixtures	Acids, corrosive materials, or other acidic materials which could release hydrocyanic acid from cyanides. Cyanides are materials with the letters "cyan" as part of their shipping name, like acetone cyanohydrin, silver cyanide, or trichloroisocyanuric acid, dry.
Nitric Acid	Other corrosive liquids in carboys (a container holding 5 to 15 gallons of liquid, often cushioned in a wooden box), unless separated in an approved manner.

If you're hauling HazMat cargo—but not explosives—you may:

- Park within five feet of the road, only if the job requires it and someone is with the vehicle at all times and that person understands the hazards involved.
- Never uncouple the trailer and leave it on a public street.
- Set out reflective triangles within 10 minutes, if you park along the roadway.
- Never park within 300 feet of an open fire.

Q. What's the difference between an "attended" and "unattended" vehicle?
A. If you have someone watch the vehicle for you, that person must be in the vehicle and must be alert—or they must be within 100 feet from the vehicle (not smoking) and within clear view.

That individual must know what to do in an emergency and must be able to move the vehicle; if necessary.

Q. Can flares be used in an emergency?
A. Never leave flares or any burning signal device around tankers used for flammables, explosives, flammable liquids, or flammable gas.

Additional Instruction to Comply with HM 126-F Requirements

An important part of knowing about transporting hazardous material is the packaging. It is an important part of the transportation process and critical to the safety of everyone who handles or transports hazardous material.

Q. What about refueling?
A. Always turn off engine before refueling. Someone must be in control of the fuel at the nozzle.

Q. Where should I keep the shipping papers while on the road?
A. They must always be in clear view in the pouch on the driver's door or where driver can reach them while the seatbelt is buckled. Shipping papers regarding HazMat information should be tagged and placed on top of all other papers.

Q. Where should shipping papers be when I am out of the truck?
A. This is a review question—they should be placed on the driver's seat or in a pouch inside the driver's side door.

Q. Are there any special inspections required when hauling HazMat Cargo?
A. Other than the pre-trip and enroute checks, stops are required every two hours or every 100 miles to check your tires and to remove any tires that are overheated. If you have a flat or a tire that is noticeably leaking, drive only as far as necessary to get it fixed.

Q. What about directions for hauling chlorine?
A. You should have an approved gas mask in the vehicle and must also know how to use an emergency kit for controlling leaks in dome lid plate fittings on the tank.

Q. What about railroad crossings?

A. *No matter what,* if you are in a placarded vehicle or carrying any amount of chlorine or have cargo tanks used to transport HazMat cargo (loaded or empty) you must stop at railroad crossings—no closer than 15 feet and no further away than 50 feet from the nearest rail. *Don't* shift gears while crossing—and it's a good practice to turn on your four-way flashers when stopping at a railroad crossing.

Q. What about route restrictions?

A. Some areas of the country require permits and special routing for carriers transporting certain materials. As the driver, it is up to you to know about these special requirements, so check with your company and always check routes before beginning a trip—you want to be permitted to travel on the roads you'll be driving. Fines are costly—against the company and against you as the driver.

Note: Anytime you're hauling explosives, (Division 1.1, 1.2 or 1.3), a written route plan is required—and you must follow that plan. The same applies when hauling radioactive materials—the carrier is responsible for telling the driver that the trailer is loaded with these materials.

HazMat Emergencies

The Emergency Response Guidebook (ERG) is used by fire fighters, police officers, industry safety personnel, and others in the event of an emergency involving hazardous materials. This book is available through the Department of Transportation (*www.dot.gov*), or you can download the forms at *http://hazmat.dot.gov/ohmforms.htm.*

When an emergency occurs, police and fire personnel must determine what type of hazardous material is involved. This is accomplished by checking the shipping papers, looking at the placards, and getting information from the driver. However, in some accidents, there may be no time to locate the shipping papers or talk to the driver. So, the only thing left is for them to look at the placards.

Once the type of hazardous material is determined, emergency personnel can then take steps to protect life and property—which is one more reason why the right placards must be used, the shipping papers must always be accurate, and the driver must be aware of what is being hauled.

Q. What do I do, as the driver, in case of an accident involving HazMat cargo?

A. The following is your responsibility at the scene of an accident involving hazardous materials:

- Warn people of danger and keep them away (Figure 11-8).
- Secure the accident scene as best you can.
- If you can do so safely, contain the spill.
- Contact the appropriate emergency response personnel (e.g., police, fire) and tell them what has happened. Be prepared to provide the following information:
  - ——Product's shipping name, hazard class, and ID number
  - ——Extent of the spill

Figure 11-8 In case of HazMat emergency, secure the accident area.

———Location
———When the accident/incident happened
———Phone number where you can be reached
———Let them hang up first—make sure they have all the information they need
———Contact your dispatcher and follow his or her instructions

Q. What do I do in case of fire?
A. Never attempt to fight a HazMat fire unless you have specific training on how to do it.

The power unit of a vehicle with placards must have a fire extinguisher with a UL rating of at least 10 B:C.

Q. What do I do in case of a leak or a spill?
A. First of all, don't touch it—because certain hazardous materials can kill you just by touching them or breathing the fumes. Determine what the HazMat cargo is by looking at shipping papers, but do not go near the spill or allow anyone else to go near it. Contact the local authorities and your dispatcher as quickly as possible. *Do not attempt to move the vehicle unless you have to because of safety concerns.*

- If you are driving and notice something leaking from the vehicle, pull as far off the road as you can, get the shipping papers, and get away from the vehicle. Then, send someone for help. Stay away from the truck but keep it in sight so you can keep others away.
- DO NOT drive to a phone if you spot a leak.

- When sending someone for help, write down your location, a description of the emergency, your name, your carrier's name and phone number, as well as the shipping name, hazard class, and ID number of the materials.
- Never smoke or allow smoking around the vehicle.

If you see leakage or damage to a HazMat package while unloading, get away from the vehicle as quickly as possible and contact your dispatcher immediately. *Do not touch or inhale the material!*

Q. How should a tank be marked for HazMat cargo?

A. For **cargo tanks**—which are attached permanently to the vehicle—loading takes place with the tank on the vehicle.

On these tanks, placard requirements include an ID number that must appear on the vehicle—either black four-inch numbers on an orange panel, or a Department of Transportation placard on a white, diamond-shaped background. And don't forget, cargo tanks must also show re-test date markings.

For **portable tanks**—which are not permanently mounted to the vehicle—loading and unloading takes place with the tanks off the vehicle.

Portable tanks show the owner's or leaser's name. The shipping name and ID number must be on opposite sides. If the tanks hold 1,000 gallons or more, the ID number must be on all four sides—in black paint and at least two inches tall.

Q. Are there any rules and regulations about loading and unloading tanks?

A. Yes. Certain rules must be followed by the person unloading. That person must:

- Be within 25 feet and have a clear view of the tanks.
- Be aware of the hazards.
- Know the procedures for an emergency.
- Be authorized and have the ability to move the cargo tank if necessary.

When loading and unloading flammable gases into tanks:

- Don't smoke.
- Turn off the engine—use the engine only to run the pump, if necessary.
- The engine should be turned on only after the product hose is hooked up and turned off before uncoupling hose.
- Secure the truck against movement.
- Secure the electrical ground wire correctly or have the ground wire attached before and after opening the fill hole.

Q. What is Performance Oriented Packaging (POP)?

A. This is a government term meaning that the packaging used for HazMat cargo must "perform" in such a way as to be safe, making it possible to handle and transport the cargo safely.

These standards require that each package be designed and produced so that when it is filled to capacity, sealed, and transported under normal conditions:

- The package will not release HazMat products.

- There will be nothing to reduce the strength or seal or cause other changes due to flucuation in temperature.
- The package itself should contain nothing that could ruin the packaging.

For additional information, check HMR, Part 173, "Shippers' General Requirements for Shipments and Packaging."

To comply with governmental regulations, all packaging must meet the above requirements and must (1) contain the manufacturer's marking (2) be marked with proper shipping name and ID number and (3) be tested and approved before use.

Let's Review

Read each question and all of the answers provided. Place the letter of the correct answer in the space provided or write your answers on a separate piece of paper so you can use these questions again as you review for the CDL. Once you have answered all the questions, check your answers against the answer key which follows.

_____ 1. When the driver is in the driver's seat with the seatbelt on, the shipping papers should be
 (A) in the glove box,   (C) in the driver's briefcase,
 (B) in a pouch in the driver's door, (D) none of the above.

_____ 2. If you are approaching a railroad crossing with a HazMat load, you must
 (A) sound the horn before crossing, (C) stop five feet from the tracks,
 (B) shift gears before crossing,   (D) none of the above.

_____ 3. True or False. Smoking is allowed around a HazMat load if you are smoking filtered cigarettes.

_____ 4. If it is necessary for you to stop at a rest stop for a few minutes, you must put the shipping papers
 (A) on the driver's seat,   (C) under the windshield wiper,
 (B) in your pocket,   (D) none of the above.

_____ 5. If you are hauling Division 1 explosives, you must not park your rig within how many feet of a fire?
 (A) 300 feet   (C) 50 feet
 (B) 500 feet   (D) 1000 feet

_____ 6. While hauling a HazMat load, you should stop every two hours to
 (A) check for leaks,
 (B) check to make sure you have enough fuel,
 (C) check the tires,
 (D) none of the above.

_____ 7. You are asked to pick up a five-pound container of "corrosives." The placards you should use are
 (A) Poison and Corrosive placards,
 (B) Poison only placards,
 (C) Poison and Dangerous placards,
 (D) no placards are required.

_____ 8. If you are a hauling a shipment containing chlorine, you should have a
 (A) cell phone,   (C) medical oxygen tank,
 (B) gas mask,   (D) none of the above.

_____ 9. If you must park a vehicle loaded with hazardous materials and leave it unattended, the best place to park it is
 (A) the shipper's lot,   (C) the consignee's lot,
 (B) the carrier's lot,   (D) all of the above.

_____10. A driver of a vehicle carrying hazardous materials can communicate with authorities by
 (A) using placards,   (C) using the CB,
 (B) calling before entering city limits, (D) all of the above.

Answers to Let's Review

1. B; 2. D; 3. False 4. A; 5. A; 6. A; 7. C; 8. A; 9. D; 10. A

Terms You Need to Know

The following terms have been taken from the contents of Chapter 11. Review them. If you see any you're not sure of, check the definition in the Glossary at the back of the book. If it helps you, keep a written list of the words and their definitions (or write in the definitions here) and review them several days prior to taking the CDL tests.

Carboy

Cargo heaters

Cargo tank

CHEMTREC

CMVSA/86

Combustible

Communicate the risk

Containment

Corrosive

Cryogenic

Cylinders

Emergency Response Guidebook (ERG)

Explosive

Flammable

Flares

Fuse

Gas mask

Hazard Class

Hazardous Material Table

Hazardous waste manifest

HazMat

Identification (ID) number

Infectious substances

Inhalation hazard

List of Hazardous Substances and Reportable Quantities

List of Marine Pollutants

NA

National Response Center (NRC)

Nonhazardous material

Other Regulated Materials (ORM)

Oxidizing substances

Placard

Poison

POP

Radioactive

Route plan

Reportable Quantity (RQ)

Safe haven

Segregation and Separation Chart

Self-reactive materials

Shipper's certification

Shipping papers

Tabbed

Tagged

Transport Index

UN

THE DISPATCH BOARD
Drive Alert—Arrive Alive

By Ron Adams, Ph.D.

Bob made it through the gauntlet, that 250 miles of I-35 from San Antonio to Dallas, one of the most congested roads in the nation and, according to most drivers, construction all the way.

As Bob sees the lights of Cowtown disappear in his rearview mirrors, he glances at his watch, "Three AM, two more hours till rest. Maybe I can make up some time after that heavy traffic north of Austin."

The throaty purr of Bob's powerful Cummings tells him all is well. "A little sleepy? I'll turn up the radio."

Bob roars though the night on the less-traveled highway. Getting more and more sleepy, he reaches for the ever-present thermos. "A shot of java'll perk me up. Damn, I'm tired." Bob rolls down his window, "Some cold air should wake me up."

Feeling the chill of the November night on his face, the veteran driver sees something in the road.

"That's the biggest damn elk I've ever seen."

Bob has been driving this run for 10 years. An avid hunter based in Colorado, he suddenly realizes there are no elk on the plains of North Texas.

Easing his rig into the next rest stop, it is definitely time to shut it down and take a nap.

A professional driver pushing to make up lost time, trying to get in that last hour before his rest . . . . An isolated incident? Some safety experts think not.

The truth is, when you are behind the wheel, being sleepy is dangerous. Sleepiness slows reaction time, decreases awareness, and impairs judgment. Sleepiness can contribute to an accident—or worse.

How safe are you about sleeping and driving? Below are seven true-false statements about sleep. See how much you really know when you check your answers below:

_____ 1. Coffee overcomes the effects of drowsiness while driving.
_____ 2. I can tell when I'm going to fall asleep.
_____ 3. I'm a safe driver, so it doesn't matter if I'm sleepy.
_____ 4. I can't take naps.
_____ 5. I get plenty of sleep.
_____ 6. Young people need less sleep.
_____ 7. Being sleepy makes you misperceive things.

Answers:

1. **False.** Stimulants are no substitute for sleep. Drinks containing caffeine, such as coffee or cola, can help you feel more alert, but the effects last for only a short time.

continues

THE DISPATCH BOARD *continued*

If you are seriously sleep-deprived, even if you drink coffee, you are still likely to have "micro-sleeps"—brief lapses that last four to five seconds. At 55 miles per hour, that's more than 100 yards, and plenty of time to kill you—or someone else.

2. **False.** If you are like most people, you believe that you can control your sleep. In one study, nearly four-fifths of people said they could predict when they were about to fall asleep. They were wrong.

 The truth is, sleep in not voluntary. If you are drowsy, you can fall asleep and never know it. When you're driving, being asleep for a few seconds can kill you or someone else.

3. **False.** The only safe driver is an alert driver. Even the safest drivers become confused and use poor judgment when they are sleepy.

 To be a safe driver you must have your eyes open—and that means staying off the road when you are sleepy.

4. **False.** Many people insist they can't nap. Yet even people who say they are not tired will quickly fall asleep in a darkened room if they have not been getting enough sleep.

 If you think you can't nap, pull over and relax for 15 minutes anyway. You may be surprised at how easily you fall asleep once you give yourself the chance. There is good scientific evidence that naps can help promote alertness.

5. **False.** Chances are good that you really aren't getting all the sleep you need. If you answered "true," ask yourself: "Do I wake up feeling rested?"

 The average person needs eight hours of sleep per night. If you go to bed late and wake up early to an alarm clock, you probably are building up a sleep debt during the week.

 If you spend eight hours in bed but still feel tired, you may have a disorder that is preventing you from getting enough sleep. Whatever the cause, avoid driving when you feel drowsy.

6. **False.** Males under age 25 are at the greatest risk for falling asleep at the wheel.

 Half of the victims of fatigue-related crashes are drivers under 25. In one study, 24 percent of the people asked said they had fallen asleep while driving— 32 percent of these were men and 13 percent were women.

7. **True.** Have you ever been driving at night and seen something you thought was an animal that turned out to be a paper bag or a leaf blowing across the road?

 That's only one of the many ways sleepy drivers misjudge their surroundings. A drowsy driver doesn't think as fast or as accurately as an alert driver and is less able to react quickly enough to avoid a crash.

Do You Have Sleep Debt? After a short nap, Bob pulls his rig back on to the interstate. "I don't know why I am so tired. I slept a lot last week when I was at home."

Sleep is not like money. You can't save it up ahead of time and you can't borrow it. But, just as with money, you can go into debt with it. If you don't sleep enough, you "owe" more sleep to yourself.

This debt can be paid off only by sleeping. You can't overcome it with willpower, and it won't go away by itself.

When your sleep debt gets big enough, there is nothing that will keep you awake. You may feel awake because you are excited, but as soon as you calm down, the sleep debt takes over and your body goes to sleep.

THE DISPATCH BOARD *continued*

This is especially likely to happen when you are sitting still and trying to be alert—like while you're driving.

Danger Signals for Drowsy Drivers.   Most people, even a veteran driver like Bob, who have a sleep debt do not realize they are tired. Drowsiness can creep up on you and you may not be aware of it.

Below are some danger signals for drowsy drivers:

- Your eyes close or go out of focus by themselves.
- You have trouble keeping your head up.
- You can't stop yawning.
- You have wandering, disconnected thoughts.
- You don't remember driving the last few miles.
- You have missed your exit.
- You keep drifting out of your lane.
- Your speed becomes variable.

If you have even one of these symptoms, you may be in danger of falling asleep. Find a safe place to stop, pull off the road, and take a nap.

Stay Alert to Arrive Alive.   Driving, especially for long distances, reveals your true level of sleepiness. At the start of a trip, excitement makes a driver feel alert, but the excitement wears off once the trip is underway.

Here are some suggestions to avoid driving tired:

1. Start any trip by getting enough sleep beforehand. If possible, take a nap shortly before you expect to go on duty.
2. Be alert for feelings of drowsiness, especially between 2 AM and 6 AM. If you feel too drowsy to drive, find a safe legal place to stop and take a nap.
3. Schedule a break every two hours or every 100 miles. Stop sooner if you show any signs of drowsiness. During your break, take a nap, stretch, take a walk, safety check your rig, and get some exercise before getting back into the cab.

Remember, Bob! Drive Alert. Arrive Alive.

(Supporting material provided by the American Trucking Association)

12 Driving Tankers and Preparing for the Tanker Endorsement

Tanker Endorsement—What You Need to Know

If you are going to pull a tanker carrying a load of liquids or compressed gas, a Tank Vehicle Endorsement will be required on your CDL.

FMCSR Part 383 defines a "tank" as a vehicle carrying liquids and compressed gases in bulk.

FMCSR Part 383 offers an additional description: A tank vehicle can be a permanently attached tank or it can be a portable tank. Both types may hold 1,000 gallons of cargo or more.

A permanent tank is loaded or unloaded while attached to the vehicle. A portable tank can be taken off the vehicle to be loaded or unloaded.

These definitions make it possible for a tank vehicle to be:

- A straight truck with a permanently attached tanker.
- A semi-trailer that is a tanker and can be coupled to a tractor.
- A flatbed trailer carrying a portable tank.

Tank vehicles are used to carry liquids ranging from milk to gasoline. They are also used to carry dry cargoes—such as lime or dry chemicals—in bulk.

Why is a separate endorsement necessary? Because pulling a loaded tank vehicle requires special driving skills. This particular job also requires the professional driver to be familiar with the type of tanker being pulled.

So, what do you need to know about tank vehicles?

When you drive a tank vehicle, you must have the knowledge and skill to handle two problems:

(1) a high center of gravity, and (2) liquid surge.

Q. What problems are caused by a high center of gravity?

A. Tank vehicles come in all sizes but they all have a high center of gravity (CG).

Translation: Most tank vehicles sit higher than other vehicles. Therefore, the load's weight is carried higher above the road (Figure 12-1). So, the load's center of gravity is always high in a tanker. And as you learned in the General Knowledge section, it is important to keep the center of gravity of a load as low as possible.

Why? To lessen the possibility of rolling over.

Because of their high center of gravity, tank vehicles are more prone to roll over on freeway on-ramps and off-ramps, on curves, and during evasive maneuvers.

Experienced tank vehicle drivers always try to enter ramps and curves well below the posted speed limits to avoid roll-over.

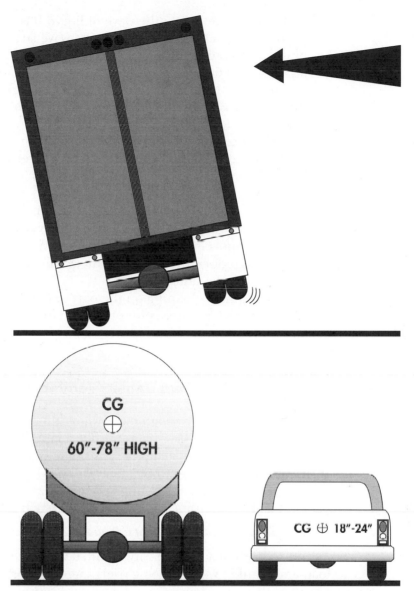

Figure 12-1   Tankers are built with a high center of gravity, making them prone to a rollover, especially on ramps and curves.

Q. What is liquid surge and what problems are caused by it?

A. Liquid surge happens when the liquid contents of partially filled tanks shift. Let's do a simple demonstration: Take a jar, fill it half-full of water, and then put a lid on tightly. Place the jar on its side. See how the liquid fills the bottom half when the jar is on its side?

Now take the jar (still in a sideways position) between your two hands. Quickly move the jar to the left and then back to the right. See how the water makes a small wave and sloshes against one end of the jar and then the other?

Now, with the same jar of water on its side and held with both hands, move the jar from side to side. What does the water do? Right! It moves higher and then lower in the jar. The same thing happens in a tanker.

In a partially filled tank vehicle, when the truck comes to a stop, the liquid contents will surge back and forth in the tank—from front to back and side to side. When the wave of liquid hits the end of the tank, it usually pushes the truck in the direction the wave is moving. So, when you are braking, the surge will push the truck forward and then pull it back until the liquid settles back down in the bottom of the tank.

If a tank vehicle is being driven on a wet highway or over ice, the liquid surge can push the stopped vehicle into the middle of an intersection or into the vehicle stopped in front of it.

One more important point: The thicker the liquid, the less the surge will be. For example, if the tank is carrying lighter weight liquids, such as milk or brine, the surge will be greater. If the cargo is a heavier liquid, like molasses or heavy oil, the surge will be less.

However, any liquid in a tank vehicle can cause very specific problems for the driver. And, as any experienced tanker driver will tell you, you should keep your movements gradual and slow. Why? Because the less sloshing that liquid cargo does, the less surge there will be—so make all shifts, turns, and stops slow and gradual.

This requires planning on the part of the driver. You must allow more time and more room to stop, more time and more room to turn, and more time and more room to shift.

Every Liquid Has Its Own Density—and Its Own Surge Capacity

As you know, some liquids weigh more than others. Once again, take out your trusty jar. First, weigh the jar. Now, measure out a cup of water, pour it into the jar, and weigh it. Do the same with a cup of syrup. The syrup will weigh more because it has a higher density and is therefore a heavier liquid.

The density of water is 8.3 pounds per gallon.

Table 12-1 shows densities of liquids measured at 60 degrees Fahrenheit.

Remember: *The higher the density of a liquid, the less the surge of this cargo will be.*

So, if you're loading a high-density liquid, it will be very heavy and you won't be able to load a full tanker without being overweight. Therefore, you will have a low center of gravity with a high-density liquid, like corn syrup or molten sulfur.

You will be able to load a greater amount of lighter density liquid—maybe even a full tank—without being overweight. However, you will have more slosh and more surge with lighter density cargoes like butane and water.

Tankers—Three Basic Designs

Tankers come in three basic designs—bulkhead, baffled, and "smooth bore" (or unbaffled). Figure 12-2 shows examples of tankers.

Bulkhead Tankers

Some tankers are equipped with bulkheads—a solid steel divider within the tank. These dividers create separate compartments within the tanker. Most gasoline tankers are equipped with bulkheads.

Table 12-1
Densities of Various Liquids at 60°F.

Substance	Pounds per gallon
Alcohol	6.8
Asphalt (transport temperature)	7.8
Butane	4.88
Corn syrup	11.82
Crude oil	6.76
Diesel fuel	7.05
Jet fuel	12.2
Liquefied chlorine	4.88
Liquid petroleum gas	4.25
Lubricating oil	7.2
Molten sulfur	16.80
Sesame oil	7.6
Tar	9.00

What is the advantage of these bulkheads?

- With these separate compartments, you can carry several different types of liquids at once. This makes it easy to service a customer who wants to buy different products at one delivery.
- Bulkheads reduce front-to-back liquid surge.

Baffled Tankers

Like bulkheads, baffles are dividers within the tanker itself. However, baffles have holes in them and do not create separate compartments.

So, why are baffles used in tankers? There is one main reason: Baffles slow down the front-to-back surge. By having holes, the baffles allow the product to move in the tank, but the partial partitions slow down the movement.

Does this mean you don't have to be as cautious when driving a baffled tank?

Absolutely not! You still must exercise the same caution you would when driving any other tank vehicle. Why? Because the side-to-side surge is still creating movement behind you—and there's still a surge factor, although it is reduced somewhat by the baffles.

"Smooth Bore" or Unbaffled Tankers

The smooth bore tank has no compartments. It is open, front-to-back, inside. Smooth bore (or unbaffled) tank vehicles are used to transport food products and certain bulk chemicals. Smooth bore tanks are easier to clean than baffled or bulkhead tanks—which is why smooth bore tanks are almost always used when hauling food-grade products.

EXAMPLES OF TANKERS

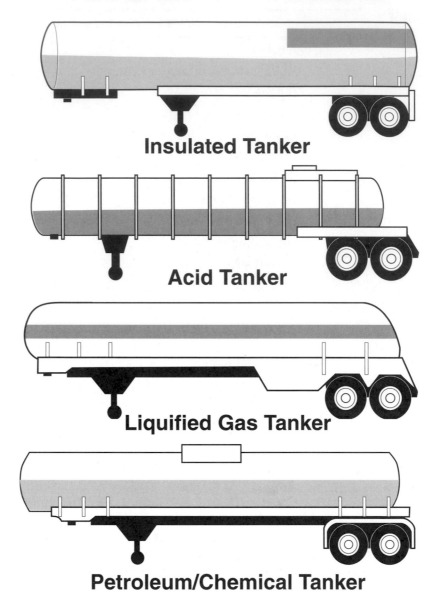

Insulated Tanker

Acid Tanker

Liquified Gas Tanker

Petroleum/Chemical Tanker

Figure 12-2 Various tanker styles are better suited to certain cargo.

So, in this type of tank, the surge factor is the most violent, the most powerful. This means you must be very cautious in starting, stopping, turning, driving curves, or entering and exiting ramps.

What You Should Know about Driving Tank Vehicles

When you're driving a tank vehicle, it will be most stable when it is empty.

A tank vehicle that is 80-percent full will be the least stable—your tank will rarely be completely full.

Why? Because liquids expand when they warm up, and there must be room for this liquid to expand. The room you leave for expansion is called "outage." The **outage** is the amount of room a certain liquid cargo requires for its expansion.

Because different liquids expand at different rates, each liquid requires a different amount of room, or outage, to expand.

When you're driving a tank vehicle, you must know the outage requirement for the bulk liquids you're carrying. This information usually comes from the dispatcher, but your employer may also give you a manual with an outage chart that provides this information for you.

As a tanker driver, you may also need to know the "innage"—this is the depth of the liquid loaded in your tank, measuring from the bottom of the tank to the surface of the liquid.

Legal Limits on Liquid Loads

Because a very dense liquid may exceed legal load limits if it fills the tank, often tank vehicle drivers only partially fill the tank with these heavy liquids. The way to know how much to load depends on (1) the outage of the liquid in transit, (2) the weight of the liquid, and (3) the legal weight limits of the tank vehicle.

Tank vehicles are required to have a liquid level-sensing device—a probe inside the tank wired to a controller. This controller is found near the other operator controls.

What You Should Know about Tank Vehicles and Brakes

In most cases, the brakes are designed to work best when a vehicle is fully loaded. The heavier the weight of the load, the better the traction will be.

If you're driving an empty vehicle, it will sometimes require twice the distance to stop the vehicle when you apply the brakes.

Warning: Brakes are more likely to lock up when you try to make an emergency stop with an empty vehicle.

The most difficult vehicle to stop is a tank vehicle with a partial, liquid load. Remember the traction rule: *A fully loaded vehicle has the best traction.*

A partial, liquid load (1) does not have the best traction and (2) will have a worse surge factor than a full load.

As mentioned earlier, the worst surge factor occurs when the tank vehicle is 80-percent full—there's enough liquid to be quite heavy and enough space for it to have plenty of surge.

A tank vehicle that is 90-percent full has more liquid and more weight—but what about outage? There probably is not enough space for the liquid to expand and move around.

In a tank vehicle that is 40-percent full, the liquid does not have enough weight nor as high a surge factor to make the vehicle go too far out of control.

Remember: With a partial load, you're giving up the traction you would have with a full load. The surge factor would also be high enough to overtake the braking power of the vehicle. In other words, that partial load would make your vehicle travel quite a distance from the time you apply your brakes to the time the vehicle actually stops.

A last word on braking: Drive slowly and carefully at all times, so that if you need to brake, you can do so gradually and steadily. Avoid braking on turns. All of these cautions will reduce the liquid surge factor. All of these precautions will help you maintain control of the vehicle as you come to a stop.

Tank Vehicles and Emergency Systems

Tank vehicles are specifically designed to avoid accidental leakage. Some emergency systems operate automatically in an accident. Others must be operated by the driver. However, if the tank is damaged—by accident or by wear and tear—certain features are included to prevent loss of the cargo. For example:

- Fittings are attached in such a way so if they were to break off, cargo does not leak out.
- A heavy-duty rear bumper protects the tank and its piping from damage in a rear-end collision.
- Openings for filling and inspection, plus the manhole, are protected from damage in case of a vehicle roll-over and safety devices prevent manhole and fill covers from opening when the tank is pressurized.
- Piping that is not protected from damage must have a stop-valve and a shear section.

Portable tanks don't have the same type of emergency systems as cargo tanks. They do have excess-flow valves—and once the flow rate exceeds the manufacturer's designated limit, they will close automatically.

The Stop Valve

A stop valve—located on the loading and unloading outlets of the tank vehicle—stops the flow of the liquid cargo. These valves are held in position by their own power supply.

Internal stop valves are self-closing. External stop valves self-close in emergencies (like fire or a broken hose).

Each stop valve also has a remote control, located more than 10 feet from the valve. These remote controls are part of the emergency system that the driver can operate manually with levers located in the operator's cabinet.

The Shear Section

A shear section will "fail" in an accident and will break away in a roll-over. In doing so, the shear section will save the important part of a pipe and its attachments. This will prevent a leak.

Shear sections are located inside the accident damage protection device but outside the stop valve.

Tank Vehicles and Pressure Relief Systems

Pressure relief systems on tank vehicles monitor the internal pressure of the tank and prevent the cargo from leaking out while the vehicle is on the road.

- The primary pressure relief system has one or more reclosing valves.
- The secondary pressure relief system will back up or assist the primary valve. Both are marked with the pressure at which they will discharge. Both are also marked with the flow rate. Their location depends on the tank's structural specifications.

What Tank Vehicle Drivers Need to Know about Department of Transportation Specifications

Hazardous materials may be carried only in authorized vehicles that meet Department of Transportation specifications. These specifications must be retested. Drivers are not involved in testing but you should know how to read the markings to comply with cargo tank regulations.

Department of Transportation specifications codes are given to tank vehicles that meet the Department's specifications. Cargo tanks are numbered in the 300s and 400s. Portable tanks are numbered 51, 56, 57, 60, IM101, and IM102.

What Tank Vehicle Drivers Need to Know about Marking

The month and year of the last test/inspection—and the type of inspection—is marked on the tank itself. It may be stamped on the certification plate using these abbreviations:

- V – External visual inspection and test
- I = Internal visual inspection
- P = Pressure retest
- L = Lining test
- K = Leakage test
- T = Thickness test

The marking—"10-01, P,V,L" means that in October 2001, the tanker was given a pressure retest, an external visual inspection and test, and a lining test.

On portable tanks, the date of the most recent retest is marked on the tank near the metal certification plate.

Tank Vehicles and Special Driving Instructions

The following are important driving instructions for tank vehicle drivers:

1. Always maintain a safe following distance—one second for every 10 feet of your vehicle's length for speeds up to 40 miles per hour—or more if necessary. Never tailgate—because of the danger of cargo surge and the amount of space required to stop with the surge factor.
2. Increase your following distance on wet pavement by one second plus one second for each 10 feet of vehicle.
3. Shift by pushing. Do not shift by pulling.
4. Always release the clutch after the surge has hit the rear of the tank when upshifting.
5. When entering a freeway entrance or exit ramp, always slow down and downshift before entering. A slow speed will reduce the risk of roll-over on a

ramp or on a curve. A minimum of 5 miles per hour below the posted speed is recommended.

6. At the top of a long hill, always downshift and select the proper gear—before you start down the grade (Figure 12-3)—and use light pressure on the brake pedal. Pumping the brakes will cause the vehicle to rock, increasing the slosh and surge of the liquid cargo.

7. If your brakes fail while going down a steep grade, use the truck escape ramp—these ramps have saved many lives, not to mention equipment and loads.

8. When hauling liquid loads, never make sudden or sharp changes in direction at any speed—especially at high speeds. This sudden action would only increase the surge factor.

9. If, for some reason, you drop off the pavement with a liquid load, never immediately return to the roadway. Instead, regain control of the vehicle and reduce your speed to a stop. This action will allow you to return safely to the roadway.

10. When driving a tank vehicle, if you are practicing good driving skills, you should never have to take sudden or sharp evasive action.

Figure 12-3   A slow speed will reduce the risk of a rollover on a ramp or a curve.

11. Experienced drivers will tell you, it is almost always safer to steer to avoid a problem than to use your brakes. But if brakes are necessary, use controlled braking, releasing the brakes as soon as the wheels lock up and then applying the brakes hard a second time.

Driving a Tanker Vehicle in Slippery Conditions

Following the same rules of slow and steady maneuvers, when driving a tank vehicle on wet or icy roads, remember that the liquid surge of your cargo is enough to cause your vehicle to lose traction. In some cases, it may be advisable—and safer—to stop and wait until the weather or road conditions clear when hauling a liquid load.

Uncoupling and Unloading

When uncoupling a tanker trailer, wait until the load settles. Otherwise, liquid surge could cause your landing gear to collapse once the trailer is uncoupled.

Let's Review

Read each question and all of the answers provided. Place the letter of the correct answer in the space provided or write your answers on a separate piece of paper so you can use these questions again as you review for the CDL. Once you have answered all the questions, check your answers against the answer key which follows.

____ 1. Liquid surge can be defined as
(A) when the tanker is filled with too much liquid,
(B) when the liquid cargo is expelled from the tank,
(C) when the liquid cargo moves back and forth as the vehicle comes to a stop,
(D) all of the above.

____ 2. A professional driver needs special skills to drive a tanker because of
(A) the cargo surge factor,
(B) the tanker's high center of gravity,
(C) the careful handling of liquid cargoes required on curves and ramps,
(D) all of the above.

____ 3. Outage is
(A) the room required in the tank for expansion of the liquid cargo,
(B) the amount of time it takes to empty the tank,
(C) the rate of leakage from the tanker,
(D) all of the above.

____ 4. A smooth bore tanker is
(A) usually used to carry food,
(B) has no bulkhead,
(C) has no baffles,
(D) all of the above.

____ 5. Baffles make handling a liquid tank vehicle slightly easier because they
(A) control forward and backward surge,
(B) are easier to clean,
(C) control side-to-side surge,
(D) all of the above.

____ 6. When taking a curve with a loaded tanker, the driver will prevent rollover by traveling
(A) at the posted speed limit,
(B) with a rollover protector,
(C) five miles per hour faster than the posted speed limit,
(D) at a speed below the posted speed limit.

____ 7. Higher density liquids
(A) can be loaded faster,
(B) will surge less than lower density liquids,
(C) have no side-to-side surge,
(D) all of the above.

____ 8. A high center of gravity means
(A) a majority of the load's weight is carried high off the ground,
(B) the vehicle will be more apt to roll over on freeway ramps,
(C) the vehicle will be more apt to roll over on curves,
(D) all of the above.

____ 9. The surge factor is worse when a tank vehicle is
   (A) 40-percent full,
   (B) 90-percent full,
   (C) 20-percent full,
   (D) 80-percent full.

____10. With a partial tanker load,
   (A) traction is less,
   (B) the surge factor may overwhelm the vehicle's braking power,
   (C) the vehicle could travel a significant distance before stopping after the brakes are applied,
   (D) all of the above.

Answers to Let's Review

1. C; 2. D; 3. A; 4. D; 5. A; 6. D; 7. B; 8. D; 9. D; 10. D.

Terms You Need to Know

The following terms have been taken from the contents of Chapter 12. Review them. If you see any you're unsure of, check the definition in the Glossary at the back of the book. If it helps you, keep a written list of the words and their definitions (or write in the definitions here) and review them several days prior to taking the CDL tests.

Baffled liquid tanks

Baffles

Bulkhead

Center of gravity (CG)

Compartment

Curves

Cylindrical

Elliptical

Evasive action

High center of gravity

Innage

Inertia

Liquid density

Liquid surge

Outage

Permanent tank

Portable tank

Portable tank emergency systems

Pressure relief systems

Ramps

Retest and marking

Shear section

Slosh

Stop valves

Uncoupling

Weight distribution

THE DISPATCH BOARD
Drivers: Front-line sales and customer service

Without a doubt, professional drivers are the top customer service representatives for their employers. You've probably heard this before, but it's worth repeating.

In many cases, when you make a delivery, you're the "face" that goes along with the company's name or its logo. It may be that the receiver never meets the president or CEO of your company. They may speak with a dispatcher or they may be called on by a sales person, but you're the person they see . . . you're the only person they may see.

So, what does this all mean?

First of all, it means that you're the company representative who sets the tone. If you're patient and friendly, if you're understanding, if you're a good listener, or a good person to contact if they have a problem, then you've done a good job of representing your employer, from the CEO on down the ladder.

So, what skills does good customer service require? Here are some suggestions that will make you not only a good professional driver, but also superior in the areas of front-line sales and customer service:

1. First and foremost, always be friendly, cordial, and courteous. If you've had a bad day, keep it to yourself.
2. Listen carefully when dock personnel or receiving supervisors make a request— then do whatever you can (within reason) to follow their wishes.
3. Find out how things work for that shipper or receiver. If they are always behind or running out of time, do what you can to help. If they want to be your last pick-up, try to make that happen too—within reason.
4. Always thank shippers and receivers for their business. Remember, they could always call one of your competitors.
5. If the dock personnel ask a question and you don't know the answer, be sure to forward the question to someone who does, and get back to them with what you find out.

continues

THE DISPATCH BOARD *continued*

6. Be well groomed—even if you've been on the road for four days. If you wear a uniform, make certain it's reasonably clean. If your boots or sneakers need replacing, don't wait until they are absolutely worn out to do so.

7. Be aware of personal hygiene. In spite of working all day, your teeth should be clean and you should put on plenty of deodorant. If you are male, you should be shaved or your beard trimmed. If you're female, your face should be clean and/or your make-up well applied. Hands should be reasonably clean, nails trimmed and neat. To make sure, chew a mint before arriving at the dock.

8. Ask for business. Anytime your company adds a new service or a new route, mention it to dock personnel. If you know of freight that you could handle, remind the supervisor that you can now pick-up and deliver for that destination. In many companies, drivers become their best sales people. Why? Because some drivers know the shipper's dock as well or better than sales personnel. They're there frequently and can spot a new shipment while making a pickup or delivery.

9. Refrain from using profanity, from sharing personal problems, and from slamming another carrier. Always be positive, cordial, polite, and once again listen closely.

10. How do you listen? Make eye contact to let them know you're listening. Mirror what they say: "So, you're planning to shut down over Easter." And check out the details. "If you're shutting down over Easter weekend, when will you be open again?"

11. Be human. If a dock worker has been in an accident or if they've told you about a sick spouse or child, ask about them the next time you visit the terminal. Be willing to take time to take interest and be compassionate. If dock personnel lose a family member or friend, ask about that, too. Work at following the company protocols, but also feel free to express yourself while a coworker is going through a hardship. Be thoughtful and courteous of the survivor's fragile state and anticipate their needs.

12. Be professional, on time, and ready to work. Listen carefully. Be responsible. If someone asks you a question and you need to get back to them with the answer, do it. Don't leave them hanging, waiting on you to help them find the solution.

13. Don't hang around the dock. Get your work done, chat with dock personnel, and then get going. If you drag your feet with the rest of your schedule, what will that mean to others in the company—that you drag your feet and that you're really not in the loop. Look for ways to keep busy. Bring your log up to date, fill out paperwork, but don't stand around getting in the way when others need to work.

14. Time is money in this business, for sure. Keep conversations brief. Don't waste a minute while you're on the clock. It will mean something later in your career if you begin developing good habits now.

13 Driving Doubles and Triples and Preparing for the Doubles and Triples/Combination Endorsement

Doubles and Triples Endorsement

Professional drivers who want to be able to drive a full range of vehicles should obtain the Doubles and Triples Endorsement. This endorsement reflects the needed knowledge and expertise in driving and working with more than one trailer, thus the name "doubles and triples."

If you plan to pull one or more trailers, you may have to take your CDL test in that vehicle with those trailers. The examiner may also test you on your knowledge of coupling (connecting the trailer combination) and uncoupling (disconnecting the combination of those trailers).

Because you have to know about more vehicle parts when you take the Doubles and Triples Endorsement and because pulling doubles and triples is so much more complicated than pulling a single trailer, a driver with a CDL and the Doubles and Triples Endorsement is highly respected and valued by many companies.

Legal Combinations

In the United States, a three-axle tractor pulling a two-axle semitrailer is the most popular over-the-road vehicle. These "18-wheeled" combinations carry most of our freight today.

Double trailers (sometimes called "pups") are acceptable in most states. Triples are legal in some states and outlawed in others.

Safe Driving while Pulling Doubles and Triples

Professional drivers must exercise extreme caution when pulling doubles and triples. The key words are "plan ahead," because planning becomes extremely important when you are pulling combinations.

There's no doubt about it—the law of averages tells you more can go wrong when you are pulling two or three trailers than if you are pulling only one trailer. Moreover, doubles and triples have proved to be less stable. Because of this, there are several areas to be aware of and concerned with at the same time.

Roll-Over

A fully loaded rig is 10 times more likely to roll over in a crash than an empty rig. This fact, in itself, is reason enough to drive a combination rig slowly and carefully.

To prevent double/triple trailers from rolling over, remember these words—slowly and gently. Much like tankers, when rounding a corner, entering a freeway on-ramp or off-ramp, or rounding a curve pulling double/triple trailers, it is important to steer gently and slow your speed. A safe speed on a curve for a tractor and single trailer combination vehicle may be too fast for a set of doubles or triples.

Avoid the "Crack the Whip Effect"

Kids on roller skates like to form chains and then "crack the whip" or make a turn so that the last person in the chain moves twice as fast as those in the center. Believe it or not, this same effect occurs when pulling doubles and triples. To avoid the last trailer being "whipped" and turning over, you must steer gently.

So what does "steer gently" actually mean? Just what it says. Avoid jerky movements, sudden veers, or other knee-jerk maneuvers. Turn corners easily and steadily, take the ramp slowly and back off the accelerator when taking the curve. Once again, the key words are "plan ahead." A quick or sudden maneuver may cause the doubles/triples to roll over or jackknife.

Keep Your Eyes on the Road and Allow Plenty of Room

It's not rocket science—when you pull double or triple trailers, your rig is going to need a lot of room for any maneuver, whether it's changing lanes or stopping at an intersection. Allow for this additional space for any maneuver. When you're entering a freeway, make sure you allow enough room between oncoming vehicles before pulling into the driving lane.

Smooth driving is required when pulling doubles and triples. Exercise defensive driving tactics. Look as far ahead as possible and slow down or change lanes slowly, steadily, and gradually when necessary.

Bad Weather Driving

In bad weather, take twice the precautions with doubles/triples. If the highway is wet or icy and you are pulling doubles and triples, remember that the hazards of these kinds of conditions double and triple for you—depending on what you're pulling. Greater length and more dead axles to pull with your drive axles create more opportunity for skidding or losing traction.

Driving with Other Motorists

When you pull doubles and triples down the highway, whether you realize it or not, you are probably causing difficulties for other motorists. Doubles and triples take longer to pass. There are also situations where the triple combination could make it difficult for other motorists to enter or exit the roadway. Why? Because the triple combination may be blocking entrance or exit ramps.

There's also something called "aerodynamic buffeting." As you drive your double or triple rig down the highway, you are cutting through the wind and, as you cut through, a "draft" is created behind you. When a smaller vehicle comes up beside you, this draft hits them and it's like getting hit by a crosswind.

Remember, too, that doubles and triples take more time to change lanes, so you need to plan so as not to "cut off" a fellow motorist in the lane you want to enter.

How to Inspect Doubles and Triples

Okay. Let's get to work. Here, we're going to use the Seven-Step Inspection Procedure to begin the inspection, and then add the inspection points for doubles and triples.

Let's review what the Seven-Step includes:

1. On approach
   - Take a look at the general condition of the vehicle.
   - Look for damage.
   - Look at the ground under the vehicle—do you see any oil, coolant, grease or fuel leaks?
   - Check around the vehicle for hazards, such as low-hanging tree-limbs, wires, or anything that would be a problem when you move the vehicle.
   - Review the last vehicle inspection report. Have the reported problems that would impact safe operation of the vehicle been repaired?
   - Inspect the vehicle to see if the problems have been fixed.
2. Check the engine
   - Check that the parking brakes are on and/or the wheels are chocked.
   - Raise the hood, tilt the cab (remember to secure all loose objects), or open the engine compartment door. Inspect the following:
     —Engine oil level
     —Coolant level in the radiator and the condition of the hoses
     —Power steering fluid level and hose condition (if necessary)
     —Windshield washer fluid level
     —Battery fluid level (if not maintenance free), connections, and tiedowns (particularly if battery is located elsewhere)
     —Automatic transmission fluid level
     —Belts and these components: alternator, water pump, air compressor. However, most air compressors today are gear driven, so if necessary, make sure that you also inspect the air compressor gears.
     —Look for leaks in the engine compartment coming from fuel, coolant, oil, power steering fluid, hydraulic fluid, and battery fluid.
     —Look for cracked and worn electrical wiring insulation.
   - Once this inspection is complete, lower the hood, cab, or engine compartment door and secure.
3. Start the engine and inspect the inside of the cab
   Start the engine
   - The parking brake should be on.
   - Always depress the clutch when engaging the starter.
   - The gearshift should be in neutral (if automatic transmission, it should be in park).
   - Listen for any unusual noises.

Look at the gauges
- Oil pressure should register normal within a few seconds after engine is on.
- Ammeter and/or voltmeter should be in normal ranges.
- Coolant temperature should begin gradually rising to normal range.
- Engine oil temperature should begin gradually rising to normal range.
- Warning lights and buzzers—all warning lights should turn off immediately except for low air pressure gauge which will turn off at about 60–80 psi.

Check the condition of the controls—look for looseness, sticking, damage, or improper setting:
- Steering wheel
- Clutch
- Accelerator
- Brake controls
  —Foot brake
  —Trailer brake (if available)
  —Parking brake
  —Retarder controls (if available)
- Transmission controls
- Interaxle differential lock (if available)
- Horn
- Windshield wiper/washer
- Lights
  —Headlights
  —Dimmer switch
  —Turn signals
  —Four-way flashers
  —Clearance, identification, marker light switches
- Check mirrors and windshield—look for cracks, illegal stickers, or other visual obstructions. Clean and adjust where necessary.
- Check emergency equipment
  ——Spare fuses, three reflective triangles, and a properly charged/rated fire extinguisher are present.
- Check for optional items
  —Tire chains (required in certain areas in the winter)
  —Tire changing equipment
  —List of emergency phone numbers
  —Accident-reporting packet

4. Turn off the engine and check the lights—make sure the parking brake is on, turn off the engine, and remove the key. Then turn the headlights on low beams, turn on the four-way flashers, and get out, taking the key with you.
   - Step to the front of the vehicle—check that the low beams are on and both four-way flashers are in working order.
   - Get back into cab, push the dimmer switch, and then check that high beams work.
5. Perform walk-around inspection—by getting back into the cab and changing lights.
   - Turn off the headlights and four-way flashers.
   - Turn on the parking, clearance, side-marker, and identification lights.
   - Turn on the right turn signal—then get out of cab and begin walk-around inspection.

General inspection:
- Walk around and inspect vehicle.
- Clean all lights, reflectors, and glass as you walk around.

For double and triple trailers:
- Shut-off valves should be open at the rear of the front trailer and closed at the rear of the last trailer.
- The converter dolly air tank drain valve should be closed.
- Check air lines—are they supported and glad hands properly connected?
- If spare tire is riding on dolly, make sure it's secure.
- Check that pintle-eye of dolly is in place in pintle hook of trailer(s).
- Check that pintle hook is latched and safety latch is in place.
- Safety chains should be secured to trailer(s).
- Check that light cords are firmly in sockets on trailers.
- Check to make sure the dolly fifth wheel is secure.

Check the left front:
- Driver's door glass should be clean.
- Locks should be in working order.
- Check the condition of the wheels, rims, and tires—there should be no missing, bent, or broken studs, clamps, or lugs.
    - ——Tires are properly inflated, valve stem and cap are in place. There are no serious cuts, slashes, bulges, or signs of tread wear (tread wear no less than $4/32''$).
    - ——Test rust-streaks lug nuts for looseness.
    - ——Hub oil level is good with no leaks.
- Left front suspension—Springs, spring hangers, shackles and U-bolts, and shock absorbers are in good condition.
- Left front brake drum and hoses are in good condition.

Check the front:
- Check the front axle for cracks or other problems.
- Check for loose, worn, bent, damaged, or missing parts of the steering system and test for looseness.
- Windshield should be free of damage and clean. Wipers should be in good working order—check for proper spring tension in wiper arms. Check blades for stiff rubber and that they are secure.
- Parking, clearance, and identification lights are clean, operational, and of the proper color—amber in front.
- Right turn signal light must be clean, operational and proper color—amber or white.

Check the right front:
- Check all items on right front as for left front.
- If you have a cab-over-engine model, all primary and safety locks should be engaged and working.
- Right fuel tank is securely mounted, with no leaks. Fuel crossover lines are secure, and there is adequate fuel in tank for trip. Caps are on and secure.
- Condition of visible parts—no leaks in the rear of engine or transmission, and the exhaust system is secure and not leaking or touching wires or lines. No cracks or bends are visible in frame and cross members.
- Air lines and electrical wiring—no visible snagging, rubbing or wearing.
- Spare tire carrier is not damaged and spare tire/wheel is the correct size and properly inflated.

- Cargo is secure—cargo is blocked, braced, tied, and chained. Header board is secure, side boards and stakes are free of damage and properly placed, canvas or tarp is secured to prevent tearing, billowing, or blocking mirrors.
- Oversized loads have required signs properly mounted and all required permits are in the driver's pouch.
- Curbside cargo compartment doors are closed and latched, with all required security seals in place.

Check right rear:

- Condition of wheels, rims, and tires—no missing, bent or broken spacers, studs, clamps or lugs. Tires are evenly matched, are of same type (no mixing of radial and bias types), and are properly inflated with valve stems and caps in place. No cuts, bulges, signs of tread wear. Tires are not rubbing and are clear of debris, and are properly spaced.
- Wheel bearing/seals are not leaking.
- Suspension—springs, spring hangers, shackles, and U-bolts are in good condition, axle is secure and powered axle(s) are not leaking gear oil.
- Check condition of torque rod arms and bushings.
- Check condition of shock absorber(s).
- If there is a retractable axle, check lift mechanism. If it is air-powered, check for leaks.
- Brakes—brake drums are in good condition and hoses have been checked for wear, rubbing, etc.
- Lights and reflectors—side-marker lights are clean, operational, and red at rear—others are amber. The same goes for side markers.

Check the rear:

- Rear clearance and identification lights are clean, operational, and red at rear. Reflectors are clean and red at rear. Taillights are clean, operational, and red at rear. Right turn signal is operating and of the proper color—red, yellow, or amber at rear.
- License plates are present, clean, and secure.
- Splash guards are properly fastened, undamaged, and not dragging or rubbing on tires.
- Cargo is secure—it is properly blocked and braced, tied, and chained. Tailboards are up and secure. End gates are free of damage and secured in stake sockets. If there is a lift gate, make sure it is also secure.
- Canvas or tarp is secured to avoid billowing, tearing, blocking rearview mirror, or covering rear lights.
- For over-length or over-width loads, have all signs and additional flags/lights in the proper position and have all required permits.
- Rear doors are closed and locked.
- Secure all trailer doors and check seal numbers.

Check left side:

Check everything you checked on the right side—and also the following:

- Batteries (if not located in the engine compartment) battery box is securely attached and the cover also is secure.
- Batteries are not damaged or leaking and there is no movement.
- Check battery fluid levels (except in maintenance-free types).
- Make sure cell caps and vents are in place, free of debris, and secure.

6. Check the signal lights.
- Get in and turn off all lights.

- Turn on stop lights (apply trailer hand brake).
- Turn on left turn signals.

Get out and check lights.

- Left front turn signal—make sure it is clean, operational, and of proper amber or white on signals facing the front.
- Left rear turn signal and stoplights—make sure they are clean, operational, and of proper red, yellow, or amber color.

7. Start engine and check brake system.
   - Get in and turn off lights not needed for driving.
   - Check all required papers, trip manifests, permits, etc.
   - Secure all loose articles in the cab.
   - Start the engine.
   - Test for hydraulic leaks—if you have hydraulic brakes, pump them three times. Then apply pressure to the pedal and hold for five seconds. The pedal should not move—if it does, there might be a leak or other problem. Fix it before beginning your trip.
   - Test air brakes.
   - Test parking brake—fasten your seatbelt, allow vehicle to move forward slowly, and apply parking brake. If it doesn't stop the vehicle, get it fixed.
   - Test service brake stopping action—move vehicle forward at about five miles per hour and push brake pedal firmly. If vehicle pulls to one side, this means possible brake trouble. Any unusual feel of the pedal or delayed stopping action could signal a problem.

Check air brakes on doubles and triples like any other combination vehicle.

Coupling and Uncoupling Double and Triple Trailers

This process isn't difficult—but it is imperative that it is done correctly every time (see Figure 13-1).

What's really involved when coupling and uncoupling a trailer?

1. Back the tractor up to the trailer so the coupling assemblies connect.
2. Then, supply the electrical power so the trailer lights are functional.
3. If air brakes are involved, the trailer needs an air supply.
4. Ensure the trailer can be controlled from the tractor.
5. Know the width of the tractor and compare it to the width of the trailer.
6. Remember the center of the fifth wheel is always the center of the tractor's frame—and the kingpin is always in the center front of the trailer (Figure 13-2).

A Word of Advice: Take time to do these procedures correctly—no short cuts. Follow every step of the procedures to the letter.

It is important to know how to couple and uncouple correctly for several reasons:

1. Time—which you never have enough of, especially when you have to go back and redo something that was done incorrectly.
2. If coupling and uncoupling are done incorrectly, a very dangerous situation is created (Figure 13-3).

Remember: For the sake of safety, the heavier of the loaded trailers should always be in the first position, directly behind the tractor. The trailer with the lighter load should always be in the rear position. This is true for doubles and triples.

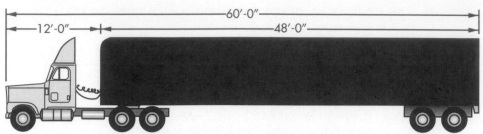

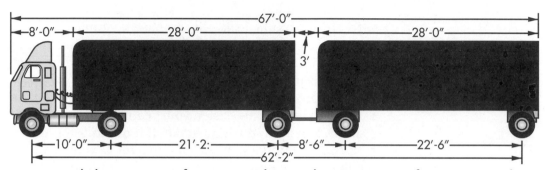

Typical dimensions of a tractor-semitrailer with a 48-foot
semitrailer

Typical dimensions of a twin trailer truck (Note: Use of conventional
tractor adds 3 to 7 feet to total length.)

Figure 13-1   Driving doubles and triples requires unique driving skills.

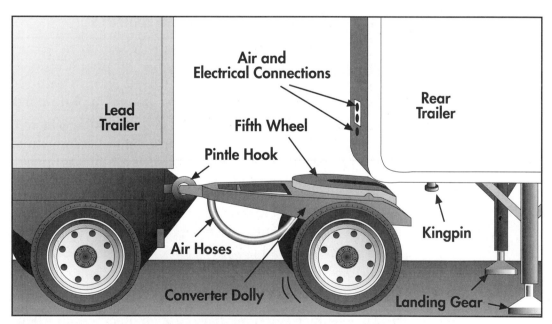

Figure 13-2   Pay close attention to step-by-step details when coupling and uncoupling.

COUPLING AND UNCOUPLING HAZARDS

VEHICLE	
HAZARD	RESULT
• Tractor Not Secured	• Damage to Brake Lines
• Trailer Brakes Not Functioning	• Trailer Pushed Into Obstruction
• Jaws Not Securely Fastened	• Trailer Breaks Loose on the Road
• Ground Not Firm for Uncoupling	• Trailer Falls and Is Damaged
• Trailer Wheels Not Chocked	• Is Pushed or Rolls Into Obstruction
DRIVER	
HAZARD	RESULT
• Climbing on Tractor	• Falls From Slippery Surface
• Working Under Unsupported Trailer (No Jackstand or Tractor Under Trailer Nose)	• Injury When Landing Gear Collapses and Trailer Drops to the Ground

Figure 13-3   Coupling and uncoupling hazards.

Steps for Coupling Doubles

There are differences between rigs—so learn the specifics for the vehicles you will be operating.

1. Before beginning a coupling procedure, walk around the trailers and the tractor. Make sure the path is clear of anything that could damage the tractor or the trailers.
2. Check the trailer kingpins—they should not be bent or broken.
3. This step is only needed for trailers manufactured before 1975:
   Secure the rear trailer—To set the emergency brakes on the second trailer:
   • Drive the tractor close to the trailer.
   • Connect the emergency line, charge the trailer air tank.

- Disconnect the emergency line. This will set the second trailer's emergency brakes if the slack adjusters are correctly adjusted.
4. Inspect the fifth wheel.
    - Look for damaged/missing parts.
    - Check that the mounting to the tractor is uncracked and secure.
    - Be sure the fifth wheel plate is greased. (Failure to keep the fifth wheel plate lubricated may cause steering problems due to friction produced between tractor and trailer.)
    - Check that the fifth wheel is in the proper position for coupling:
        —The wheel is tilted down toward the rear of the tractor.
        —The jaws are open.
        —The safety unlocking handle is in the automatic locking position.

Note: *If using a sliding fifth wheel, it should be in a locked position.*

5. Chock trailer wheels. If trailer has spring brakes, make sure they are on.
6. Make sure cargo is secured against movement during coupling.
7. Position tractor directly in front of the trailer.
    - Never couple a trailer by backing under it at an angle. This could shove the trailer sideways and break or damage the landing gear.
    - Check the position, using outside mirrors—look down both sides of the trailer.
8. Back under the trailer slowly. Back until fifth wheel touches trailer, then stop. Don't hit the trailer!
9. Secure tractor—put on parking brake and shift transmission into neutral.
10. Check kingpin and fifth wheel—they should be aligned.
11. Check trailer height—if it is too low, the tractor could hit and damage the nose of the trailer. If it's too high, it may not couple correctly. The trailer should be low enough to be raised slightly when the tractor backs under it.
12. Connect air lines to trailer.
    - Check glad hand seals and connect the tractor's emergency air lines to the trailer emergency glad hand (Figure 13-4).

Figure 13-4   Connecting air lines to the trailer.
(Photo courtesy of ATA Associates, Inc.)

- Check glad hand seals and connect the tractor's service air line to the trailer service glad hand.
- Check that air lines are safely supported and won't be crushed when the tractor is backing under trailer.

13. Get into cab and supply air to trailer.
    - Move tractor protection valve control from "emergency" to "normal" position—or push in the "air supply" knob.
    - Wait until air pressure reaches "normal."
    - Check brakes for crossed air lines by shutting off engine so you can hear brakes. Apply and release trailer brakes—listen to hear brake move and air escape when released.
    - When brakes are working, start engine.
    - Check to see that air pressure is normal.
14. Lock trailer brakes—pull out "air supply" knob or move tractor protection control from "normal" to "emergency" position.
15. Back under trailer *slowly*—using lowest reverse gear—to avoid hitting kingpin too hard. Stop when kingpin is locked into fifth wheel.
16. Check connection for security by raising trailer landing gear slightly off ground and pulling the tractor *slowly* forward while trailer brakes are still locked.
17. Secure rig—shift transmission into neutral, with the parking brakes on. Then, shut off engine and take your key with you as a safety precaution (so someone else can't move your truck while you're inspecting the coupling).
18. Inspect coupling—use a flashlight at night.
    - Ensure there is no space between upper and lower fifth wheel. If you see space, something is wrong—the kingpin may be on top of the closed fifth wheel jaws and the trailer could come loose in transit. Check to find the problem.
    - Get under trailer and look back to fifth wheel—make sure jaws are closed around the shank of the kingpin.
    - The locking lever should be in the "lock" position—and the safety catch should be in position over locking lever.
    - On some fifth wheels, the catch must be positioned over the locking lever by hand.

Note: If coupling isn't done correctly or if coupling devices are damaged, don't drive the unit. Get it fixed!

19. Connect electrical cord and check air lines:
    - Plug electrical cord into trailer and fasten safety catch.
    - Check both air lines and electrical line for damage.
    - Check to make sure air and electrical lines will not hit moving parts of the rig.
20. Raise front trailer landing gear—if available, begin with low gear range and when free of the weight, change to high gear range.
    - Raise landing gear all the way—never move a rig with landing gear partially up. It could catch on railroad tracks or other elevated portions of the roadway.
    - When full weight of trailer is held by tractor, check for turning clearance between rear of tractor frame and landing gear.

- Make sure there is enough clearance between top of tractor tires and nose of the trailer.
- Remove wheel chocks and store.

21. Position the converter dolly in front of the second or rear trailer:
    - Open the air tank petcock and release dolly brakes. (If dolly has spring brakes, use the dolly parking brake control.)
    - Wheel dolly into position so it is in line with kingpin (if it is a short distance away).
    - If distance is too great, use tractor and first trailer to pick up the converter dolly.
    - Position tractor and first trailer as close as possible to converter dolly.
    - Move the dolly to the rear of first trailer and couple it to the trailer:
        - ——Lock the pintle hook.
        - ——Secure the dolly support—in the raised position.
        - ——Position the dolly as close as possible to the nose of the second trailer.
        - ——Lower the dolly support.
        - ——Unhook dolly from the first trailer.
        - ——Wheel dolly into position—in front of the second trailer, aligned with kingpin.

22. Connect converter dolly to front trailer. Back first trailer in front of the dolly tongue. Hook the dolly to front trailer. Then, lock pintle hook and secure converter gear support in raised position.

23. Connect converter dolly to rear trailer. Check the trailer brakes—they should be locked and wheels chocked.
    - Make sure trailer height is correct—slightly lower than the center of the fifth wheel so that trailer is raised when dolly is pushed under.
    - Back converter dolly under the rear trailer.
    - As a precaution, raise landing gear slightly off the ground to prevent damage if the trailer moves.
    - Test coupling by pulling against the pin of the second trailer.
    - Take the transmission out of gear. Set the brakes and get out.
    - Visually check the coupling—there should be no space between the upper and lower fifth wheel and the locking jaws closed on the kingpin.
    - Connect safety chains, air hoses, and light cords.
    - Close converter dolly air tank petcock.
    - Close the shut-off valves at rear of second trailer (service and emergency).
    - Completely raise the landing gear.
    - Push "air supply" knob in and check for air at rear of second trailer. To do this, open the emergency line shut-off. If there is no air pressure, the brakes won't work and something is wrong.

Steps for Uncoupling Doubles

Uncoupling the Rear Trailer

To uncouple double or triple trailers, begin with the rear trailer and use the following steps, working slowly and surely to avoid damage to vehicles or injury to yourself and others:

1. Park rig on level ground and in a straight line.

2. Apply the parking brakes.
3. Chock wheels of second trailer (if it doesn't have spring brakes).
4. Lower landing gear of second trailer—enough to take some of the weight off the dolly.
5. Close air shut-offs at rear of the first trailer and on the dolly. Then, disconnect all dolly air and electric lines and secure.
6. Release dolly brakes, either by pushing the brake release button or draining all the air from the dolly air tank.
7. Release converter dolly fifth wheel latch.
8. Slowly pull the tractor and first trailer and dolly from under the rear trailer.

Uncouple the Converter Dolly

1. First, lower dolly's landing gear.
2. Disconnect safety chains.
3. Chock wheels or apply converter gear spring brakes.
4. Release pintle hook on first trailer and pull clear of dolly.

Remember: *When the dolly is still under the rear trailer, never unlock the pintle hook. This may cause the dolly tow bar to fly up—which is dangerous in itself. But, it may also make it difficult to recouple.*

Let's Review

Read each question and all of the answers provided. Place the letter of the correct answer in the space provided or write your answers on a separate piece of paper so you can use these questions again as you review for the CDL. Once you have answered all the questions, check your answers against the answer key which follows.

___ 1. When coupling, the fifth wheel jaws should close around
    (A) the head of the kingpin,   (C) the shank of the kingpin,
    (B) the bottom of the kingpin,   (D) none of the above.

___ 2. Before backing the vehicle under a trailer, make sure to
    (A) turn on the lights,   (C) drain the air hose,
    (B) lock the trailer's brakes,   (D) all of the above.

___ 3. When the dolly is still under the rear trailer in doubles or triples, never unlock the pintle hook because this may cause
    (A) the dolly to collapse,   (C) the dolly tow bar to fly up and make coupling difficult,
    (B) damage to the trailer,   (D) nothing to happen.

___ 4. In coupling doubles or triples, if the trailer does not have spring brakes, it is necessary to
    (A) install temporary brakes,   (C) chock the wheels,
    (B) apply air brakes in the cab,   (D) all of the above.

___ 5. When you are inspecting the rig after coupling, how much space should there be between the upper and lower fifth wheel?
    (A) 12 inches or less   (C) 1 foot
    (B) 18 inches   (D) no space.

___ 6. The device used in coupling that connects the service and emergency air lines from the tractor to the trailer is called
    (A) glad hands,   (C) C-clamps,
    (B) fifth wheel,   (D) none of the above.

___ 7. To reduce the risk of roll over,
    (A) perform each maneuver quickly,
    (B) select a route that has no curves,
    (C) keep the center of gravity as low to the ground as possible,
    (D) all of the above.

___ 8. When coupling a trailer and a tractor, before backing the tractor under the trailer, you should check the trailer height, which should be
    (A) lower than the tractor's,
    (B) raised slightly by the tractor as it backs under the trailer,
    (C) two feet higher than the tractor,
    (D) none of the above.

___ 9. "Aerodynamic buffeting" happens as the tractor-trailer(s) push through the wind, causing the vehicles behind to
    (A) go more slowly than usual,   (C) gently nudge the trailer,
    (B) go faster than usual,   (D) none of the above.

___10. When coupling doubles and then inspecting a fifth wheel, you should
    (A) look for damaged/missing parts,
    (B) check that mounting to the tractor is uncracked and secure,
    (C) both A and B,
    (D) neither A or B.

Answers to Let's Review

1. C; 2. B; 3. C; 4. C; 5. D; 6. A; 7. C; 8. B; 9. D; 10. C.

Terms You Need to Know

The following terms have been taken from the contents of Chapter Thirteen. Review them. If you see any you're unsure of, check the definition in the Glossary at the back of the book. If it helps you, keep a written list of the words and their definitions (or write in the definitions here) and review them several days prior to taking the CDL tests.

Aerodynamic buffeting

Air tank petcock

Chock

Converter dolly

Converter gear

Coupling

Cross-wind

Dead axles

Dolly support

Dolly tongue

Doubles

Drive axles

Emergency line

Fifth wheel

Kingpin

Landing gear

Pintle hook

Pups

Safety chains

Slack adjusters

Spring brakes

Steer-countersteer

Triples

Twins

Uncoupling

THE DISPATCH BOARD
The Driver's Visual Search Pattern: A Necessity for Safety

Above all things, a driver must always be safe. To properly drive any vehicle, a driver must use a systematic visual search pattern. That's a pattern moving forward or backward, surveying the roadway, the traffic or any hazards in your path and behind the truck, as well.

Many times drivers use mirrors only as an afterthought when, in fact, they must be used at least every six to eight seconds.

Paying strict attention to the direction the vehicle is traveling (common sense), the driver should use this same approach to the visual search.

A great set of principles a driver should use is I.P.D.E. What does it stand for?

I = Identification
P = Prediction
D = Decision
E = Execution

These principles are taught in beginning driver education classes throughout the country, but these same principles will serve the professional driver equally well. So, how are they used in professional driving?

The "identification" portion is to reveal anything that might possibly be a problem to the driver. "Prediction" is how would this or these problems occur and how would they impact the safety of all concerned. "Decision" is simply, "What must I, (the driver), do to avoid the predicted problem, and "Execute" is the action required to avoid the unsafe problem or situation.

A vehicle traveling forward must avoid those deadly head-on and rear-end crashes by scanning a distance of 12–15 seconds ahead, or to the horizon and avoid tailgating any vehicle in front of *yours* (now I've made it personal—we're talking about you, the driver).

A safe following distance is one second for every 10 feet of length of your vehicle plus an additional second if you are traveling over 40 miles per hour.

THE DISPATCH BOARD *continued*

Now, how to use those mirrors! "Systematic" is the watchword. Scan the road ahead for traffic, then use the left mirror. Now scan ahead and use the right mirror. This is a driving process. Every fifth or sixth time you scan, take time to scan your important gauges.

Many times a driver will go through this visual search by habit and really look at the mirrors instead of seeing what the mirrors reveal. The driving process is a continual mental one, so it is important to stay away from automatic habits and to become aware of everything you do. This means always being aware of how you're doing what you're doing—and why you're doing it.

When you drive, you'll find blind spots everywhere and only a systematic visual search reveals them.

To eliminate blind spots at the front and rear of your vehicle, always do a walk-around before entering the vehicle, searching in front and behind the vehicle to reveal any potential dangers.

Never back a vehicle unless necessary and always use a ground guide (a person who can clear your areas and safely guide you into the parking area).

Always Get Out And Look (GOAL) before backing.

Remember, too, to always check for overhead dangers and obstacles that could cause damage to the top or underside of the rig.

Remember to successfully use IPDE, you must take the time and must have the space to use the IPDE process.

It would do no good to identify a problem if you did not have the time and space to predict how the situation effects you, to decide what to do, and to execute an action that would prevent the incident or accident.

Why do you even want information about how to do these things? For your own personal safety, your career as a professional driver, your rig, and its cargo. Your well being and your career depend on your constant attention to safety.

We've covered the who—which is you, the what—which is safety, the when—which is constantly, and the where—which is everywhere.

Accidents can happen anywhere a vehicle is moving. Your personal safety and the safety of those around you are the foremost concerns of the authors of this book.

Learn to drive safely! Then drive safely to earn!

14 Driving Passenger Vehicles and Preparing for the Passenger Endorsement

Who Needs a Passenger Endorsement?

Drivers operating buses and vans that seat more than 15 people, including the driver, must have a CDL. The exception would be those driving family members for personal reasons, not for a salary or for profit.

Bus drivers are also required to have a Passenger Endorsement on their CDL. This includes passing the General Knowledge Tests, the Skills Test, and the Air Brakes Endorsement—if the bus has air brakes—plus the written Passenger Endorsement.

Like any commercial vehicle driver, the bus or van driver ensures the safety of the vehicle by making a pre-trip inspection. This would include checking problems reported by previous drivers.

If the problems reported earlier have been corrected, then the next driver should sign the previous driver's report. This serves as the driver's certification that previous problems have been corrected.

During each pre-trip check, the driver should ensure good working order and safe function of the following items:

- Parking brake
- All lights and reflectors
- Horn
- Windshield wiper(s)
- Rear-view mirrors
- Steering mechanism
- Tires (no recapped or regrooved tires on the front wheels)
- Wheels and rims
- Service brakes (including hose couplings if bus has a trailer/semi-trailer)
- Coupling devices
- Emergency equipment
    - ——Close all open emergency exits
    - ——Close access panels (for engine, restroom service, baggage)

Drivers should check the interior for safety and working order of the following:

- Aisles and stairwells are clear.
- Floor coverings have no gaps or tears.
- Handholds and railings are intact.
- All emergency exit handles are secure.
- All signs/signaling devices are operational—including the restroom emergency device.
- All seats are securely fastened to the floor (one exception—a charter bus for farm workers may have up to eight temporary folding chairs).

- All emergency exit doors and windows are closed.
- All emergency exits are clearly marked with signage.
- Red emergency light must be working and clearly visible—drive with it on at night or any time you use outside lights.
- Roof hatches should be locked in partly open position, but do not leave them open as a general rule.
- The fire extinguisher and emergency reflectors are present, as required by law.
- Unless bus is equipped with circuit breakers, it must have spare electrical fuses on board.

Loading Passengers and Cargo

Passengers must be seated and all baggage must be stored under the seats. No carry-on baggage is allowed in the stairwell or the aisle.

All carry-on baggage must be stored to allow free movement about the bus and must not block emergency exits or windows.

Carry-on baggage should be stowed to protect riders from injury if carry-ons fall or shift.

No passenger should stand in the area adjacent to the driver. Most buses have a marked "standee line" that is placed even with the rear of the driver's seat. All riders should stand behind this line.

When on the road, mention the company's safety rules and regulations, including "No smoking," "No drinking," and other rules designed for the comfort of passengers, such as the use of computers, cell phones, radios, and tape or CD players.

When You Arrive at the Destination

Once you've arrived at the destination, the driver's job is to:

- Announce the location.
- Announce the reason for stopping.
- Announce the next departure time.
- Announce the bus number.
- Remind passengers to watch their step.
- If aisles are on a lower level than the seating, remind passengers to step down when they are disembarking.
- Remind riders to take carry-ons with them.
- To prevent theft, don't allow pre-boarding riders on the bus until departure time.

What Bus Drivers Need to Know On the Road

While driving, occasionally scan the interior of the bus, and if any passengers are not following the rules, remind them—explain the "why" of the rules. This may prevent problems down the road.

If a passenger is disorderly—for whatever reason—your responsibility is to ensure that person's safety as well as that of other passengers.

Never let a passenger out in an area that is unsafe or desolate. Wait until the next scheduled stop—in a well-lighted area—to discharge him or her from the bus.

When the Bus Should Stop

- All buses must stop between 15 and 50 feet from a railroad crossing. Stop no closer than 15 feet and no farther than 50 feet away. Look and listen in both directions—open your front door if this allows you better vision and allows you to hear an oncoming train. If a train passes, before proceeding, look and listen again to make sure another train isn't following close behind the first one.
- If bus has manual transmission, never change gears while crossing a track.
- Stop at all drawbridges—at least 50 feet before the draw of the bridge—that are not controlled by a signal light or traffic control officer. Proceed when the draw is completely closed.
- Buses are not required to stop but to slow down and check for any other oncoming vehicles:
  - ——At streetcar crossings.
  - ——At railroad tracks used exclusively for industrial switching.
  - ——When a police or railroad flagman is directing traffic.
  - ——If the traffic signal shows green.
  - ——At crossings that are "exempt crossings."
- Buses are also required to slow down when:
  - ——The traffic light shows green.
  - ——The bridge has an attendant who controls traffic when the drawbridge opens.

Don'ts for Bus Drivers

Under *no* circumstances should a driver:

- Refuel the bus with riders on board—and never refuel in a closed building with riders on board.
- Engage another passenger in conversation or any distracting activity. Your duty is to drive the bus.
- Tow a bus with passengers on board—and never allow passengers to ride in a towed vehicle.
- Most companies would allow a bus loaded with passengers to be towed out of danger—check the company manual to find out other rules.

Driving a Bus Defensively

Bus crashes immediately grab front-page headlines—and if you've seen any of these news articles, you may know that bus crashes usually happen at intersections. This means: Use caution.

Many bus crashes occur in icy or rainy weather. Be aware that excessive speed can also be a "killer" on curves and on any wet or icy road. For any questionable stretch of road, reduce your speed. Even with good traction, the bus may roll over. With poor traction, it may slide off the road.

How do you know if your speed is excessive? If the bus leans toward the outside of a banked curve, you're going too fast!

Give yourself plenty of room for each maneuver. Newspapers often report a school bus ripping off the safety mirrors of passing vehicles—or even hitting other vehicles in passing.

Remember how much clearance your bus needs and carefully accelerate when merging with traffic. Never assume the driver with the flashing right-turn signal will actually turn right.

Brake-Door Interlocks

All bus drivers—especially urban mass transit drivers—should be aware of brake and accelerator interlock safety systems. What do they do? The brake-door interlock system applies the brakes and holds the throttle in an idle position each time the door is opened.

When the door closes, the interlock releases. Some drivers use this feature in place of the parking brakes.

One word says it all: *don't!*

Hazardous Materials On Board Buses

As a responsible driver, it is your job to watch for baggage or other cargo containing hazardous materials, because most are not allowed to be transported by buses.

Here's a list of some of those hazardous materials that are forbidden in spaces on the bus occupied by people:

- Class 2 poison, Class 6 liquid poison, tear gas, irritating materials
- More than 100 pounds of solid Class 6 poisons
- Explosives, except for small-arms ammunition
- Labeled radioactive materials
- More than 500 pounds total of allowable hazardous materials—no more than 100 pounds of any one class.

Note: Some travelers may board a bus with unlabeled hazardous materials. They may not realize how unsafe it is to carry these materials. Do not allow passengers to carry on common hazardous materials—like batteries or gasoline.

The Federal Hazardous Materials Table

The Federal Hazardous Materials Table designates which materials are hazardous to transport. They have been designated as "hazardous materials" because they endanger the health, safety, and property of those around them during their transport.

Federal rules require the originating shipper to mark any hazardous materials with the material's name, ID number, and hazard label.

There are nine different hazard labels. They are about four inches square and are diamond-shaped.

When you see the diamond-shaped labels on a container of material to be shipped, don't allow that container on your bus unless you are sure the material is allowed.

Post-trip Vehicle Inspection

After passengers have disembarked, inspect the bus. Interstate carriers require a written inspection report from each driver at the end of every shift. These reports list any problems with the bus systems or any damage done during the last shift.

Double check areas that passengers may have damaged in transit, such as loose handholds, seats, emergency exits, and windows.

Report this damage at the end of the shift so repairs can be completed before the next trip.

If you drive for a mass transit organization, also look to see if the following are in working order:

- Passenger signaling units
- Brake-door interlocks

Let's Review

Read each question and all of the answers provided. Place the letter of the correct answer in the space provided or write your answers on a separate piece of paper so you can use these questions again as you review for the CDL. Once you have answered all the questions, check your answers against the answer key which follows.

____ 1. While driving a bus, you should
(A) invite passengers to come to the front of the bus for conversation so you can get to know them,
(B) keep your eyes on the road,
(C) keep your eyes on the road and periodically scan the interior of the bus,
(D) all of the above.

____ 2. If a passenger becomes drunk and obnoxious, as a bus driver you should
(A) stop the bus and put the passenger off the bus,
(B) tell the passenger to come to the front of the bus so you can find a compromise,
(C) in a loud voice, ask the passenger to quit drinking,
(D) none of the above.

____ 3. Federal regulations say a bus must have a fire extinguisher and
(A) emergency reflectors,   (C) a bathroom,
(B) a gun,   (D) all of the above.

____ 4. An announcement about company policy and rules regarding smoking, CD players, etc., should be made
(A) before the bus has traveled into another state,
(B) when passengers complain about another passenger,
(C) at the beginning of the trip,
(D) all of the above.

____ 5. To refuel a bus, the optimum situation is
(A) while passengers are engaged in conversation and don't notice you are refueling,
(B) when you find cheap gas,
(C) in an enclosed structure,
(D) none of the above.

____ 6. At a railroad crossing, the bus should stop
(A) at least 15 feet before the crossing,
(B) 25 feet before arriving at the crossing,
(C) 100 feet before the crossing,
(D) none of the above.

____ 7. During your post-trip inspection, be sure to check
(A) the handholds and seats,
(B) any lunch bags that have been left behind,
(C) the restroom signal,
(D) all of the above.

____ 8. At the pre-trip inspection, the driver must check
(A) all bus systems,
(B) the horn, brakes, and emergency mirror,
(C) the reflectors,
(D) all of the above.

____ 9. If a problem is found on the pre-trip inspection, the driver should
    (A) report the problem and await repair,
    (B) say nothing to the passengers,
    (C) fix it himself,
    (D) all of the above.

____10. After stopping, when you pull the bus back into traffic, you should
    (A) wait for a space in traffic to open,
    (B) honk your horn before pulling back into traffic,
    (C) simply pull into traffic—it will wait for you since your bus is probably larger than most vehicles,
    (D) find an intersection where a policeman is directing friends in and out of the traffic.

Answers to Let's Review

1. C; 2. D; 3. A; 4. C; 5. D; 6. D; 7. A; 8. D; 9. A; 10. A.

Terms You Need to Know

The following terms have been taken from the contents of Chapter 14. Review them. If you see any you're unsure of, check the definition in the Glossary at the back of the book. If it helps you, keep a written list of the words and their definitions (or write in the definitions here) and review them several days prior to taking the CDL tests.

Access panels

Brake-door interlock

Bridge traffic control officer

Bus

Carry-on baggage

Coupling device

Departure

Destination

Drawbridge

Emergency exit

Federal Hazardous Materials Table

Handhold

Passenger supervision

Post-trip vehicle inspection

Railroad crossing

Roof hatch

Seatbelt

Standee line

Streetcar crossing

THE DISPATCH BOARD
Outstanding Driver Who Went above and beyond the Call of Duty

Houston METRO Bus Operator Vincent White helped a young couple during one of the most disastrous floods to hit the Houston area. Flooding from Tropical Storm Allison in June 2001 was so severe, the region was proclaimed a disaster area.

White's actions give new meaning to METRO's Safe Haven Program, in which people who believe they are in danger or need emergency help can find a safe haven with METRO. The program, sponsored by METRO's Department of Police & Traffic Management, allows people to flag down a METRO bus—not just at a bus stop but wherever they might be—if they're feeling threatened or believe they're in an unsafe environment. Originally begun in 1988, the program was promoted again in 2000 to re-emphasize METRO's concern for providing a safe environment for its patrons in the community.

White started his shift on the 82 Westheimer route at 1:17 AM on Saturday, June 9, in a torrent of rain, expecting not to even make pullout. The couple and their newborn baby are glad he did.

Before he could get very far, White received a bulletin from his facility's dispatch office to wait since the road ahead was turning into a river with about 8 to 10 inches of water. He sat in the bus for about two hours until the water seemed to be receding. At around 4 AM, he was driving on Westheimer Road in the central part of the city with only four passengers and received another bulletin telling him to come back to the West Facility, located in far southwest Houston.

At about that time, a frantic man waved down the bus and told White he and his pregnant wife, who was having contractions five minutes apart, had been waiting for a long time for an ambulance to arrive. White knew he had to help them if he could and immediately called his dispatcher for permission to take the bus to the hospital through high water if necessary. He transferred the remaining passengers onto another METRO bus before starting a harrowing drive to the Texas Medical Center amid torrential rain and ever-rising water.

All the way to Ben Taub Hospital, one of the few medical facilities that was accepting patients during the storm, White kept his cool while trying to "stay on the yellow line." He used a few tricks the veteran operators had taught him, like pumping the brakes. "It was the worst I've ever seen in my 9-½ years as a bus operator," he said. "People were stranded, cars were stalled. It was like a war zone out there."

But White, who was born in 1967, had confidence in his bus, which happened to be number 4067. He was able to get the young couple to the hospital in time, although they didn't get around to exchanging names. He told them "good luck" and the man called him a hero. Then he returned safely to the West Facility.

"Maybe I shouldn't have been out there. But it felt good to be called a hero," he said. "Now, I can't say don't come out in those kinds of conditions because you never know."

Although his story may be the most dramatic, White is among a number of METRO Bus Operators who went above and beyond the call of duty to help victims of the flood.

Courtesy of Houston Metropolitan Transit Authority.

PART III

Practice Tests and Review

15 Tips for Passing the CDL

Congratulations—you're almost there!

Studying and reviewing do not take as much physical effort as mental effort—so we know that when you have reached this point, you've spent many hours preparing yourself for the CDL General Knowledge and Skills Tests, as well as for one or more of the endorsements.

The following are aids and tools to make studying less demanding and more efficient. Don't rush through this portion of your preparation. It may be the most important information in the book!

Here we go!

Read through this information before beginning your review. It will help you take the tests and accurately measure your areas of strength and weakness.

The following are some suggestions to help you pass the written CDL tests:

- Each of the test questions will be either true-false or multiple choice—usually having four possible answers. Only one is right.
- Read the question. Then read it again.
- First, answer all questions where you are 100-percent certain you know the answer.
- When you answer a question, don't go back and change it. Chances are, your first impression is the most accurate.
- If your test sheet will be graded by a machine, and you do change an answer, completely erase the old answer before marking the new answer.
- As you go through the test, make certain you're marking the right question with the right answer.
- Sometimes you can find a question further down the page that will give you the answer to a question or will help you fill in the blanks for a question you're not sure you know.
- If the right answer does not come to you immediately, narrow down the choices.
- Never leave a blank—a blank will count as an incorrect answer. Put down something—wild guesses sometimes are right!

Most states give written CDL tests. Some use computers—you read the question and then push button A, B, C, or D to indicate your answer.

Q. What should I do to review?
A. Everybody is different. Some will want to quickly read major chapters. Others may want to re-take tests at the end of each chapter.

Use the review tests at the end of the chapters and the book to review everything you have read and learned.

If one chapter gave you problems, go back and scan the chapter. If you highlighted information as you read, go back over all highlighted information.

Q. Do review tests really help?

A. They do two things—first, they help you review and recall information from earlier readings. Second, the review tests help you determine where you are strong (need less work) and where you are weak (need more work in these areas).

Finally, taking review tests helps you prepare for the day you'll actually be taking test. It gives you a "practice run" so you can get the feel of taking the written tests.

CDL Tests—Questions and Answers

The following questions are some of the questions most frequently asked by CDL applicants. Read through carefully to make certain you are aware of this information.

Q. How do I arrange to take the CDL tests?

A. This process depends on the state where you are taking the test. You can get the best information from the local branch of the state department of transportation (see Appendix A for telephone numbers, addresses, and websites).

You can almost always take the written Knowledge Test on a walk-in basis—you don't need an appointment. However, in many states, you *must* have an appointment to take the Skills Test.

Q. How much does it cost to take the CDL?

A. The costs differ from state to state. Table 15-1 shows the average cost for some of the tests.

Q. Where will I take the CDL tests?

A. You will almost always take the written test at the Department of Motor Vehicles driver's license stations. Some of the stations, however, will not be

Table 15-1
Average cost of CDL tests

License	First CDL or Renewal with Written Exam	Renewal (No Written Exam)	Road Test
Class A	$25.00	$15.00	$25.00
Class B	$25.00	$15.00	$25.00
Class C	$12.50	$10.00	$12.50
Endorsement			
HazMat	$10.00	$10.00	None
Passenger	$10.00	No Charge	$5.00
Tanker	$10.00	No Charge	None
Tanker/HazMat	$20.00	$10.00	None

equipped to conduct the Skills Test. In this case, the Department of Motor Vehicles will tell you where the Skills Tests are conducted.

In some communities, an authorized company or individual may give you the skills test.

We encourage you to visit the test site a day or two before taking the test, just to find out where it is located and so you can be familiar with the area prior to going in for testing. Be sure and ask permission to just visit the site—usually no problem with this.

Q. How old do I have to be when I take the CDL tests? Is there an age limit?
A. In most states, CDL applicants must be 21 years of age to take the CDL General Knowledge and Skills Tests. In a few states, drivers between 18 and 21 years of age can apply for a Restricted CDL, which limits them to driving within that state only.

There is no maximum age limit for applicants wishing to take the CDL.

Q. How long do I have to take the CDL tests?
A. Usually, there are no time limits, but check with your local Department of Motor Vehicles to make certain this is the case in your state. In any case, make certain to give yourself enough time to complete the test—which means arriving well before the licensing site closes for the day.

Ask the Department of Motor Vehicles about its hours of operation.

Then, plan to take the test. You may need to take off work for a half-day to have enough time to take the test. Whatever you do, be prepared and don't rush yourself.

Q. Can I take my children with me while I take the written CDL tests?
A. It's not a good idea. If child care is a factor, don't try to take these tests with your children wandering around the testing facility. You won't do as well—and getting a babysitter or making other arrangements for something this important just makes good sense.

Q. What identification and other documents do I need to bring when I take the CDL tests?
A. If you already have a CDL and are going in for renewal, make sure your medical card has not expired. If it has, you'll need to get a Department of Transportation physical—and many states require that you have it before you apply for your CDL.

You should also take a driver's license or some type of photo ID and your Social Security Card.

If you are testing for endorsements—particularly the Tank and Hazardous Materials Endorsements—some states require other documents, licenses, and certificates. Check with the Department of Motor Vehicles for specifics.

Q. Is there any way I could take an oral test rather than a written one?
A. Some states offer these. Find out if they are available from the Department of Motor Vehicles. You will probably need to make an appointment.

Q. What is a passing grade on the CDL Knowledge Test?
A. Federal law states you must score 80 percent or better to pass the CDL Knowledge Test. Your state may require an even higher score to pass the CDL. Ask about your state's requirements when you call to make an appointment to take the test.

Q. Can I take the Skills Test, even if I don't pass the Knowledge Test?

A. Well, we know you're going to do well, so don't worry about this question, but since you're asking . . .

Rule #1: You can't take the Skills Test until you pass the Knowledge Test.

Some states allow you to take parts of the Skills Test even if you don't do well on one part. Other states end the Skills Test session if you fail one section.

Very few states set a limit as to the number of times you can retake the tests. However, most will charge a fee for each retake, so it could get expensive. To find out the exact rules of your state, contact the Department of Motor Vehicles.

Q. Are there any suggestions about taking the Skills Test?

A. Just one: Listen carefully to the examiner's instructions—make sure you understand them. If you don't understand what the examiner wants you to do, ask for more information. If you ask the examiner to restate the instructions or to explain what he or she wants, it will not be held against you . . . and it won't cost you any points.

Q. Are there any Last Words of advice?

A. We don't want to sound like your third grade teacher, but . . .

- Read slowly and carefully—know exactly what the question is asking.
- Write neatly—so anybody can read your writing.
- Don't leave any blanks. Give it your best guess if you just don't know.
- Don't make any marks—other than marking your answers on the answer sheet.
- Ask questions—such as what kind of pencil is required? What grade average is required? Don't be pesky, but find out what you need to know to be comfortable taking the test.

Testing Styles

As you may remember, there are many approaches to testing—essay, multiple choice, true-false, fill-in-the-blank. Here are some tips on these various types of tests:

True/False

Usually written in the form of statements, true-false test questions are often seen as the easiest type of testing.

Wrong! In a true-false test, you must check to see if all parts of the statement or question are true. If one part is false, the entire statement is false and should be marked "false" even though the majority of the statement is true.

Look for words like "always," "never," "complete," and "all." When you see these words in the test, read the statement several times. Whatever the answer, it should cover the entire statement, not just part of it.

Multiple Choice

A favorite of testers and those taking the test, multiple choice questions are easier to deal with if you follow these eight steps:

1. Read the question.
2. Read the question and the first answer. Does this combination make a true statement? If not, go to the next choice.
3. Generally, only one combination makes a true statement.
4. If more than one answer appears true, use the process of elimination or make a "smart guess" by eliminating those answers you absolutely know to be wrong. Does a remaining answer have the word "every," "always," "all," or "never"? Remember—it's rare that something is *always* or *never* the case. That narrows the choice.
5. If you are left with two possible answers, a "wild" guess gives you a 50-50 chance of getting the answer right.
6. If an answer is much shorter or much longer than the others, it is often the correct answer.
7. When one of the choices is "all of the above," choose this answer only if you are convinced that all the answer choices are correct. It may be that only one answer completes a true statement with the question.
8. There may be questions where none of the possible combinations makes a true statement. Be careful and make sure no answer choice is correct before choosing "none of the above."

Matching

When you are asked to match one item with another, look at the instructions carefully. You may be asked to match the first list of terms with a second list of definitions. Or you may be asked to match a heading in one list with several items in the second.

First, know what you are being asked to do. If there are an equal number of items in each list, you probably are being asked to make a one-to-one match. If there are more items in one list, expect to have some leftovers or items with more than one match. Then, follow these steps:

1. Scan the two lists quickly—make any matches that are obvious.
2. As you match, you may want to mark through those choices you've used.
3. Next, take the remainder of each list and try to answer each heading with what you know—then check the other list to find anything close.
4. Make all the matches you can—skip the ones for now that you can't answer at all.
5. For the terms you just can't match, line them up with the remaining choices and pick the best match.

Remember: Never leave any blanks.

Essay Questions

This type of question is answered with a lengthy written piece. In this kind of test, you can use your own words. Some of the questions the examiner asks on the Skills Test are like essay questions—they're asking you to explain something in your own words.

Fill-in-the-Blank

You won't see too many of these or essay questions on the General Knowledge Test, but in this type of question, a statement is given that is missing a word. Where the word is missing, you will see a blank space. Sometimes you are given possible words to fit into the blank. Choose the item or word that makes the sentence a true statement.

Preparing Yourself and Your Vehicle for the CDL Skills Test

Q. What tools should I take for the Skills Test?
A. For the inspection, take a flashlight, tire pressure gauge, tire tread depth gauge, and a pair of gloves.

Q. What are some suggestions about taking the Skills Test?
A. Have the right vehicle. Have that vehicle in good working condition—and be familiar with that entire vehicle, from door to door and wheel to wheel.
   If you're taking the Skills Test for a Class A CDL, you must take the Skills Test in a Class A vehicle. If you plan to take the Air Brakes Endorsement and don't want the air brakes restriction on your CDL, you need to have air brakes on your vehicle.

Q. Will the examiner provide a vehicle if I don't have one?
A. No state and no CDL examiner will provide a vehicle. You must bring your own—no ifs, ands, or buts.

Q. Should I work on the vehicle before taking the Skills Test?
A. Part of the Skills Test is to conduct an inspection—a bad time to find a problem with the brakes, transmission, tires, etc.
   Conduct several inspections before you go for your Skills Test and have the vehicle in the best working condition possible.

Q. Should I try to get the vehicle cleaned up before I take the CDL Skills Test in it?
A. It sure wouldn't hurt. You want to make a positive first impression. Tighten all loose nuts and bolts, and repair any problems. Wash the vehicle. It won't get you extra points, but a clean vehicle is easier to inspect than a muddy one.

Q. How well should I know the truck in which I take the CDL Skills Test?
A. Very, very well. If it's a new truck, spend as much time as posssible learning where all the controls are and get a feel of how each lever, pedal, and switch responds.
   Know which noises are normal for the vehicle and which could indicate trouble.
   Be prepared—the examiner could ask you to name or explain every lever and switch in the cab. It won't be too impressive if you're clueless about which switch does what.
   To prepare, read over the owner's manual. Sit in the cab and familiarize yourself with every control, right down to the windows and door locks.

Q. What else will help me do my best on the tests?
A. Study, prepare, and one last thing . . . be organized for test day. What does organization have to do with anything? Here are a few suggestions:

1. Have information from the Department of Motor Vehicles about the tests, where to go, and when to show up.
2. Make a "dry run" to the test site. How long does it take to get there? When you go, what time of day will it be—and what will traffic be like?
3. Find the parking, find the building, and go in so you can see the test site, if you have permission.
4. Don't be rushed—take your time. If you need to take a half-day off work, do it.
5. Give yourself enough time to arrive at the test site for your appointment.
6. The night before taking the CDL, get a good night's sleep—no late night TV, no partying.
7. Eat a balanced breakfast the morning of the test.
8. Watch coffee/tea/caffeine intake. The same goes for chocolate.
9. Be positive—make positive statements about the test and yourself.
10. Be committed—be responsible for studying and reviewing. Be committed about doing a good job so you can get on with your career plans . . . and the next exciting chapter of your life.

THE DISPATCH BOARD
He Didn't Have to Stop but He Did

He drove the same road four times a week for a local grocery chain. Most trips were uneventful. He liked that. He also liked being at home most nights. But this night would be different.

Heading back to the terminal after making his last delivery, he turned the CB down and slipped a Linda Ronstadt tape into his tape player. The moon was shining, skies were clear, and the weather was cool enough to let in a little fresh air. He felt good. He'd be home soon.

Heading down State Highway 71, he drummed his fingers to the beat of the music. What could be better—a job he loved, going home every night, and a family who loved him.

But his thoughts were interrupted.

In the middle of a field he had passed a hundred times or more was something different. He slowed down, stopped, and turned around. It was worth checking out.

The usually dark field was lush with maize in the spring and fall. He had often admired the fullness of the heads of the plants, and wondered if the farmer who plowed and planted that field knew something other farmers didn't.

Tonight, however, something else caught his eye. He looked hard in the direction of the field, toward a red light glowing almost dead center in the now fallow field. "What in the heck is that," he said out loud to no one in particular. He strained again and parked the truck.

Knowing it was against company rules to stop without a mechanical reason in the middle of a dark night, he bounded out of the cab, grabbing his flashlight as he did.

His gloved hands easily won the battle with the barbed wire fence and he instinctively walked toward the light. "For some reason I wasn't afraid for myself," he would say later. "I just needed to know what that light was doing in the middle of that field."

continues

THE DISPATCH BOARD *continued*

It was almost 2 AM

Walking several hundred yards over the furrowed ground, he finally got close enough to figure out the source of the red light. Just ahead was a late model Camero. But what was it doing in the middle of the field?

"Could be kids making out," the driver thought as he kept moving ahead. But he couldn't see any people in the car. He was now at the door of the car. Nobody was around.

"Really strange," he whispered aloud. "Really strange."

He stood and listened for a moment, hearing nothing but gusts of wind whip over the landscape. Then he heard something else, a moan or a sob that sounded more human than animal.

The driver flashed his light around and under the car. Still he found nothing.

He walked around the car, and then made increasingly wider circles until he found the source of the moan. There, on the ground, was the body of a young woman, barely breathing and bloodied from her apparent airborne trip from her car. Kneeling to assess her condition, he asked if she could hear him. There was no reply.

He pulled his cell phone from his pocket and dialed 911, finding a nearby emergency service and giving his location as well as a promise to meet them on the highway.

When he heard the wail of the sirens, he told the woman that help was on its way and then ran, stumbling, across the field in the direction of the highway and the flashing lights.

It would take several months of hospitalization until the young women was allowed to go home. The extent of her injuries could have cost her life, but quick thinking by an alert professional driver saved her life and shortened her rehabilitation by months.

The driver was later recognized for his assistance that night. He blushed as he received the hero's award while his family cheered with pride.

He didn't have to stop—but he did—and in doing so, made it possible for one very lucky young woman to return to college that next fall and go on with her life.

Her family offered the driver money and other rewards, but the driver refused. As he told a fellow driver long after the hoopla had died down, "Heck, I was just doing my job. Sure, I didn't have to stop, but I did, and I'm glad I did."

16

The CDL Skills Test—A Final Review

If you plan to obtain a Class A CDL, you will be asked to take the Skills Test in the tractor-trailer or truck you plan to drive.

What Is the Skills Test?

Just like it says, this examination will test your skills as a professional driver. It is divided into three parts:

- **The Pre-trip Inspection Test**—A test to determine if you know how to correctly conduct an inspection of your vehicle. It will also test your ability to determine if the vehicle is safe to drive.
- **The Basic Control Skills Test**—A test to show the examiner if you can safely back, park, and judge vehicle length.
- **The Road Test**—An actual driving test where you will go on the road to test your ability to safely handle the vehicle in almost any road condition.

There are some exceptions as far as skills test requirement goes:

- If you're applying for the Class C CDL, you won't be required to take the road test part of the skills test.

Note: For the Basic Control Skills Test and the Road Test, you will be required to take the test in the same vehicle as the type of CDL for which you are applying.

Some General Information about the Skills Test

1. Most of the Skills Test must be done by making an appointment.
2. Some procedures differ by state—contact your state Department of Motor Vehicles to find out where the test is conducted, what tests are offered, and when.
3. Some states use third party examiners—so the test may be held at a trucking school or trucking company.
4. The Skills Test is designed to thoroughly test your driving skills. It isn't easy—so don't take your Skills Test without preparing and practicing.

The Pre-trip Inspection

Before going to take your Skills Test, you must do a thorough pre-trip inspection of your vehicle. Don't get to the examiner's station and discover a defect in the vehicle. The examiner will not allow you to use that vehicle for the road test—which means you lose your appointment time and will have to reschedule another appointment in several weeks.

To do a good job on the pre-trip inspection, bring the following with you:

- Tire pressure gauge
- Tread depth gauge
- Tire "billy"—tire "checker"
- Wheel chocks
- Shop rag (to clean lights and reflectors)
- Gloves
- Vehicle registrations
- Proof of insurance (in certain states)
- Any applicable permits to operate in the state
- Your current driver's license

When you arrive at the testing center, the examiner will give you instructions (they will be similar to those below):

During this test, you will be examined in three areas—a vehicle inspection test, a basic control skills test, and an on-the-road driving test. For the vehicle inspection test, you will be asked to perform a thorough inspection of the vehicle. For the basic control skills test, you will do backing, parking, and turning exercises. And for the road test, we will go out on the road for a trip that will take 30 to 45 minutes.

At all times when you are behind the wheel during this test, you are in charge of the vehicle. I will never ask you to do something that is either unsafe or illegal.

I will give you instructions as we go along. If you have any questions, please ask. If you don't understand a direction, ask me for more information.

When it is time to begin the pre-trip inspection, the examiner will say:

Please conduct a complete and thorough inspection of the vehicle. You may use the Vehicle Inspection Memory Aid from the Driver's Manual, if you want to use it. As you do the inspection, point out or touch the things you are inspecting and explain what you're looking for as you inspect it.

Start by inspecting the engine compartment. Then climb into the cab and start the engine. After you have done the start-up checks in the cab, turn off the engine and do the rest of the inspection. Do you have any questions? Then, go ahead and start the vehicle inspection.

The keys to doing a proper pre-trip inspection are:

- Do it all the time.
- Practice.
- Know all the systems and components.

Practice your pre-trip inspection and do this the same way each time. By doing the pre-trip inspection this way, you'll develop a rhythm or routine. If you miss checking something, you'll know it because you'll feel "off" or "off rhythm".

Practice until you have the routine down to the minute. It will usually require 45 to 60 minutes.

When you're taking the pre-trip inspection test, the examiner will ask you to do it in the following manner:

- Inspect the engine compartment.
- Start the engine and perform the in-vehicle checks.
- Shut down the engine and perform the external inspection.

It is possible that the examiner will have you check only one side of the vehicle, because if you can do one side correctly, then you'll know how to do the other one as well.

On a straight truck or tractor-trailer, it will be left to the examiner's choice which side he or she wants checked. A bus will be inspected on the passenger door side only.

If you have a cab-over vehicle, the examiner will not require you to jack up the cab. However, if you are not able to check an item due to the cab not being raised, tell the examiner you are not able to check that part and just tell him or her what you would normally look for—this will give you credit for having checked that item.

While doing the inspection, the examiner will be taking notes, but don't get paranoid about what he or she is writing down—don't get in a hurry, and don't get nervous.

As you perform your pre-trip inspection, call out what you are inspecting and what you are going to be looking for in that area. Here's an example:

"I'm checking the wheel, lugs, and nuts. I'll be looking for any cracks, any rust—which could indicate a loose nut—or any missing lugs or nuts."

If the examiner doesn't know what you're checking or what you're looking for, you may not get credit for it. Go slowly and be precise. Prove to the examiner that you know what you're doing.

Review the 7-Step Pre-trip Inspection (Figure 16-1)

- **Step one: Approach the vehicle**—As you walk toward the vehicle, look for signs of damage, leaks, and whether the vehicle is leaning. Then, check the surrounding area for any hazards.
- **Step two: Check the engine compartment**—Check all components: fluid levels, wiring, belts, hoses, steering controls, front brakes, and suspension, etc.
- **Step three: Start the engine and check the cab interior**—With the transmission in neutral (or in park if it is an automatic transmission), apply brakes, depress clutch, and start the engine. Check all gauges and controls and all emergency equipment. Make certain you have the vehicle registration (this is part of your inspection).
- **Step four: Turn off the engine and check the lights**—Check headlights (both low and high beams) and four-way flashers on the front of the vehicle. Then, turn off the headlights and flashers and turn on all marker/clearance lamps and the right-turn signal.
- **Step five: Complete a walkaround inspection**—Beginning at the driver's side of the cab, begin checking all items—lights, fuel tanks, wheels, mirrors, coupling devices, suspension, air line connections and air lines, brakes, doors, etc. Each axle must be inspected thoroughly.
- **Step six: Check the signal lights**—Turn off all body lights, turn on brake lights and the left-turn signal. Then, get out and check them.
- **Step seven: Start the engine and check the brake system**—You're almost done now. Turn off all lights and perform a brake check. If you have air brakes, remember to turn your engine off before pumping the brakes to check your low air pressure warning light/signal.

WALKAROUND SEQUENCE

1. Left Side of Cab Area
2. Front of Cab Area
3. Right Side of Tractor Area
4. Right Saddle Tank Area
5. Coupling System Area
6. Right Rear Tractor Wheels Area
7. Rear of Tractor Area
8. Front of Trailer Area
9. Right Side of Trailer Area
10. Right Rear Trailer Wheels Area
11. Rear of Trailer Area
12. Left Rear Trailer Wheels Area
13. Left Side of Trailer Area
14. Left Saddle Tank Area

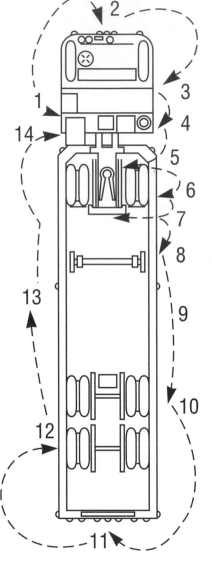

Figure 16-1   Pre-trip Walk-Around Sequence

The way to pass your pre-trip inspection test is to do the following:

1. Practice—until you can complete your pre-trip inspection in about 45 to 60 minutes.
2. Be consistent—use the same routine to do your pre-trip inspection every time.
3. Study all the information on pre-trip inspections.
4. Be certain the examiner knows what you're inspecting and what you'll be looking for in each area.
5. Be prepared. Check the truck before you go to the examining station. Take a tire pressure gauge, tread depth gauge, wheel chocks, shop rag, gloves, and all registrations, permits, and your driver's license.

Remember: *Do all of the required brake checks.*

Some states have added a simulated downgrade question. This is done after the pre-trip inspection and before you go out on the road test. In this question, the examiner will ask you to simulate going down a long downgrade. The examiner will ask you what you would do. You must tell the examiner:

- "I would test my brakes before beginning the downhill."
- "I would downshift to the proper gear before I start."
- "I would not clutch or shift while going down the grade."
- "I would check my mirrors constantly."
- "I would use light, steady braking pressure."

Mention each of these steps—each one is important!

Preparing for the Basic Control Skills Test

Q. Why is this test given?

A. Basically, this test is to determine whether or not you can operate and control a truck safely and on the road with other traffic.

There are six exercises the examiner can ask you to complete. You will be asked to do about four of these. The examiner will be looking to see if you can judge the length of your vehicle and if you can judge its position in relationship to others.

You will have time to practice before you are tested. Learn and practice all six exercises ahead of time. They are:

- Right turn
- Backward serpentine
- Parallel parking (driver's side)
- Parallel parking (passenger's side)
- Alley docking—backing into a dock
- Straight line backing—forward stop line

Veteran examiners have this to say about this test:

People who are confident in their skills do very well.

Some people get nervous—too nervous. So practice until you know you've got it down to a science.

The Basic Control Skills Test comes after the pre-trip inspection and before the road test. At some test sites, examiners prefer to start the road test and then, along the way, will have you stop and do the Basic Control Test.

Q. What can I expect from the Basic Control Tests?

A. The examiner will tell you this:

This is a test that is made up of a series of basic control moves. Try not to go over any lines or hit any cones or dividers—which represent our boundaries. Remember it is better to do a pull-up than it is to drive over a boundary.

"As we do each exercise, I will give you directions—and when you finish the exercise, sound your horn and set your brakes to let me know you've completed the maneuver."

"If you see me raise my arm with my palm facing you, stop your vehicle."

After the examiner provides these instructions, you will begin the Basic Control Skills Test.

For Straight Line Backing (Figure 16-2)

The examiner will tell you: "Drive forward through the alley and stop with your front bumper as close as possible to the painted line at the end without going past the line and without leaning out of the window or the door. You may stop only once—and I will wave you forward when I get to the end of the alley."

When this maneuver is completed, the examiner will provide the following instructions:

"Now, back your vehicle down the alley, avoid touching either side of the alley and stop with your front bumper even with the stop line at the end of the alley."

Hints to Help

- When you pull forward, go slowly. Keep your vehicle straight and centered between the boundaries or the sides of the alley.

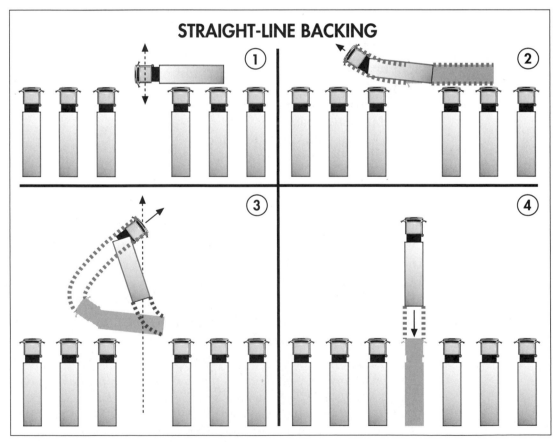

Figure 16-2   Straight-Line Backing

- When you stop, do so gently and deliberately—how you stop your vehicle counts in the exercise, so do it smoothly.
- Remember, stopping within two feet of the stop line is just as important as backing down the alley without touching the sides.
- The alley length is 100 feet and the width between boundaries is 12 feet.

Parallel Parking (Figure 16-3)

The examiner will start the exercise:

(For tractor-trailers)—Drive by the parking spot and back the trailer into it. You are only required to get the trailer into the space. Try to get your trailer as close as possible to the rear and to the curb without striking any boundaries or crossing the lines. You may jackknife your trailer, but get the trailer into the space. When you see me wave you forward, start the exercise. Sound your horn and set your brakes when you have completed it.

Hints to Help

- The parking space will be 10 feet longer than the trailer.
- The width of the parking space is 12 feet.
- To pass, get the trailer within 18 inches of the rear stop line and as close to the curb (really a painted line) as possible.
- Practice makes passing this test easier.

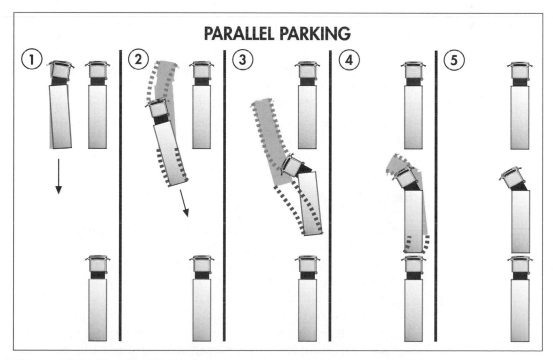

Figure 16-3 Parallel Parking

Alley Dock Exercise

For this exercise, the examiner will say:

Drive by the entrance to the alley with the alley on your left side. Kick your truck to a 45-degree angle. Stop and back into it. When you are straight, attempt to get as close to the back of the alley as possible, but don't back past it. I will stand near the entry to the alley. When I wave you forward, you may begin the exercise. Sound your horn and set your brakes when you've completed the maneuver.

Hints to Help

- Go past the entrance to the dock.
- As the middle of the tractor passes by the entrance, make a hard right by turning the steering wheel.
- Use soft braking throughout the maneuver—and go slowly.
- Use the lowest reverse gear.
- Head toward the cone on a 45-degree angle and stay left of the cone.
- Stop when the truck and trailer are straight and at a 45-degree angle to the dock.
- Begin backing slowly—making minor adjustments with the steering wheel to keep from over correcting, back into alley.
- Watch the trailer swing!
- Stop within two feet of the rear of the alley.
- Once the vehicle's rear passes the clearance line, you are within two feet of the back of the alley.
- Stay within all boundaries.

The Right Turn (Figure 16-4)

This exercise is included to simulate a right turn at an intersection and to test your ability to make a right turn safely.

The examiner will say: "Drive forward and make a right turn around the cone, trying to bring your rear wheels as close as possible to the cone without hitting it. I will wave you forward from the cone."

Hints to Help

- To make a successful right turn, stay toward the center of the street but in your lane.
- As you pass the turn, begin to turn to the right. The turn will be determined by how much your vehicle off-tracks—and a tractor-trailer will off-track much more than a small straight truck.
- Get your right rear tires as close to the cone as possible without touching it— you'll lose points if you touch the cone *or* swing too far out.
- Before going for your test, practice turning with the vehicle you will drive for the test.
- Go slowly.

MAKING A RIGHT TURN

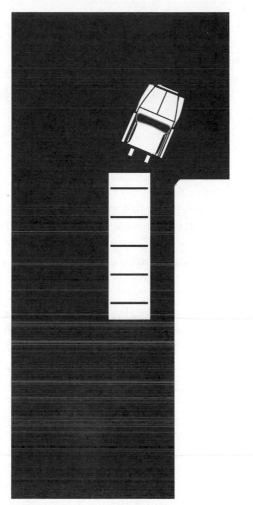

- Assume Proper Speed and Position

- Shift into Proper Gear

- Begin Turn When Cab is Halfway Past Corner

- Watch Right Mirror During Turn

Figure 16-4   Making a Right Turn

- Don't touch or drive over any boundaries.
- After turning, continue forward until the vehicle is straight, and wait for further instructions.

Backward Serpentine

The total distance of this course is 270 feet and the distance between the traffic cones is the length of your vehicle. The distance from the traffic cones to either outside boundary is 35 feet and the total distance from boundary to boundary is 70 feet.
  The instructor will say:

> *I will adjust the distance between the cones for your vehicle. When I signal, move forward, driving along the right side of the row of cones. Stop when your entire vehicle is past the third cone, then back up in a serpentine in this diagram until you back past the first cone. Try not to touch any cones or allow any part of your vehicle to pass over any cone, and keep your vehicle within the painted boundaries.*

Hints to Help

- If you get to a point where you are going to hit a cone, stop and reposition the vehicle by pulling forward.
- Each pull-up costs you points, but it's much better to pull up than to hit a cone.
- Don't cross any boundary lines.
- Practice, practice, practice!
- Go slowly—there's no time limit!

Passing the CDL Road Test

Two parts down and one—the fun part—to go. The Road Test will determine if you can safely drive your vehicle in actual over-the-road situations and conditions.

The CDL Road Test will require approximately 30 to 45 minutes and will involve a number of road conditions and maneuvers, such as right turns, left turns, various grades, railroad crossings, two-lane country roads, commercial areas, and interstate highways.

If the road condition is not available, the examiner may ask you what you would do in certain driving situations. In these roadside simulations, the examiner will give you instructions to set up the situation and then ask you describe what you would do in that particular case.

The examiner will never ask you to do anything that is unsafe or that may cause an accident. But, you are the driver—the individual responsible for the vehicle and its safety. So, if the examiner asks you to do something that you are not entirely comfortable doing, you can ask questions or even politely refuse to follow the instruction. But, you must have a reason why you refuse.

The examiners will not try to cross you up or trick you, but they are only human and sometimes all of us make mistakes. Again, politely explain why you feel that what the examiner is asking is unsafe.

On the CDL Road Test, here are some of the instructions you will hear:

> *During this test, I will always give directions for maneuvers as far in advance as possible. As we're driving, I may point out a location and ask you to pretend it is the top of a steep hill or maybe a railroad crossing. I will then ask you to go through the motions of what you would do if it were a real railroad crossing or steep grade. And at the same time you're going through the motions, tell me what you are doing and why.*
>
> *During the test, I will not give you trick directions or instructions to do something illegal or unsafe. During the test, I will also be marking the test form, but don't let this make you uncomfortable, because a mark does not mean you've done something wrong.*
>
> *Just concentrate on your driving.*

Q. What happens if I have an accident during the test?
A. You get an automatic failing grade—so study for the Road Test and practice, and study for the General Knowledge Test by answering the several tests in that chapter.

On the Road Test, if you make a mistake or two, don't worry. The examiner mainly wants to see if you can handle a commercial vehicle safely. A few minor glitches won't set you up to fail.

Q. During the CDL Road Test, what will the examiner be looking for?
A. The examiner will be checking the following:

1. Starting and stopping
   - Do you do these maneuvers smoothly without jerking or bouncing?
2. Shifting
   - Do you shift without grinding gears or jerking the vehicle?
   - Do you use the clutch and double-clutch?
3. Engine control
   - Do you maintain proper revolutions per minute without overspeeding or lugging? If you're driving a new engine that shifts at a lower rpm, point this out to the examiner.
4. Proper following distance
   - Do you maintain a safe following distance at all times?
5. Turn signals
   - Do you signal in advance of a lane change or turn? Do you turn off the turn signal immediately after the maneuver?
6. Proper set-up
   - When making turns, is your vehicle in the correct position?
7. Intersections
   - Do you move into the intersection cautiously? Are you prepared to stop?
   - Do you turn your head to check for approaching vehicles or foot traffic?
   - Do you stop within the stop lines? Do you keep your transmission in neutral and your foot off the clutch at traffic lights and stop signs? Do you stop at the stop line and then slowly move ahead?
8. Transmission control
   - Is your truck in gear at all times—no coasting to a stop and no coasting through a turn?
9. Braking
   - Do you brake smoothly, using the brake pedal—never the hand valve?
   - Do you check the mirrors when braking to see if anyone is following too closely?
10. Traffic signs and traffic control
    - Do you always observe speed limits and all traffic control devices, including stop lights, stop signs, etc.?
11. Curves
    - Do you slow down to negotiate a curve? Never allow truck to lean while going through a curve.
12. Interstate driving
    - Do you stay in the far right lane except when moving to the left to allow traffic to enter the freeway from an on-ramp or to pass a slow vehicle?
    - Do you check mirrors often?
    - Do you merge smoothly?
    - Do you use turn signals when merging and changing lanes and then turn them off promptly after the turn is made?

- Do you look 12 to 15 seconds ahead?
- Is your vehicle centered in your lane?

13. Upgrades
    - Do you maintain correct rpm and downshift when appropriate?
    - Can you start up an upgrade without rolling back?
    - When stopped, do you turn on your four-way flashers?

14. Downgrades
    - Do you maintain speed using a lower gear and steady, light braking?
    - Do you check your brakes before beginning a long downgrade?
    - Do you check the mirrors for signs of the brakes overheating?

15. Turns
    - Do you signal in advance of a turn and turn off your signal as soon as the turn is completed?
    - Do you stay in your lane?
    - Are both hands on the wheel when turning?
    - Do you stay in the same gear—no shifting—on a turn?

16. Railroad crossings
    - Do you look left and right and then look left and right again?
    - Do you roll down your window to listen?
    - If you are hauling HazMat cargo or passengers, do you stop at least 15 feet from the tracks—and no more than 50 feet?
    - Do you shift gears while crossing the track?

17. Underpasses and bridges
    - Do you check all bridge weight signs and height clearances?
    (Once you've cleared an underpass, the inspector may want to know the clearance on the underpass or height or weight limit. Be sure to look.)

Avoid These Bad Habits!

When taking the Road Test:

- Don't forget to put on your seatbelt.
- Don't drive with one hand on the wheel.
- Don't exceed speed limits.
- Don't allow the vehicle to roll forward or backward when stopped.
- Don't forget to slow down and look both ways at an intersection or railroad crossing.
- Use turn signals, but don't forget to turn them off.
- Use the clutch, but don't ride the clutch.
- Don't take the transmission out of gear and coast to a light or stop sign.
- Don't run over a curb while turning.
- Don't forget to slow down on rough roads. (Bouncing the examiner will not help you score points.)
- Don't forget to maintain a safe following distance.

17 The CDL Knowledge Test—A Final Review

General Knowledge Questions

The following statements are either true or false. Mark your answer in the blank provided. Then, check your answers using the key at the end of the chapter.

____ 1. Your vehicle and cargo weight cannot be regulated by state laws.

____ 2. It is okay to load tires beyond their rating.

____ 3. An empty vehicle is likely to go into a rear-wheel skid.

____ 4. A vehicle that is overloaded to the rear is likely to cause a rear-wheel skid.

____ 5. A vehicle is likely to tip over if it has a high center of gravity.

____ 6. You are required to keep a log of your time.

____ 7. Once you receive your CDL from one state, you do not have to report any traffic violations you are convicted of in a different state.

____ 8. A driver will lose his or her CDL for a year if he or she is convicted of driving under the influence (DUI), driving while intoxicated (DWI), or driving while on drugs.

____ 9. If a driver uses a commercial motor vehicle to commit a felony involving controlled substances, then the driver will lose his or her CDL for over a year.

____10. Drivers who operate commercial motor vehicles in an unsafe manner cannot earn a CDL.

____11. To obtain a CDL, drivers must take the General Knowledge Test.

____12. You do not have to list all the names and addresses of all employers who ever hired you to apply for a job driving a commercial motor vehicle.

____13. Drivers may still drive a commercial motor vehicle even if they are disqualified.

____14. Serious driving violations in a commercial motor vehicle include excessive speeding, reckless driving, or any traffic offense that causes a fatality.

____15. If you refuse to take a drug test from any employer, it is the same as if you tested positive.

____16. Once a driver passes an employer's road test, he or she does not have to pass the CDL Skills Test.

____17. Unless a vehicle is placarded for hazardous materials, it does not have to carry a fire extinguisher.

____18. The CDL Skills Test can be taken in any vehicle.

____19. A driver must know the CDL laws and meet the requirements in FMCSR Part 391.

____20. After a serious illness or injury that affects your driving ability, you must renew all medical certificates.

____21. Carriers do not have to test drivers for drugs before they hire them.

_____22. Brakes that lock up are usually the result of the driver panicking, not faulty equipment.

_____23. Tires that are flat or have leaks may be used on a commercial motor vehicle only with caution.

_____24. Drivers of a commercial motor vehicle must signal 50 feet before making a turn.

_____25. When stopped on the highway, drivers must put on the four-way flashers and keep them on until returning to the road.

_____26. Commercial motor vehicles require service brakes, emergency brakes, and parking brakes.

_____27. All of the warning lights on the dash should come on when you first start your vehicle.

_____28. The battery box on a commercial motor vehicle must have a secure cover.

_____29. A few beers have about the same effect as a couple of shots of hard liquor like scotch.

_____30. The best cure for fatigue is caffeine.

_____31. Rust around the wheel nuts often indicates that the nuts are loose.

_____32. Upshifting at a higher rpm as you reach higher gears is called progressive shifting.

_____33. Turn signals facing forward can be either white or amber.

_____34. Use a special coolant tester to check your antifreeze during winter weather.

_____35. Ice on the radiator shutters will melt after the engine warms up.

_____36. The normal oil pressure while idling is 5 to 15 psi.

_____37. Vehicles marked "Dangerous" are classified as carrying hazardous materials.

_____38. Drivers should turn vehicle lights on one half-hour after sunset until one half-hour before sunrise.

_____39. After opening the circuit breaker, you must replace it.

_____40. Vacuum pressure creates the braking force in the braking system.

_____41. Check the tire pressure when the tire is cold.

_____42. Total stopping distance is the vehicle length plus reaction time distance plus braking distance.

_____43. Driving down the highway alongside other vehicles makes it difficult to change lanes and can cause you to get trapped.

_____44. When headlights become dirty, visibility can be reduced by 50 percent.

_____45. When an oncoming vehicle has its high beams on, you should flash your high beams at the driver.

_____46. When a driver is using drugs or alcohol, he or she will drive too fast, too slow, or change speed for no reason.

_____47. To avoid steering into a crash, apply the brake while turning.

_____48. During hot weather, tire pressure can become higher than normal, so you should let air out of your tires when the pressure exceeds 105 psi.

_____49. During hot weather, roads can become slippery and dangerous because of bleeding tar on the road.

_____50. Be careful when downshifting while going down a steep incline, because you might get stuck in neutral.

_____51. An emergency vehicle is marked with lights and siren.

_____52. Bridge laws control traffic on a bridge.

____53. Tire load means the maximum weight that a tire can safely carry.

____54. Even if your load is sealed, you are still responsible for exceeding gross weight or axle limits.

____55. The lighter your load, the shorter your stopping time and distance will be.

____56. Slam on the brakes to avoid a front-wheel skid.

____57. Releasing the brake is the first step to correcting a drive-wheel braking skid.

____58. If you have to leave the road to avoid another vehicle, make sure to turn widely.

____59. The most common type of skid occurs when the rear wheels lose traction due to over-braking or acceleration.

____60. To determine the best engine speed for shifting, you should use the information in the vehicle's owner's manual.

____61. Turn the retarders off whenever road conditions are hazardous, like when roads are wet, icy, or covered with snow.

____62. You should exceed the posted speed limit to make lane changes, turns, merges, and tight maneuvers.

____63. As a courtesy, you should signal other drivers to let them know when it is safe to pass.

____64. It is illegal to drive your vehicle in a way that would cause an accident or cause it to break down.

____65. Blocking, which is secured to the cargo compartment floor, is used to prevent cargo from moving or shifting.

____66. To protect your cargo and others on the road, you should use a tarp.

____67. After starting a trip, you should check your cargo after traveling 50 miles.

____68. It is important to perform a post-trip inspection after every run on every vehicle you operate.

____69. You should check your cargo securement devices whenever you stop during a trip.

____70. The lighter your load, the less traction your vehicle will have.

____71. Just because size and weight distributions are legal does not mean that they will ensure safe operation in bad weather.

____72. To secure cargo, use as few tiedowns as possible.

____73. The drive tires of your vehicle must have ¼ inch of tread.

____74. Steering axle tires must have at least ¼ inch of tread.

____75. Poisonous fumes entering the cab are a dangerous hazard of exhaust system leaks.

____76. A bent tie rod is a steering system defect.

____77. All mud flaps should touch the ground.

____78. Dry bulk tanks are stable in curves and turns.

____79. A state official has the authority to put your vehicle "out of service" if he or she conducts a roadside inspection and finds your vehicle to be unsafe.

____80. Normal clutch travel distance is more than two inches.

____81. During a pre-trip inspection, check the brake lights by pulling the red knob.

____82. After you have completed the seven-step inspection, regardless of your vehicle, you are ready to roll.

____83. In some states, you may be required to have snow chains mounted during winter months.

____84. A few seconds after starting the engine, the oil pressure should come up to normal.

____85. The average engine temperature ranges from about 180 to 250 degrees Fahrenheit.

The following statements are multiple choice. Mark your answer in the blank provided. Then, check your answers with the key at the end of the chapter.

____ 1. In a pre-trip inspection, what should your tires look like?
   (A) Tires are not mismatched in size and ply, and tires are not worn or damaged.
   (B) Tread depth should be less than 4/32 inch on the front tires, and 2/32 inch on all other tires.
   (C) Dual tires should be touching.
   (D) All of the above.

____ 2. In a pre-trip inspection, what should you check for in your wheels and rims?
   (A) Look for rust around wheel nuts, which indicates looseness.
   (B) Cracked or damaged wheels or rims.
   (C) Mismatched or bent lock rims.
   (D) All of the above.

____ 3. During a pre-trip inspection, check your brakes and suspension system for:
   (A) Brake shoes and pads with fluid in them.
   (B) Shoes worn thinner than 1/4 inch.
   (C) Cracked, missing, or broken parts.
   (D) All of the above.

____ 4. Federal and state laws prohibit driving an unsafe vehicle, so you should make sure that you fix which of the following problems?
   (A) A small leak of power steering fluid.
   (B) Steering wheel play of more than 10 degrees (2 inches on a 20-inch wheel).
   (C) A leak in the exhaust system.
   (D) All of the above.

____ 5. You should always have which of the following emergency equipment in your vehicle?
   (A) At least one fire extinguisher.
   (B) Warning triangles.
   (C) Spare electrical fuses.
   (D) All of the above.

____ 6. During a pre-trip inspection, don't inspect which of the following in your engine compartment?
   (A) Valve clearance.
   (B) Electrical wire insulation.
   (C) Engine oil level.
   (D) Hose condition.

____ 7. Before the trip and while traveling, what should you check for?
   (A) Cargo securement.   (C) Tires.
   (B) Vehicle gauges.   (D) All of the above.

____ 8. During an enroute inspection, what should you check?
   (A) Brakes and tires.   (C) Cargo.
   (B) Coupling devices.   (D) All of the above.

___ 9. How do you start your vehicle on an uphill grade?
   (A) Let the vehicle roll backwards and then engage the clutch.
   (B) Use the parking brake to hold the vehicle from rolling backwards and then engage the clutch.
   (C) Slip the clutch slowly while accelerating.
   (D) Take your foot off the brake and shift quickly.

___10. How should you accelerate?
   (A) Accelerate until you feel a jerking motion.
   (B) Accelerate smoothly so you won't cause coupling damage.
   (C) Accelerate quickly when traction is poor.
   (D) All of the above.

___11. When you start after stopping and your drive wheels begin to spin, what should you do?
   (A) Apply the brakes.   (C) Turn your engine off.
   (B) Take your foot off the accelerator.   (D) All of the above.

___12. How should you hold the steering wheel?
   (A) You can put your hands anywhere on the steering wheel.
   (B) With both hands close to the bottom of the wheel.
   (C) With both hands on 3 o'clock and 9 o'clock.
   (D) With both hands on 12 o'clock and 6 o'clock.

___13. How should you adjust your speed when it is raining or snowing?
   (A) On packed snow, keep your speed constant.
   (B) On a wet road, use caution.
   (C) Allow extra time for stopping, because it takes longer and it will be harder to turn without skidding.
   (D) All of the above.

___14. Hydroplaning:
   (A) Occurs when water or slush forms a film between the tires and the road.
   (B) Can occur at any speed.
   (C) Is more likely to occur when tire pressure is low.
   (D) All of the above.

___15. At night you should always:
   (A) Watch the vehicles that are approaching.
   (B) Make sure that your stopping distance is within your sight distance.
   (C) Drive faster with low beams than high beams.
   (D) All of the above.

___16. What can cause you to skid?
   (A) Over accelerating.   (C) Not using your brakes.
   (B) Turning too slowly.   (D) All of the above.

___17. To correct a tractor drive-wheel acceleration skid, you should:
   (A) Countersteer.
   (B) Apply more power to the wheel.
   (C) Apply the brakes.
   (D) Stop accelerating and push in the clutch.

___18. How do you correct a tractor rear-wheel braking skid?
   (A) Turn into the skid.
   (B) Don't brake, turn quickly, and countersteer.
   (C) Slide sideways and stop.
   (D) Slide sideways and spin out.

___19. Retarders:

(A) Provide emergency braking.

(B) Apply extra braking power to the nondrive axles.

(C) Help slow the vehicle and reduce brake wear.

(D) Prevent skidding.

___20. When using retarders, what is a major concern?

(A) They cause extra brake wear.

(B) They may cause the drive wheels to skid when the traction is poor.

(C) Their use may be illegal on some highways.

(D) They can cause the steering axle brakes to quit.

___21. While driving, you should look ahead:

(A) 1 to 3 seconds.   (C) 12 to 15 seconds.

(B) 6 to 9 seconds.   (D) 20 to 25 seconds.

___22. When traveling at highway speed, you should look ahead:

(A) ⅛ mile.   (C) ¼ mile.

(B) ¹⁄₃₂ mile.   (D) ¹⁄₁₀ mile.

___23. You should check the mirrors to see:

(A) The location of the rear of your vehicle in a turn.

(B) The condition of some of your tires.

(C) Traffic gaps when merging.

(D) All of the above.

___24. What is important to remember about using mirrors?

(A) Even when using mirrors, there may be "blind spots."

(B) You should check your mirrors twice before making a lane change.

(C) Convex mirrors make things look closer.

(D) Look in the mirror for several seconds each time.

___25. Which of the following is true when using your turn signal?

(A) When turning, turn your signal off as you turn.

(B) When turning, signal early.

(C) Use your turn signal only when changing lanes in heavy traffic.

(D) All the above.

___26. Which of the following is true about using your vehicle lights?

(A) During the day, use headlights when it's raining or snowing.

(B) Flash your brake lights to warn those behind you that you are stopping.

(C) Turn on your lights when you are parked on the side of the road.

(D) All of the above.

___27. Which of the following is true about how to mark a stopped vehicle?

(A) If you are stopped longer than 10 minutes, put out reflective triangles at 10, 100, and 200 feet from the vehicle.

(B) Keep the vehicle taillights on.

(C) Place a triangle back beyond a hill that prevents oncoming traffic from seeing your vehicle within 250 feet.

(D) Don't use the four-way flashers in daylight.

___28. Avoid using your horn because:

(A) It does not do a good job of letting people know where you are.

(B) It may startle other drivers.

(C) It takes air pressure away from the air brakes.

(D) All of the above.

____29. Speed and weight have what type of effect on stopping distance?

(A) Empty trucks have a shorter stopping distance.

(B) When you double your speed, it will take three times the distance to stop.

(C) The heavier the vehicle, the more the brakes have to stop.

(D) All of the above.

____30. Who is responsible for making sure that cargo is not overloaded?

(A) The driver.   (C) The shipper.

(B) State and federal agents.   (D) All of the above.

____31. Why should you cover the cargo?

(A) Federal and state laws require it.

(B) To protect the cargo and keep it from spilling.

(C) Department of Transportation specifications.

(D) All of the above.

____32. What is important to know about loading cargo?

(A) Make sure that the cargo is low and even.

(B) Put lighter cargos toward the back.

(C) The higher the center of gravity, the safer the cargo is.

(D) All of the above.

____33. On the freeway during rush hour where most cars are going 35 miles per hour, the safest speed for your vehicle is

(A) 20 miles per hour.   (C) 35 miles per hour.

(B) 25 miles per hour.   (D) 45 miles per hour.

____34. Whenever you are tailgated you should:

(A) Increase the space in front of you.

(B) Go faster.

(C) Slow down.

(D) Flash your taillights.

____35. During hot weather, your tires

(A) Can be cooled by driving if they overheat.

(B) Decrease in air pressure as the weather gets warmer.

(C) Should be inspected every 150 miles or three hours.

(D) All of the above.

____36. If your engine begins to overheat, what should you do?

(A) Stop the vehicle and remove the radiator cap.

(B) Finish your trip, then check your engine.

(C) Stop as soon as possible and shut off your engine.

(D) Keep your engine running.

____37. When traveling down a steep hill, how should you use your brakes?

(A) Pump the brakes lightly.

(B) Pump the brakes using lots of pressure.

(C) Use strong pressure that increases as you move downward.

(D) Light, even, and steady pressure.

____38. What is the meaning of the red triangles with an orange center on the back of a vehicle?

(A) This vehicle is an emergency vehicle.

(B) The vehicle is slow moving.

(C) The driver is a student.

(D) The cargo of the vehicle is hazardous.

____39. To avoid a crash, you should:
   (A) Steer with one hand and downshift with the other.
   (B) Apply the brakes as you steer and turn.
   (C) Don't turn any more than needed to avoid a crash.
   (D) Avoid countersteering.

____40. Countersteering is:
   (A) Turning the wheel counter-clock wise.
   (B) Steering back and forth several times.
   (C) Turning the wheel more than needed.
   (D) Turning the wheel back in the other direction, once you've passed something in your path.

____41. If an oncoming vehicle drifts into your lane on a two-lane road, what should you do?
   (A) Steer away from the vehicle to the left, trading places.
   (B) Maintain your position until you're seen.
   (C) Brake hard.
   (D) Steer to the right to avoid the vehicle.

____42. When can you use your brakes if you must leave the road in an emergency?
   (A) Only when you feel the vehicle start to tip over.
   (B) When your speed drops to about 20 miles per hour.
   (C) As soon as possible.
   (D) When one wheel is still on the pavement.

____43. If you are on the right shoulder going 55 miles per hour, what is the safest way to get onto the road?
   (A) Stay on the shoulder if it is clear and come to a stop, then return to the road when it's safe.
   (B) Brake hard and steer sharply onto the road.
   (C) Maintain your speed and steer gently onto the road.
   (D) Countersteer.

____44. What is controlled braking?
   (A) Gently tapping on the brakes.
   (B) Locking the brakes for a short time.
   (C) Keeping the vehicle in a straight line when braking.
   (D) All of the above.

____45. If your hydraulic brakes go out, what should you do?
   (A) Try pumping the brakes to generate pressure.
   (B) Downshift.
   (C) Use the parking brake.
   (D) All of the above.

____46. Sign(s) of tire failure is(are):
   (A) A loud bang.   (C) Vibration.
   (B) Heavy steering.   (D) All of the above.

____47. If you have a blow out in your front tire on a level highway at 50 miles per hour, what should you do first?
   (A) Quickly drive to the shoulder.
   (B) Countersteer.
   (C) Stay off the brake until the vehicle slows.
   (D) Press hard on the brakes.

____48. Which of the following is true about backing?
   (A) Helpers should be used.
   (B) Back toward the driver side of the vehicle when you have a choice.
   (C) Avoid backing whenever you can.
   (D) All of the above.

____49. Which of the following is true about double-clutching and shifting?
   (A) Use your tachometer and road speed to tell you when to shift.
   (B) Double-clutch only on slippery roads.
   (C) If you miss a gear when upshifting, bring your vehicle to a stop.
   (D) Double-clutch only with a heavy load.

____50. What is important about downshifting?
   (A) Downshift after you go down a hill.
   (B) Downshift before you enter a curve.
   (C) When you double clutch, let the engine rpm decrease while the shift lever is in neutral and the clutch is released.
   (D) All of the above.

____51. During a front wheel skid, what will the vehicle do?
   (A) Continue to go straight, even when you steer.
   (B) Start spinning.
   (C) Go into a spin if you apply the brakes.
   (D) Go into a spin if you steer.

____52. What can cause a truck fire?
   (A) Tires with low air pressure.
   (B) Electrical short circuit.
   (C) Flammable cargo.
   (D) All of the above.

____53. Use the B:C fire extinguishers on:
   (A) Burning liquids and electrical fires.
   (B) Wood and paper fires.
   (C) Cloth fires.
   (D) All of the above.

____54. Use the A:B:C fire extinguishers on:
   (A) Burning liquids and electrical fires.
   (B) Wood and paper fires.
   (C) Cloth fires.
   (D) All of the above.

____55. You can use water on what type of fires:
   (A) Electrical fires.
   (B) Gasoline fires.
   (C) Tire fires.
   (D) All of the above.

Check Yourself—General Knowledge Review Questions Answer Key

True/False			
1. F	36. T	72. F	21. C
2. F	37. T	73. F	22. C
3. T	38. F	74. F	23. D
4. F	39. F	75. T	24. A
5. T	40. F	76. T	25. B
6. T	41. T	77. F	26. D
7. F	42. F	78. F	27. A
8. T	43. T	79. T	28. B
9. T	44. T	80. F	29. C
10. F	45. F	81. F	30. A
11. T	46. T	82. F	31. B
12. T	47. T	83. T	32. A
13. F	48. F	84. T	33. C
14. T	49. T	85. F	34. A
15. T	50. T		35. C
16. F	51. F	**Multiple Choice**	36. C
17. F	52. F	1. A	37. D
18. F	53. T	2. D	38. B
19. T	54. T	3. D	39. C
20. T	55. F	4. D	40. D
21. F	56. F	5. D	41. D
22. T	57. T	6. A	42. B
23. F	58. F	7. D	43. A
24. F	59. T	8. D	44. C
25. T	60. T	9. B	45. D
26. T	61. T	10. B	46. D
27. T	62. F	11. B	47. C
28. T	63. F	12. C	48. D
29. T	64. T	13. C	49. A
30. F	65. T	14. D	50. B
31. T	66. T	15. B	51. A
32. F	67. F	16. A	52. D
33. T	68. T	17. D	53. D
34. T	69. T	18. B	54. D
35. F	70. T	19. C	55. C
	71. T	20. B	

18 CDL Endorsement Tests—A Final Review

To help you prepare for the various Endorsement Tests, a number of review questions are included. These are not the actual test questions, but they are similar to those you will see on the written endorsement tests. You may write the answers next to each question or you may opt to use an additional sheet of paper, putting the answers next to the number corresponding to the question. Then you can use these tests several times, if necessary.

Review Questions for Air Brakes Endorsement

The following statements are either true or false. Mark your answer in the blank provided. Then check your answers with the key at the end of the chapter.

_____ 1. Fanning air brakes increases the air pressure.

_____ 2. Even if your air compressor stops working, you should have air pressure stored in the air tanks.

_____ 3. The air brake system safety relief valve opens at 60 psi.

_____ 4. If your air brake system safety relief valve opens a couple of times, you should have your system repaired.

_____ 5. When the brakes are hot, you should not set the parking brake.

_____ 6. Spring brakes should come on automatically if you pump the air pressure down to 60 psi.

_____ 7. When the low air pressure warning device comes on, you should do nothing until you get to a service station.

_____ 8. The breakaway valve is also called the tractor protection valve.

_____ 9. When your brakes are out of adjustment, your service, parking, and emergency braking power will be poor.

_____10. Spring brakes are not affected by air pressure.

_____11. Air brakes of most large vehicles have spring brakes that are part of the emergency brake and parking brake system.

_____12. The trailer hand brake can also be used as a parking brake.

_____13. If you have one, a front brake limiting valve control should be in the "normal" position under all road conditions.

_____14. The service brake system is the pump and check valves that keep the air tank pressure in check.

_____15. In a single brake system that has a fully charged air system, the air pressure should not drop more than 5 psi per minute after the initial drop.

_____16. Brake drums or discs should not have cracks longer than half the width of the friction area.

_____17. Slack adjusters never need adjustment.

_____18. The service brake glad hands are color-coded blue.

___19. You should have your vehicle's single brake system adjusted if the governor stops between 100 and 125 psi.

___20. The emergency brake glad hands are color-coded blue.

___21. Unless you have a dual air system, the spring brakes will come on if the emergency brake air lines ruptures.

___22. Unless you have a dual air system, the spring brakes will come on if the service air lines break.

___23. To adjust the slack, you should always apply the service and parking brakes.

___24. To test the brakes on a single air system, start the engine and let it run at a fast idle to charge the air system—you should see an increase in pressure from 50 to 90 psi in three minutes.

___25. When testing the brakes on a dual air system, start the engine and let it run at a fast idle to charge the air system—you should see an increase in pressure from 85 to 100 psi in 45 seconds.

The following statements are multiple choice. Mark your answer in the blank provided. Then check your answers with the key at the end.

___ 1. Air brakes take more time to activate than hydraulic brakes because:
   (A) It takes air longer to flow through the lines.
   (B) Air brakes use a different type brake drums.
   (C) Air brakes are located further from the wheels.
   (D) An air brake system is composed of multiple systems.

___ 2. Why is the stopping distance for air brakes longer than hydraulic brakes?
   (A) Reaction time.   (C) Effective braking distance.
   (B) Brake lag distance.   (D) All of the above.

___ 3. What affects the power of spring brakes?
   (A) The condition of the emergency brakes.
   (B) The adjustment of the spring brakes ensures the power.
   (C) Weather conditions.
   (D) The condition of the parking brakes.

___ 4. When the driver uses the brake pedal, which brake system applies and releases the brakes?
   (A) Parking.   (C) Dual.
   (B) Service.   (D) Emergency.

___ 5. A combination of service, parking, and _____ systems comprise modern air brakes.
   (A) Hand.   (C) Drum.
   (B) Emergency.   (D) Dual.

___ 6. What does the air compressor governor control?
   (A) Air pressure applied to the brakes.
   (B) Air compressor speed.
   (C) The brake chamber release pressure.
   (D) Air pumped into the air tanks.

___ 7. You should drain water from compressed air tanks because:
   (A) Water mixed with oil can cause brakes to slip.
   (B) Water cools the compressor excessively.
   (C) Water can get into the oil of the compressor.
   (D) Water can freeze and cause brake failure.

___ 8. In cold weather, what should you do to an alcohol evaporator?

(A) Remove the alcohol.

(B) Check the alcohol for oil.

(C) Check and fill the alcohol level.

(D) Clean the evaporator air filter.

___ 9. In an air brake system, a brake pedal:

(A) Connects the shock adjuster.

(B) Controls the air pressure applied to the brakes.

(C) Joins the service and parking brake systems.

(D) Joins the parking and emergency brake systems.

___10. What do all air brake-equipped vehicles have?

(A) An air supply pressure gauge.   (C) At least one brake heater.

(B) A hydraulic system.   (D) An air use gauge.

11   The air supply pressure gauge indicates:

(A) The pressure going to the brake chamber.

(B) How much air has been used in the trip.

(C) The pressure in the air tank.

(D) The amount of air the air tank can hold.

___12. The purpose of dual parking control valves is:

(A) To balance pressure to the brakes.

(B) To utilize the service brake system when parked.

(C) To balance parking power.

(D) To release the spring brake in an emergency.

___13. On a long downgrade, how can you tell if your brakes are fading?

(A) You begin to hear squeaking noises when you apply the brakes.

(B) You have to push harder to control your speed.

(C) The brakes don't cool sufficiently between applications.

(D) All of the above.

___14. How should the free play of manual slack adjusters on S-cam brakes be checked?

(A) Park on level ground and set the emergency brake.

(B) Park on level ground, chock the wheels, turn off the parking brakes.

(C) Set the parking brake, drain off air from the service brake.

(D) Park on an incline and set only the emergency brake.

___15. What does the application pressure gauge show?

(A) The pressure in the air tanks.

(B) The amount of air in the air tank.

(C) How much air pressure you are applying to the brakes.

(C) The pressure applied to the brake pedal.

___16. The air pressure warning light should come on before the pressure gets below:

(A) 60 psi.   (C) 30 psi.

(B) 90 psi.   (D) 100 psi.

___17. What are spring brakes held back by?

(A) Water pressure.   (C) Springs.

(B) Air pressure.   (D) Centrifugal force.

___18. If there is a leak in the air brake system, the parking or emergency brake can be held in position only by:

(A) Spring pressure.   (C) Foot pressure.

(B) Water pressure.   (D) Centrifugal force.

____19. With the engine off and the service brake released, a straight truck air brake system should not leak at a rate greater than:

(A) 0 psi per minute.   (C) 2 psi per minute.

(B) 1 psi per minute.   (D) 3 psi per minute.

____20. You have a problem if you are testing the service brakes and you notice that:

(A) There is an unusual feel.   (C) Stopping action is delayed.

(B) The vehicle pulls to one side.   (D) All of the above.

____21. The dual air brake system operates on which axle(s)?

(A) Rear axle.   (C) The trailer.

(B) Front axle.   (D) All axles.

____22. What should you do if the secondary system of a dual air brake-equipped vehicle fails?

(A) Bring the vehicle to a safe stop and get the system fixed.

(B) Slow down and continue using the primary system.

(C) Drive to the nearest garage for repairs.

(D) Continue to the next convenient place to stop.

____23. When checking to make sure that the spring brakes come on automatically, the parking brake knob should pop out when:

(A) You start the truck.

(B) The air pressure falls to between 20 to 40 psi.

(C) You step on the foot brake.

(D) All of the above.

____24. During an emergency stop, how should you brake?

(A) Use the full power of the emergency brakes and service brakes.

(B) Brake so that you can steer and stay in a straight line.

(C) Always brake hard and fast.

(D) Maintain constant pressure on the brakes.

____25. Emergency stab braking is:

(A) The same as controlled braking.

(B) Putting on the brakes hard without locking the wheels.

(C) Repeatedly braking until the wheels lock, then releasing pressure.

(D) Braking lightly several times in a row.

____26. Why is controlled or stab braking better than short, light brake pedal pressure on long downhill grades?

(A) Steady pressure works better with a vehicle that is in low gear.

(B) Air usage is less with controlled or stab braking.

(C) Light pressure heats up the brakes.

(D) All of the above.

____27. When the low air pressure warning comes on, you should:

(A) Stop and park as soon as possible.

(B) Continue on to your destination.

(C) Use the parking or emergency brake to stop.

(D) Tap the air pressure gauge to see if it is working.

____28. When do you use the parking brake in an air brake-equipped vehicle?

(A) Only when parked on a hill.

(B) Only in an emergency.

(C) Any time you park.

(D) To inspect the service brake.

____29. If it is not done automatically in your vehicle, how often should you drain your air tanks?
   (A) Everytime you stop for more than 10 minutes.
   (B) At the end of each day of driving.
   (C) Every two hours of driving.
   (D) At least once a month.

Review Questions for Combination Vehicle/Doubles/Triples Endorsement

The following statements are either true or false. Mark your answer in the blank provided. Then check your answers with the key at the end of the chapter.

____ 1. The dolly support carries the dolly air lines.
____ 2. It is impossible to check if the entire brake system of a triple is charged.
____ 3. Triples have the most rearward amplification.
____ 4. The first step to coupling is apply the trailer brakes.
____ 5. To finish the coupling process, begin in high gear to roll up the landing gear.
____ 6. Double and triple trailers should be inspected carefully because they have more parts.
____ 7. You might eventually get a service line air leak if your glad hand on your blue air line doesn't have a seal.
____ 8. Uncoupling is much easier if you park the trailer at an angle.
____ 9. When you finish coupling, always make sure there's no slack in the air lines.
____10. To prevent roll-over, make sure your load is low and centered between the trailer sides.
____11. A converter dolly should be treated as an axle with a fifth wheel and may have its own air tank.
____12. Your brakes will not work at all if you cross your air lines on a new trailer equipped with spring brakes.
____13. The tractor protection valve should close automatically when you reduce the air pressure to 60 psi.
____14. You can test the trailer emergency brake system if you charge the trailer brakes, then push in the blue round knob.
____15. To make a right turn with a long vehicle, you should use another lane to avoid hitting the curb.
____16. When coupling doubles, it is best to back the converter dolly under the second trailer.
____17. In double or triple trailers, you will find shut-off valves only in the emergency air lines.
____18. You can injure yourself if you unhook the pintle hook with the converter dolly still under the trailer.
____19. You can test the trailer service brakes by pulling the red, eight-sided knob.
____20. To make sure that your air lines are not crossed, you should turn off your engine, apply and release the trailer brakes with the hand valve, and then listen for brake movement and air release.

____21. You are having problems when you turn a corner and your trailer wheels go a different way than your tractor wheels.

____22. Release the trailer brakes if your vehicle starts to skid.

____23. When coupling doubles, there is nothing you can do if the second trailer does not have spring brakes.

____24. You should check your path for hazards before you begin coupling.

____25. It is possible to damage your landing gear if you back under the trailer at an angle.

The following statements are multiple choice. Mark your answer in the blank provided. Then check your answers with the key at the end of the chapter.

____ 1. When driving doubles or triples, what should you remember about looking ahead?
(A) Allow more following distance.
(B) Look far ahead so you can slow down gradually.
(C) Looking ahead increases your safety.
(D) All of the above.

____ 2. To maintain safety when hauling a double or triple, you should:
(A) Use special care in bad weather and mountain driving.
(B) Be ready to stop at the last minute.
(C) Watch only the brake lights of the car in front of you.
(D) All of the above.

____ 3. You can prevent a roll over by keeping the cargo as close to the ground as possible and:
(A) Steering hard and applying the brakes around curves.
(B) Making sure your brakes function properly.
(C) Going slow around curves.
(D) Keeping your tires properly inflated.

____ 4. Why are "bobtail" tractors harder to stop?
(A) The back of the vehicle is shorter.
(B) The vehicle is lighter.
(C) There are fewer wheels to stop the tractor.
(D) There are less brake systems.

____ 5. On a combination vehicle, to stop a jackknife:
(A) Brake hard.
(B) Do not use the trailer hand brake.
(C) Turn the steering wheel in the opposite direction of the skid.
(D) All of the above.

____ 6. Offtracking is:
(A) When the rear wheels follow a different path than the front wheels.
(B) The process of taking the tracks off a tractor.
(C) When a driver fails to keep the wheels on track.
(D) An error in keeping track of the hours and miles driven.

____ 7. When pulling a 100-foot double at 30 miles per hour, how many seconds of space should you keep between you and the vehicle in front of you?
(A) At least two seconds.   (C) At least seven seconds.
(B) At least five seconds.   (D) At least 10 seconds.

___ 8. When pulling a 100-foot triple at 50 miles per hour, how many seconds of space should you keep between you and the vehicle in front of you?
(A) At least two seconds.   (C) At least 11 seconds.
(B) At least five seconds.   (D) At least 15 seconds.

___ 9. When the trailer wheels of a double go into a skid, what is likely to happen?
(A) The trailer will tip over.
(B) The trailer will jackknife.
(C) The brakes will squeak.
(D) The front wheels of the tractor will skid.

___10. Which of the following is true about quick steering movements with doubles and triples?
(A) Stab braking is always used in quick steering.
(B) Double and triples tip over easily from quick steering.
(C) Counter-steering is easier with doubles and triples.
(D) None of the above.

___11. When driving doubles and triples, which of the following is correct?
(A) The rear trailer of a triple is less likely to tip over than a double.
(B) Rearward amplification prevents a crack-the-whip effect.
(C) A sudden steering movement can result in the rear trailer tipping over.
(D) All of the above.

___12. You need _____ times more stopping distance when stopping a combination at 40 miles per hour than at 20 miles per hour.
(A) Three times.   (C) Eight times.
(B) Four times.   (D) 10 times.

___13. When emergency braking doubles or triples, what should you do?
(A) Use only the tractor brakes.
(B) Brake hard.
(C) Use controlled or stab braking.
(D) Use lock braking and steering.

___14. The trailer air supply:
(A) Controls the tractor air supply.
(B) Controls the air supply to the protection valve.
(C) Supplies the trailer with air.
(D) Supplies air to the tractor control.

___15. The service air line:
(A) Controls the tractor air brakes.
(B) Controls the air supply.
(C) Carries air to the tractor brakes.
(D) Carries air to the trailer brakes.

___16. What color are the emergency line couplers?
(A) Red.   (C) Blue.
(B) Yellow.   (D) Black.

___17. Why should you connect the air hose couplers together?
(A) To maintain a constant air supply.
(B) To keep the dirt and water out of the lines.
(C) To keep the rubber seals from drying out.
(D) None of the above.

___18. What happens when you cross the air lines of an older trailer without spring brakes?

(A) The brake pedal will not work.

(B) You will not be able to start the vehicle.

(C) The hand valve will cause the trailer brakes to come on when you use the air brakes.

(D) You could drive away, but have no trailer brakes.

___19. Why do many trailers built before 1975 have no parking brakes?

(A) They don't have air brakes.

(B) They don't have spring brakes.

(C) They use the emergency brake for a parking brake.

(D) Shut-off valves were not available then.

___20. If the service air line comes apart while driving but the emergency line is okay, what happens immediately?

(A) The same thing as when there's a leak in the emergency line.

(B) The emergency trailer brakes will come on immediately.

(C) Nothing is likely to happen until you press the brakes.

(D) The emergency tractor brake will come on.

___21. You should always grease the fifth wheel because:

(A) It makes it easy to couple.

(B) It makes it easy to uncouple.

(C) It prevents steering problems.

(D) It prevents rust and corrosion.

___22. What should you do just before the tractor is coupled?

(A) Make sure that the trailer and tractor line up.

(B) Chock the trailer wheels.

(C) Connect the emergency and service air lines.

(D) None of the above.

___23. In coupling, where should the tractor be lined up?

(A) In front of the kingpin.

(B) Slightly to the right of the trailer.

(C) Directly in front of the trailer.

(D) None of the above.

___24. In coupling, the trailer is at the right height when:

(A) The top of the kingpin is even with the top of the fifth wheel.

(B) The kingpin is two inches above the fifth wheel.

(C) The trailer landing gear is fully extended.

(D) The trailer is lifted slightly when the tractor connects.

___25. During coupling, how do you lock the trailer brakes before you back under the trailer?

(A) Push in the air supply knob.

(B) Pull out the air supply knob.

(C) Apply the air brakes.

(D) None of the above.

___26. To make sure that the kingpin and the fifth wheel connection are secure, what should you do?

(A) Slowly drive forward with the trailer brakes locked.

(B) Back up slowly.

(C) Pull ahead, steering left and right.

(D) Jerk the vehicle forward.

____27. When coupling is complete, how much space should there be between the upper and lower fifth wheel?
    (A) About one inch.   (C) ⅛ inch.
    (B) At least two inches.   (D) No space.

____28. When the fifth wheel locking lever is almost in the locking position but will not lock, what should you do?
    (A) Have it repaired before driving.
    (B) It's not a problem—the locking lever is only a safety precaution.
    (C) Keep working with the lever.
    (D) None of the above.

____29. After the tractor is coupled, you should not move it until you push in the air supply knob and:
    (A) Hear a loud click.
    (B) Wait until the air pressure is normal.
    (C) The tractor protection valve.
    (D) Flush all moisture from the system.

____30. After coupling, you can make sure the air lines are not crossed because:
    (A) When you pump the brake you will hear the brakes move and air escape.
    (B) The tractor will move easily forward and back.
    (C) The tractor protection valve will pop out.
    (D) All of the above.

____31. When the engine and brake are off, the air leakage rate for combination vehicles must be less than:
    (A) 0 psi per minute.
    (B) 3 psi per minute.
    (C) 6 psi per minute.
    (D) None of the above.

____32. The maximum leakage rate for a combination vehicle with the engine off and brakes on is:
    (A) 1 psi per minute.
    (B) 2 psi per minute.
    (C) 4 psi per minute.
    (D) 10 psi per minute.

____33. You should use the trailer hand valve:
    (A) To test the trailer brakes.
    (B) Only when the trailer is fully loaded.
    (C) To complete an emergency stop.
    (D) In combination with the foot brake.

____34. Why do you need a tractor protection valve?
    (A) It keeps air in the tractor if the trailer breaks away or develops a bad leak.
    (B) It protects the tractor from damage.
    (C) It is a back-up for the trailer air supply control.
    (D) All of the above.

____35. The tractor protection valve will close automatically when:
    (A) You push in the trailer air supply control.
    (B) The air pressure is low (20 to 45 psi).
    (C) The air pressure is too high (70 to 90psi).
    (D) The emergency brakes are turned on.

_____36. How do you keep the trailer from moving when hooking a combination to a second trailer?
(A) By using the trailer emergency brakes.
(B) By using the trailer spring brakes.
(C) By using wheel chocks.
(D) Any of the above will work.

_____37. When connecting two or more trailers to the tractor, the heaviest trailer should be placed:
(A) In the front, closest to the tractor.
(B) In the rear, as the last trailer.
(C) Don't connect trailers that are not the same weight.
(D) None of the above.

_____38. Which of the following statements is true about converter dollies?
(A) They usually need glad hand converters.
(B) They have little braking power because they're small.
(C) They do not have spring brakes.
(D) All of the above.

_____39. During coupling, when you connect a trailer to a converter dolly, what is the correct height for the trailer?
(A) The locking jaws and the kingpin flange should be the same height.
(B) It must be slightly lower than the center of the fifth wheel.
(C) The trailer must be higher than the top of the dolly.
(D) The fifth wheel should be the same height as the kingpin.

_____40. How can you supply air to the air tanks of the second trailer?
(A) Open the shut-off valve at the rear of the first trailer and close the valve at the rear of the second.
(B) Open the shut-off valve of both trailers.
(C) Close the shut-off valve of both trailers.
(D) None of the above.

_____41. After coupling doubles, you can make sure that air has reached the last trailer by:
(A) Opening the hand valve and listening to the air.
(B) Looking at the air gauge for each trailer.
(C) Opening the emergency line shut-off valve at the rear of the last trailer.
(D) There is really no way to tell until you begin driving.

_____42. What will happen if you unlock the pintle hook with the dolly still under the rear trailer?
(A) The dolly may roll back.
(B) The dolly tow bar may fly up.
(C) The brake lights will come on.
(D) The pintle hook may break.

_____43. During a walk-around inspection, what is the position of the pintle hook and the dolly air drain valve?
(A) Open, free.
(B) Closed, free.
(C) Open, latched.
(D) Closed, latched.

_____44. What should you hear when you inspect the trailer brakes of a double, turn the hand valve on, and open the service line valve at the rear of the rig?

(A) A high-pitched whistle.

(B) The tractor protection valve open.

(C) Air escape from the open valve.

(D) Nothing at all, if things are okay.

_____45. When testing the trailer emergency brakes, you should charge the air brake system, check that the trailer rolls freely, and:

(A) Open the emergency brake air lines.

(B) Pull out the trailer air supply control.

(C) Push in the trailer air supply control.

(D) None of the above.

_____46. After you have turned the hand brake on, how do you check the trailer brakes?

(A) Bring the air pressure up to normal.

(B) Turn the parking brakes off.

(C) Move slowly forward to see if the vehicle slows down.

(D) All of the above.

Review Questions for Tank Vehicle Endorsement

The following statements are either true or false. Mark your answer in the blank provided. Then check your answers with the key at the end of the chapter.

_____ 1. Outage is dangerous.

_____ 2. Retest markings are stamped on the tank itself.

_____ 3. To avoid roll-over with a tanker, you should speed through a curve.

_____ 4. A smooth bore tanker is one that is a long, hollow tube with no sharp corners.

_____ 5. Because bulk liquid tankers have a high center of gravity, they are hard to handle.

_____ 6. Baffles are located inside tankers that have openings at the top and bottom.

_____ 7. Baffles eliminate side-to-side liquid surge.

_____ 8. Cylindrical is the most stable liquid tanker shape.

_____ 9. A retest marking reading of "12-01, P, V, L" says that in December 2001, the cargo tank received and passed a pressure retest, external visual inspection and test, and a lining inspection.

_____10. In case of emergency, the stop valves will close in the cargo tanks.

The following statements are multiple choice. Mark your answer in the blank provided. Then check your answers with the key at the end of the chapter.

_____ 1. Why does hauling liquids in tankers require special care?

(A) Because the center of gravity is low.

(B) Because the center of gravity is high.

(C) Because the center of gravity is wide.

(D) Because the center of gravity is flat.

____ 2. When exiting the freeway with a tanker, you should drive below the posted speed because:
(A) The exit speed posted may be too high for your particular load.
(B) Your tanker may roll over.
(C) Liquid surge may make your tanker hard to handle.
(D) All of the above.

____ 3. Liquid surge in a tanker affects handling by:
(A) Moving the vehicle in the direction of the surge.
(B) Making cornering easier.
(C) Increasing vehicle power downhill.
(D) Causing the tanker to move slower.

____ 4. What should you do when loading a tanker equipped with bulkheads?
(A) Nothing special.
(B) Check your weight distribution.
(C) Watch your power usage.
(D) Don't drive unless they are all filled.

____ 5. The advantage of baffled bulkheads is:
(A) There will be less side-to-side surge.
(B) There will be more side-to-side surge.
(C) There will be less front-to-back surge.
(D) There will be more front-to-back surge.

____ 6. Baffles in liquid cargo tanks do not prevent surges:
(A) Top-to-bottom.   (C) Back-to-front.
(B) Side-to-side.   (D) In-and-out.

____ 7. What can happen when you are transporting liquids and have a side-to-side surge?
(A) Engine overheat.   (C) Brake failure.
(B) Tire failure.   (D) Roll overs.

____ 8. When can smooth bore liquid tankers be very dangerous?
(A) When you are starting or stopping.
(B) When you are driving against the wind.
(C) When you are loading or unloading.
(D) When you are going downhill.

____ 9. Why should you know the outage of your tanker load?
(A) Liquids evaporate at different speeds.
(B) Some liquids expand more than others when warm.
(C) Some heavy liquids don't require outage.
(D) You don't need to know the outage of your tanker load.

____10. How much liquid can you load in a tanker?
(A) It depends on the weight of the liquid.
(B) It depends on the amount the liquid will expand.
(C) It depends on the legal limit.
(D) All of the above.

Review Questions for Hazardous Materials

The following statements are either true or false. Mark your answer in the blank provided. Then check your answers with the key at the end of the chapter.

_____ 1. When loading and unloading cargo tanks, the person in attendance must be within 50 feet of the tanker.

_____ 2. Column 1 of the Hazardous Materials Table shows how to ship an item.

_____ 3. A driver is allowed to run the vehicle engine while loading explosives.

_____ 4. Drivers carrying Class A or B explosives must have a floor liner that doesn't contain iron or steel.

_____ 5. The Separation Distance Table explains how far packages of hazardous materials should be located from people and cargo space walls.

_____ 6. When a consignee refuses a shipment of hazardous materials, the only thing you can do is return it to the shipper.

_____ 7. The word "waste" is written before the name of the materials on the shipping papers.

_____ 8. Anyone can drive a vehicle placarded for hazardous materials.

_____ 9. Class A is the least dangerous type of explosive.

_____10. ORM B is regulated because it can damage your vehicle.

_____11. The Segregation and Separation Chart lists hazardous materials that are prohibited to be carried in combination.

_____12. Smoking is prohibited within 25 feet of a vehicle loaded with hazardous materials.

_____13. When hauling hazardous materials in a vehicle with dual tires, you should check the tires often.

_____14. Drivers should always be aware that hazardous materials pose a risk to health, safety, and property during transportation.

_____15. Tankers used to transport hazardous materials must be marked with a manufacturer's date.

_____16. Black III indicates the highest level of radioactivity.

_____17. You will need a "Dangerous" placard when transporting pressurized liquid oxygen.

_____18. The Uniform Hazardous Waste Manifest must have a copy of the loading plan.

_____19. A vehicle placarded for Class A or B explosives must never be left unattended.

_____20. Proper shipping names are shown in plain type and in alphabetical order on the Hazardous Materials Table.

_____21. When placarding a vehicle, you must put placards on the front, back, and both sides.

_____22. To communicate risks, make sure that the right shipping papers, package labels, and placards are included with hazardous materials.

_____23. Always refuse shipments that are leaking hazardous materials.

_____24. When an accident occurs on a trailer containing explosives, make sure to remove all the explosive material before pulling the vehicles apart.

_____25. If your vehicle is leaking hazardous materials, stop the vehicle and go get help.

_____26. If an accident occurs while transporting hazardous materials, your responsibility as a driver is to limit the spread of the material, even if it puts your safety at risk.

_____27. The National Response Center should be called if someone is killed, injured, or sent to the hospital or if property damages exceed $50,000 because of an accident involving hazardous materials cargo.

____28. The National Response Center is a resource center for police and fire fighters who must assist in a hazardous materials incident.

____29. Call the Department of Transportation if you are involved in a hazardous materials spill.

The following statements are multiple choice. Mark your answer in the blank provided. Then check your answers with the key at the end of the chapter.

____ 1. Who makes sure that the shipper has correctly named, labeled, and marked a HazMat shipment?
   (A) Driver.   (C) Shipper.
   (B) Carrier.   (D) All of the above.

____ 2. What can drivers, shippers, and carriers use to find out if materials are regulated?
   (A) List of Hazardous Substances and Reportable Quantites.
   (B) Hazardous Material Table.
   (C) Both A and B.
   (D) Neither A nor B.

____ 3. Drivers who carry radioactive material or flammable cryogenic liquids must have special training within how many years?
   (A) One-half year.   (C) Two years.
   (B) One year.   (D) Five years.

____ 4. The shipper is not responsible for which of the following?
   (A) Labeling.   (C) Placarding.
   (B) Packaging.   (D) Preparing shipping papers.

____ 5. You cannot describe a nonhazardous material by:
   (A) Using a hazard class or ID number.
   (B) Slang words.
   (C) Abbreviations.
   (D) Code words.

____ 6. What is the correct placard if you're carrying 500 pounds of class A and B explosives?
   (A) "Dangerous".   (C) "Explosive" B.
   (B) "Explosive" A.   (D) "Explosive and Dangerous".

____ 7. What is the correct placard if you are carrying 600 pounds of organic peroxide and 500 pounds of oxidizer?
   (A) "Dangerous".   (C) "Oxidizer".
   (B) "Organic peroxide".   (D) None of the above.

____ 8. What should you do when a common carrier transport material is classified as "Forbidden" on the Hazardous Material Table?
   (A) Transport it anyway and report it to the Department of Transportation.
   (B) Make sure that the quantity does not exceed 500 pounds.
   (C) Transport it as a normal shipment, but be extremely careful.
   (D) Never transport the material.

____ 9. What is the proper way to placard two liters of "Flammable Liquid" labeled "Poison-Inhalation Hazard" on the shipping paper?
   (A) Placard as a poison gas.
   (B) Use a poison placard and the proper hazard class placard.
   (C) Both A and B are correct.
   (D) Neither A nor B is correct.

___10. What does it mean when you see an "X" or "RQ" in the HM column of a shipping paper entry?
  (A) The cargo will not be shipped.
  (B) The driver must report the shipment to the Department of Transportation.
  (C) The shipment is regulated by hazardous materials regulations.
  (D) None of the above.

___11. The correct order of description of hazardous materials on the shipping paper is:
  (A) Shipping name, hazard class, ID number.
  (B) Hazard class, ID number, shipping name.
  (C) ID number, shipping name, hazard class.
  (D) The order does not matter as long as all three descriptions are present.

___12. What special equipment should the driver carry when carrying chlorine in cargo tanks?
  (A) A kit that measures chlorine levels.
  (B) A cell phone.
  (C) A gas mask and emergency kit for leak control.
  (D) No special equipment is required.

___13. The shipper certifies that he or she has packaged the material according to the regulations, except when:
  (A) The shipper is a private carrier carrying his own product.
  (B) The driver's cargo compartment is sealed.
  (C) The vehicle will not cross state lines.
  (D) The shipment is hazardous waste.

___14. You know a shipment includes hazardous material if:
  (A) You talk to the shipper.
  (B) You inspect every package.
  (C) You check the hazardous material table.
  (D) You look at the shipping papers.

___15. Why do you need a uniform hazardous waste manifest?
  (A) It indicates that you're carrying hazardous material.
  (B) It is exactly the same as a shipping paper.
  (C) None of the above.
  (D) All of the above.

___16. A vehicle that is carrying hazardous materials must have _____ placard(s)?
  (A) One.   (C) Eight.
  (B) Four.   (D) Ten.

___17. When a vehicle carrying explosives is stopped on the side of the road, what type of emergency warning device can be used?
  (A) Reflective triangles.   (C) Traffic cones.
  (B) Flares.   (D) Any of the above.

___18. When a vehicle carrying flammable liquids or gas is stopped on the side of the road, what type of emergency warning device can be used?
  (A) Reflective triangles.
  (B) Flares.
  (C) Traffic cones.
  (D) Any of the above.

_____19. When loading hazardous materials, you should always:
  (A) Double wrap wet boxes in plastic.
  (B) Never smoke within 50 feet of explosives, oxidizers, and flammables.
  (C) Never use hooks.
  (D) Keep bystanders 100 feet away.

_____20. When you are loading explosives, you should check the cargo space:
  (A) To make sure there are no sharp objects or points.
  (B) To make sure cargo heaters are working and ready.
  (C) To make sure the floor liners are loose.
  (D) All of the above.

_____21. You cannot transport Class A explosives with:
  (A) A large wheelbase trailer.
  (B) A placarded cargo tanker.
  (C) Two or more trailers.
  (D) A vehicle containing food.

_____22. You should load cylinders of compressed gas by:
  (A) Putting them in boxes that won't allow them to turn over.
  (B) Putting them in racks attached to the vehicle.
  (C) Holding them upright or braced lying down flat.
  (A) Any of the above.

_____23. What does the transport index on the labels of radioactive II packages mean?
  (A) It is used by Department of Transportation inspectors only.
  (B) It means nothing and can be covered or removed.
  (C) It indicates the correct placard to use.
  (D) It indicates the degree of control needed during transportation.

_____24. In a single vehicle, the total transport index of all radioactive material cannot exceed:
  (A) 0.   (C) 25.
  (B) 15.   (D) 50.

_____25. A vehicle carrying animal and human food must not be loaded with:
  (A) Poisons.
  (B) Explosives.
  (C) Oxidizers.
  (D) All of the above.

_____26. What should you immediately do before you move a cargo tank of hazardous material?
  (A) Double check the air brake system.
  (B) Close all manholes and valves.
  (C) Call CHEMTREC at (800) 424-9300.
  (D) No other safety precautions are necessary.

_____27. You must park at least _____ feet away from an open fire if your vehicle is placarded.
  (A) 50.   (C) 200.
  (B) 100.   (D) 300.

_____28. When monitoring a placarded vehicle, you must:
  (A) Be awake and in the vehicle or within 100 feet of it.
  (B) Be aware of the hazards of the load.
  (C) Know what to do in an emergency.
  (D) All of the above.

____29. When should you check the dual tires on a placarded vehicle?
    (A) Twice per day.
    (B) Once per day.
    (C) At the beginning of the day.
    (D) Every two hours or 100 miles, whichever is less.

____30. When transporting Class A or B explosives, a driver must always have:
    (A) Shipping papers.
    (B) A copy of FMCSR Part 397.
    (C) A written route plan and emergency instructions.
    (D) All of the above.

____31. If a permit or special route is needed to transport a HazMat load, whose responsibility is it to get it?
    (A) The Department of Transportation.
    (B) The shipper.
    (C) The driver.
    (D) All of the above.

____32. If you are transporting hazardous materials, when should you check your route about permits or restrictions?
    (A) Whenever you stop to fill up for gas.
    (B) As the need arises.
    (C) Before you start the trip.
    (D) When you see highway signs noting restrictions.

____33. It is impossible for a placarded vehicle to drive near an open flame unless:
    (A) It can pass safely without stopping.
    (B) It has a table 2 placard.
    (C) The cargo compartment is sealed.
    (D) The wind is blowing toward the road.

____34. When transporting hazardous materials, a written route plan is required:
    (A) Always.
    (B) When transporting class A and B explosives.
    (C) Only when the carrier is Class B.
    (D) Never.

____35. If you are smoking, how close can you be to a placarded vehicle carrying explosives, oxidizers, or flammables?
    (A) You should never smoke around this cargo.
    (B) Not within 25 feet.
    (C) Not within 50 feet.
    (D) As close as you like.

____36. When refueling a placarded vehicle with the engine off, always remember to:
    (A) Make sure that you pay before you pump.
    (B) Have someone stand near the pump shut-off valve.
    (C) Be at the nozzle, controlling the fuel flow.
    (D) Watch for persons smoking.

____37. In the power unit of a placarded vehicle, what type of fire extinguisher rating is required?
    (A) UL rating of 10 B:C or more.   (C) UL rating of 40 B:C or more.
    (B) UL rating of 25 B:C or more.   (D) UL rating of 100 B:C or more.

Review Questions for Passenger Transport

The following statements are either True or False. Mark your answer in the blank provided. Then check your answers with the key at the end of the chapter.

____1. All buses should stop between 15 and 50 feet from a railroad crossing.
____2. Stop at all drawbridges at least 10 feet before the draw of the bridge.
____3. Hazardous materials are not allowed to be transported by buses.
____4. All carry-on baggage must be stored to allow free movement about the bus and must not block emergency exits or windows.
____5. Passengers must be seated and all baggage must be stowed under the seats.
____6. When the bus is full, carry-on baggage is allowed in the stairwells or in the aisle.
____7. Buses are required to slow down when the traffic light shows green.
____8. A bus driver may engage another passenger in conversation while driving.

The following statements are multiple choice. Mark your answer in the blank provided. Then check your answers with the key at the end of the chapter.

____ 1. Curved (convex) mirrors on buses:
    (A) Are against the federal laws.
    (B) Make things appear farther away than they are.
    (C) Make things appear larger.
    (D) All of the above.
____ 2. During a pre-trip inspection, you should check:
    (A) Rider signaling devices.
    (B) Handhold railing.
    (C) Emergency exit handles.
    (D) All of the above.
____ 3. When carrying farm workers, how many folding aisle seats can the vehicle have?
    (A) None.   (C) Five.
    (B) Ten.   (D) Eight.
____ 4. Church buses can have how many unsecured seats?
    (A) None.   (C) Five.
    (B) Ten.   (D) Eight.
____ 5. Bus emergency exits must:
    (A) Have exit signs that are clearly marked.
    (B) Be unlocked.
    (C) Keep doors and windows closed.
    (D) All of the above.
____ 6. While operating a bus, you should always have which of the following emergency equipment?
    (A) Emergency reflectors.   (C) Spare electrical fuses
    (B) At least one fire extinguisher. (D) All of the above.
____ 7. You should wear your seatbelt:
    (A) During short trips.   (C) Always.
    (B) For highway driving.   (D) During bad weather.

_____ 8. How should you secure baggage on a bus?
(A) Packages can be only one-foot tall so when they are in the aisle they can easily be stepped over.
(B) You can secure luggage in front of the emergency exit.
(C) The packages should be stowed away so that the packages don't fall on passengers.
(D) All of the above.

_____ 9. What type of cargo is prohibited on a bus?
(A) Chickens.
(B) Ammunition labeled ORM-D.
(C) Irritating materials or tear gas.
(D) All of the above.

_____10. The maximum weight of all hazardous materials that can be transported on a bus is:
(A) 500 pounds.   (C) 1000 pounds.
(B) 150 pounds.   (D) 50 pounds.

_____11. If a rider wants to board your bus and is carrying a closed gas can, what should you do?
(A) Store the gasoline in the front of the bus.
(B) Collect an extra fare for baggage.
(C) Don't allow the rider to board.
(D) It's okay to let the rider on board as long as the can is closed and kept away from the engine.

_____12. Passengers should not stand:
(A) In the handicapped passenger space.   (C) More than six deep.
(B) They can stand anywhere.   (D) In front of the standee line.

_____13. Disorderly or out-of-control riders should be discharged:
(A) In a safe place.   (C) As soon as possible.
(B) Near a police station.   (D) At the next bus stop.

_____14. Based on statistics, where do most bus crashes happen?
(A) While the bus is parked.   (C) At intersections.
(B) On two-lane roads.   (D) When the bus stops.

_____15. How do you keep control of the bus on curves?
(A) Press hard on the brake and turn sharply.
(B) Slow to a safe speed before the curve, then accelerate slightly.
(C) Countersteer.
(D) Brake all through the curve.

_____16. A bus driver should stop at a railroad crossing _____ feet before the nearest track?
(A) 50 to 100.   (C) 15 to 50.
(B) 10 to 15.   (D) 10.

_____17. You should stop _____ feet in front of a drawbridge that has no attendant?
(A) 50.   (C) 175.
(B) 20.   (D) 100.

_____18. A bus cannot be fueled while:
(A) Near an open flame.
(B) The engine is on.
(C) Passengers are on board.
(D) All of the above.

___19. It is illegal to tow or push a bus with passengers unless:
  (A) The tow truck is larger than 20,000 VWR.
  (B) Discharging passengers would be unsafe.
  (C) Followed by an escort vehicle.
  (D) The distance is less than one mile.

___20. When traveling at 50 miles per hour in a 40-foot bus, how many seconds of space should you keep between you and the vehicle in front of you?
  (A) Two seconds.
  (B) Eight seconds.
  (C) Five seconds.
  (D) Three seconds.

Check Yourself—Answers to Endorsements Tests

Air Brakes True/False
1. False
2. True
3. False
4. True
5. True
6. False
7. False
8. True
9. True
10. False
11. True
12. False
13. True
14. False
15. False
16. True
17. False
18. True
19. False
20. False
21. True
22. True
23. False
24. True
25. True

Air Brakes Multiple Choice
1. A
2. B
3. B
4. B
5. B
6. D
7. D
8. C
9. B
10. A
11. C
12. D
13. B
14. B
15. C
16. A
17. B
18. A

19. C
20. D
21. D
22. A
23. B
24. B
25. C
26. C
27. A
28. C
29. B

Combinations/Triples/ Doubles True/False
1. False
2. False
3. True
4. False
5. False
6. True
7. True
8. False
9. False
10. True
11. True
12. False
13. True
14. False
15. True
16. True
17. False
18. True
19. False
20. True
21. False
22. True
23. False
24. True
25. True

Combinations/Triples/ Doubles Multiple Choice
1. D
2. A
3. C
4. B
5. B

6. A
7. D
8. C
9. B
10. B
11. C
12. B
13. C
14. C
15. D
16. A
17. B
18. D
19. B
20. C
21. C
22. C
23. C
24. D
25. B
26. A
27. D
28. A
29. B
30. A
31. B
32. C
33. A
34. A
35. B
36. D
37. A
38. C
39. B
40. A
41. C
42. B
43. D
44. C
45. B
46. D

Tank Vehicle True/False
1. False
2. False
3. False
4. True

5. True

6. True

7. False

8. False

9. True

10. True

Tank Vehicle Multiple Choice

1. B

2. D

3. A

4. B

5. C

6. B

7. D

8. A

9. B

10. D

Hazardous Materials True/False

1. False

2. False

3. False

4. True

5. True

6. False

7. True

8. False

9. False

10. True

11. True

12. True

13. True

14. True

15. False

16. False

17. True

18. False

19. False

20. True

21. True

22. True

23. True

24. True

25. False

26. True

27. True

28. True

29. False

Hazardous Materials Multiple Choice

1. B

2. C

3. C

4. C

5. A

6. B

7. A

8. D

9. B

10. C

11. A

12. C

13. A

14. D

15. A

16. B

17. A

18. A

19. C

20. A

21. B

22. D

23. D

24. D

25. A

26. B

27. D

28. D

29. D

30. D

31. C

32. C

33. A

34. B

35. B

36. C

37. A

Passenger Transport True/False

1. True

2. False

3. False

4. True

5. True

6. False

7. True

8. False

Passenger Transport Multiple Choice

1. B

2. D

3. D

4. A

5. D

6. D

7. C

8. C

9. C

10. A

11. C

12. D

13. A

14. C

15. B

16. C

17. A

18. D

19. B

20. B

Appendix A

State Departments of Transportation

These addresses will be helpful, not only for finding out answers to questions but in providing printed information to help you with the CDL.

US Department of Transportation (DOT)
www.dot.gov
400 7th St, SW
Washington, DC 20590
Information: 202-366-4000
Hearing Impaired TTY: 202-755-7687

Alabama Department of Transportation
www.dot.state.al.us
1409 Coliseum Blvd
Montgomery, AL
Phone: 334-242-6358

Alaska Department of Transportation
www.dot.state.ak.us
3132 Channel Dr
Juneau, AK 99801-7898
Phone: 907-465-3900

Arizona Department of Transportation
www.dot.state.az.us
PO Box 2100
Phoenix, AZ 85001-2100

Arkansas Department of Transportation
www.ahtd.state.ar.us
Mailing Address: PO Box 2261
Little Rock, Arkansas 72203
Location: 10324 Interstate 30
Little Rock, Arkansas 72209
Phone: 501-569-2000

California Department of Transportation
www.dot.ca.gov/
Mailing Address: PO Box 942873
Sacramento, CA 94273-0001
Location: 1120 N St
Sacramento, CA
Phone: 916-654-5266

Colorado Department of Transportation
www.dot.state.co.us
4201 E Arkansas Ave
Denver, CO 80222

Connecticut Department of Transportation
www.state.ct.us/dot/
2800 Berlin Turnpike
Newington, CT 06131-7546
Phone: (860) 594-2000

Delaware Department of Transportation
www.state.de.us/deldot/
800 S Bay Rd
PO Box 778
Dover, DE 19903
Phone: 302-760-2080 or 800-652-5600

Florida Department of Transportation
www.dot.state.fl.us/
605 Suwannee St
Tallahassee, FL 32399 0450
Phone: (850) 414-4100

Georgia Department of Transportation
www.dot.state.ga.us/
#2 Capitol Square
Atlanta, GA 30334-1002
Phone: 404-656-5267 or
808-532-3700

Hawaii Department of Transportation
www.hawaii.gov/icsd/dot/dot.html
869 Punchbowl St
Honolulu, HI 96813

Idaho Transportation Department
www.state.id.us/itd/itdhmpg.htm
3311 W State St
PO Box 7129
Boise, ID 83707-8606
Phone: (208) 334-8000

Illinois Department of Transportation
www.dot.state.il.us
2300 S Dirksen Parkway
Springfield, IL 62764

Indiana Department of Transportation
www.ai.org/dot/

Motor Carrier Services Division
www.in.gov/dor/mcs/
Indiana Department of Revenue
5252 Decatur Blvd, Ste R
Indianapolis, IN 46241
Phone: (317) 615-7200

Iowa Department of Transportation
www.dot.state.ia.us
800 Lincoln Way
Ames, IA
Phone: 515-239-1111
Fax: 515-239-1120

Kansas Department of Transportation
www.ink.org/public/kdot/
915 Harrison, Room 754, Docking State
    Office Building
Topeka, KS 66612-1568
Phone: 785-296-3585

Kentucky Transportation Cabinet
www.kytc.state.ky.us/
501 High St
Frankfort, KY 40622
Phone: 502-564-4890

**Louisiana Department of Transportation
    and Development**
Mailing Address: PO Box 94245
Baton Rouge, LA 70804-9245
Location: 1201 Capitol Access Rd
Baton Rouge, LA 70802-4438
Phone: 225 379-1100

Maine Department of Transportation
www.state.me.us/mdot
16 Statehouse Station
Augusta, ME 04333
Phone: (207) 287-2551

Maryland Department of Transportation
www.mdot.state.md.us
PO Box 8755
BWI Airport, MD 21240
Phone: 888-713-1414

**Massachusetts Department of
    Transportation**
www.magnet.state.ma.us/mhd/home.htm
10 Park Plaza
Boston, MA 02116

Michigan Department of Transportation
www.mdot.state.mi.us
State Transportation Building
425 W Ottawa St
PO Box 30050
Lansing, MI 48909
Phone: 517-373-2090

Minnesota Department of Transportation
www.dot.state.mn.us/ or
    motorcarrier@dot.state.mn.us
395 John Ireland Blvd
St. Paul, MN 55155-1899
Phone: 800-657-3774

Mississippi Department of Transportation
www.mdot.state.ms.us/
401 N West St
Jackson, MS 39201
601-359-7001
Fax: 601-359-7050

Missouri Department of Transportation
www.modot.state.mo.us
105 W Capitol Ave
PO Box 270
Jefferson City, MO 65102
Phone: 888-275-6636 or 1-573-751-2551 (out
    of state)

Montana Department of Transportation
www.mdt.state.mt.us
PO Box 201001
2701 Prospect Ave
Helena, MT 59620-1001
Phone: 406-444-6200

Nebraska Department of Roads
www.dor.state.ne.us
PO Box 94759
1500 Hwy 2
Lincoln, NE 68509-4759
Phone: 402-471-4567

Nevada Department of Transportation
www.nevadadot.com
1263 S Stewart St
Carson City, NV 89712
Phone: 775-888-7000

**New Hampshire Department of
    Transportation**
www.state.nh.us/dot
John O. Morton Building
1 Hazen Dr
Concord, NH 03302-0483
Phone: (603) 271-3734

New Jersey Department of Transportation
www.state.nj.us/transportation
1035 Parkway Ave
PO Box 600
Trenton, NJ 08625
Phone: 888-486-3339 or 609-292-6500 (out of state)

New Mexico State Highways and Transportation Department
www.nmshtd.state.nm.us
1120 Cerrillos Rd
PO Box 1149
Santa Fe, NM 87504-1149
Phone: 505-827-5100

New York Department of Transportation
www.dot.state.ny.us

Region 1
84 Holland Ave
Albany, NY 12208
Phone: 518-474-6178

Region 2
Utica State Office Building
Genesee St
Utica, NY 13501;
Phone: 315-793-2447

Region 3
Senator John H. Hughes
State Office Bldg
333 E Washington St
Syracuse, NY 13202
Phone: 315-428-4351

Region 4
1530 Jefferson Rd
Rochester, NY 14623-3161
Phone: 716-272-3300

Region 5
General William J. Donovan Office Bldg
125 Main St
Buffalo, NY 14203
Phone: 716-847-3238

Region 6
107 Broadway
Hornell, NY 14843
Phone: 607-324-8404

Region 7
Dulles State Office Building
317 Washington St
Watertown, NY 13601
Phone: 315-785-2333

Region 8
Eleanor Roosevelt State Office Bldg
4 Burnett Blvd
Poughkeepsie, NY 12603-2594
Phone: 914-431-5750

Region 9
New York State Office Bldg
44 Hawley St
Binghamton, NY 13901
Phone: 607-721-8116

Region 10
New York State Office Bldg
Veterans Memorial Hwy
Hauppauge, NY 11788;
Phone: 510-952-0032

Region 11
Hunters Point Plaza
47-40 21st St
Long Island City, NY 11101;
Phone: 718-482-4526

North Carolina Department of Transportation
www.dot.state.nc.us
Mailing Address:
1503 Mail Service Center,
Raleigh, NC 27699-1503
Location: 1 S Wilmington St,
Raleigh, NC 27611
Phone: 919-733-2522

North Dakota Department of Transportation
www.state.nd.us/dot
608 E Boulevard Ave
Bismarck, ND 58505-0700
Phone: 701-328-2500

Ohio Department of Transportation
www.dot.state.oh.us
1980 W Broad St,
Columbus, OH 43223
Phone: 614-466-7170

Oklahoma Department of Transportation
www.okladot.state.ok.us
200 NE 21st St
Oklahoma City, OK 73105
Phone: 405-425-2026

Oregon Department of Transportation
www.odot.state.or.us
355 Capitol St, NE
Salem, OR 97301-3871
Phone: 888-ASK-ODOT

Pennsylvania Department of Transportation
www.dot.state.pa.us
PO Box 2047
Harrisburg, PA 17105-2047
Phone: 800-932-4600 or 717-391-6190 (out
    of state)

**Rhode Island Department of
    Transportation**
www.dot.state.ri.us
Two Capitol Hill
Providence, RI 02903-1124
Phone: 401-222-1362

**South Carolina Department of
    Transportation**
www.dot.state.sc.us
955 Park St
PO Box 191
Columbia, SC 29202-0191
Phone: 803-737-2314

**South Dakota Department of
    Transportation**
www.state.sd.us/dot
700 E Broadway Ave
Becker-Hansen Bldg
Pierre, SD 57501
Phone: 605-773-3265

Tennessee Department of Transportation
www.tdot.state.tn.us
505 Deaderick St
Nashville, TN 37243
Phone: 615-741-2848

Texas Department of Transportation
www.dot.state.tx.us
125 E 11th St
Austin, TX 78701-2483
Phone: (512) 465-3500

Utah Department of Transportation
www.sr.ex.state.ut.us
Calvin Rampton Building
4501 S 2700 West
Salt Lake City, UT 84119-5998
Phone: 801-965-4000

Vermont Agency of Transportation
www.aot.state.vt.us
120 State St
Montpelier, VT 05603-0001
Phone: 802-828-2000

Virginia Department of Transportation
www.vdot.state.va.us
1401 E Broad St
Richmond, VA 23219
Phone: 804-786-2716

Washington Department of Transportation
www.wsdot.wa.gov
Location: 310 Maple Park Ave SE
Olympia, WA
Mailing Address: PO Box 47308
Olympia, WA 98504-7308
Phone: 360-705-7070

**West Virginia Department of
    Transportation**
www.wvdot.com
Bldg 5, Room A110
1900 Kenawha Blvd E
Charleston, WV 25305
Phone: 304-558-3456

Wisconsin Department of Transportation
www.dot.state.wi.us
4802 Sheboygan Ave
PO Box 7910
Madison, WI 53707-7910
Phone: 608-266-2353

Wyoming Department of Transportation
http://wydotweb.state.wy.us
5300 Bishop Blvd
Cheyenne, WY 82009-3340
Phone: 307-777-4375

Appendix B

Major Trucking Firms and Transportation Companies

C. R. England
800-338-0575

Smithway Motor Xpress
800-247-8040

Watkins Shepard
800-548-8895

Danny Herman Trucking Inc.
800-325-0253—Midwest
800-331-3725—Southwest

CRST
800-553-2778

Star Transportation Inc.
800-416-5912

Werner Enterprises
888-493-7637

Stevens Transport
800-333-8595

MS Carriers
800-231-5209

Willis Shaw Express
800-564-6973

Van-Pak
888-736-4879

C.H. Dredge and Co., Inc.
800-348-8224

Dick Simon Trucking
800-993-7483

PGT Trucking, Inc.
800-832-6748

JB Hunt
800-2JB-HUNT

Roehl Transport Inc. (pronounced rail)
800-585-7073

US Xpress
800-USXPRESS

Cannon Express
800-845-9390

Schneider Transportation
800-752-5318

Arrow Trucking Co.
800-444-6116

FFE Transportation Svcs., Inc.
800-569-9233

M.W. McCurdy & Co.
800-323-8810

Contract Freighters, Inc.
800-641-4747

Sunflower Carriers
800-775-7005

Swift Transportation Inc.
800-669-7943
www.swft.com

Merit Distribution Services Inc.
800-771-2507

Melton Truck Lines
800-545-8669

Ozark Motor Lines, Inc.
800-264-4100

Glossary

Accelerator   Located just under the steering wheel, you can operate this pedal with your right foot to control engine speed.

Access panels   Panels granting access to controls, vehicle parts and storage for tools and other items.

Administrator   The Federal Highway Administrator, the chief executive of the Federal Highway Administration, an agency within the Department of Transportation.

Aerodynamic buffeting   As you drive your double or triple rig down the highway, you are cutting through the wind and, as you cut through, a "draft" is created behind you.

Air backflow   If the tractor air supply develops a problem, air from the trailer air supply would have a tendency to "back flow" and fill the tractor's air supply. If this happens, both tractor and trailer would be left powerless.

Air bag suspension   A trailer suspension system that uses air bags instead of traditional springs.

Air brakes   These brakes use air instead of fluid to stop or brake. They require special handling and an additional permit on your CDL.

Air compressor   Compresses air and pumps it into the air tanks. Air brakes use compressed air to brake the vehicle.

Air compressor governor   Maintains constant air pressure in the air tanks—between 100 psi and 125 psi.

Air leakage rate   The rate at which air leaks from the air brakes. Use the air leakage rate to test brake pressure.

Air pressure   Compacting air and storing it in a small space. Compressing it creates energy and this energy operates the air brakes.

Air storage tanks   Also called "air tanks" or "air reservoirs." These tanks hold compressed air produced by the air compressor. These tanks have enough air to stop the vehicle several times, even if the air compressor stops working.

Air tank drains   Air tanks are equipped with drains, usually located at the bottom of the tank. Oil and water accumulate in the tanks and must be drained daily.

Air tank petcock   A valve on a tank that can be opened to drain the tank.

Alcohol concentration (AC)   The concentration of alcohol in a person's blood or breath. When expressed as a percentage, it means grams of alcohol per 100 milliliters of blood or per 210 liters of breath.

Alcohol evaporators   Designed to automatically inject alcohol into the system to reduce the chance that water in the air brake system will freeze.

Alcohol or "alcoholic beverage"   Beer, wine, distilled spirits, or liquor.

Alternator   Keeps the battery charged and powers the truck's systems while it is running.

Ammeter   Used to measure the flow of electrical currents.

Amperage   The number of amperes generated by the vehicle's electrical system.

Amphetamines   Stimulant drugs used to stay awake. Also called "Bennies," "speed," or "pep pills"—they are illegal.

Application pressure gauge   Lets the driver know how much air pressure is being applied to the brakes.

Automatic drain   An air tank drain that is activated automatically. From time to time, you will hear these drains blow out the air and any accumulated oil and water.

Axle weight   Weight transmitted to the ground by one axle or one set of axles. Axle weight is not how much the axles themselves weigh! Axles support the vehicle and its load.

BAC   Blood alcohol level.

Backing   The process of putting a vehicle in reverse.

Backup lamp   One white light located at the rear of buses, trucks, and truck tractors. It is a signal to other drivers that you are backing up.

Baffled liquid tanks   Tanks with dividers designed to slow down front-to-back surge.

Baffles   Dividers in a tanker that keep the load from shifting.

Balanced load   Cargo that is evenly distributed from top to bottom, front to back, and side to side.

Bank   A sloped area that causes the highway or road to slant slightly.

Battery   Converts chemical energy to electricity. It is used to start the engine.

Belted bias ply   Tires on which the plies cross at an angle and there's an added layered belt of fabric between the plies and the tread. Belts make the tread more rigid than bias ply tires and the tread will last longer.

Bias ply   Tires in which the plies are placed at a criss-crossed angle. This makes the sidewall and the tread very rigid.

Binders   Used to bind down loads on flatbed trailers.

Black ice   A thin coating of ice that is usually invisible because you can see the roadway through it.

Bleeding tar   Tar that bleeds to the driving surface and can be very slippery.

Blind spot   An area that you can't see with your rearview mirrors—usually from the rear axle to midway up the trailer and from midway down the door to the ground.

Blocks   Also called "chocks." They prevent trucks from moving unexpectedly; used in testing brakes and loading and coupling trailers.

Bobtail tractor   The lead tractor and power supply when towing trailers or other tractors.

Braces and supports   Devices used to prevent the load from moving. Whether the vehicle is a flatbed or drybox, the load must be blocked or braced to prevent moving on all sides.

Bracing   A method that prevents movement of the cargo in the trailer or any other cargo compartment.

Brake cam shaft   The brake slack adjuster is attached to the push rod at one end and the cam shaft at the other end. When the slack adjuster is pushed, the cam shaft twists, forcing the brake shoes away from each other to press on the side of the brake drum.

Brake chamber   When the driver applies the brake and air is applied to the braking system, air is pumped into the brake chamber and pushes out the "push rod"—which is attached to the "slack adjuster." When the driver takes his or her foot off the brake pedal, the air is released from the brake chamber and the return spring pulls the brake shoes away from the drum.

Brake drums   Located at the ends of the axle. The drums contain the braking mechanism and the wheels are bolted to the drums.

Brake fade   When it takes more and more pressure on the brake pedal to slow the vehicle.

Brake failure   Brakes do not work.

Brake lag distance   Distance the vehicle travels once the brake has been applied and the brakes begin to work.

Brake linings   These press against the drum, creating enough friction to slow or stop the vehicle.

Brake pedal   Located just to the left of the accelerator and operated with your right foot. When you press down on the pedal, the brakes are applied and the vehicle slows down.

Brake reservoirs   For air or vacuum braking systems, the reservoirs (or tanks) store the compressed air until it is needed.

Brake shoes   These press against the drum, creating enough friction to slow or stop the vehicle.

Brake-door interlock   Applies the brakes and holds the throttle in an idle position each time the door is opened.

Brakes   Used to stop the vehicle.

Braking   Process of using brakes.

Braking distance   The perception time plus the reaction time plus the brake lag—needed to stop a rig. Usually calculated to include speed.

Braking force   A percentage of the GVWR or the GCWR.

Braking performance   A combination of how quickly the brakes stop the vehicle and how far the vehicle travels before it stops. Braking performance is also measured by how much force must be applied to the brakes before the vehicle stops.

Braking rate   The ability of a vehicle's brakes to stop the vehicle when traveling at a certain speed; these specifications are provided for the manufacturer and the vehicle must at least meet the required braking rate.

Bridge icing   In cold weather, bridges usually become icy before roads do. Drive slowly over bridges in cold weather.

Bridge traffic control officer   Individual stationed at a drawbridge to direct traffic and to stop traffic just prior to the bridge being raised.

Bulkhead   A solid steel divider within the tank.

Bus   Vehicle that carries more than 15 passengers.

Cab   The part of the vehicle where the driver sits.

Cables   Wires, chains, or other connectors from the tractor to the trailer.

Canceling the turn signal   Shutting off the turn signal.

Carboy   Glass, plastic, or metal container used to carry between 5 to 15 gallons of liquid.

Cargo doors   Doors located at the back or side of trailer where cargo may be loaded or unloaded.

Cargo heater   Heater used to keep cargo warm.

Cargo securement   Making sure that the cargo does not shift or fall.

Cargo securement devices   Tie-downs, chains, tarps, and other methods of securing cargo in a flatbed.

Cargo shift   Cargo moves from its original position.

Cargo tank   Tank used to hold liquid or compressed gas.

Carry-on baggage   Luggage, bags, and packages brought onto a bus by passengers. Carry-on baggage must be kept out of the aisle and not impede the movement of passengers.

It is also imperative that carry-on baggage be stowed in a secure manner to avoid injuring passengers if the bus stops or lurches suddenly.

Center of gravity   The point where weight acts as a force. Center of gravity affects the vehicle's stability.

Centrifugal force   A natural force that pulls liquids or objects away from the center.

Chains   Used for tiedown to secure cargo.

Checklist   List of parts of the vehicle to check or inspect.

CHEMTREC   The acronym for the Chemical Transportation Emergency Center in Washington, DC. It has a 24-hour toll-free line and has evolved to provide emergency personnel with technical information and expertise about the physical properties of hazardous products. The number for CHEMTREC is 800-424-9300.

Chock   A block (usually made of wood) used to hold a tire in place and keep a vehicle from moving.

Clearance lights   Lamps that outline the length and width of the vehicle. These lights are found at the highest and widest part of the sides, back, and front of the vehicle.

Climbing lane   Extra lane used by slower vehicles trying to climb a hill.

Closed circuit   An electrical circuit in a completed loop in which electricity's positive and negative poles are connected. This allows the current to travel from the source to its usage point.

Clutch pedal   Located to the left of the brake pedal, the clutch pedal is operated with the left foot. You press the clutch pedal to disengage the clutch, and release the pedal to engage the clutch.

CMVSA/86   Commercial Vehicle Safety Act of 1986—requires all 50 states to meet the same minimum standards in testing and licensing of all commercial drivers and requires that all commercial motor vehicle drivers must pass and obtain the CDL.

Coil spring suspension   Dampens wheel vibration with coils that absorb "bounce" between the road and the tires.

Cold start and warm-up switch   Found on diesel engines. When the engine is cold, there's a start-up lag time. Turning the key allows the ejectors in the engine to warm up. A light comes on, letting you know the engine is warm enough to start.

Combustible   Any material that can ignite or burn.

Commerce   Any trade, traffic, or transportation within the jurisdiction of the United States between a place in a state and a place outside of that state, trade, traffic, and transportation in the United States, which affects any trade, traffic, and transportation.

Commercial driver's license (CDL)   A license issued by a state or other jurisdiction to an individual, which authorizes the individual to operate a specified class of commercial motor vehicle.

Commercial Driver's License Information System (CDLIS)   Established by FHWA pursuant to section 12007 of the Commercial Motor Vehicle Safety Act of 1986.

Commercial motor vehicle (CMV)   A motor vehicle or combination of motor vehicles used in commerce to transport passengers or property if the vehicle has a gross combination weight rating of 11,794 kilograms or more (26,001 pounds or more) inclusive of a towed unit with a gross vehicle weight rating of more than 4536 kilograms (10,000 pounds); or is designed to transport 15 or more passengers, including the driver.

Communicate the risk   Attaching proper placards to the vehicle.

Communicating with others   The use of lights, horns, and hand signals to let other drivers know your intentions.

Compartment   Enclosed space where certain items are kept.

Compressed gas   Gas held under pressure.

Containment   The ability to keep any situation or substance from moving from its original site; "containment" of a fire means restricting its movement from its origin; "containment of a liquid" means preventing liquid from spreading farther from its origin, as in a spill.

Controlled braking   Accomplished by squeezing brakes firmly *without locking the wheels.*

Controlled substance   Includes all substances listed on schedules I through V of 21 CFR 1308 (Secs. 1308.11 through 1308.15).

Converter dolly   Used to connect the trailer to the tractor or to another trailer.

Converter gear   Part of the converter dolly used to couple the tractor and the trailer, or the trailer to another trailer.

Conviction   A determination that a person has violated or failed to comply with the law in a court of original jurisdiction or a violation of a condition of release without bail, regardless of whether the penalty is rebated, suspended, or probated.

Coolant   Liquid used to keep the engine cool.

Corrosive   Includes materials that cause destruction or irreversible damage to human skin tissue on contact—can be liquid or solid.

Countersteering   Once you've steered around an obstacle in your path, you will turn the wheel back in the other direction.

Coupling   Connecting two sections of a vehicle or trailer.

Coupling device   A device—called a converter gear or dolly—that makes it possible to attach one trailer to another or to a tractor.

Cross-wind   Wind currents traveling from side to side—particularly dangerous on mountain roads.

Cryogenic   Maintaining materials by freezing.

Curves   Where the highway bends in another direction. Usually includes a slight bank, which may cause a load to shift; curves should be taken below the normal speed limit.

Cut-in/cut-out levels   Governor on the air compressor. When air pressure drops below a certain psi, the governor will cut in and build the pressure back to its necessary level. Then, the compressor will automatically cut out.

Cylinders   A pressurized tank designed to hold gases.

Cylindrical   In the shape of a cylinder—usually referring to anything long and round.

Dashboard   Control panel just beyond the steering wheel that houses all gauges, knobs, and other operating information so that the driver may operate the truck safely.

Dead axles   Axles pulled by the drive axle that do not give power to the wheels. Without the drive axle, these axles would be stationary.

Deceleration   Slowing the vehicle.

Defroster or defrosting device   An element associated with the vehicle's heating unit that clears the windshield of any ice or foggy distraction.

Departure   The time the vehicle is scheduled to leave the facility.

Destination   Arrival location.

Differential   Gears that allow each wheel to turn at a different speed on the same axle for easier manageability while turning.

Dimmer switch   Located on the floor to the left of the brake pedal (if it isn't on the dashboard). This switch allows you to move the headlights from low beam to high beam.

Disc brakes   Brakes that have a power screw, which is turned when air pressure is applied. This causes the power screw to clamp the disc between the caliper's brake lining pads.

Disqualification   The suspension, revocation, cancellation, or any other withdrawal by a state of a person's privilege to drive or a determination by the FHWA, under the rules of practice for motor carrier safety—that person is no longer qualified to operate a commercial motor vehicle.

Dolly support   The device that holds up the front end of a dolly when it is uncoupled from a tractor.

Dolly tongue   A part of the dolly converter that goes under the trailer, linking it to the tractor or another trailer.

DOT   Department of Transportation.

Double   A vehicle carrying two trailers or tankers.

Downgrade   A steep downward slant in the road, usually around mountains or hill country.

Downhill grade   See downgrade.

Drawbridge   Bridge that can be lifted to accommodate tall water vessels by pulling one-half of the bridge up, thereby interrupting traffic flow.

Drive axle   The axle that provides all of the power to the wheels and pulls the load.

Driveaway-towaway   A method of hauling in which the cargo is one or more vehicles with one or more sets of wheels on the roadway.

Driver applicant   An individual who applies to a state to obtain, transfer, upgrade, or renew a CDL.

Driver's license   A license issued by a state or other jurisdiction to an individual which authorizes the individual to operate a motor vehicle on the highways.

Driver's record of duty status   A form submitted by the driver to the carrier after completing a 24-hour period of work.

Driving a commercial motor vehicle while under the influence of alcohol   Driving a CMV with a blood alcohol concentration of 0.04% or more, driving under the influence of alcohol, as prescribed by state law; or refusal to undergo such testing.

Drop-off   An uneven highway where new pavement makes part of road higher than the rest, creating a "drop-off" that may be a driving hazard.

Dry bulk tanks   Tanks that have a high center of gravity, which means the driver will use special care, particularly when rounding curves and when entering or exiting a freeway by using an on-ramp or off-ramp.

Dual air brake systems   The truck has two separate air brake systems—the primary system and the secondary system—but only one set of controls.

Dual parking control valves   Some vehicles (mainly buses) have auxiliary air tanks that can be used to release the spring brakes so the vehicle can be moved to a safe place. Vehicles with dual parking control valves have two control knobs on the dash—one is a push-pull knob used to apply the spring brakes for normal parking. The other is spring-loaded in the "out" position.

Dummy coupler   Seals the air brake hose when a connection is not in use.

Dunnage   Loose packaging material.

DUI   Driving under the influence.

Effective braking distance Distance the vehicle will travel once the brakes make contact with the drum. With good braking technique and brakes perfectly adjusted on good, dry pavement, a vehicle going 55 miles per hour will travel 150 additional feet before coming to a complete stop.

Electron A tiny particle carrying a negative charge of electricity.

Elliptical An oval shape sometimes found on "fish-eye" mirrors.

Emergency brake system The system that stops the vehicle in an emergency situation—usually caused by failure of the braking system. The emergency brake system uses parts of the service and parking brake systems.

Emergency brakes Stops the vehicle in an emergency situation—usually caused by failure of the braking system.

Emergency equipment Equipment needed during an emergency. For a commercial motor vehicle, the emergency equipment consists of a fire extinguisher, reflective emergency triangles, fuses (if needed), tire change kit, accident notification kit, and a list of emergency numbers.

Emergency exit Exit used for emergency purposes only.

Emergency line Air line between the tractor and the trailer. If the service line becomes disconnected, the emergency line becomes the air supply to the trailer brakes. If the emergency line is broken, it will cause the trailer brakes to lock.

Emergency Response Guidebook (ERG) Used by fire fighters, police officers, industry safety personnel, and others in the event of an emergency involving HazMat cargo. This book is available through the Department of Transportation.

Employee Any operator of a commercial motor vehicle, including full-time, regularly employed drivers; casual, intermittent, or occasional drivers; leased drivers; and independent, owner-operator contractors.

Employer Any person or entity (including the United States, a state, the District of Columbia, or a political subdivision of a state) who owns or leases a commercial motor vehicle or assigns employees to operate such a vehicle.

Endorsement An authorization to an individual's CDL that is required to permit the individual to operate certain types of commercial motor vehicles.

Endorsements Optional tests that allow drivers to add permits for certain vehicles or cargo.

Engine compartment Area where the engine is located.

Engine retarder Also called "Jake Brake", "Williams Blue OX Brake"—engine retarders allow the engine to be used to help slow the vehicle down, particularly if brake fade occurs on a downgrade.

Engine temperature gauge Usually marked "Temp" or "Water Temp." This gauge indicates the temperature of the engine's cooling system in degrees.

En route During travel or on the way.

EPA Environmental Protection Agency.

Escape ramp A ramp—usually at the bottom of a down-grade—which drivers may use to stop their vehicle if the brakes fail.

Etiologic agents Microorganisms (also known as germs) that can cause disease.

Evasive action Action taken to avoid an accident, hitting debris on the road, or a dangerous situation—often involves swerving, braking, sudden lane changes, etc.

Exhaust system Required on all motor vehicles and used to discharge gases created by the operation of the engine.

Explosive   Material or a mixture that can explode.

Fail-safe brakes   Also known as spring brakes. The most commonly used emergency brake and/or parking brake system on tractors and buses. They must be mechanical, because air can leak off.

Federal Hazardous Materials Table   Designates which materials are hazardous to transport. They have been designated as "hazardous materials" because they endanger the health, safety, and property of those around them during their transport.

Federal Motor Carrier Safety Regulations (FMCSR)   Governs the operation of trucks and buses by common, contract, and private motor carriers.

Felony   An offense under state or federal law that is punishable by death or by imprisonment for a term exceeding one year.

Field of vision   The area in which you can see in front of you.

Fifth wheel   Controls how much weight is distributed on each axle of the tractor. It is part of the locking device that is used to connect a trailer and a tractor.

Fire extinguisher   Safety device used to put out fires.

"Fish-eye" mirror   Convex mirror, positioned on the side of the truck, usually providing driver with wider view of the back of trailer; makes vehicles and objects appear smaller and farther away than they are.

Fishyback   Carrying trailers and containers by ship.

Flags   Used to mark over-length or over-wide vehicles.

Flammable   Material that can burst into flames.

Flammable cargo   Cargo that can ignite if exposed to a fire or flame.

Flares   Burning signal device—part of safety equipment.

Flash point   The lowest temperature at which a substance can give off flammable vapors that can ignite if the vapors come in contact with a fire or a spark.

Flatbed   Truck or trailer without sides or a top.

Fluid pressure   The nature of fluids is to flow; when they cannot, pressure is created—fluid pressure is used to operate hydraulic brakes.

FMCSR Part 393   Describes parts and accessories needed to safely operate a commercial motor vehicle.

Foreign   Outside the 50 United States and the District of Columbia.

Foundation brakes   Used at each wheel—parts of the brake that don't rotate. The most common is the S-cam drum brake; wedge and disc brakes are less common.

Four-way flashers   Two amber lights located at the front and two amber lights or red lights located at the rear of the vehicle. These are usually the front and rear turn signal lights, equipped to do double duty as warning lights.

Frame   The metal infrastructure of any vehicle—creates the underpinnings to support the rest of the vehicle.

Friction   The rubbing together of two objects which causes resistance.

Front brake limiting valve   Vehicles built before 1975 have a front brake limiting valve control switch on the dash. The valve has two positions—"normal" and "slippery." Putting the valve in the "slippery" position reduces the normal air pressure to the front brakes by 50 percent—and in doing so, reduces the braking power of front brakes by 50 percent.

Front clearance lamps   Two amber lamps located at each side of the front of large buses, trucks, truck tractors, large semi-trailers, full trailers, pole trailers, and projecting loads.

Front identification lamps   Three amber lights located at the center of the vehicle or cab. Required on large buses and trucks and truck tractors.

Front side marker lamp   Two amber lights located to each side or near the center of the vehicle between the front rear side marker lamps. Required for buses, trucks, semi-trailers, full trailers, and pole trailers.

Front side reflectors   Two amber reflectors located on each side toward the front of buses and trucks, tractors, semi-trailers, full trailers, and pole trailers.

Front turn signals   Two amber signals located to the left and right front of the tractor. Can be above or below headlights. Required on buses, trucks, and truck tractors.

Front wheel skids (drive wheel skids)   The most common type of skid, resulting from over-braking or over-acceleration—can be stopped by taking foot off accelerator. If road conditions are slippery, push the clutch in.

Fuel and fuel system   Provides energy to the engine so that it will run.

Fuel injectors   Spray the fuel into the combustion chambers.

Fuel lines   Carry the fuel from the pump to the cylinders.

Fuel pump   Delivers the fuel to the engine.

Fuel tank   Holds the fuel.

Fuse   Device that completes the electrical circuit and prevents overheating by breaking the circuit, thus reducing the risk of fire damage.

Gas mask   A safety device carried in vehicles transporting hazardous materials—in case of an accident, the driver will use the gas mask to avoid inhaling poisonous or harmful fumes.

Gear   Pertaining to the transmission. Each gear supplies a certain speed to the vehicle. The lower the gear, the slower the vehicle's speed and the greater pulling power.

Gearshift   The stick or lever located inside the tractor that the driver uses to select the gear.

Generator   Changes mechanical energy into electricity to power batteries and other electrical systems.

Glad hand   Air hose brake connection between the tractor and the trailer.

Glare   A condition caused by sun or bright lights reflecting off pavement or a vehicle's glass or metal parts, causing difficulty in a driver's vision; particularly a problem when driving west as the sun is setting.

Groove pattern   The area between the tread ribs.

Gross combination weight rating (GCWR)   The value specified by the manufacturer as the loaded weight of a combination vehicle. In the absence of a value specified by the manufacturer, GCWR will be determined by adding the GVWR of the power unit and the total weight of the towed unit and any load thereon.

Gross vehicle weight (GVW)   Total weight of a single vehicle and its load.

Gross vehicle weight rating (GVWR)   The value specified by the manufacturer as the loaded weight of a single vehicle.

Grounding   Provides an alternate safe path for an electrical current if the normal path is accidentally broken.

Handhold   On buses, what passengers use to hold onto while standing in the aisle.

Hazard   Harmful item or situation.

Hazard Class   Indicates the degree of risk associated with a particular material.

Hazardous Material Table   A list of hazardous materials outlining federal guidelines.

Hazardous materials   A group of materials that the Secretary of Transportation judges to pose a threat or risk to safety, health, or property while it is being transported in commerce; the meaning such term has under section 103 of the Hazardous Materials Transportation Act.

Hazardous waste manifest   Any cargo containing hazardous waste must be accompanied by a hazardous waste manifest—and this must be signed by the driver.

HazMat   Hazardous material(s).

Headache rack or header board   Protects the driver from the freight shifting or crushing him or her in an accident or a sudden stop.

Headlights   Two white headlights, one to the right and one to the left, located on the front of the tractor—required on buses, trucks, and truck tractors. Used to illuminate the vehicle to help the driver see and to help others see the vehicle.

Heater   Warms the cab of the vehicle.

High beams   Lights used at night to see long distances. Use only when other cars are far away from you.

High center of gravity   The majority of a load's weight is high off the ground.

Horn   Used to communicate with other motorists.

Hydraulic brakes or hydraulic braking system   Brakes that use fluid pressure to stop.

Hydroplaning   Occurs when water or slush collects on the roadway and the vehicle's tires ride on top of the water, instead of the roadway itself, causing the driver to lose control of the vehicle.

Identification lights   Lights located on the top, sides, and back of a truck to identify it as a large vehicle.

Identification (ID) number   Number used to identify hazardous materials on shipping papers. ID numbers begin with UN—except those loads traveling between the United States and Canada, which are identified by an NA number.

Ignition point   The point at which a flammable substance will catch on fire (ignite).

Ignition switch (or starter)   Supplies electricity to the engine and other systems. When the key is turned, it turns on the accessory circuits. As soon as the engine starts, release the key. If you have a "false start," let the engine cool for 30 seconds before giving it another try.

Inertia   The tendency of an object to remain in the same condition, either in motion or standing still, until it is acted on by an outside force (e.g., applying the brakes to stop a truck).

Infectious substances   May cause disease or death in animals or humans. This includes human or animal excretion, secretions, blood tissue, and tissue components.

Inhalation hazard   A material that can be harmful if inhaled.

Innage   The depth of the liquid loaded in your tank, measuring from the bottom of the tank to the surface of the liquid.

Inspection routine   List of steps you go through to inspect your vehicle—in the same way each time—so that you do not forget a step.

Insulation   Material used to maintain certain temperatures within trailers; particularly important in refrigerated units to maintain cool temperatures.

Intermodal containers (fishyback/piggyback)   Containers sealed by the shipper, transported by boat, and then loaded on trailers for final delivery. Shippers prefer containers because they resist pilferage (theft) and other problems.

Johnson bar   Most tractors have a handle attached to (or near) the steering column—called a "Johnson bar" or "trolley valve"—used to apply the trailer's brakes.

Kingpin   Used in coupling, a hardened steel pin on a trailer that locks into the fifth wheel.

Knowledge Tests   Written tests that a driver must pass in order to receive a CDL or special permits.

Landing gear   Supports for the front of a trailer when it is not attached to a tractor.

Leaf spring suspension   Dampens wheel vibration; all the leaves must be intact to provide this comfort. During inspection, look for missing or broken leaves.

Length and width limits   Limitations on the length and width of a truck or tractor trailer rig. Combinations exceeding these limits must have special permits and travel irregular routes or have a route plan.

License plate lamp   One white light located at the center rear—on buses, trucks, tractors, semi-trailers, full trailers, and pole trailers.

Lights   Help others to see you, help you to see others, to signal intentions (such as lane changes, slow down or stop), and communicate with other vehicles.

Liquid density   Liquid in a tanker that has a high mass for its volume.

Liquid surge   The movement of a liquid in a tanker, created by the physics of forward motion. When tanker stops, the force of the liquid surge can actually move the entire vehicle several feet forward.

List of Hazardous Substances and Reportable Quantities   A list of hazardous materials that drivers should learn if they consistently haul such materials.

List of Marine Pollutants   A list of materials that are harmful to marine life or—if they enter the water table—or humans.

Livestock   Live animals, such as cattle, hogs, horses, sheep, and goats.

Load rating   Refers to the strength of the tire.

Locking device   Keeps the towed trailer and towing tractor together until you're ready to uncouple them. This locking device is called the "locking jaws" and it locks around the shaft of the trailer's kingpin.

Locking jaws   Another name for Locking Device.

Low air pressure warning signal   On all vehicles equipped with air brakes—signals when air pressure falls below 60 psi.

Low beams   Normal headlight setting used to illuminate the vehicle to help the driver see and to help others see the vehicle.

Manifest   A document describing cargo in the vehicle.

Manual drain   An air tank drain that is operated by turning a knob (or petcock) a quarter turn—or by pulling a cable.

Mirrors   Used to see what is behind and to the sides of the vehicle.

Modulating control valve   This is controlled by a handle on the dash board and is used to apply the spring brakes gradually. The more the handle is moved, the more the brakes are applied. This valve is designed to use in case service brakes fail while driving.

Motor vehicle A vehicle, machine, tractor, trailer, or semi-trailer propelled or drawn by mechanical power, used on highways, except that such term does not include a vehicle, machine, tractor, trailer, or semi-trailer operated exclusively on a rail.

MPH Miles per hour.

NA Initials preceding identification numbers that are used only in shipments between the United States and Canada.

National Response Center Has the ability to contact the proper law enforcement agency and the proper containment or clean-up personnel. The National Response Center phone number is 800-424-8802.

Net weight Weight of a package, not including the packing materials.

Night driving Driving at night.

Noise levels The concentration of noise.

Non hazardous material Material that by itself or in bulk does not create any hazard to health or the environment.

Nonresident CDL A CDL issued by a state to an individual living in a foreign country.

Normal stopping In a normal stopping situation, you apply pressure to the brake pedal until the vehicle comes to a stop. Pressure is applied smoothly and steadily.

N.O.S. Not otherwise specified.

"Nose factor" When carrying livestock, remember that your cargo does have an odor, and you should try to park your vehicle downwind of other vehicles or truckstops to keep everyone happy.

"No zone" The area to each side of the truck where it is not possible to see approaching traffic.

Odometer Keeps track of the total miles the vehicle has traveled.

Oil pressure gauge Gauge that measures oil pressure.

Oil temperature gauge Gauge that shows the temperature of the oil.

On-ramp/off ramp Ramps leading on and off freeways. Some ramps may bank, so it is recommended that you enter and exit a ramp at speeds below the posted speed limit.

ORM (Other Regulated Materials) These materials are not considered hazardous materials, by definition, but are dangerous when transported in commerce, so they must be regulated.

Out of service order A declaration by an authorized enforcement officer of a federal, state, Canadian, Mexican, or local jurisdiction that a driver, a commercial motor vehicle, or a motor carrier operation may not continue to operate.

Outage Space in a tanker that allows for liquid loads to expand. Drivers must know outage requirements for each product they haul.

Overacceleration Too much power supplied to the drive wheels—driving too fast and not adjusting your speed to the road and traffic conditions.

Overbraking Braking too hard and locking the wheels, causing a skid.

Overload More weight than your vehicle can carry or that is legally allowable.

Oversteering Turning the wheels more sharply than the vehicle can handle.

Oxidizing substances Substances that react with oxygen.

Pallet Flat wooden support structure used to group an amount of cargo together for shipping and stacking.

Parking brake controls   In older vehicles, the parking brake will be controlled by a lever. In newer models, the driver applies the parking brakes (spring brakes) using a diamond-shaped, yellow push-pull knob—you pull the knob out to apply the parking brakes and push it in to release.

Parking brake system   The system used when applying the parking brake.

Parking brakes   Brakes used when you park the vehicle.

Parking lamps   Two amber or white lights located just below the headlights on small buses and trucks.

Passenger supervision   Providing passengers information necessary for their safety during trip. This includes movement in the vehicle, storage of luggage, placement of carry-ons, and general behavior.

Perception distance   Distance the vehicle will travel from the time driver sees a hazard and the time the driver reacts (presses the brake pedal).

Permanent tank   A tank that is attached to the vehicle and must be loaded with the vehicle.

Piggyback   Trailers or containers that are first carried by rail.

"Pigtail"   Detachable connections—electrical connections between towing and towed vehicles—made by simply twisting wires together with shielded cables.

Pintle hook   Used in coupling, at rear of the fifth wheel—used to tow trailers.

Pitman arm   A lever attached to the steering box—moves the front wheels back and forth.

Placard   A sign placed on cargo to indicate that the shipment contains hazardous materials. These signs must be visible from all angles.

Plies   Separate layers of rubber-cushioned cord.

Poison   This hazardous material class includes materials that are toxic to humans or so toxic that they pose a health hazard during transportation. The class also includes materials presumed hazardous to humans because of laboratory tests. It also includes irritants, such as tear gas and infectious substances.

Pole trailer/pulpwood trailer   A trailer that is composed of a telescopic pole, a tandem rear wheel unit, and a coupling device used to join the trailer to a tractor.

POP   Performance oriented packaging.

Portable bulkheads   Bulkheads that can be removed from the trailer or moved in different configurations.

Portable tank   The tank can be taken off the vehicle and loaded and unloaded.

Portable Tank Emergency Systems   Systems that will lessen the impact of an accident by automatically sealing the tank.

Post-trip inspection   Driver's inspection of rig after each trip.

Pressure relief systems   Monitor the internal pressure of the tank and prevent the cargo from leaking out while the vehicle is on the road.

Pre-trip inspection   Before you begin to drive, a check of your vehicle to make sure that all systems are damage free and working properly to ensure safe driving.

Projecting loads   Cargo that has projecting items which need flags to warn others of the protruding objects. The load must extend more than four inches from the sides of the truck or four feet beyond the rear of the truck. Flags used to mark projecting loads must be at least 12 inches square and must be red.

Psi   Pounds per square inch.

Psia   Pounds per square inch absolute.

PTO lever   Power take-off lever.

Pullup   Stopping and remaneuvering to the correct position.

Pups   Double trailers.

Push rod   Attached to one end of the slack adjuster.

Pyrometer   Displays the engine exhaust temperature.

Radial ply   Ply that does not cross at an angle but is laid from bead to bead, across the tire. Radial tires have a number of belts and their construction means the sidewalls have less flex and less friction—which requires less horsepower and saves fuel.

Radiator shutters   Outer portion of the radiator; if the shutters freeze shut, the engine may overheat and stop. Remove ice when this happens.

Radioactive   Substances that give off radiation rays that are usually harmful.

Railroad crossing   Where the street crosses a railroad track.

Ramps   Entrances or exits to major roadways; may be slightly graded or banked.

Reaction distance   Time it takes for driver's foot to get off the accelerator and stomp on the brake.

Rear bumper   The protective apparatus that prevents shorter vehicles from running under taller ones. Clearance between the bumper and the ground is no more than 30 inches, measured when the vehicle is empty.

Rear clearance lamps   Two red lights located at the top right and top left of the rear of large trucks and buses, tractors, semi-trailers, full trailers, pole trailers, and projecting loads. These lamps outline the overall width. Not required on smaller vehicles.

Rear identification lamps   Three red lights centered on the top rear of large buses and trucks, large semi-trailers, full trailers, and pole trailers. Not required on smaller vehicles.

Rear reflectors   Two red reflectors located on the lower right and lower left of the rear of small and large buses and truck trailers, full trailers, and pole trailers.

Rear side marker lamps   One red light located on each side of the lower left and lower right rear of the side of buses and trucks, semi-trailers, full trailers, and pole trailers.

Rear side reflectors   Red reflectors located just below the rear side marker lamps— required on buses, trucks, semi-trailers, full trailers, and pole trailers.

Rear tail lamps   Lights located at the rear of the truck—amber in color.

Rear turn signal lamps   Two amber or red lights, each located at the lower right and lower left of the rear of trucks and buses, tractors, semi-trailers, full trailers, pole trailers, and converter dollies.

Rear-end projection   Projection four feet beyond the rear of the truck. Flags used to mark projecting loads must be at least 12 inches square and must be red.

Rear-view mirrors   Mirrors used to see on the sides and behind the vehicle.

Rear-wheel skid   Occurs when the rear drive wheels lock and have less traction, causing the rear of the vehicle to slide sideways. To correct, let off the brakes, allowing the rear wheels to roll again, and turn quickly. When the vehicle begins to slide sideways, quickly steer in the direction you want the vehicle to go.

Reefers (refrigerated units)   Truck or tanker used to carry refrigerated cargo or perishables.

Representative vehicle   A motor vehicle which represents the type of vehicle that a driver applicant operates or expects to operate.

Reservoirs   Air tanks.

Retarder controls   Controls that allow the engine to slow the speed of the vehicle, particularly on a downgrade.

Retest and Marking   Specified by the Department of Transportation, requires a regular testing and remarking schedule for tanks authorized to carry HazMat cargo—usually the responsibility of the carrier.

Return spring   Pulls the brake shoes away from the drum.

Right-of-way   The right of a person or vehicle to go before another.

Rim   Part of the wheel that holds the tire in place.

Roof hatch   Opening in the top of a bus to let air in.

Route plan   Prescribed route prior to the trip, usually when the vehicle is carrying hazardous materials or irregular loads. The driver may use less-traveled roads or comply with times during which hazardous materials may be hauled on certain roadways.

RPM   Revolutions per minute. Read by a tachometer and indicates when to change gears.

RQ   Reportable quantity.

Saddle mounts   A steel assembly that couples a towed vehicle (trailer or semi-trailer) with the towing vehicle.

Safe speed   Posted as the speed limit.

Safe-haven   A location approved for parking an unattended vehicle loaded with explosives.

Safety chains   Usually used in pairs with a tow-bar connection to keep trailers from accidentally separating.

Safety valve   Located in the first tank the air compressor pumps air into. This valve will release excess air and protects the air system from exceeding psi limitations (and possibly damaging the system.)

S-cam brakes   The usual configuration of brakes on modern vehicles. Pushing the brake pedal causes the S-cam to force the brake shoes away from the drum. On releasing the brake pedal, the S-cam twists back, returning the wheels to free motion.

SCF   Standard cubic foot.

Seatbelt   Safety harness that holds the driver into the seat. Seatbelts should always be worn when driving—make sure and put it on before you start the vehicle.

Segregation and Separation Chart   Requires certain hazardous materials be loaded separately.

Selector knob   An air-assisted lever on the gearshift which takes the transmission from low-range to high-range.

Self-reactive materials   Materials that are thermally unstable and that can undergo a strong decomposition and may even detonate without participation of oxygen (air).

Serious traffic violation   A conviction received when operating a commercial motor vehicle for excessive speeding, reckless driving, improper or erratic traffic lane changes, following the vehicle ahead too closely, or a violation arising in connection with a fatal accident.

Service brake system   The system that applies and releases the brakes as you apply and release pressure on the service brake.

Service brakes   The vehicle's main braking system—used to stop the vehicle in regular driving situations.

Shaft of the kingpin   Coupling device on the trailer around which the jaws of the locking device are placed for a secure connection.

Shear section   Will save the important part of a pipe and its attachments, thus preventing a leak.

Shipper's certification   A written statement saying that the cargo was prepared according to the law.

Shipping papers   Documents that include any information that is required by FMCSR Parts 172.202, 172.203, and 172.204.

Shutting down the engine   Actually turning off the ignition and allowing the engine to cool.

Side marker lamps   Two amber lights located to each side or near the center of the vehicle between front rear side marker lamps. Required for buses, trucks, semi-trailers, full trailers, and pole trailers.

Side reflectors   Two amber reflectors located on each side or near midpoint of the vehicle between the front and rear side reflectors of buses and trucks, large semi-trailers, large full trailers, and pole trailers.

Skid control   The ability to control the movement of the vehicle once it has entered a skid. Usually done by steering—never by braking.

Skills Test   The actual driving test to make sure that a driver can operate a trailer or tanker.

Slack adjuster   Attached to one end of the push rod and on the other to the brake cam shaft. When it is pushed out, it causes the brake cam shaft to twist, which will cause the S-cam to turn. This forces the brake shoes away from each other and presses them inside the drum, causing the vehicle to stop.

Slack adjusters   Located on the brake chamber push rod, this adjustment device compensates for brake shoe wear.

Slosh   Term used to describe the action of liquids in a tanker—moving front to back or side to side.

Spare tire   Additional tire used as a precaution in case something happens to the vehicle's tires.

Speedometer   Shows the vehicle's road speed in miles per hour (mph).

Spindle   Another word for axle.

Splash guards (mud flaps)   Rubberized sheaths hanging behind the wheels that lessen amount of water or mud kicked up in back of a trailer or truck.

Spotting mirror   Same as convex mirrors—objects appear smaller and farther away than they really are. Always check and adjust prior to each trip.

Spring brakes   Also known as fail-safe brakes. The most commonly used emergency brake and/or parking brake system on tractors and buses. They must be mechanical because air can leak off. Otherwise, they are the conventional brake chambers.

Stab braking   Apply the brakes as hard as possible, release the brakes when the wheels lock, and when wheels start rolling again, reapply the brakes hard—repeat this process as often as necessary.

Standee line   A line behind the driver's seat of a bus that passengers should stand behind.

State   A state of the United States and the District of Columbia.

State of domicile   The state where a person has his or her true, fixed, and permanent home and the principal residence to which he or she has the intention of returning whenever he or she is absent.

Steer-countersteer   Once you've steered around an obstacle, you will turn the wheel back in the other direction.

Steering   The actual directing of the vehicle's movement—rolling frontward or backward.

Steering axle   An axle that steers vehicle—can be powered or nonpowered.

Steering column   Connection between the steering wheel and the steering box.

Steering gear box   The housing between the steering column that holds the power steering pump to make the wheels turn right and left.

Steering system   The steering wheel, steering column, gearbox, Pitman arms, tie-rod ends, and front axle make up the entire steering system.

Steering wheel   The wheel that allows you to direct the front wheels of the vehicle.

Steering wheel knuckles   Found on Pitman arms and tie-rod ends. Connection allows them to swivel.

Steering wheel lash   Usually caused by hitting an object or hole—causes the steering wheel to lash back in the opposite direction. To prevent injury, keep your thumbs outside the steering wheel when wrapping your hands around it.

Stop lamp switch   Stop lights come on when the brake pedal is applied. The electrical switch that turns on the stop lights is activated by air pressure.

Stop lamps   The same as "stop lights." Located on the back of the tractor/trailer—indicate you are stopping the vehicle.

Stop valves   Located on the loading and unloading outlets of the tank vehicle—stop the flow of the liquid cargo.

Stopping distance   The time it takes for a vehicle to stop.

Storage tanks   Air tanks.

Straps   Proper tiedown equipment.

Streetcar crossing   Where the street crosses a streetcar rail.

Supply pressure gauge   Tells the driver the amount of air pressure (measured in pounds per square inch—psi) in the system. If the vehicle has dual air brakes, there will either be one gauge with two needles or two separate gauges.

Suspension   Springs used to support a vehicle and its axles.

Swinging meat   A side of beef or any other meat that can be extremely unstable when hanging in a refrigerated trailer (reefer).

Tabbed   Same as Tagged—a way of marking shipping papers indicating a portion of the cargo is hazardous material.

Tachometer   Instrument located on the dashboard indicating the number of engine revolutions per minute (rpm). RPM is often used to indicate when to shift gears.

Tagged   Shipping papers marked to show that a cargo contains hazardous materials are "tagged" with colored tags or other special markings.

Tailgate   Slang term for a vehicle following too closely.

Tank vehicle   Any commercial motor vehicle that is designed to transport any liquid or gaseous materials within a tank that is either permanently or temporarily attached to the vehicle or the chassis.

Tanker   Special trailer used to carry liquids or dry bulk loads, such as grains, chemicals, etc.

Tarp or tarpaulin   Material used to cover most freight—tied down with rope, webbing, or elastic hooks.

Television receiver   Device that receives television signals. FMCSR states that a television set must be installed behind the driver's seat or otherwise outside of the driver's line of vision while he or she is driving. The regulation further states that the television set must be placed in such a manner that the driver will have to leave the driver's seat to watch it.

10 o'clock and 2 o'clock position   If the steering wheel were a clock, these two times would be where your hands would be placed.

Throttle   A cable connected to the carburetor which acts like an accelerator, causing the engine to go faster when the knob on the dash board is pulled out. When pushed in, the throttle will slow the engine.

Tie-downs   A category of chains, ropes, and other implements used to secure cargo.

Tie-rod   Part of the steering mechanism, connecting devices on the steering column to enable the steering column to turn the wheels of the tractor or truck.

Tire chains   Chain grids used on tires to provide additional traction on snowy or icy roadways.

Tire failure   When tires fail due to tire damage or defects.

Tire pressure   Amount of air pressure enabling tires to support their maximum weight.

Tires   Provide traction and reduce road vibration, transferring braking and driving force to the road.

Torsion bar suspension   A steel rod, bar, or arm assembly that acts as a spring instead of a leaf or coil spring to create suspension over the rear tractor wheels.

Total stopping distance   Distance from the time you see the hazard until your rig has stopped—about the length of a football field. If you're traveling faster than 55 miles per hour, you're going to increase the distance it takes to stop. If you double your speed, it will take you four times the distance to stop.

Tow bars   Part of a full trailer that allows the trailer to be coupled to the tractor or another trailer with a locking device and safety chains or a cable to prevent accidental separation.

Tow-away operation   Trucking operation offering towing services to disabled vehicles or to transport several tractors/trucks at one time using one vehicle.

Traction   The ability of your tires to "grab" the road.

Transmission control lever   Another name for Gear Shift.

Transport index   Tells the degree of control necessary during transportation—and the total transport index of all packages in a single vehicle cannot exceed 50.

Tread   Series of tie bars and fillets in the outer covering of the tire to improve traction. Tread depth should be at least $\frac{2}{32}$ inch.

Triple   A vehicle carrying three trailers or tankers.

Trolley valve   Most tractors have a handle attached to (or near) the steering column called a "Johnson bar" or "trolley valve." It is used to apply trailer brakes.

Turn to the right   The most difficult maneuver because the driver can't see what is happening to the right of the vehicle.

Turning space   Turn wide at the beginning of the maneuver or, if there is not enough room, turn wide as you complete the turn.

Twins   Disconnecting a trailer or combination of trailers.

U-bolts   Used to hold the springs on the frame and hold the springs onto the axle.

U-joints   Located between the drive shaft and the transmission and the drive shaft and the differential.

UN   The first part of a hazardous materials ID number. If the letters are NA, you know the shipment is traveling between the U.S. and Canada. All other ID numbers begin with UN.

Uncoupling   The act of unhitching the trailer/trailers from the tractor.

United States   The term United States means the 50 states and the District of Columbia.

Upgrade   A steepening of the road, usually found around mountainous terrain or in hill country; the opposite of a downgrade.

Vacuum brakes   Type of brakes usually found on trailers, operated by knob control from the tractor and requiring air tanks to operate.

Vehicle group   A class or type of vehicle with certain operating characteristics.

Vehicle   A motor vehicle, unless otherwise specified. Also, any wheeled contraption, including motorcycles, automobiles, trucks, and tractor-trailer rigs.

Viscosity   The tendency of a liquid not to flow. Low viscosity liquids flow easier than those with high viscosity.

Visual awareness   A driver's constant checks of the right and left rear view mirrors and in front of vehicle to avoid obstacles, accidents, or situations that would endanger the driver and/or the load.

Voltmeter   Shows voltage in the alternator or generator; device registering the amount of electricity being produced that goes to the battery.

Warm up   Allowing the engine and fluids to heat up to normal running temperatures before starting the vehicle.

Weaving   Going back and forth between lanes.

Webbing   Used to hold tarps in place.

Wedge brakes   The wedge is pushed by a push-rod between the ends of the brake shoes. The push-rod shoves the shoes apart and presses them against the brake drum. Wedge brakes have one or two brake chambers.

Weight distribution   Percentage of weight carried on each axle according to how the cargo is loaded.

Wheel   To be inspected with each trip; carries a tire and is attached with lugnuts.

Wide load   A trailer carrying a wider-than-usual load that requires more land width on the highway.

Wig-wag   Another type of low air pressure warning. This is a metal arm located above the driver's sight-line—attached at the top of the windshield near the visor. When the air pressure reaches around 60 psi, the wig-wag will swing in front of the driver's face.

Winch   Device used in loading and tying down cargo; also used to tow vehicles or to move heavy cargo from one place to another.

Windshield wipers   Used to remove precipitation from the windshield.

Work zones   Roads or highways that are under construction.

Index